GALLIPOLI

VICTOR RUDENNO

GALLIPOLI

ATTACK FROM THE SEA

YALE UNIVERSITY PRESS
NEW HAVEN AND LONDON

For information about this and other Yale University Press publications, please contact:
U.S. Office: sales.press@yale.edu www.yalebooks.com
Europe Office: sales @yaleup.co.uk www.yaleup.co.uk

Set in Minion by SX Composing DTP, Rayleigh, Essex
Printed in Great Britain by St. Edmundsbury Press Ltd. Bury St. Edmunds.

Library of Congress Cataloging-in-Publication Data

Rudenno, Victor.
    Gallipoli : attack from the sea / Victor Rudenno.
      p. cm.
    Includes bibliographical references and index.
    ISBN 978–0–300–12440–8 (alk. paper)
    1. World War, 1914–1918—Campaigns—Turkey—Gallipoli Peninsula. 2. World War,
    1914–1918—Campaigns—Turkey–Marmara, Sea of 3. World War, 1914-1918—Naval
    operations—Submarine. I. Title.
    D568.3.R83 2008
    940.4'26—dc22

                                                                        2007042539

A catalogue record for this book is available from the British Library.

10 9 8 7 6 5 4 3 2 1

Contents

Illustrations

Nos 3, 5, 6, 7 and 8 courtesy of the Australian War Memorial Collections. Nos 9, 10, 11, 12 and 14 courtesy of the Royal Navy Submarine Museum, Gosport.

Maps and Tables

Maps

Tables

Acknowledgements

I wish to thank all those who have given me support and understanding in the writing of this book. Most of all I thank my wife, Sue, who has always supported me unreservedly in all my endeavours. Special thanks go to my father-in-law, Alan O'Neil, who undertook the onerous task of proofreading a first draft of the manuscript and has provided many helpful suggestions; and to my mother, Christa, who has offered generous help in the translation of German documents.

I also wish to express my gratitude to the following individuals and institutions: in the UK to the staff and management at the Public Records Office; the Royal Submarine Museum; the Imperial War Museum; and the British Library; in the US to the National Archives; in Australia to the Australian War Memorial and the Mitchell Library. Finally, I wish to thank all those at Yale University Press who have contributed to the production of this book – in particular Heather McCallum, Rachael Lonsdale, Manuela Tecusan and Lucy Isenberg.

Introduction

The advent of modern submarines has resulted in a major shift in naval warfare strategy and has greatly increased the public awareness of, and interest in, this exciting and intriguing aspect of naval service. The U-Boat Campaign of the Second World War and the American submarine service actions against Japan are well known to those interested in naval warfare. As a youth I became intrigued by the adventures of the submarine service, especially through TV shows such as 'The Silent Service'. The clandestine nature of the combat and the risks taken by the crews – Allied, German and Japanese – made for exciting stories.

It was not until some time later that I became aware of a fact which is certainly less well known amongst the general public: that the Battle of the Atlantic of the Second World War had already been fought some twenty-five years earlier, in the Great War. As in the Second World War, the German U-boats of the First World War had achieved significant successes in sinking over 11 million tons of shipping. Certainly the advent of sonar during the Second World War increased the risks for submarines, but the loss of German submarines during the First World War was high, with 178 sunk out of a total of 375 constructed, and with the loss of 5,400 officers and men.

The Gallipoli campaign of the First World War plays an important part in Australian culture since it is generally regarded as a time when a new nation came of age through the tragic sacrifice of its young men. Like many Australians, I had little knowledge of the contributions made by other nations such as Britain and France to the campaign, and knew little or nothing about the efforts of their navies. I was also surprised to find that in the nearby Sea of Marmara, linked to the Aegean by the Dardanelle Straits, the British submarine service undertook one of the most courageous and exciting campaigns of the war. Even more amazing was the discovery that an Australian submarine played a role at a critical point of the campaign.

Few books have been written in recent times, either from an offensive or a defensive point of view, about these naval and submarine events, perhaps due to the lack of written material from that period and to a perception of the submarine technology as primitive. Clearly, from the tonnage sunk by the Allied submarines in the Sea of Marmara, including the number of naval ships, the offensive technology was no less successful than that employed during the Second World War. No submariners before or since have had to traverse such a narrow expanse of water as the Dardanelles, against strong currents and through minefields and nets, to reach their hunting grounds and then had to make the return journey on completion of a patrol.

As will be seen in the following narrative, the impact of the Allied submarine campaign on the Turkish merchant navy in the Sea of Marmara was significant, although not conclusive. At certain times, particularly during major land engagements, Turkish forces were under considerable pressure, but this did not stop their war machinery or the final dispatch of men and materials to the front. By the end of the ten-month Gallipoli campaign, nearly half of the Turkish transports had been sunk, so that a much reduced level of men and materials was transported by sea; instead, they had to take the longer 260-mile overland route. The Allies, however, had an even greater distance to cover, from the colonies to Great Britain, on to Alexandria, then on to Lemnos and finally to Gallipoli. As will be described later, they also suffered at the hands of German and Austrian U-boats.

The submarines did play a very important part in improving the morale of the Allied troops and in causing some initial panic amongst the Turkish populace. However, it was not only submarines that played an important role, but also the British and French navies, which provided fire support to the troops onshore and, most importantly, supplied them with the food, water and munitions to wage the campaign. Aircraft also played an increasingly supporting role and for the first time detailed planning evolved for modern naval landings on hostile shores.

To write this book, I have obviously relied on more source material than is listed here; but I shall refer in particular to the individual British and German submarine patrol reports and to the books by Shankland and Hunter (1964) and Wilson (1988) on *E11* and *E7*'s patrols. For general naval actions I have relied on the *Dardanelles Dilemma* by Chatterton, while for the land battles the book by James has been a primary source. I have in general kept to imperial units and to the British naming of Turkish locations current at the time; for Turkish ships I have relied on an excellent work by Langensiepen.

1

The Beginnings

Modern chaos theory would suggest that the tiny movements of a butterfly's wings could result in a hurricane thousands of kilometres away. In our story, the butterfly was the German battlecruiser *Goeben*, and the resulting hurricane that produced so much suffering and death was the Gallipoli campaign. Although major naval actions played a part in the Great War, their role gradually diminished, as in the Second World War, to one of blockade by the Germans, who used primarily submarines, and to one of containment and anti-submarine warfare by the Allies.

The steps leading to the First World War are well documented, with the killing of Archduke Franz Ferdinand on 28 June 1914 seen as a pivotal point. On 5 July the rulers of Austria–Hungary (Austria) received approval from their ally Germany to take a strong line against Serbia, which had been suspected of masterminding the assassination. Although perhaps not intended initially as a prelude to war,[1] an ultimatum was sent to Serbia on 23 July. Serbia accepted this ultimatum with some reservations on 25 July. However, not satisfied with this, Austria declared war the following day. The critical issue at this juncture, given that the armies of Austria could not be mobilized for several weeks, was the reaction of Serbia's protector, Russia.

Russia's reaction was a general mobilization to protect herself from any additional threat from Germany, which only served to produce a chain reaction. As part of Germany's longer-term strategy, a war on two fronts was considered unwinnable, so Russia had to be convinced to stand down its armies. When Russia refused to demobilize, Germany declared war on 1 August. Germany's plan of action called for a quick victory in the west, so on 2 August she demanded free passage through Belgium to attack France, which was refused. Germany declared war on France on 3 August and Britain entered the war on 4 August. Thus the First World War truly began out of 'sabre rattling' rather than from any clear intention.

Both Germany and the Allies (the Entente) realized that, in the event of war,

Russia would be dependent on the supply of arms and munitions to be transported from the Mediterranean Sea to Russia's Black Sea ports via the straits called the Dardanelles. Also important was the fact that, at the time, 90 per cent of Russia's grain and 50 per cent of all of her exports came by this route. The Dardanelles, in turn, were controlled by the Ottoman Empire, today known as Turkey. On 2 August, the imperial German ambassador to Constantinople (Istanbul), the capital of the empire, and the Grand Vizier of the Ottoman Empire signed a *secret* treaty of alliance between their two governments, which was directed against Russia. Germany's success in negotiating this alliance, and hence in putting a stranglehold on Russia, was achieved by recourse to a predetermined and orchestrated policy.

The Ottoman Empire was founded in the fourteenth century AD by a Turkish tribe whose leader was named Osman, and reached its zenith in the seventeenth century AD. From that point on it slowly began to contract, as Britain, France, Austria and Russia all whittled away at its territory. At its peak, the empire extended from Hungary and the Balkans to include Greece, and ran down to the Persian Gulf and across the northern parts of Africa, as far west as Algeria.

All the major powers had their eyes fixed on the weakening empire, but could not agree on how it should be divided between them. Hence, at different times, they rushed to defend it, as for example in the Crimean War of 1854–6 when Britain and France opposed Russia's annexing of Ottoman territory. British and French naval forces on that occasion were able to sail through the Dardanelles and up the Bosphorus into the Black Sea and attack Turkish coastal towns. By 1910, 'the sick man of Europe',[2] as the empire was often called, had lost Algeria to France, Egypt to Britain and Tripoli to Italy. Next, the Balkans were lost to the forces of Bulgaria, Greece and Serbia in 1912–13.

Between 1896 and 1908, the Young Turk Movement had developed which had the aims of preventing the further disruption of the Ottoman Empire and of reconstructing it on a liberal, national basis. The Young Turks, who were mostly exiles living in France, England and Switzerland, were hampered by factional disputes. Yet in July 1908, an insurrection in the Ottoman army, led by Enver Pasha, was finally successful and the Sultan was forced to re-enact the constitution of 1876. The first parliament assembled on 17 December 1908, with the Young Turks holding a large majority.

Rear Admiral Sir Douglas Gamble arrived on 18 September 1908 to take over the British Naval Mission in Constantinople. His role was to continue with the British training programme, to obtain additional purchase orders for 'suitable' British warships and to protect British interests. He attempted to improve the operations of the Ottoman navy, which was riddled with officers who saw the navy purely as an extra source of income. Due to political infighting and to Gamble's outspoken manner, his influence weakened, and Rear Admiral Williams replaced him on 3 May 1910. Admiral Williams fared no better as the Ottoman navy minister, Albay Mehmet Muktar, refused to cooperate with the British at every turn.[3]

On 10 December 1909, Grand Vizier (*Sadrazan*) Osman Pasha met Major von Stremple, the German military attaché, with the aim of acquiring an armoured cruiser and several destroyers. The British had been reluctant to supply the cruiser, which perhaps explained the animosity of the navy minister. The German government had little difficulty in supplying the destroyers, but, like Britain, it also equivocated on the cruiser because of concern over the Ottoman navy's ability to handle such a large ship. After a number of false starts, on 15 July 1910 Grand Admiral von Tirpitz announced that four reconditioned battleships of the Brandenburg class were available, two of which were selected by Constantinople. Although there was considerable protest from opposition parties over the cost of the two battleships,[4] the latter arrived in late 1910.

Germany had thus strengthened its relationship with the Ottoman Empire by providing naval ships to help to improve its position against the Greek navy. However, by 1911 the Ottoman government had started discussions with the British government for the purchase of additional naval vessels, most likely due to lack of available ships from Germany. The Balkan War in 1912 terminated these discussions but, by 1913, the Ottoman government had already approached German banks for funding to purchase British-built ships. Needless to say, Berlin did not approve the provision of funds for the purchase of any foreign shipping. However, Constantinople was successful in acquiring, from the British ship-builders Armstrong and Vickers and at a cost of £7.5 million, the nearly complete *Rio de Janeiro*,[5] which the original purchaser, Brazil, no longer wanted. The arrangement included the subsequent purchase of a second ship, in exchange for allowing Armstrong to modernize the arsenal at the Golden Horn and to establish a modern arsenal and floating dockyards in the Gulf of Ismid.

The *Rio de Janeiro* was renamed *Sultan Osman-i Evvel* and a 500-strong crew arrived at Newcastle on 27 July 1914, with the official handing over scheduled for 3 August. At the outbreak of hostilities, the Royal Navy seized the ship on 2 August and renamed it *Agincourt*. The second ship was renamed *Erin*. This action proved to be a critical mistake in British relations with the Ottoman Empire. The ships had been paid for primarily from public subscriptions, and the failure by Britain to secure their delivery was a blow to Turkish national pride.

After the 1908 Revolution, the Sultan remained a figurehead. However, in 1913, Enver and his followers staged a *coup d'état* and assumed control. Enver effectively became the new ruler of the Ottoman Empire and took the title of 'Pasha', equivalent to 'Lord' (the other members of his triumvirate were Talaat Bey, minister of the interior and later grand vizier and Djemal Pasha, head of the admiralty). Most importantly, he had spent some time in Germany as a military attaché and greatly admired the country. Germany was keen to develop a strong relationship with Enver Pasha, particularly given the increasing importance of oil for her navy. By 1913 Constantinople had convinced Germany to send a military mission to the Dardanelles, led by General Liman von Sanders, a move which caused conflict with other European powers. Although it is unlikely that German industry counted on any meaningful military contracts that Constantinople could afford given its past history, the strategic benefits must have played a significant part in Germany's planning. From Constantinople's point of view, the German mission was probably seen as a critical deterrent to both Greece and Russia from future expansion into the Ottoman Empire, particularly given the increasing cooperation between Britain and Russia.

Early naval action in the Mediterranean

In November 1912, the Kaiser decided that the German navy should have a presence in the Mediterranean. The Mittelmeerdivision or Mediterranean Division was created, and the battlecruiser *Goeben*, which was undertaking sea trials, and the light cruiser *Breslau* were sent to the Mediterranean. Effectively, the trip was used as a shakedown cruise for both ships.[6] They arrived in Constantinople on 15 November, with the *Goeben* suffering from faulty boiler tubes. Although perhaps initially a minor event in the eyes of the British and the French, the presence of the most powerful ship in the Mediterranean greatly enhanced German prestige in Turkey.

British sea power had peaked in the Mediterranean at the turn of the century, with fourteen battleships in 1902. However, in view of the increasing competition with Germany in home waters and of the stronger presence of the French, the battleships were gradually withdrawn from the Mediterranean. When Winston Churchill became the First Lord of the Admiralty in October 1911, he continued this policy, proposing in March 1912 that the Mediterranean fleet move from Malta to Gibraltar and the Atlantic fleet from Gibraltar to home waters. After some debate and the realization that no squadron of battleships would be available till 1915, it was decided to maintain three or four battlecruisers in the Mediterranean.

The Anglo-French Naval Agreement, signed on 10 February 1913, saw naval control in the Mediterranean become the responsibility of the French. The British forces were to be under French control and were expected to lend

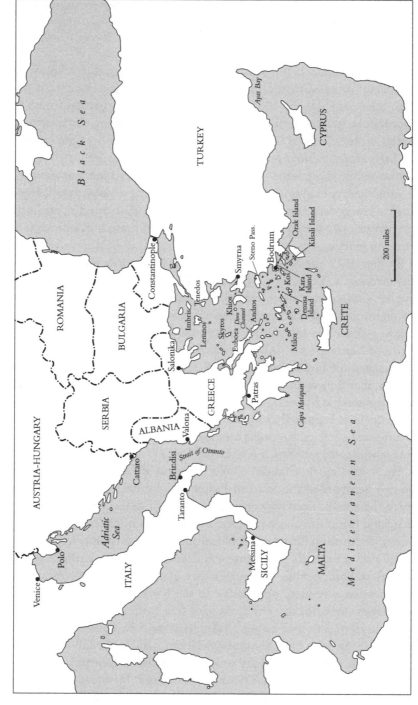

Map 1.1 The eastern Mediterranean

support against any threat from Austro–Hungarian forces, or any potential threat from a neutral Italy. (Italy declared its neutrality on 2 August 1914.) The French–British forces exceeded the German–Austrian forces by some 26 per cent shortly after the outbreak of hostilities.[7]

In late October 1913, Rear Admiral Wilhelm Souchon took over the command of the Mittelmeerdivision. Souchon proved to be a most formidable opponent in the upcoming hostilities and, perhaps even more importantly, an excellent diplomat, winning over many Turks with lavish parties on the decks of the *Goeben*. He spent much of his time cruising the Mediterranean, visiting ports and getting to know the area. In 1913–14 the *Goeben* visited Iskenderun (Alexandretta), and the harbour was surveyed as a possible German naval base. In March 1914 Souchon and Admiral Haus, the Austro–Hungarian commander-in-chief, agreed that during any hostilities the first priority would be to disrupt the flow of French troops from North Africa to France.

By June 1914 the *Goeben* had to put into Pola (now Pula in Croatia) for major repairs to her boilers. Material and workmen were sent from Germany and her 4,500 boiler tubes were replaced, but these repairs were not all carried through to completion. On 29 July the *Goeben* departed Pola heading for Trieste, which she left on 30 July, heading south. Meanwhile the *Breslau* departed Durazzo on 31 July. The Kaiser had warned his forces in early July to be prepared for hostilities; however, Souchon was still convinced, up until 1 August, that they would not be drawn into the war.[8] On 2 August Souchon's two ships were at Messina, where small supplies of coal were commandeered. After finally accepting that war with France was imminent, he set sail in the evening and received a wireless message confirming a declaration of war with France while still at sea on 3 August.

The following morning at 6.08 a.m., while off the coast of Algeria, the *Goeben* bombarded the town of Philippeville for ten minutes, and at daybreak the *Breslau* fired on Bone for nineteen minutes, with the French guns returning fire. Thus the war in the Mediterranean had begun. At the same time Vice-Admiral Chocheprat, in command of Group A, which consisted of about half of France's Mediterranean fleet including six battleships, was on his way to Philippeville. Although aware of the attack by *Goeben*, Group A still sailed at a reduced speed, due to mechanical difficulties of one of its battleships (even though the remaining five battleships, together with four armoured cruisers and eleven destroyers, were in good order). Souchon feinted to the west after the bombardment, which initially confirmed the French view that he would try to leave the Mediterranean. It is likely that the east wing of Chocheprat's Group A passed within 40 nautical miles of the *Goeben* heading east. A unique opportunity to engage the *Goeben* was thus missed by the smallest of margins. Indeed, Vice-Admiral de Lapeyrere, the French commander-in-chief with Group B, had sighted the *Goeben*'s mast and smoke at a distance of 25 to 30 miles, but didn't give chase as he believed he could not catch her.[9]

On the afternoon of 4 August Souchon received another wireless message advising that an alliance with the Ottoman Empire had been concluded and that he should therefore proceed to Constantinople. He requested approval to take on additional coal before heading back to Messina. Due to the continuing concern that Souchon might break into the Atlantic, Admiral Milne, commander-in-chief of the British Mediterranean forces, acting under orders from the Admiralty, sent two of his battlecruisers[10] from Malta to Gibraltar. On the morning of 4 August, the two battlecruisers were north of Bone when they sighted the *Breslau*, followed shortly afterwards by the *Goeben*. However, at this crucial point, war had not been declared between Britain and Germany. The Germans had marched into Belgium on the morning of 4 August; by midday, Britain had sent its ultimatum advising that, if Germany did not withdraw, a state of war would ensue between the two countries from midnight GMT, 4 August. Once again, luck had been on Souchon's side. The British ships followed the *Goeben*, but Churchill informed Milne that no act of war should be committed before midnight. Later, Milne was informed of Italy's neutrality and therefore that his ships should not come within 6 miles of her coastline.

Meantime Souchon arrived at Messina on 5 August, having outstripped his pursuers thanks to the tireless efforts of his crew to shift coal from the bunkers into the boilers – only to discover that Italy had declared its neutrality. No coal was therefore available from Italian sources. German sources, however, managed to provide some coal, and the captain of a British collier was also persuaded to sell his cargo.[11] Both from Souchon's wireless transmissions and from the British consulate, Milne was made aware of the location of *Goeben* and *Breslau*, when hostilities formally opened between Britain and Germany. Milne committed his forces to the north of the Strait of Messina, still convinced that Souchon would ultimately head west. This left only the light cruiser *Gloucester* to cover the south for an easterly retreat. Souchon requested support from Austrian naval forces in the Adriatic Sea, but none was forth-coming. On the afternoon of 5 August, *Goeben* and *Breslau* broke out to the south and were sighted by the *Gloucester*, which began to follow them, while Milne's forces proceeded around Sicily in a vain attempt to catch the Germans.[12] On the evening of 5 August, still shadowed by *Gloucester*, *Goeben* changed course to the south, away from her previous northerly course to the Adriatic. In the meantime, the light cruiser *Dublin* and two destroyers had left Malta heading north-east and at midnight sighted the *Breslau*. Over the next few hours, the *Dublin* searched in vain for the *Goeben*, which, warned by the *Breslau*, had earlier passed the *Dublin* to the east. Souchon had been lucky once again.

Milne still had no idea what Souchon's intentions were, despite a message from the *Dublin* that it had heard the *Goeben* signalling for Constantinople. The message from the *Dublin* had not been received.[13] On 2 August, Milne had dispatched Rear Admiral Troubridge with the bulk of the British Mediterranean fleet into the Adriatic, to cover the Austrian fleet. On 6 August, Troubridge headed south-east with his four armoured cruisers, to intercept the *Goeben*. Anticipating contact with *Goeben* at 6 a.m. on 7 August, Troubridge withdrew at 4 a.m. He later claimed that he did not engage because he felt that little good would be served, given the *Goeben*'s superior firepower, which would probably have destroyed his battle group. This attitude was certainly not in the typical British naval tradition, where a more numerous, although perhaps weaker, force would seek to inflict as much damage on the enemy as possible. A further consideration concerned orders, originally sent from the Admiralty to Milne, which forbade engaging with superior forces. These orders had been passed on to Troubridge, but there has been much debate as to whether that was sufficient to prevent him from attacking this very important target,[14] although Troubridge was exonerated at a subsequent court-martial. Souchon had been lucky again, especially given that the head of the British Naval Mission in Greece was aware, on 7 August, of the intended destination of the *Goeben* and the *Breslau*. However, he was reluctant to forward the information in case it compromised King Constantine of Greece.[15]

In the meantime, the *Gloucester* was still shadowing the *Goeben* and, although ordered by Milne to fall back, Captain Kelly of the *Gloucester* continued to dog both German ships. On the afternoon of 7 August the *Gloucester* and the *Breslau* briefly engaged with each other, and one shot hit the *Breslau* although she sustained little damage.[16] Following a further order from Milne, and now low on coal, Kelly finally gave up the chase. Due to a misunderstanding over the transmission of premature signals from both the Admiralty and Milne over the commencement of hostilities with Austria, Milne did not re-engage wholeheartedly in the search for Souchon until the afternoon of Sunday 9 August. By that time, the *Goeben* and *Breslau* were in the neutral harbour of Rousa Bay on Denusa Island, where they met up with a disguised German collier to refuel.[17] This renewal of the search was too late for Milne and his forces, and the *Goeben* and the *Breslau* sailed into the Dardanelles on the evening of 10 August.[18]

Milne was then ordered by the Admiralty to blockade the Dardanelles, but, as Britain was not at war with the Ottoman Empire, Milne questioned his orders. The Admiralty informed him that his 'blockade' was only to watch carefully the entrance, in case the enemy cruisers came out. The light cruiser *Weymouth* was sent into the Dardanelles to gauge the Turkish reaction, which was not positive. Her captain was informed that the *Goeben* and the *Breslau* had been purchased by the Turkish navy and renamed the *Yavuz Sultan Selim* and the *Midilli*.

Table 1.1   Approximate naval forces in the Mediterranean, August 1914

	England	France[a]	Greece	Italy	Russia[b]	Germany	Austria	Turkey
Battleships	–	21	–	11	5	–	13	2
Cruisers	11	28	2	21	1	2	7	2
Destroyers	16	84	14	33	26	–	18	8
Torpedo boats	–	187	17	85	10	–	40	9
Submarines	–	75	2	22	11	–	6	–

[a] Most of which were stationed in the Mediterranean.   [b] Black Sea fleet.
Primary source: Halpern 1987

On the day *Goeben* and *Breslau* returned to Messina to coal before their final and successful dash to the Dardanelles, an Anglo–French convention was held in London where it was decided that the French would be responsible throughout the Mediterranean for the protection of both French and British shipping; they would safeguard the Suez and Gibraltar straits; and, most importantly, they would act against the Austrian fleet, should it venture out and down the Adriatic. On 10 August France declared war on Austria, and two days later Britain did the same. Vice-Admiral Boué de Lapeyrere became commander-in-chief of the Mediterranean fleets and, though Malta was placed at his disposal, the operations at the Dardanelles were excluded from his area of control and remained under British command.

The French fleet assembled at Malta, since at this time it was not clear whose side Italy would join. In mid-August, the French fleet met up with Rear Admiral Troubridge's First Cruiser Squadron, conducted a sweep up the Adriatic as a show of strength and succeeded in destroying the Austrian cruiser *Zenta*,[19] with her escort destroyer *Ulan* escaping to the north. The primary Austrian ports of Trieste, Fiume, Pola and Cattaro on the eastern side of the Adriatic faced the Italian shore to the west. Since 1913 the Austrian navy had been in the process of building up her fleet and, when hostilities broke out, she possessed three first-class battleships, ten other capital ships, seven cruisers including the *Zenta* and four modern light cruisers. Additionally, she possessed some modern destroyers and torpedo boats. Amongst her submarine fleet, she had three classes: *UI* and *UII*, with displacements of 216 tons and with three torpedo tubes; *UIII* and *UIV*, of 237 tons and with two torpedo tubes; and *UV* and *UVI*, of 235 tons and with two torpedo tubes. A private submarine in Fiume owned by the torpedo firm Whitehead & Co. was confiscated and renamed *UXII*.

There was no question that the Allies had mastery over the Mediterranean, particularly while the Austrian fleet was holed up in the Adriatic. This allowed for the safe passage of the many supply and troop transports that regularly traversed the Sea. The only real threat was from submarines, with the first hint of what was to come occurring on 17 October, when the French armoured cruiser *Waldeck Rousseau* was attacked – but not sunk – by an Austrian submarine in the Adriatic. On 21 December 1914, while travelling through the Otranto Straits, the French Dreadnought *Jean Bart* was torpedoed by *UXII*, under the command of *Linienschiffsleutnant* Egon Lerch, but managed to limp back to Malta. The impact of these incidents was to force the battleships into the safety of the Malta harbour, and also to force the blockade to be entrusted to the French cruisers, destroyers and submarines.

The French submarines also tried to score a success against the Austrian fleet, which relied on harbour defences to protect their battleships, just like the French. The *Cugnot*, a steam-driven submarine under the command of Lieutenant de Vaisseau Dubois, entered the Gulf of Cattaro in November, having passed through two minefields and an anti-submarine net. But the submarine was detected and spent three hours trying to get into the inner harbour; then she finally managed to escape. In the following month, on 16 December, the *Curie*, under the command of Lieutenant de Vaisseau Gabriel O'Byrne, entered Pola and, after passing the first anti-submarine net, got caught on a second one, when the vessel rose to periscope depth. After doing all that was possible to break free, with both electric motors burnt out, with the air so foul that the ship's dog collapsed and died, and with sea-water mixed into the battery acid to form a deadly chlorine gas, there was little for her to do but surface. The crew managed to escape before scuttling her.[20] It was not long before the Austrians re-floated the submarine and after a refit she was commissioned in March 1915 as *UXIV*. This submarine was of 554 ton displacement, had twin diesels and carried eight torpedoes – a significant improvement on Austria's other submarines.

Political moves

In early August 1914, von Wangenheim, the German ambassador to Constantinople, was still concerned about the entry of the *Goeben* into the Dardanelles. Even though the secret treaty had been signed, debate continued in the Turkish government over the justification for this move. Although Britain had money and control of the seas and an alliance with France, it was her alliance with Russia, which was a sworn enemy of Turkey. The possible arrival of the *Goeben* and *Breslau* would put some pressure on Turkey with regard to its neutrality, but ultimately, to allay the concerns of the Allies, the problem was overcome by announcing the purchase of the two ships for 80 million marks.

Turkey also assured the Allies that she would remain neutral, return the German crews and not use the vessels in the Black Sea or in the Mediterranean. Shortly after arriving, Souchon was appointed commander-in-chief of the Turkish navy and then lobbied the Turkish authorities to have the British Naval Mission expelled. On Sunday 16 August the *Goeben* and the *Breslau* steamed to Constantinople, where the ships were 'handed over' to the Turkish navy. The practical reality was that the ships still belonged to Germany and were crewed by German sailors, with a token Turkish complement. The German ambassador was to comment later to the US ambassador that he had never experienced having to sign such big cheques in order to keep the two ships in operation since their arrival.[21]

The Germans were in command both of the Turkish army (under General Liman von Sanders) and of the navy, while the most powerful ship in the Mediterranean was in an ideal position to support naval action against the Russians. Germany also had a secret treaty, according to which Turkey would immediately go to war with Russia. Enver, who supported the agreement with Germany, and von Sanders were in favour of an early declaration of war against Russia, while the Grand Vizier Said Halim was against war. Additionally, Constantinople required time to bring her military forces and defences into a state of readiness and requested assistance from Berlin on mine and torpedo warfare, and gunnery experts for the gun emplacement and fortifications on the Dardanelles and the Bosphorus. Berlin agreed and sent six hundred specialists in disguise to Turkey.

The Ottoman fleet was not in very good condition when Souchon took over operations. The Germans believed that the British Naval Mission had done a poor job in training the fleet. After the British commenced their close watch of the Dardanelles, Souchon and his colleagues considered the possibility of attacking the British forces, but, given the poor condition of the Turkish fleet, this was considered too risky a venture. Souchon then directed his attention to the possible damage that could be inflicted upon the Russian fleet in the Black Sea. At the same time, the defences of the Dardanelles and the Bosphorus were considered a major priority; they had to ensure that the rear flank was protected during any future operations against the Russians. By 1 September the position of the British Naval Mission under Vice-Admiral Limpus was becoming untenable, with the Germans everywhere in authority, so Churchill gave permission for the mission to leave Turkey. Accordingly, at 5 p.m. on 16

September 1914, the mission left Constantinople on the neutral Italian steamer *Sardegna*.

The British, however, remained suspicious of the Germans on account of the continued presence of the *Goeben* and the *Breslau*. The British Admiralty and Cabinet gave orders that, should either ship attempt passage into the Mediterranean, they were to be intercepted and destroyed irrespective of what flag they were flying. The British also informed the Turkish government by late September that any Turkish ships which came out of the Dardanelles would be considered a threat to British interests and could therefore be attacked. The British naval squadron blockading the Dardanelles included the *Indomitable*, commanded by Captain Kennedy, who proposed a plan to send an officer up the straits on a merchantman, to spy on the *Goeben* and to endeavour to find out what her intentions were.

However, the British Vice-Consul C. E. Palmer (who lived in the town of Chanak on the Asiatic side of the Narrows – we shall hear more of him later) had reported that the *Goeben* was taking on coal, but was concerned that German agents and Turkish officials were watching him, which made spying difficult. A code was therefore established so that Palmer could continue to send information to Kennedy.[22]

The stand-off was bound to lead to more difficulties and on 26 September a Turkish torpedo boat was stopped at the entrance to the Dardanelles by the destroyers *Rattlesnake* and *Savage*. She was found to have German sailors on board and was sent back by the British blockading force. The Turkish reaction was to close the Dardanelles completely on 29 September by the addition of several mines to the outer minefield. This closed off all shipping to Russia via the Black Sea. The decision for the closure, which surprised even the Turkish Cabinet, has been attributed either to Weber Pasha, the German general commanding the fortifications, or to Javad Bey, the Turkish commandant of the Dardanelles, who would have been persuaded to do this by his German advisor, Vice-Admiral Murten. Escalation of hostilities was now only a matter of time, and by early October Souchon and his colleagues considered the possibility of using torpedo boats to attack the British ships off the Dardanelles, but abandoned this idea because, again, it was considered too risky.

A less difficult decision was to attack their old enemy Russia via the Black Sea, so the first Turkish–German naval attack took place on 29 October, when Turkish naval forces, including the *Goeben*, attacked Sebastopol, Novorossisk, Feodosia and Odessa. Only minor damage was inflicted on the Russian force, with the sinking of two small warships and six merchant vessels. However, from a diplomatic point of view, the Germans saw the operation as a success. On the same day the Allies severed relations with the Ottoman Empire and sent an ultimatum. By 2 November Russia had declared war on the Ottoman Empire, with Great Britain and France following suit on 5 November 1914.

However, prior to the formal declaration of war, the British squadron was ordered to shell the outer forts on 1 November. On that day British destroyers sank one minelayer yacht, and on 3 November Vice-Admiral Carden,[23] the British squadron commander in the Aegean, carried out the first bombardment against the forts at the entrance to the Dardanelles, more perhaps in order to punish the Turks for their choice of allies than from a meaningful attempt to secure the straits. Two battlecruisers, *Indefatigable* and *Indomitable*, used their 12-inch guns to attack, from a safe distance, the six 11-inch and 10-inch guns of the ancient castle at Sedd el Bahr and the two 9.4-inch guns of the modern Cape Helles fort. These defences and the battery of 5-inch howitzers at Tekke Burnu to the north-west comprised the outer defences on the European side. The battlecruisers were successful in destroying several of the enemy's guns, and the fort was damaged due to the fortunate explosion (from the attackers' point of view) of a powder magazine. On the Asiatic side, two French battleships, *Suffren* and *Vérité*, with their 12-inch guns, fired on the fort at Kum Kale, which had nine guns ranging from 6 inches to 11 inches. To the south-west they also attacked Orkanie, which was on higher ground, with a couple of 9.4-inch guns. The French ships achieved only moderate success.

There is some uncertainty about who ordered the attack on 3 November. Churchill had been warned earlier by Major-General Callwell[24] that the capture of the Dardanelles would have to be primarily an army task. The same conclusion had also been reached previously by the Greek general staff, the details of which were shown to General Ian Hamilton (who eventually was to command the land forces). Without apparent consultation, Churchill is believed to have ordered this first attack. Lieutenant Colonel Maurice Hankey, later Secretary of the Committee of Imperial Defence and of the War Council, suggested that it was not clear who had actually made the decision to attack,[25] and went further to say that it seemed improbable that the War Cabinet or War Committee would have sanctioned such a minor operation, one 'that was unlikely to achieve any useful strategical or political purpose and would only serve as a warning to the Turks'. There have been many debates on the relative merits of this attack, given its inability to achieve any substantial damage, while possibly putting the Turkish forces on alert and ultimately convincing them that it would be wiser to strengthen the inner defences of the Dardanelles.

During this time, the Russian forces in the Black Sea were relatively active, bombarding Turkish ports and mining numerous locations, thus denying Turkey vital coal and oil, and by 5 November Russian destroyers had mined

the entrance off the Bosphorus. The first major naval engagement between the
Turkish and Russian fleets occurred off the Crimean coast on 18 November.
The Russians succeeded in hitting the *Goeben*, which resulted in the deaths of
sixteen sailors, while the Russian battleship *Evstafiy* was hit four times and was
put out of commission for a lengthy period. The effectiveness of mines, both
in the Black Sea and, later, in the Dardanelles, became increasingly obvious.
This was best demonstrated on 26 December, when the *Goeben* hit two newly
laid Russian mines while approaching the Bosphorus. Although 600 tons of
water entered the battlecruiser, trim was maintained and the ship made
port safely. However, since there were no docking facilities at Constantinople,
the *Goeben* was out of action for some four months while repairs were
undertaken.

Churchill considered the forcing of the Dardanelles as a decisive point in
putting pressure on Turkey and defending Egypt. At the outbreak of hostilities
a Turkish army of 100,000 advanced into the Caucasus and, on 2 January
1915, the British Ambassador in Petrograd received a telegram to the effect
that the Russians were under pressure in the Caucasus. To relieve the tension,
a demonstration against the Turks was requested.[26] Shortly afterwards the
Turkish forces were defeated, which strengthened the Allied view that they
made poor soldiers. By February 1915 Turkish forces had also reached the
eastern side of the Suez Canal. Although their attack was not successful, Lord
Kitchener, supreme commander of the British forces, was concerned at this
turn of events. At the War Council's first meeting on 25 November 1914,
consideration had been given to the best approach for forcing the Dardanelles,
both by naval forces alone and through a combined effort of land and naval
forces. This was at the request of Churchill, who thought it was an ideal
method of defending Egypt. The idea was later rejected by Kitchener, who
pointed out there were simply not enough troops to be diverted to another
front,[27] although the War Council made no effort to confirm his assertion.

No action was to be taken at this stage with regard to assembling ships for
any potential operation. In early January, the possible occupation of Bulgaria
from the German side and the threat to Serbia were ongoing considerations
for the War Council. Support for Serbia would have to be by way of the Greek
seaport at Salonika (now Thessalonika), with the permission and, it was
hoped, the military support of Greece. However, given that Russia would have
the upper hand in any post-war redistribution of the Ottoman Empire which
would be against Greece's national interest, no real support was ever forth-
coming. Greece therefore had to tread a tightrope of neutrality, which resulted
in passive resistance being offered to both sides. The fact that there was a single
railway line from Salonica to Serbia meant that only an army of 200,000 could
be supported, and so the Dardanelles began to appear as a suitable alternative

in the east, particularly as significant naval support could be incorporated. If successful, the capture of the Dardanelles and the defeat of Turkey would re-establish communications with Russia and possibly draw Greece, Bulgaria and Romania into war on the Allies' side. Kitchener's initial estimate of the troops required at that time was 150,000. By the time the Russian appeal had reached the War Council in January, Churchill, Kitchener and Prime Minister Lloyd George were of the opinion that something had to be done to relieve the pressure on Russia. The question was how this was to be accomplished.

With the lack of suitable ground forces, the only realistic alternative was to launch a naval attack on the Dardanelles forts in an effort to break through to the Sea of Marmara. The British Grand Fleet had bottled up the German High Seas Fleet, the French fleet contained the Austrian fleet in the Adriatic and the impact of U-boats had not had any dramatic effect on naval planning, so from a naval standpoint a new arena of action was plausible. Churchill approached Admiral Carden for his opinion on whether it was practical for ships alone to force the Dardanelles. Carden was cautious, pointing out that a large number of ships and considerable effort would be required to succeed. When the War Council met on 5 January 1916, interest was shown in this form of attack. Lord Fisher, the First Sea Lord, was more circumspect as to the likelihood of success and ultimately predicted a naval loss of twelve ships. This eventually proved to be close to the mark. He was also concerned about weakening the British Grand Fleet in the North Sea, and even wanted a flotilla of destroyers to be brought back from the Dardanelles. Perhaps more importantly, he always favoured another military objective – a landing on the Baltic Coast of the unprotected northern seaboard of Germany. For this purpose he was building heavily armoured landing barges and monitors, but the scheme was dependent on getting one Russian army and on containing the German fleet, neither of which was ever to happen.

Admiral Carden was therefore asked to provide information as to what forces would be required for success. The French were concerned that any Allied offensive other than on the western front might weaken the Allies' determination in France. They were therefore keen to see another major onslaught on the western front, an idea in which Kitchener saw little value. The various theatres of war were therefore reviewed, an attack on the Dardanelles being considered to be the one with the best prospects for success.

Admiral Carden's staff (Captain Sowerby and two staff officers, Commander Ramsay and Captain Godfrey of the Royal Marines) provided detailed plans to the Admiralty on 11 January. These consisted of a four-stage attack, involving a direct and indirect naval bombardment of the forts, the clearing of the minefields, with the naval squadron eventually proceeding into the Sea of Marmara. Churchill was very supportive of the plan, which involved a steady reduction of the forts one by one rather than rushing the Dardanelles. Although commentators have argued that he was 'responsible' for the plan, Churchill would later claim that it was fashioned and endorsed by technical authorities and approved by the First Sea Lord, and that he 'seized upon it and set it on the path of action; and thereafter espoused it with all my resources'.[28]

The plan called for aerial reconnaissance and a considerable expenditure of ammunition, but it was impossible to estimate how much time would be needed to complete the operation. Carden asked for a fleet of twelve battleships, three battlecruisers, three light cruisers, sixteen destroyers, six submarines, four seaplanes, twelve minesweepers and other miscellaneous craft. This was considerably larger than his force of two battlecruisers, four French battleships, three light cruisers, fifteen destroyers, four submarines, one torpedo depot ship and some merchant auxiliaries which he possessed at the time. Coincidentally, at the time the *Majestic, Canopus, Formidable* and *Duncan* class battleships were all marked for decommissioning within fifteen months. Although considered to be of little use against the more modern German battleships which might be encountered in the North Sea, they were regarded as suitable for attack against the Turkish forts. Additionally, it was proposed that the new *Queen Elizabeth* (super dreadnought), then the most powerful battleship afloat, should carry out her final gunnery and calibration tests on the Dardanelles forts.

On 13 January 1915, Churchill put the proposal for a naval attack on the Dardanelles to the War Council. This was favourably received,[29] although he later stated that had he known that 80,000, to 100,000 troops would have been available three months later, he would have argued for a combined operation. The Admiralty was asked to consider an action in the Adriatic against the Austrian navy and to prepare for a naval expedition in February, to bombard and take the Gallipoli Peninsula. It was also decided that, if the western front remained one of stalemate by spring, troops should be dispatched to another theatre, although the Dardanelles was not discussed as a specific objective at that time.

By February there was a subtle but important change in the view of the British ministers and the War Council. During this time, the military advisors to the War Council had failed to put forward their views, as they considered that it was not their place to comment, unless asked by their political leaders. It was now proposed by Kitchener that 29 Division could be spared to bring Greece into the war. Although this plan to send troops to Salonika didn't materialize when negotiations with the Greeks failed on 15 February, it was only a small step to consider sending them the extra distance to Gallipoli. By mid-February, Fisher's concerns about the plausibility of winning the

Dardanelles by a naval action alone became more apparent. So on 16 February an informal meeting of six of the ten members of the Council, including Lloyd George, Grey, the Secretary of State for Foreign Affairs, Kitchener, Churchill and Fisher, decided that 29 Division should be sent to the Greek island of Lemnos. Additionally, units of the Australian and New Zealand Army Corps (Anzac),[30] which were in Egypt, should be dispatched to the same destination.

The possible siding of Bulgaria with Germany and Austria was also of concern, and thus it was estimated that a show of strength in the Dardanelles might cause Bulgaria to pause. It was decided that the navy should acquire suitable transport for the conveyance of these troops and it was proposed that this operation should be predominantly carried out by lighters (large open boats used for loading and unloading ships), and Rear Admiral Wemyss was instructed to proceed to Lemnos for the purpose of making preparations for the arrival of the army. However, this force was intended to support the naval operation, by occupying the forts once they had been defeated by naval action, as outlined in the request by the War Office to the Admiralty on 24 February:

Though troops should always be held in readiness to assist in minor operations on both sides of the Straits in order to destroy masked batteries and engage the enemy forces covering them, our main army can remain in camp at Lemnos till the passage of the Straits is in our hands, when holding Bulair lines may be necessary to stop all supplies reaching the peninsula.[31]

In a fashion not dissimilar to the poor organization of the British army at the time, little forward planning was undertaken before the dispatch of troops to Lemnos. On arrival, Wester Wemyss found that there were no suitable facilities and insufficient infrastructure to support what was a major operation. On 4 March he received the first detachment of 5,000 Australian troops sent from Egypt, who had of necessity to remain on board their ships as there was no accommodation on land. By 9 March he discovered that a French division was on the way, and a few days later units of the Royal Naval Division arrived. These had to be sent to Alexandria, as by this time there were not enough wharves to handle all the arriving ships. In the meantime, Kitchener had become concerned that German activity would increase on the western front due to the failure of the Russians in the east, and therefore 29 Division was now to be committed to the western front.

On 19 February, Admiral Carden opened his naval attack on the outer defences of the Dardanelles, which from a military viewpoint, as we will see later, was initially a failure, though it did have a dramatic political effect in the region. As hoped, the Bulgarians broke off their discussions with Austria and Germany (although they were later to join them); the Greeks offered three divisions for the attack on the Gallipoli Peninsula, although this offer never materialized; the Russians spoke of attacking Constantinople from the east; and the Italians showed a more positive attitude towards the Allies. The Russians insisted that their arch-rival, the Greeks, could under no circumstances be allowed to participate in any advance on Constantinople, and on 10 March the British government, with later consent from the French, secretly agreed to hand over Constantinople to Russia after the war.

By 24 February, Kitchener made it clear that, if the navy failed to break through the Dardanelles, the army would have to take over the operation. When the War Council met that day, the general consensus was that the job of taking control of the Dardanelles should be seen through to the end.[32] Lieutenant General Sir John Maxwell, commander-in-chief in Egypt, was given the task of coordinating the army. There was still some confusion as to how many men would be available, what their objectives would be and at what stage operations would start. This confusion was brought about by Kitchener's vacillation over the deployment of 29 Division (it was not until 10 March that Kitchener released it), and also over when exactly the army operation should be undertaken. By 8 March, Maxwell wrote despairingly: 'who is coordinating and directing this great combine?'[33]

Another objective under consideration, heightened by the possibility of the arrival of German submarines, was Smyrna (now Izmir), which was the largest Turkish port on the Mediterranean. On 5 March, Vice-Admiral Peirse commenced an attack on the port with the cruiser *Euryalus*, the Russian cruiser *Askold*, the seaplane carrier *Aenne Rickmers* and minesweepers in support. An attempt was made to negotiate with the Vali of Smyrna, who was thought to be pro-Allied, but it came to nothing. The resulting action proved to be very similar to actions in the Dardanelles, where the naval forces were unable to destroy the forts because of the minefields, while the minefields could not be removed because of the hidden mobile guns. The Turkish defensive measures included the sinking of five steamers in the channels blocking the port while the Turkish torpedo boat *Demir Hissar* sneaked out of the Dardanelles and attacked and disabled the *Aenne Rickmers*. With the port effectively blocked and with increasing demands for naval forces in the Dardanelles, the Allied force was ordered to return on 15 March.

Early submarine activity

As mentioned previously, once hostilities commenced British forces blockaded the Dardanelles, attacked Turkish ships and bombarded the fort at Sedd el Bahr. Three British submarines were originally located at Malta: *B9*, commanded by Lieutenant Warburton; *B10*, commanded by Lieutenant

Gravener; and *B11*, commanded by Lieutenant Holbrook. Moved to the island of Tenedos and supported by the merchant ship *Hindu Kush*, these relatively old and small submarines[34] were used as part of the blockade under the command of Lieutenant Commander Pownall. Four French submarines, *Faraday*, *Le Verrier*, *Coulomb* and *Circé*, were also attached to the *Hindu Kush*. The submarines commenced their patrol at the mouth of the Dardanelles at about 4 a.m. each morning and remained on patrol till after dark, in the hope of attacking the *Goeben* or the *Breslau* in case these made any attempt to re-enter the Mediterranean.

B11: 13 December 1914

During their patrols, the submarine commanders could see Turkish activity at the Narrows, which was located 25 miles to the north-east. The officers, no doubt, often considered the possibility of going to the Narrows to engage the enemy. However, they were acutely aware that at the time there were five lines of Turkish mines placed across the Narrows to act as a major deterrent to both submarines and surface ships. The French submarine force was showing some interest in attacking the Narrows, but Pownall felt that it was important for the British to be the first to attempt the attack, and initially considered commanding the mission himself. However, he eventually approached Holbrook, as the eight-year-old *B11* had the strongest battery in the submarine squadron, having been replaced in Britain just prior to her departure for the Mediterranean. A strong battery was required because of the continuous flow of fresh water down the Dardanelles into the Mediterranean. When submerged, the best the *B11* could achieve at full speed was only 5 to 6 knots for about two hours. At its cruising speed of 2 knots, the battery would last for twenty-four hours. The current in the Dardanelles was believed to be 2 to 3 knots, which could increase to 4 in the Narrows themselves.[35] Battery endurance therefore was a limiting factor.

The two officers discussed the approach with Captain Coode, commander of the destroyer flotilla to which the submarines reported. The objective was to attack enemy shipping as far as Chanak. Captain Coode was later to report to the Vice-Admiral that, if the *Lilly Rickmers* was still at Chanak, an attempt should be made to sink her, as he understood from Mr Palmer that the German staff were still living aboard.

A further difficulty was created by the numerous projections on the B class submarine, which had no guards to prevent fouling the mine cables. Holbrook therefore decided that the first and essential issue was to fit some guards to his boat. A 'jumping wire' to protect against horizontal wires, ropes and the like, was run from a mooring eye-plate at the bow to the head of the vertical rudder at the stern to prevent the conning tower catching any obstructions. A jumping pole was secured in the exhaust-ventilating pipe on the conning tower, to hold the jumping wire, thus creating an inverted 'v' shape over the length of the submarine. Additional lengths of 15 foot curved steel rods were shaped and fitted around each of the actuating spindles, which bore the rods that moved the two diving rudders at the stern. Guards were fitted over the flanges of the exhaust pipes, and shaped guards were also bolted to each of the permanent hydroplanes on either side of the bow, to prevent wires from getting in between the existing guards and the hydroplanes. A nosepiece made up of 3/8-inch steel plate in the shape of the bow was screwed on, with rounded head bolts and nuts designed to protect the torpedo tube caps from catching any wires or ropes when open. A 1.25-inch stay was fitted, running from the point of the plate which overhung the bows to the stern of the boat below the water line, to prevent any horizontal wires from catching underneath the plate.

Holbrook tested the anti-fouling equipment by charging his submarine against a mock-up of a mooring wire, which comprised a mine sinker, suspended by wire from the old cruiser *Blenheim*'s main derrick. These tests showed that the equipment had successfully protected the submarine. The strength of the current in the Narrows was not accurately known, so it was impossible for Holbrook to forecast how far his boat could go. He therefore took an anchor with him, so that at night he could hold his position on the surface while he recharged his battery. The obvious difficulty was whether or not the Turkish forces would provide him with an opportunity to utilize this unusual contrivance.

On 13 December, at 3 a.m., *B11* cast off from the *Hindu Kush* and by 4.15 a.m. was on the surface, three miles outside the Dardanelles, waiting for the Turkish searchlights to finish their evening sweep of the straits. She then travelled on the surface for as long as possible. (Some authors have suggested that she was trimmed down, so the decks were awash and only the conning tower was visible.) At 5.22 a.m., when within a mile of Cape Helles, the boat started to dive. Holbrook decided to keep close to the European or northern shoreline, which was relatively straight, whereas the Asiatic or southern side was more irregular and shallow. Within fifteen minutes he noticed a vibration, and surfaced to discover that the guard on the port forward hydroplane had twisted around and would act as a hook. The guard was quickly removed by flooding the stern trim tanks and by raising the bows, so that a crewman, attached to the submarine by rope, could unbolt the guard. This exposed the hydrofoil, but Holbrook elected to continue on his mission.

He kept to a depth of around 50 feet, at a speed of 3 to 4 knots, which resulted in a speed of about 2 knots over the ground. Because of the opposing current, he found it necessary to rise to periscope depth every forty-five minutes or so, to check his position quickly by periscope. This required considerable effort in keeping the boat in trim and manipulating the hand worked hydroplanes. Fortunately, Holbrook had an extra petty officer (W. C. Milsom) on board from a spare submarine crew, and he was able to take turns on the after hydroplanes. The continued checking was necessitated by the relative unreliability of the compass. This was located in a brass box outside the hull, with the bearing illuminated by an electric lamp and then reflected by prisms to the interior of the boat. It was important that Holbrook remained submerged at the greater depths for as long as possible so as to be able to travel underneath the minefields, as the five lines of mines were expected to be located at a depth of 16 to 30 feet off Kephez Bay.

The first part of the submerged trip took four hours, during which time the crew ate breakfast in shifts, and Holbrook ate half a lobster which had been presented to him by the French submarine captains on his departure.[36] For the last hour, the submarine descended to 80 feet to avoid the minefield, but during this time the sound of the scraping mooring cables of the mines could be heard along the side of the submarine. At 9.40 a.m. Holbrook estimated that he should be somewhere near the Narrows and, rising to periscope depth, found his estimate to be correct. On his starboard quarter on the Asiatic side, in Sari Siglar Bay, he spotted a two-funnelled grey painted man-of-war, approximately one mile away.[37] Given the difficulty of the strong currents, he decided to try to get closer to this impressive target before firing his torpedo. Holbrook altered course; when he checked his position after five minutes, he discovered that the currents had taken him further down the straits, almost back into the minefield, and that the target was now on his port bow. Turning to port, by 9.53 a.m. B11 was about 800 yards distant and one point (11.25 degrees) abaft the ship's beam. The ship was flying the Turkish ensign, so Holbrook fired one torpedo from his starboard tube, and then turned to port. He observed the torpedo track through his periscope, but at the moment before impact the submarine dipped a little deeper, and the explosion was obscured. The noise which resulted shortly after was a clear indication that something had been hit. When the periscope broke surface once again, Holbrook observed a big cloud of smoke on his starboard beam. At this point the enemy saw his periscope and commenced firing. The periscope dipped below the surface once more and, when Holbrook was again able to observe the ship a little while later, it was on his port bow. The firing had stopped and the enemy ship was settling down by the stern.

At this point, things became somewhat difficult for Holbrook and his crew. Firstly, it was reported that the compass had become unreadable beyond a few black specks, due to moisture on the lenses. Using his periscope, Holbrook determined the appropriate westerly course in order to get back into the main channel before proceeding south, and he ordered the helmsman (Thomas Davey) to use the appropriate black speck on the compass for his bearing. He ordered the submarine to go deeper, but due to her more easterly location, *B11* suddenly struck the bottom at 38 feet. Holbrook ordered a hard turn to starboard, and called for full power from his electric motors. After bumping along the bottom from 10.10 a.m. to 10.20 a.m., the submarine at last submerged into deeper water.

Having reached deeper water, but without his compass, Holbrook now needed to use his periscope to determine his position and the direction in which he intended to go. Choosing what appeared to be the high ground on the European shore, the boat was set on that course. After about ten minutes he spotted a break in the land on the port side, which he assumed was the entrance to the Dardanelles, and so turned south towards it. With the current now in his favour, he maintained a depth of 60 feet, with occasional sightings through his periscope. Once again, he crept under the minefields, arriving at the entrance to the Dardanelles at 2.10 p.m.; there he blew his main ballast and came to the surface. The trip had taken nine hours in total, using up so much of the oxygen in the submarine that it was impossible to restart the engines until the boat was fully ventilated ten minutes later.

Holbrook himself casually reported the above events in 1976 as follows:

As a fisherman I knew that despite the strength of the current in midstream if I crept in close to the [north] shore there would be slack water. We dived to 60 feet at the Narrows, waited a while and then moved up and through. I came up to periscope depth and saw on the starboard quarter a large old Turkish battleship. We went down again but the tide got up and swept us into Sari Siglar Bay and now the ship was on our port bow. I altered course and it needed full speed to combat the current and get into position for a shot. I fired one torpedo and then had to reduce speed because the lights were getting low and obviously our batteries were failing. We then found ourselves aground stern first and I could see the ship down by the stern and smoke from the shore suggesting that fire was being directed at us. By using full revs. we got off but I couldn't see the way out of the bay. I looked for the farthest bit of land through the periscope but the Coxswain said the spirit compass lenses had packed up and all he could see was black spots. I told him to follow them and at full [submerged] speed in twenty minutes a sea horizon appeared on our port bow. We made for it and were more or less swept out of the Straits having dived off course through the Narrows. We had been underwater for nine hours. What a wonderful crew, each a first-class man, but we had been very lucky.[38]

Meanwhile, on the *Mesudiye* (which, ironically, prior to the war had flown the flag of the British admiral in charge of the naval mission to Turkey), the crew manned her guns after the torpedo struck and opened fire on the nearly stationery periscope, which had been observed on her port side. However, shortly after commencing firing, the ship began to list heavily to port as the stern began to sink. Firing ceased, and her men scrambled for a hold as the boat slowly rolled over 10 minutes after being hit. The boat did not turn over completely, as her masts had struck the bottom and held her in place, allowing many of the crew to escape death. At the time of the sinking, the American Vice-Consul, Mr G. Van H. Ingert, happened to be rowing his small boat nearby. He pulled over and helped pick up a number of the survivors, and then heard shouts from men trapped in one of the gun batteries. On investigating he found one porthole to be uncovered and this, he discovered, led straight to the gun deck where the men were trapped. With the aid of oars and ropes he was able to save fifty or sixty of the men, a task for which he was not thanked.[39] Some time later, the German naval officer in command of the Dardanelles, Vice-Admiral Merten, admitted to Mr Ingert that the British had undertaken a 'mighty clever piece of work'.[40] Fortunately, from the Turkish point of view, casualties were light, and the *Mesudiye*'s six 6-inch and 3-inch guns were later recovered.

For his heroic deeds, 26-year-old Holbrook received the first Victoria Cross (VC) in the history of the submarine service, having negotiated the minefields, successfully sunk a man-of-war[41] and avoided Turkish guns and patrol boats. His executive officer, Lieutenant Sydney Thornhill Winn, was made Companion of the Distinguished Service Order (DSO), and the 13-man crew each received a Distinguished Service Medal (DSM) or Distinguished Conduct Medal (DCM). Following their success, the Admiralty telegraphed: 'Communicate to the officers and men of *B11* their Lordships high appreciation of the daring and skilfulness which have achieved this exploit.' The French commander-in-chief signalled: 'Please accept my warmest congratulations for the glorious deed of the submarine *B11*.' Holbrook became a household name in England and spent a considerable part of his spare time responding to the large volume of congratulatory mail he received. As well as mail, he was also sent gifts – for instance a scarf, which proved useful in the bitterly cold climate at the time. The Dardanelles might have been seen as exciting by the outside world, but Holbrook considered it 'a shocking place and I am bored stiff with it, it blows one continual gale here'. He had also not been ashore for five months.

This first submarine action was a prelude and a strong confidence builder to a major submarine campaign, particularly by the British, to disrupt Turkish supply lines in the future defence of Gallipoli against Allied ground forces.

Although the sinking of the *Mesudiye* was not a major military loss for Turkey, it did play an important role in lifting the morale of the Allied forces and in heightening the concern of the Turkish and German defenders as to the capability and potential threat of a small submarine.

Saphir: 15 January 1915

The French submarine *Saphir*, under the command of Lieutenant de Vaisseau Henri de Fournier, arrived at Tenedos to reinforce the Dardanelles blockade on 17 December 1914, after having been fitted with mine-guards in Malta. While at Malta, de Fournier had shown his plans for forcing the straits to the British commander-in-chief. At Tenedos he reported to the French commander, *Contre-Admiral* Guépratte, seeking permission to make his attempt, but was first ordered to undertake some patrols off the entrance to the straits, to become familiar with the conditions. On 15 January *Saphir* departed on its first patrol, but de Fournier could not resist the temptation to break through the Narrows and immediately headed up the straits. By 7.20 a.m., *Saphir* had run aground in Eren Keui Bay, swept in by the current, but de Fournier managed to get his boat off the gently sloping sandy bottom. When he judged he was approaching the Kephez minefield, he went down to 70 feet, and twice between 8 a.m. and 9 a.m. the sound of scraping mine-mooring cables was heard along the submarine's hull.

The submarine successfully passed under the minefields, as *B11* had done previously. Unfortunately, a leak had started behind some electrical cables; it was due to loosening glands and rivets, which had been repaired some weeks earlier at Malta. The leak was inaccessible, and the bilge pumps were not performing well enough to control the water inflow. Nevertheless de Fournier carried on, proclaiming 'we will put things right this evening in the Marmara',[42] and at 11.30 a.m. *Saphir* came to periscope depth in Sari Siglar Bay. She then went back to 70 feet, intending to remain at that depth for another thirty-five minutes in order to get above Chanak and through the Narrows. Thirty minutes later the submarine hit the Asiatic side of the shore near Chanak, where she ran up the shallow shoals, and the bow broke the surface at an angle of 35 degrees, with the hydrophones in full view. With the engines going full astern, *Saphir* would not budge, so de Fournier ordered the blowing of the forward ballast tanks. This action was successful in getting the submarine off the shoals, but with the loss of trim. Before trim could be re-established, the submarine sank by the stern at a 45-degree angle, until she hit the bottom at 230 feet, where she levelled off. During the descent, acid from the batteries spilled out into the bilge, where it mixed with the sea-water to form deadly chlorine gas.

The water depth was greater than *Saphir*'s limits and more leaks appeared, with sea-water reaching ankle depth in the control room. De Fournier ordered the main ballast tanks to be blown, but this had no apparent effect. He then ordered the release of two emergency 10-ton drop keels (a rare safety device of that time, not incorporated on modern submarines), which achieved the desired effect of sending the submarine to the surface. On reaching the surface, the main tanks were flooded again, to submerge the submarine. At this point, she came under attack from the nearby motorboat *Canakkale*, gunboat *Isa Reis* and minelayer *Nusret*.[43] *Saphir* was not hit but, once submerged, conditions in the boat became very bad and proper trim could not be maintained because of the release of the drop keels. De Fournier had little choice but to surface, so he manoeuvred the submarine to the centre of the Narrows and ordered the crew to abandon ship, once *Saphir* had surfaced for the last time.

The executive officer, Cancel, was the last to leave the surfaced submarine, but not before having flooded the ballast tanks; then *Saphir* sank to the bottom of the Narrows. The *Nusret* came alongside and rescued thirteen out of the twenty-seven members of the crew. De Fournier, who could not swim, his executive officer and twelve other crew members did not survive the cold water and the swift current of the Narrows. Although the submarine was lying only 300 metres from the shore, salvage attempts by the Turks proved impossible due to the strong currents and a water depth of 60 metres.

2

Naval Attack on the Dardanelles

Making for impregnable defences

It is important to recognize the difficulties faced in the planning and implementation of naval operations for the bombardment and destruction of the forts defending the Dardanelles. The Dardanelles are 35 miles in length, running in a north-easterly direction. The entrance is 2.5 miles wide, with the town of Sedd el Bahr on the western or European side and Kum Kale on the Asiatic or eastern side. Over the next 4 miles, the straits head in a north-easterly direction and widen to a maximum width of four and a half miles (into Eren Keui Bay on the Asiatic side), and then narrow to less than a mile, 15 miles from the entrance. At this point, which is the Narrows, the strait turns sharply, heading in a northerly direction and being bordered on both sides by high ground and steep cliffs. The Narrows extend for 4 miles to Nagara Point (on the Asiatic side), and then widen to 3 miles, before turning again sharply to the north-east. They continue on for another 20 miles, to the town of Gallipoli (Gelibolu on the European side), before entering the Sea of Marmara.

Defensive fortifications ran along both sides of the Dardanelles, from the opening at the Aegean up to the Narrows. There were three defensive groups. The first consisted of the outer defences on either side, at the mouth of the Dardanelles. On the northern side these were located at Sedd el Bahr and to the south at Kum Kale, making a total of four long-range and twenty medium-range guns. The intermediate defences were arranged between the entrance to the Dardanelles and Kephez Point, and comprised only seven medium-range guns in two batteries, together with one or two field batteries. Inner defences at the Narrows were grouped in batteries around Kilid Bahr on the western or Gallipoli shore, and Chanak on the eastern or Asiatic side. They comprised nearly eighty guns, of which only eight were long-range. These batteries were originally all poorly sited, with no attempt at concealment and with exposed magazines. They were manned by inexperienced gun crews, using poor-range finding equipment, and possessed little in the way of telecommunications. Once German expertise became available, however, these deficiencies were quickly remedied.

As previously mentioned, there has been considerable debate amongst historians and military experts as to the usefulness of the initial naval attack on the outer defences on 3 November. The destruction of the guns at Sedd el Bahr was, to a large extent, due to a lucky shot that hit one of the munitions bunkers, hence damaging the fort. In his explanation to the Gallipoli Commission after the war, Churchill attempted to justify this attack as having been motivated by a need 'to know accurately the effective ranges of the Turkish guns, and the conditions under which the entrance to the blockaded port could be approached'.[1]

However, the German military appreciated the impact of the naval attack and sent Field-Marshal von der Goltz to become the Sultan's adjutant general; von der Glotz reached Constantinople on 12 December. Additionally, Vice Admiral von Usedom was sent from Germany to Constantinople as inspector general of the coast artillery and mines and also, as mentioned earlier, naval artillerymen and mine warfare specialists. Any opportunity for a surprise attack by the Allies on the peninsula, using both navy and army resources, had clearly been lost.[2] Furthermore, the easy destruction of the Sedd el Bahr fort had given the British-navy planners a false impression of the ease with which the operation could be brought to a successful conclusion using ships alone. At a range of 12,000 yards, the chance of hitting an individual gun was 2 to 3 per cent.

Given the Turkish concern over the relative ease with which damage had been inflicted on the outer fort, the balance of the Dardanelles defences was shifted to the intermediate and inner defences, although the outer forts were not abandoned. Additionally, Djevad Bey, the Turkish commander in the straits, shifted the emphasis from defence by guns to defence by mines. The minefields were to be concentrated higher up in the straits, while the field of fire of the principal forts would be below the minefields. In this way a barrage could be maintained on ships entering the straits, before they could reach the mines and remove them. In fact the guns were to protect the mines, and the mines were to prevent any penetration of ships up the Dardanelles and through the Narrows. However, mines were in short supply and, up until November 1914, only 191 contact mines had been laid in five lines across the straits. By March 1915, the number had increased to eleven lines, with a total of 344 contained mines. In addition, three 18-inch torpedo tubes were installed on a pier at Kilid Bahr, which could be used to fire across the straits.

When howitzers began to arrive, they were deployed as mobile batteries on both sides of the straits, to provide cover fire for the minefields. By March there were twenty-four of these mobile batteries, with buffalo teams established to drag the guns to new emplacements, whenever the British located them. Additionally, smoke canisters were placed at various intervals to confuse the British and to draw fire away from the mobile batteries. Although the mobile units were unlikely to hit moving targets, they were to prove effective against anchored ships and smaller mine-sweepers. The German technicians and gunnery experts delivered the required expertise to improve the range finding and communications systems and to train the Turkish crews in their use. So by March 1915 the only way battleships would be able to pass through the Dardanelles successfully was by the removal of the minefields. It was this situation, as James states,

> which was never fully grasped by the British, and which has not been understood by some historians of the campaign. The British, both in London and at the Dardanelles, persisted in treating the forcing of the Dardanelles in terms of knocking out the main established batteries at the Narrows.[3]

Mine defences

At this point it is worth describing in greater detail the mine defences employed by the Turks. Responsibility for the successful deployment of the minefields in the Dardanelles fell to Vice-Admiral Merten of the German navy, who arrived in November 1914. Up until 18 March 1915 the minefields were not protected by any obstructions, and therefore could be parted from their mooring cables by efficient mine-sweepers. However, as mentioned, they were protected by coordinated onshore batteries of seventy guns and six searchlights, which even at night provided a withering rate of fire at short range against any mine-sweepers attempting to clear the mines. During the day, these batteries were protected from the Allied fleet by the large-calibre guns of the forts. The large-calibre guns, in their turn, were protected from the fleet by the movable howitzers, which prevented a ship from mooring in one place in order to concentrate its fire against the forts.

In the minds of the British commanders, the minefields therefore presented an obstacle: they prevented a rush by the fleet through the straits, and they did it in a way that the guns of the forts alone were never strong enough to achieve. The question which remains, however, is whether the minefields were truly capable of preventing a determined fleet from getting through. Analysis by the committee appointed to investigate the attacks on the enemy's defences[4] suggests that there were five lines of mines off Kephez Point that had to be passed to reach Sari Siglar Bay below the Narrows, with odds of 15 to 1 against a ship reaching that point. Then to get to the Narrows a further five lines of mines would have to be passed, increasing the odds to 100 to 1 against success. If this assessment is correct, it is unlikely that any ship from the fleet would have succeeded in passing through the Narrows unless the mine-sweepers had managed to remove the mines.

The approximate timing and strength of the mine deployment is summarized in Table 2.1 below.

Table 2.1 Turkish mine deployment

Date of deployment	Mine line number	Location	Number of mines
3 Aug. 1914	6	off Kephez Point	38
	5	Sari Siglar Bay	47
24 Aug. 1914	9	below Kephez Point	48
24 Sept. 1914	10	below line 9	29
1 Oct. 1914	2	Narrows	23 (29)
	5	strengthened	n.a.
9 Nov. 1914	8	off Kephez Point	16 (18)
Dec. 1914	7	off Kephez Point	50
	3	Narrows	28
	4	Narrows	39
26 Feb. 1915	1	Narrows	53
8 March 1915	11	Eren Keui Bay	20
18 March 1915	12	Domuz Deresi	10
	13	Tenker Dere	9
May 1915	14	Narrows	8
	15	Narrows	31
Aug. 1915	16	Nagara Submarine Net	n.a.
15 Sept. 1915	(24?) 17	White Cliffs	47
Dec. 1915	18	White Cliffs	48
Total			544–52

Primary source: 1921 Report of the Committee Appointed to Investigate the Attacks Delivered on the Enemy Defences.

The mines were generally spaced 44 to 55 yards apart, except for line 11, where the mines were 110 to 165 yards apart. Lines 14 and 15 comprised two deep lines of mines, intended to sink submarines.

Both German naval and Russian naval mines were employed, but the majority were from the German manufacturer Carbonit. These employed hydrostatic depth gear, which was suitable for use in a constant current and reliable in its depth setting. The latter was generally 13 to 15 feet. The mine was attached to its 1,000-pound sinker by a single, high quality, steel mooring wire of 2/10-inch diameter, with a breaking strain of 5 to 6 tons. These mines tended not to be dragged by the currents, and only a few broke from their moorings. The mine had a positive buoyancy of 250 to 400 pounds and carried explosive charges of 180 to 220 pounds. Up until the Allied evacuation from the Dardanelles, a total of about 400 Carbonit Type 1 mines were employed, being supplemented by 50 older German naval Type C. 77 mines and 50 modern Russian mines, retrieved from the Black Sea.

Floating mines of four types were also deployed in the Dardanelles. The Ramis floating mine consisted of a float, with a 165-pound Trotyl charged mine suspended about 10 feet below. If the tin float, which was filled with cork, was bumped with sufficient force to dent the rim, it closed an electric circuit and detonated the mine. The Bulgarian floating mine was conical and carried a 220-pound Trotyl charge. It was weighted until it floated just below the surface. The Sautter-Harlé mine was employed in a similar fashion. The periscope floating mine was a decoy, to suggest the presence of a submarine and to entice surface ships to ram it. A long zinc tube was attached vertically to a submerged mine, with approximately 18 inches of the tube protruding above the surface to mimic the appearance of a periscope. Only fifty to sixty floating mines were laid during 1915, with no recorded sinkings. However, given the outflowing surface current of the Dardanelles, if the Turks had had a sufficient number of floating mines to deploy once the Allies were committed to a breakthrough, these could have posed a significant threat.

The February offensive

On 8 February, Rear Admiral de Robeck (Admiral Carden's second in command) arrived at Tenedos and immediately set off on the destroyer *Mosquito* to inspect the Dardanelles entrance. Numerous ships continued to arrive via Malta to strengthen the fleet for this massive enterprise. One such was the *Triumph*, which came from the China Station. One of her officers observed that when she was employed in the siege of Tsing To,

it was clearly demonstrated early in the operations that ships were almost entirely ineffective against modern land fortifications. It was impossible even to see the forts, which had no difficulty in hitting ships at considerable ranges, the adequacy of the forts' fire being most marked.[5]

Other incidents, for instance the torpedoing of the French battleship *Jean Bart*, also forewarned of the dangers that were likely to occur at the Dardanelles. The Admiralty had decided that, in view of the mine menace which would have to be accepted in the Dardanelles, battleships, while in dry dock, should be fitted with 'cow catchers' to their bows, in the hope of sweeping away or detonating any mines encountered. Needless to say, this measure was quite ineffective and clumsy; neither the officers nor the crew of the *Majestic*, which had been so fitted, considered it worthwhile, and mostly because it made the ship much more difficult to steer. Another optimistic innovation was to place several 6-inch mortars on the top of the turrets, so that, if the ship was sunk – and it was assumed she might be, the mortars could be used at close range to attack the Turks. Weather was also a concern: winds of hurricane force in the Aegean during the month of February made the coaling of ships extremely difficult. Even the *Inflexible* was rehearsing her gunnery with a very realistic silhouette of the *Goeben* for a target, in the mistaken belief that she might make a dash for open waters.

With the arrival of this massive armada of 12 battleships (including the 15-inch gunned *Queen Elizabeth*) and an array of cruisers and destroyers, there

Map 2.1   The Dardanelles

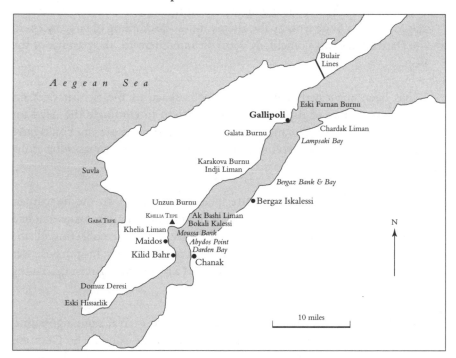

was certainly no chance of surprise. During the three months from the initial Anglo-French naval sorties in November, Turkey had removed many of its modern guns from the Bosphorus to the Dardanelles, having now been convinced that the real attack would come from the Anglo-French forces and not from the Russians. The minefields had been strengthened by sweeping up mines that the Russians laid at the northern end of the Bosphorus and re-laying them in the Dardanelles – a risky business for those undertaking it. However, the German advisers still believed that the Dardanelles could be forced, although a large number of ships might have to be sacrificed by the Allies. There was, however, an important proviso. General von Sanders was clearly worried about the oncoming attack, but he remained cool and in his assessment of the situation stated:

> Even in case the allied fleet forced a passage and won the naval battle in the Sea of Marmara, I judged that it would be in a nearly untenable position so long as the entire shores on the Dardanelles strait were not held by strong allied forces. Should the Turkish troops succeed in holding the shores of the strait, or in regaining them, the regular supply of food and coal would become impossible. But for a successful landing of troops near Constantinople, where they might avail themselves of the resources of the country, the defensive arrangements left little hope of success. A decisive success could not be won by the enemy unless the landing of large forces in the Dardanelles was coincident with, or antecedent to, the passage of the fleet.[6]

It has been suggested that the simple presence of the British fleet off Constantinople may of itself have been sufficient to eliminate the need for support from the land. The mere fact that a liberator was present could have created conditions for a revolution in Turkey. As the US Ambassador at the time stated:

> As soon as the guns began to fire, placards appeared on the hoardings, denouncing Talaat and his associates as responsible for all the woes that had come to Turkey. Bedri, the Prefect of Police, was busy collecting all the unemployed young men and sending them out of the city; his purpose was to free Constantinople of all who might start a revolution against the Young Turks.[7]

So, although success may have been achieved by a naval campaign alone, the full situation had not yet become obvious to the Allies. The Germans were busily fortifying the Dardanelles and strengthening emplacements everywhere, even though many of the guns were extremely old. The citizens of Constantinople were very concerned that the Dardanelles would be forced, but everything that could be done to prepare the fortifications and deploy infantry had already been done. It was now up to the Allies to make the next move.

Admiral Carden planned the first major attack on the outer forts for 19 February. His plan provided for the following stages in the operation:

1 reduction of the defences at the entrance to the straits, in Bashika Bay and on the north coast of Gallipoli.
2 sweeping the minefields and reducing the defences up to the Narrows.
3 reduction of the Narrows.
4 sweeping the principal minefield (which was off Kephez).
5 silencing the forts above the Narrows.
6 passing the fleet into the Sea of Marmara.
7 operations in the Sea of Marmara and patrolling the Dardanelles.[8]

By early February, seaplane support became available through the arrival of the converted carrier *Ark Royal*, which was later replaced by the carrier *Ben My Chree*. These ships were effectively floating hangers and would lift the seaplanes in and out of water by cranes. However, the seaplanes were not very effective, given their performance characteristics: they could only take off in calm seas, when some wind was blowing to aid their lift-off; and even then, they could only ascend to a low altitude, where they were often hit by rifle fire. The most reliable aircraft was Short No 136, which, during twenty-six flights made between 17 February and 31 May, had sixteen engine failures.[9] Aircraft operations were to increase over time but were never fully exploited.[10]

At 7.30 a.m. on the 19 February the first seaplane took off for a reconnaissance flight, being followed by the destroyer *Basilisk*. Two additional destroyers also went close to shore for detailed reconnaissance. By 7.58 a.m. the two destroyers were under fire from the Orkanie Battery 4, at its maximum range of 11,000 yards. By 9 a.m., the bombarding squadrons, carrying 178 guns of 5.5 inches and upwards, arrived at their designated positions. The French battleship *Suffren*, supported by *Gaulois*, was off Kum Kale in the south, with the *Bouvet* to the north-west, spotting for them, about six miles from the target. The *Cornwallis* was to tackle Orkanie, while the *Triumph* was to the north attacking Cape Helles. The *Inflexible*, out of range to the west, bombarded Sedd el Bahr, while the *Vengeance* was to the north-west of *Cornwallis*.

Table 2.2 Forts of the Dardanelles

Forts	Name	Number	Armaments	Location
Outer forts	Helles	1	two 9.4-inch guns	European side
	Sedd el Bahr	3	six 9.4 to 11-inch guns	European side
	Orkanie	4	two 9.4-inch guns	Asiatic side
	Kum Kale	6	six 9.4 to 11-inch, one 8-inch and two 6-inch guns	Asiatic side
Intermediate forts	Messudieh	7	three 5.9-inch guns	European side
	Suan Dere	7a	four 4.7 inch guns	European side
	Dardanos	8	five 5.9-inch guns	Asiatic side
	Djevad Pasha		four 4.7-inch guns	European side
Inner forts	Yildiz	9	six 6-inch guns	European side
	Rumili Meddjidieh	13	two 11-inch guns and four 9.4-inch guns	European side
	Hamidieh II	16	two 14-inch guns	European side
	Namazieh	17	one 11-inch, one 10-inch, eleven 9.4-inch and three 8.2-inch guns	European side
	Hamidieh I	19	two 14-inch, and seven 9.4-inch guns	Asiatic side
	Chemenlik	20	two 14-inch, one 9.4-inch and one 8.2 inch guns	Asiatic side
	Medjidieh Avan	23	six 8.3-inch mortars	Asiatic side
	Derma Burnu	22	six 9.4-inch guns	European side
	Anodalu Medjidieh	24	three 11-inch, four 10.2-inch, two 9.4-inch and two 8.2-inch guns	Asiatic side

Primary source: Admiralty Naval Staff Gunnery Division, 1921

At 9.51 a.m. the signal to open fire was hoisted by the flagship, and within minutes the *Cornwallis* began shelling Orkanie. Ten minutes later *Triumph* opened fire on the No. 1 fort at Helles, and thirty minutes after that *Suffren* commenced shelling No. 6 fort at Kum Kale. By 10.40 a.m., new orders arrived for a modification of tactics. Under instructions to use his ammunition with economy, and given that little seemed to have been achieved in the early stages of the bombardment, Admiral Carden ordered his ships to anchor and carry on their firing from fixed positions, in the hope of gaining greater accuracy. *Cornwallis*'s capstan was defective, so *Vengeance* took her place. Due to strong winds and currents, it was necessary in some cases, such as with the *Vengeance*, to use a 'spring'. This involved dropping another cable from the stern and hauling it in, so that the ship was turned to provide a full broadside to the target. *Vengeance* fired three or four shots, one of which was seen at 12.38 p.m. to hit the enemy's guns with no reply of shot.

By 2.30 p.m., Admiral Carden decided that the ships would need to come in closer to the forts. The ships weighed anchor, and by 3 p.m. were once again attacking the forts, at the closer range of 8,000 yards, although not at anchor. *Triumph*, which had the task of attacking Helles, encountered great difficulty in locating the well-concealed fort. Eventually *Inflexible* took her place at a range of 12,000 yards, and fired twenty-one rounds into Helles with some success. Later in the afternoon, when she went to the assistance of *Vengeance*, she fired a further nineteen rounds at Orkanie.

Suffren was to attack Kum Kale at a range of 7,000 yards with her secondary armament, and then to come within 5,000 yards of Orkanie, while supported by *Vengeance*. By 3.50 p.m., *Suffren* had made three runs at Kum Kale and Admiral Guépratte asked permission to shorten the range. He then moved closer and at 4.10 p.m. increased his rate of fire. In twenty minutes the southern side of the fort was a shambles.

At this time *Vengeance* was also firing on the fort and then, in company with *Cornwallis*, attacked the forts at Orkanie and Helles, using their secondary armament. With no sign of life from the forts, Admiral Carden signalled *Suffren* to close in on them and *Vengeance* to ceasefire and examine the forts. Unfortunately, *Suffren* misunderstood the signals and assumed that she was to ceasefire and close on *Inflexible*. At that time, *Suffren* was in an excellent position to destroy the Orkanie battery, which was intact and visible to her. Admiral de Robeck in *Vengeance*, in response to his orders to 'examine the forts', was coming into the centre of the entrance to the straits, when suddenly he came under heavy fire from both Helles and Orkanie. Immediately, *Bouvet* fired salvos over *Vengeance* and *Cornwallis* in support, *Suffren* reopened on Helles and *Gaulois* fired at Orkanie at 9,000 yards. By 5.15 p.m. *Inflexible* had moved in to attack Orkanie, which was the most active of the forts. The *Agamemnon*, which had just joined the fleet with the *Queen Elizabeth*, arrived in the nick of time to lend its support to *Cornwallis*.

It must have been a violent scene, with the group of ships returning fire in *Vengeance*'s defence filling the air with smoke and the smell of cordite.[11] However, sunset was approaching, and at 5.20 p.m. the flagship hoisted the recall and reluctantly the squadron steamed off. De Robeck in *Vengeance* asked for permission to continue the fight but was also recalled by the signal to cease fire at 5.30 p.m.

The following day at 10.30 a.m., Admiral Carden summoned his captains for a debriefing of the previous day's events. A review of the events highlighted the following:

- Ships did not dominate the forts;
- Ships underway, even at slow speed, could not obtain accurate results;
- *Triumph*'s firing over land at Helles failed because indirect shooting could not be relied upon;
- Notwithstanding the large number of successful hits, enemy guns were not permanently silenced;
- The enemy had not wasted shots but waited until the ships were at close range;
- Turkish gunners had been forced away from their guns into shelters by the long-range bombardment, but returned at the appropriate time to return fire.

Although the plan was relatively sound, the execution proved poor. Several ships, such as the *Albion* and *Amethyst*, didn't take part, while some, like the *Vengeance*, were not in action all the time, and the forts were given time on some occasions to undertake repairs when there was a lull in the battle. After the action it was found that poor staff work had failed to establish that the guns of *Triumph* could not reach Helles from her assigned position and that *Cornwallis* could neither anchor at her assigned position nor bombard Helles at 14,000 yards. Although there had been eleven hours of sunlight that day (6.48 a.m. to 5.40 p.m.), the engagement lasted only seven hours and three quarters. Given that weather conditions would deteriorate over time, it was important for Admiral Carden to make the most of any good weather in attacking the forts.[12]

It may already have started to become obvious to those present, even at this early stage, that the navy could not compete against the forts unless they were supported by land-based forces. On the western front the success of the destruction of Belgium forts by the Germans, using 38-centimetre howitzers which fired their rounds at an angle over 45 degrees, gave the impression that forts could be easily destroyed by new and increased firepower and then quickly seized and held by follow-up troops.

The howitzer had several important advantages over ship-mounted guns, including:

- a higher, and thus more obtuse, projectile trajectory, which could get over parapets or vertical defences;
- penetration of any overhead protection;
- ability to clear hills and hit enemy gun positions in valleys.

The disadvantages of howitzers included their lack of accuracy, which required them to be in a fixed position and to be used at a relatively short range, and which had the consequence that the trajectory could be influenced by strong winds. The advantages of ship-mounted guns included:[13]

- longer range and greater accuracy;
- higher velocity and hence greater penetration.

The next bombardment occurred on Thursday 25 February, the delay being due to a strong southerly gale and bad visibility. Prior to the storm, seven mine-sweepers sent from England began sweeping for mines off the peninsula, to secure a safe area from which the newly arrived *Queen Elizabeth* could use her 15-inch guns. For this next phase of the operation, once it was realized that indirect fire would not be successful, long-range bombardment on Orkanie would be carried out by *Irresistible*; on Helles, by *Agamemnon*; on Sedd el Bahr by *Queen Elizabeth*; and on Kum Kale by *Gaulois*. The preliminary long-range bombardment was to be followed by two pairs of battleships going in at close range, in order to engage with secondary armament. The battleships taking part in this stage of the operation were *Vengeance, Cornwallis, Albion, Triumph* and *Inflexible,* and the two French ships, *Suffren* and *Charlemagne.* The idea was that, having driven away the gunners by the initial bombardment, the guns could then be destroyed by the secondary engagement.

The fleet left Tenedos at 5 a.m. and the long-range bombardment commenced at 10.14 a.m., when the *Queen Elizabeth* opened fire, her shot falling short. Simultaneously the *Gaulois* commenced firing and got a hit on Kum Kale, while *Agamemnon* fired on Helles, which immediately returned fire. By 10.28 a.m., *Irresistible* was attacking Orkanie and *Gaulois* was hitting Kum Kale. Helles concentrated its fire on *Agamemnon*, hitting her several times, whereupon *Queen Elizabeth* opened fire upon Helles. *Agamemnon* was hit seven times and suffered casualties but managed to hit her target twice. The *Queen Elizabeth*, to her north-west, had found the range on Helles, so by 11 a.m. had hit the fort on four occasions and by noon another five times. The light cruiser *Dublin*, which had been spotting for *Queen Elizabeth*, was compelled by 10.50 a.m. to move further out to sea as the guns on shore had already straddled her. By 11.25 a.m., *Irresistible* was hitting her target effectively, and struck both 9.4-inch guns of the fort. The *Queen Elizabeth* had also successfully destroyed one gun and damaged another at Sedd el Bahr and Helles.

Around noon, the second phase of the attack commenced. First *Vengeance* and then *Cornwallis* made a run, until they reached a position 4,000 yards from Kum Kale in the mouth of the Dardanelles, fired all guns, turned to port and returned out of range of the fort's batteries. By using this approach, they were able to bring both port and starboard guns to bear, firing on the forts to the south and north of the entrance. Chatterton reported the action, as described by an officer on the *Vengeance*:[14]

No. 1 (Helles) had stopped, but no one knew if they'd open when we got close. By 12.45 we were on our course, and other ships began firing to support us. We went in at 12 knots, and at 12.54 *Vengeance* opened fire, slowly, with her starboard 6-inch at Orkanieh, and with her port 6-inch at Helles, beginning at 6500 yards. Five minutes later Sedd-el-Bahr open fire on *Vengeance*, to which our port guns replied. The after turret also came into action. From [1.30 p.m. til 1.54 p.m.] we were turning out to port, being distant about 2500 yards from Kum Kale (that is, about 1500 yards later than ordered), and in turning threw a few into Kum Kale as well as Sedd-el-Bahr. A good hit on Orkanie was seen just as we finished turning out.

It is unlikely that the Turks expected the ships to rush through the outer defences, but, once they observed them turning to port, they opened fire. During this first bombardment, the *Cornwallis* fired 140 12-inch and 6-inch shells. At 2.15 p.m., the French ships *Suffren* and *Charlemagne* undertook the same form of attack, achieving some good hits on Kum Kale. To complete the operation, the British battleships *Albion* and *Triumph* were then sent in, to follow up at a range of 2,000 yards. At this stage a considerable number of hits were observed on most of the forts, with *Albion* punishing Kum Kale and Orkanie and *Triumph* pounding Sedd el Bahr. By this time, *Albion* and *Triumph* were firing into the ruined forts at point-blank range – *Triumph* at a range of 200 yards! By 6.30 p.m., Sedd el Bahr was in ruins, Kum Kale was badly damaged, and both Helles and Orkanie were out of action, with barracks and forts ablaze.

The next phase of the operation was to clear any mines in the mouth of the Dardanelles so that the intermediate defences could be attacked. Due to the lack of dedicated mine-sweepers, North Sea fishing trawlers, with their civilian crews, were sent to the Dardanelles to do the job, utilizing the same procedures as mine-sweepers. Effectively, the approach was to string a cable or 'sweep-wire' between two trawlers, below the surface, with the aim of cutting the cables connecting a mine to its sinker. Each of the trawlers

drags a 'kite', a heavy, prismatic wooden appliance which dives under water when towed, in precisely the same way as an ordinary kite rises in the air due to wind pressure.

The kite, towed from an ordinary steam winch, goes down to the depth permitted by the amount of wire paid out. The actual sweep-wire passes through rings on the kites towed by a pair of vessels, thus forming a span of wire roughly parallel to the sea bottom but well beneath the surface. The actual distance apart at which sweepers can work – generally three to five hundred yards - naturally depends upon their power, towing capacity and the state of the weather.[15]

When compared to navy mine-sweepers, they suffered from a number of additional difficulties. These small boats were slow to start with, having an average speed of about 9 knots. Moreover, having to tow the sweep wire as well as to negotiate the Dardanelles current reduced their speed to about 3 or 4 knots, thus making them easy targets for any guns or howitzers on shore. The trawlers were also unarmed, unarmoured and crewed by fishermen who had no training in, or experience of, mine-sweeping or coming under fire. To increase the risk for the trawler crews, mine-mooring cables were not always cut, so that the mines had to be dragged to shallower water and sunk or detonated by rifle fire. Clearly, more suitable vessels than the twenty-one converted fishing trawlers should have been sent to the Dardanelles for what was to become a difficult operation.

Because of the trawlers' slow speed and lack of natural protection, it was decided that any sweeping of the channel would be conducted at night, under the protection of battleships and destroyers. Lieutenant Commander John Waterlow was one of a number of Royal Navy personnel temporarily appointed to the trawlers, to strengthen their resolve as they were bathed in searchlights upon their entry to the minefields. He wrote:

A 6-inch shell hit the funnel so close to my head that scraps of paint and smuts covered me. Another shell passed through the after cabin, where two or three of the men were, going in one side and out the other without bursting, and hit no one. The noise was deafening and made one's head ache.[16]

On the night of 25 February, the mine-sweepers were assigned the *Albion*, *Triumph* and *Vengeance* together with half a dozen destroyers. Some steel plating had been added to the trawlers for protection. As had occurred on the 19th, when the mine-sweepers cleared for *Queen Elizabeth* on the north-western side of the peninsula, they found no mines at the entrance to the Dardanelles.

Admiral Carden decided that on the following day, 26 February, the initial attacks on the intermediate defences should commence. The battleship *Albion* was directed to concentrate fire on Kum Kale, and the *Triumph* to aim its attack at Sedd el Bahr. The newly arrived *Majestic* was to destroy a bridge that spanned the Mendere River, which flowed to the east of Kum Kale and connected it with the road to Chanak. By this time the previous bombardment had dismounted both of the 9.4-inch guns at Helles and forced the garrisons to abandon the forts. However, no more than one third of the biggest guns had been put out of action at Sedd el Bahr and Kum Kale, while at Orkanie one of the 9.4-inch guns had been destroyed and the other damaged.

Initially, *Vengeance* was off Kum Kale, with Admiral de Robeck directing operations. He had been joined by Commodore Roger Keyes, who had just been appointed chief of staff to Admiral Carden, having spent the previous six months in charge of submarines at Harwick. The attack opened at 8.40 a.m., with the *Albion* and destroyers shelling forts at Sedd el Bahr. At 9.50 the *Majestic* used its 6-inch guns to shell the Mendere Bridge; but, because it was constructed from wooden trusses, it took some time before damage of any significance was achieved. The mine-sweepers, protected by destroyers, now moved inside the straits in their turn, to protect the battleships from any potential minefields. The primary objective for the day was an attack on the modern battery at Dardanos,[17] located on the Asiatic side of the Dardanelles, near the restricted passage at Kephez. At noon, *Majestic* and *Albion* opened fire with their 12-inch guns. At a range of approximately 11,000 yards the battleships repeatedly hit their target and, after completing their pounding of the battery, slowly started taking their turn to retreat out of the Dardanelles. As they were doing so, a mobile battery of howitzers at Eren Keui, which had been silent up to that stage, commenced firing. The *Majestic* was hit on the port side by shrapnel from one of the nearby shell bursts. She continued to suffer shrapnel damage from the shot falling around her, but no major hits were taken.

In the afternoon, demolition parties supported by Royal Marines were sent ashore to destroy the guns at Kum Kale and Sedd el Bahr once and for all. At 2 p.m. *Vengeance* landed the demolition party and fifty marines on the Aegean side, to the south of Kum Kale. The shore party was fired upon, but the *Dublin*, which was in support, put down suppressing fire. The demolition party under the command of Lieutenant Commander Robinson destroyed several anti-aircraft guns near Orkanie and next the remaining 9.4-inch gun, but there had been insufficient time to deal with the guns at Kum Kale. At 2.53 p.m. the *Irresistible* fired several rounds into Sedd el Bahr, before landing her demolition party. Four of the original six guns at Sedd el Bahr, which ranged from 11-inch to 9.4-inch, had at that stage suffered little from the bombardments. With four terrific explosions, the landing party ensured the destruction of the guns as well as the magazines, so that the fort was finally put out of commission. All landing parties returned to the ships, with only one dead and a few minor injuries. These operations were a clear indication of what could be achieved in the early stages by a combination of naval and ground forces in the systematic destruction of the forts.

On the afternoon of 27 February, after the weather had improved from the morning's storm, *Irresistible* landed a second demolition party to the east of Sedd el Bahr. *Irresistible*'s 6-inch guns again provided firing cover as the landing party destroyed four Krupp howitzers and two mortars. On the following day another demolition party was landed on the Asiatic side and was able to destroy all nine guns at Kum Kale. When the destruction was complete the demolition party made a run for it, escaping from the Turks as they arrived from the Yeni Shehr village nearby.

Over those few days the forts at Sedd el Bahr, Kum Kale and Orkanie were considerably weakened, if not, for all practical purposes, put out of action. The Turks brought in reinforcements which prevented future raids by small landing parties. However, the larger calibre guns that had been destroyed could only be replaced by much smaller batteries such as howitzers.

The March offensive

Of equal concern was the inability of the naval bombardment adequately to destroy the secondary defences, especially the mobile guns. Previously, on 1 March, *Irresistible*, flying Admiral de Robeck's flag, *Albion*, *Triumph*, *Ocean* and the *Majestic* were involved in an operation to destroy the guns along the southern shore, especially the howitzers and field guns in the neighbourhood of Eren Keui. On numerous occasions, having thought that they had silenced the guns and hence moving on to new targets, the previously attacked onshore batteries would recommence firing. Often the batteries would not reply until some time later, confirming the enemy's ability to remain relatively unde-tected and unscathed. Admiral Carden had been warned to use his munitions carefully, and this German-inspired ruse by the Turks increased the usage and waste of this valuable resource.

On the evening of 1 March, six trawlers were sent to sweep an area which would enable battleships to steam up as far as Kephez and attack the inter-mediate defences. The mine-sweepers, protected by the light cruiser *Amethyst* and by four destroyers, got within 3,000 yards of Kephez. At that point, the enemy's searchlights spotted the ships and commenced firing at point-blank range. The trawlers cut their wires and headed out of the Dardanelles as quickly as possible, while the escorts provided covering fire. The 'Catch 22' situation was becoming more obvious; the battleships could not destroy the fortifications without sweeping of the minefields, while the minefields could not be swept until the minefield's defensive batteries were destroyed, and they in turn could not be destroyed while the long-range guns of the forts kept the fleet at a distance.

On 2 March, *Canopus*, *Swiftsure* and *Cornwallis* engaged batteries 7 and 8, while the mine-sweepers continued trying to clear the minefields, but with little progress. Meanwhile, during these two nights, the French squadron reconnoitred the Gulf of Saros (Xeros). *Suffren* and *Gaulois* then bombarded the forts along the Bulair Lines and *Bouvet* bombarded the bridge over the Kavak River, while French mine-sweepers swept along the coast, finding no mines. Again, on 3 March, in support of the trawlers, *Albion*, *Prince George* and *Triumph* attacked batteries 7 and 8 once more, with little success but with no casualties or damage. A small reconnaissance party was landed at Sedd el Bahr and found a concealed battery of six 15-pound field guns, which were destroyed before the party returned safely.

Optimism was still running high when Admiral Carden sent a message to London to the effect that, subject to fine weather, he hoped to get through to Constantinople in about two weeks. This had the immediate impact of removing all reservations at the Admiralty and War Council, while in Chicago the price of wheat fell, on expectations of renewed exports from Russia once the Dardanelles was reopened.[18] But in reality Carden lacked the required determination, as on 2 and 3 March only three out of the eighteen available battleships engaged the intermediate defences and during the first three weeks no more than a quarter of the squadron was in action against the forts at any one time.[19]

To ensure the final destruction of the forts and of their guns, two demolition parties, each one supported by 250 marines, were landed on 4 March, one at Kum Kale and the other at Sedd el Bahr. Early that morning, a seaplane reconnaissance flight over the two forts disclosed no movement of troops. The recently arrived *Lord Nelson* was placed off Helles, *Ocean* near Sedd el Bahr and the *Majestic* further east, to cover the northern shore. *Irresistible* and *Cornwallis* were off Kum Kale, in Morto Bay, at the entrance to the Dardanelles; *Dublin* and *Armageddon* were further south, past the western end of the bay. At 9.30 a.m. the marines and demolition parties embarked for Sedd el Bahr. As the small boats approached the shore, they came under strong Turkish fire. Naval fire was used to suppress the Turkish activity, but, once ashore, Major Palmer commanding the marine party requested another 200 men in support. Admiral de Robeck decided that the risks were too great and ordered the withdrawal of forces. The landing party was removed at 3 p.m. with the loss of three men killed and one injured. The operation had achieved no more than the smashing of two small Nordenfeldt guns.

To the south, at Kum Kale, the enemy resistance was even greater and their numbers larger. The landing party was driven back before they were able to destroy any of the guns. The evacuation from Kum Kale proved more difficult than at Sedd el Bahr as the enemy held the high ground. Two seaplanes attempted to locate the enemy trenches without success, with one seaplane being hit eight times and the other twenty-eight times. Destroyers had to be moved in to cover the retreat, and at dusk *Scorpion* and *Wolverine* landed a recovery party to look for survivors. They successfully recovered two officers and five men who had been left behind. Even with the support of a significant naval bombardment, casualties for these raids amounted to seventeen killed, twenty-four wounded and three missing. These landings had failed even though they encountered only small pockets of Turkish resistance, which had not been quelled by naval fire. The ability of small groups to repulse such landings was, as it turned out, a forewarning of things to come.

On 5 March, *Queen Elizabeth* began a bombardment of Rumili Meddjidieh, which was situated at the Narrows on the European side. This fort consisted of half a dozen guns, including 11- and 9.4-inch ones. Also slightly further to the north was Namazien, with 11-inch, 10.2-inch and a few 9.4-inch guns. The operation was planned to be an indirect bombardment by *Queen Elizabeth*, utilizing her 15-inch guns at the limit of her effective range of 22,000 yards. She was anchored two and a half miles to the south-west of Gaba Tepe, and supported by *Inflexible* and *Prince George*. *Queen Elizabeth* came under howitzer fire, but her escorts quickly suppressed it. As it was an indirect bombardment, spotting of the fall of shot was required. The initial plan was to do this from the air, but difficulties arose when the propeller of one seaplane disintegrated and the plane crashed from a height of 3,000 feet. Fortunately, both pilot and observer survived. Further difficulties arose with the wounding of a second seaplane's pilot, while a third provided only one observation before darkness prevented further activity. *Irresistible*, *Canopus* and *Cornwallis* were therefore sent up the straits to spot the fall of shot and to wireless back their results. The battleships came under attack from howitzers and various other guns from shore; hence, in order to share the risk, each took the lead in turn. From the twenty-eight rounds fired by *Queen Elizabeth* at Rumili Meddjidieh there were eleven hits, and only one from the five rounds aimed at Namazien. Although the forts were severely damaged and the gun crews shaken, not one of the guns was put out of action.

Next day, the bombardment by *Queen Elizabeth* resumed at 12.30 p.m. with fire directed at Chemenlek, which lay on the Asiatic side of the Narrows, opposite the previous day's targets. Chemenlek contained two Krupp 14-inch cannons, as well as 9.4-inch and 8.2-inch guns and howitzers. This was one of the three most powerful forts at the Narrows. Firing from the same location as on the previous day, *Queen Elizabeth* got off only one round before she was hit half a dozen times by shore fire and forced to move out a further 2,000 yards. At this new station she was hit a third time and continued to move off-shore, until she was 21,000 yards from her target and again near the limit of her 15-inch guns. At this range, the chances of hitting the individual guns at the fort were obviously very low, especially with the poor level of spotting provided. In the course of that day *Queen Elizabeth* was hit no fewer than seventeen times by the concealed 6-inch howitzers on shore. On the same day, the Turks decided to retaliate in a similar fashion, and moved their battleship *Barbaros Hayreddin* down to the Narrows, firing her 11-inch guns over the Gallipoli Peninsula and using observers at Gaba Tepe. The *Barbaros* then retreated back to the safety of the northern end of the Narrows.

After the *Barbaros* had finished her bombardment, the British battleships *Vengeance*, *Albion*, *Prince George* and *Majestic*, together with the French *Suffren*, made four runs above Eren Keui Bay. At a range of 13,000 yards they fired on Rumili Meddjidieh, on the European side of the Narrows and Dardanos on the Asiatic side. Both forts replied, achieving hits on the *Vengeance* and the *Majestic*. That evening around midnight, the British trawlers, supported by the light cruiser *Amethyst* and destroyers, renewed their efforts to reach the mines. However, enemy fire, aided by searchlights, was too intense and the trawlers withdrew. On Sunday 7 March, *Agamemnon* and *Lord Nelson* came up to within 13,000 yards of Rumili Meddjidieh, followed by the *Suffren*, *Charlemagne*, *Gaulois* and *Bouvet*, which fired on the howitzers and field guns. This action finished for the day at 3 p.m. *Lord Nelson* was hit below the water-line by howitzer fire and, listing slightly to port, had to return to Mudros for repairs. That evening the French mine-sweepers, covered by seven destroyers, also tried to reach the minefields but got the same reception as their British counterparts, and were forced to retreat under intense fire.

The above narration clearly shows that, at this stage, the Anglo-French naval forces had achieved little for the expenditure of significant amounts of ammunition and undue wear of their guns. The actions were also relatively repetitive, with ships entering the Narrows, and then using the wider lower end at Eren Keui Bay as a turning area, while they fired on the intermediate and inner defences. At 5 a.m. on 8 March, following the repulse of the French mine-sweepers the previous evening, the 380-ton Turkish naval steamer *Nusret*[20] travelled down the straits to Eren Keui Bay. She had been fitted with twenty (or, from Turkish records, twenty-six) Carbonit mines and, under the direction of Colonel Geehl, she started laying these mines. They were not placed in a line across the Narrows but down the Narrows, within Eren Keni Bay on the Asiatic side, at approximately 100-yard intervals. She returned to

Chemenlek at 8 a.m. The mines were set at a depth which would hit the battleships but allowed the keels of the destroyers and trawlers to pass over without harm. It may have been considered more effective to lay one or two lines of mines straight across the straits; but mines were in short supply. Also, placing the mines down the straits, within the 'turning' area for the capital ships, was to result in considerable confusion for the Allies.

By one of those many quirks of fate, *Queen Elizabeth* entered the straits for the very first time on 8 March, with the purpose of firing on the forts at the Narrows. Fortunately the pride of the British navy did not proceed very far into the straits and thus avoided contact with the newly laid minefield. However, the *Irresistible*, one of her five supporting ships, observed several mines, which had possibly come loose from their moorings. Due to bad light and difficulty of spotting, *Queen Elizabeth* concentrated her fire on Rumili Meddjidieh, which resulted in only one effective hit before she withdrew at 3.30 p.m. That evening trawlers made another effort to sweep off the Kephez area but, as previously, were driven back. At this stage Admiral Carden, who had been flying his flag on the *Queen Elizabeth*, decided that bombardment of the forts would be suspended for several days. On 9 March *Albion*, *Prince George* and *Irresistible*, accompanied by destroyers, did go into the straits to mop up some minor targets, and that evening three trawlers once again attempted without success to sweep the area off Kephez.

On the evening of 8 March, after much discussion between the admiral and Commodore Keyes, who continued to press the point that the mines had to be removed without further delay, the admiral sent a telegram to the Admiralty which included the following text:

To sum up the situation. We are for the present checked by absence of efficient air reconnaissance, the necessity of clearing the minefield, and the presence of a large number of movable howitzers on both sides of the Straits, whose positions up to the present we have not been able to locate. Meanwhile, every effort will be made to clear the minefield by night, with two battleships in support. Two battleships watch the shore on both sides of the entrance by day and prevent the enemy from collecting in that locality or bringing up guns.

Until it is considered advantageous to resume bombardment on a large scale, it is not desirable to send battleships far inside by day, as it only affords practice to the enemy's howitzers. . . . Our experience shows that gunfire alone will not render forts innocuous; most of the guns must be destroyed individually by demolition.[21]

Admiral Carden was clearly having second thoughts about dominating the forts by naval fire alone and saw increasing need for intervention by troops on the ground to complete the job. As Bean wrote:

> The fierce shriek of a great high-velocity shell swishing low overhead, and the dust and noise of the burst, may have frightened the gunners of the forts to cover; but when, time after time, the shells burst harmlessly a hundred yards behind the target, or merely threw up large earth-clouds from the other side of the grass ramparts, such shellfire was an experience to which in this war brave men very soon became accustomed.[22]

By this stage, it was also becoming apparent to the War Council that troops had to be sent to the Dardanelles. The role of such troops, however, was regarded as being more in the nature of a supporting naval action than of an army land offensive supported by the navy. In the view of the War Council, troops would take and hold territories effectively won by naval bombardment, but no more than that. By 10 March, Kitchener had also agreed to the initial sending of the experienced 29 Division, and informed the War Council that a total force of 128,700 could be deployed. However, this figure included 47,600 Russian troops which were never to be made available, and was well below his original estimate of 150,000.[23] Kitchener believed that the Turks would evacuate the peninsula once the fleet passed through the Dardanelles, but that a force would be required to take the Bulair Lines, to prevent the Turks from re-invading the peninsula. The rest of the force would approach Constantinople and take control of the Bosphorus, so that the British fleet could deal with the *Goeben*. The Russian fleet and its army would then attack and take control of Constantinople.

The need to remove mines from the straits became increasingly apparent. On the evening of 10 March, the trawlers *Escallonia, Manx Hero, Syringa, Beatrice II, Soldier Prince, Avon* and *Gwellian*, with four escorting destroyers, the light cruiser *Amethyst* and the battleship *Canopus*, entered the straits. This time there was a change in tactics, with the trawlers heading for an area above Kephez and then using the current to proceed downstream. The first pair of trawlers, having just put out their sweeps, caught several mines in the dark waters. These exploded, sinking the *Manx Hero*, although the crew was saved. Overhearing the explosion, the enemy turned on their powerful searchlights and opened fire with their 6-inch guns. *Canopus* fired back at the batteries but was unable to destroy the searchlights. During the engagement two more trawlers were hit and, under intense fire, the other trawlers quickly abandoned their sweep and departed under the cover of the destroyers.

On the evening of 11 March, six more trawlers were again found by searchlights and, under fire, withdrew for home without conducting any sweeps. Up until this time the trawlers had been manned by the fishermen who operated them in the North Sea. On the evening of Saturday 13 March, the trawlers and picket-boats[24] were manned for the first time by volunteers from the Royal Navy and the Royal Naval Reserve (RNR). The trawlers were to pair off on the European side, as far above Kephez Point as possible, and then sweep downstream, each pair slightly overlapping the next one ahead. The picket boats were to go beyond Kephez Point, turn around, deploy their sweeps and blow up anything on their way down, before returning back upstream. Protected by the light cruiser *Amethyst* and by destroyers, they once again attempted to sweep for mines and once again they came under a tremendous barrage from the guns on shore; ultimately they were forced to retreat. Only one pair of trawlers was able to deploy the sweeps. Four trawlers and one picket boat were put out of action by the guns recovered from the torpedoed *Mesudiye*. The *Amethyst* also suffered a number of hits, which resulted in twenty-four dead and thirty-six injured. A further five men were killed on the trawlers.

Until March, the only secure base of operations for Allied ships was in Alexandria in Egypt, or in Malta. On 7 March the island of Lemnos (including its major port of Mudros) was occupied by troops sent from Egypt. The Greeks had captured the island during the Balkan Wars, and now, with the support of the pro-Allied Greek Prime Minister Venizelos, the Greek garrison was withdrawn, leaving the defences undisturbed for the British to occupy.[25] The island had technically become Turkish again once the Greeks had withdrawn. Although the Greek Prime Minister resigned at this time on account of his king's refusal to support any Greek military activity, the island was still occupied by the British. As mentioned previously, Rear Admiral Wemyss was selected as military governor. Wemyss, during the coming months, took charge and built up the base around the great natural harbour of Mudros.

Admiral Carden decided on 14 March that a major attack on the forts would be carried out on 18 March. This decision was no doubt influenced by a telegram from the First Lord, stating that the Admiralty had information that the Turkish forts were short of ammunition; that German officers were making desperate appeals (for further assistance); and that the dispatch of a German or Austrian submarine was under consideration. He was ordered to make haste while the opportunity presented itself, before the arrival of enemy submarines, which would complicate the situation. He should therefore press forward methodically and resolutely, by day and by night. The Admiralty obtained the information from Room 40 of Naval Intelligence, through the decoding of the German emperor's telegram to Admiral Usedom on 13 March. The message read:

. . . HM the Kaiser has received the report and telegram relating to the

Dardanelles. Everything conceivable is being done to arrange for the supply of ammunition. For political reasons it is necessary to maintain a confident tone in Turkey. The Kaiser requests you to use your influences in this direction. The sending of a German or Austrian submarine is being seriously considered.[26]

Therefore during the intervening four days, between 14 and 18 March, particularly by daylight, the lower straits would have to be cleared of any mines by the trawlers. The French sent in nine trawlers, later followed by the British trawlers, to sweep out south-east from Suan Dere. Again, the trawlers came under heavy fire and were often prevented from doing their job. However, by 18 March the commanding officer of the British mine-sweepers reported that no mines had been found between Kephez Bay and the White Cliffs at the northern end of Eren Keui Bay (a distance of about 1.5 miles), and the French reported finding none below the White Cliffs. Unfortunately, neither of them had towed their sweeps across into Eren Keui Bay. As part of the increasing importance of the Dardanelles front, the British and French were quickly assembling additional mine-sweepers, to be sent as soon as possible to assist with the clearing. Between 14 and 16 March seaplanes were also used to search for mines and reported the appropriate areas as clear. The ability of seaplanes to spot mines at a depth of 18 feet from a height of 3,000 feet was tested on 15 March, to ensure the effectiveness of their use. However, the results, which were regarded as successful, were probably bogus (or so they were described by the Mitchell report). This was because the background against which the visibility of the mines had been tested was probably a shallow sandy bottom seen through clear water. In contrast, the straits presented a dark rocky bottom, against which the mines were most unlikely to become visible.[27] The seaplanes were now used not only to detect the presence of mines, but, more dangerously, their absence.

Divisions of infantry were being steadily assembled, and on 17 March General Sir Ian Hamilton arrived to meet Admiral Carden. He had been appointed by Kitchener as commander of the Allied ground forces on 12 March, by which time Kitchener had become more convinced that the navy was unlikely to force the straits on its own. Hamilton was one of Britain's most experienced generals, having been Kitchener's chief of staff in the Boer War, and was attached to the Japanese army during its war with Russia. He had a reputation for bravery, since he had been recommended for the Victoria Cross on two occasions. He had served in most capacities in the army, except as commander-in-chief.

On 16 March, Admiral Carden, who had been under intense pressure, took sick leave and command was handed over to Rear Admiral de Robeck.

Although Admiral Wemyss was de Robeck's senior, he agreed to de Robeck taking command of the attack on the Dardanelles because of his superior first-hand knowledge. De Robeck was promoted acting Vice-Admiral, while Wemyss continued in his role as administrator of operations on Mudros. As matters turned out, this continuation was perhaps one of the most unfortunate cases of largesse during the war.

Admiral de Robeck was committed to the major offensive of 18 March; his ships and men were getting tired. Apart from battle damage, some ships had guns that had to be replaced due to excessive wear. At 8.30 a.m., in a light southerly wind, the fleet left its base. Two hours later, the first line of ships, *Queen Elizabeth*, *Agamemnon*, *Lord Nelson* and *Inflexible*, preceded by destroyers fitted with light sweeps, entered the lower part of the Dardanelles. The north flank was guarded by *Prince George* and the southern flank by *Triumph*. As reported by one of the participants: 'It looked as if no human forces could withstand such array of might and power.'[28]

The plan of attack was for the four British battleships to go in advance of the French battleships and silence the enemy. Then the French battleships *Suffren*, *Bouvet*, *Gaulois* and *Charlemagne* were to close on the forts and destroy them. Because of the mobile howitzers, ships were not to anchor but rather to keep moving slowly ahead, against the current. *Ocean*, *Irresistible*, *Albion* and *Vengeance*, supported by *Swiftsure* and *Majestic*, were then to relieve the French formation and to continue the bombardment. It was hoped that this concentrated and continuous fire would do the job. With the main forts and light batteries having been brought under control, three pairs of trawlers, supported by the battleships *Cornwallis* and *Canopus*, were to sweep along the Asiatic side to Sari Siglar Bay, to enable the fleet to bring its fire power to bear against the Narrows at close range.

At 10.10 a.m. the first of the battleships proceeded up the straits, with *Queen Elizabeth* on the western flank. *Agamemnon*, *Lord Nelson* and *Inflexible* bombarded Yildiz, Rumili Meddjidieh, Hamidieh II and Namazieh, on the European side of the Narrows. *Triumph* on the Asiatic flank and *Prince George* on the European side silenced the fire from howitzers, which had started at 10.58 a.m. By 11.28, *Queen Elizabeth* had initiated her long-range attack on Hamidieh I, followed by an attack on Chemenlik, while *Lord Nelson* concentrated on Hamidieh II. The other battleships on the European side of the Narrows, together with *Prince George* and *Triumph*, attacked the forts of Messudieh, Yildiz and Dardanos. Although the forts did reply sparingly with their ammunition, the mobile howitzers and field artillery represented the greatest difficulty for the battleships. After an hour of bombardment, at 12.15, the French ships were ordered to close in. *Queen Elizabeth* was hit three times by the Turkish forts, and then at 12.30 the *Gaulois* was hit by a 14-inch shell fired from the Narrows, which caused her to retire; finally she had to beach herself on Rabbit Island outside the Dardanelles. Turkish gunfire intensified as it was realized that the arrival of fourteen capital ships signalled the start of a major Anglo-French initiative.

The *Chicago Daily News* reporter Raymond Swing and several other journalists were seated on a hill to the north of Chanak with a perfect view of the events unfolding. Swing was later to recall:

> Viewed as a picture, the battle was a sight of overpowering grandeur. The skies were cloudless, the sun shone down from near the zenith on the war ships, the waters were a deep clear blue, the Hellespont hills were a dark green. The picture was in many hues, the gray–white smoke of the explosions, the orange smoke of firing cannon, and the black of flying earth in eruption, all set off by the white geysers of water as they rose after the immersion of shells. The accompaniment of sound was both oppressively insistent and varied. There was the roar when guns fired, the deafening detonations of the shells when they hit, the whistle of shells in flight, the shriek of flying splinters. We were close enough on our hill site to see and hear the firing of shells and their burst almost simultaneously.[29]

In the formation of British ships, *Inflexible* was on the southern or Asiatic side, closest to the line of mines laid by the *Nusret*. Turkish howitzer fire therefore concentrated on her, in an attempt to get her to move further south into the minefield. *Inflexible* was hit on numerous occasions, set on fire, and suffered significant other damage and a number of casualties. *Lord Nelson* moved to her aid, firing on the howitzers at Eren Keui. At 1.25 p.m. *Inflexible* withdrew to put out the fire and resumed her attack at 2.36 p.m. The *Agamemnon* also came under heavy attack, and was hit twelve times below her armour belt, five times on the amour and seven times above. However, by 2 p.m. the Turkish barrage had abated, partially due to very low levels of ammunition, so Admiral de Robeck decided to send his mine-sweepers forward. Again the Turkish fire increased, this time directed at the small trawlers, so that they had to be recalled, having failed to reach Kephez Point.

The second group of British battleships was now ordered to relieve the French battleships. The situation facing the Turkish defenders at that time was best described by the Turkish general staff as follows:

> By 2 p.m. the situation had become critical. All telephone wires were cut, all communication with the forts was interrupted, some of the guns had been knocked out, others were half buried, others again were out of action with

their breech mechanism jammed; in consequence the artillery fire of the defence had slackened considerably.[30]

The relief of the French battleships played into the hands of the Turks, because during the change-over the French ships turned to starboard towards the Asiatic shore. The *Bouvet* was the battleship furthest to the south and she ran straight into the minefield. As reported by one of *Queen Elizabeth*'s officers:

A cloud of white smoke was seen over the forecastle of the *Bouvet*, heeling over to about 15 degrees to starboard, and listing rapidly to 30 degrees. Men could be seen running up over her bottom. She turned turtle, went down stern first, her bow remaining for a few seconds upright, and then she was completely gone. Of her total complement (between 600 and 700) only 5 officers, 10 petty officers, and 51 men were saved.[31]

Incredibly, the ship only took two minutes and thirty-five seconds to sink! In her death throes, the *Bouvet* most likely also dislodged a number of mines that now floated with the currents down the straits, narrowly missing nearby ships.

At 2.30 p.m. *Vengeance, Albion, Irresistible* and *Ocean* began to engage the forts at ranges of 11,500 to 13,000 yards, being supported by *Swiftsure* and *Majestic*. At 3.14 p.m., the *Irresistible* either struck a mine or was hit by a shell. A quarter of an hour later she was observed to have a list, but kept up her fire on the forts. By this stage, the trawlers had got out their sweeps and were proceeding up the straits. They exploded three mines. *Inflexible* had received a number of hits from the enemy's shore batteries, which had put one of her 12-inch guns out of action. Earlier on, a shell had fallen close to her port side and caused a leak in a couple of compartments. At 3.45 p.m. the battlecruiser struck a mine on the starboard bow. The inrush of water killed thirty-nine men as the ship took on two thousand tons of water and was forced to leave her position after six hours of action. She returned safely to Tenedos, where it was discovered that twenty compartments had flooded through a rectangular opening to the sea of 30 by 26 feet.

Some thirty minutes after the *Inflexible* had struck the mine, it was the turn of the *Irresistible*. She got to within 10,000 yards of Rumili Meddjidieh and had turned towards the Asiatic side to increase her range, when she entered the northernmost part of *Nusret*'s mined area. Almost immediately, she hit a mine and was holed underneath her starboard engine room, losing all headway. Under heavy enemy fire, the destroyer *Wear* rescued 28 officers and 582 men. The captain and a skeleton crew remained aboard, while the *Ocean*, under the command of Captain Hayes-Sadler, was ordered to prepare to take her in tow. When she made no apparent effort to help the *Irresistible*, she was ordered to withdraw. *Ocean* had still not withdrawn by 6.05 p.m., when she also struck a mine on her starboard side, about a quarter of the distance in from the northern end of the line of mines. Simultaneously, a shell destroyed her steering, forcing her to be abandoned. The destroyers *Clone*, *Chelmer*, *Kennet* and *Jed* rescued the crew. When it became dark, the captain of the *Irresistible* returned to his ship in the *Jed* and recovered four men who had been left behind. By 7.20 p.m. the two battleships were abandoned. Turkish reports state that the *Ocean* drifted into Morto Bay and sank at about 10.30 p.m., while the *Irresistible* drifted into range of the Narrows forts and was sunk by 7.30 p.m.[32] The next day an aerial search for the two vessels failed to find them; it was assumed at the time that the ships had been sunk by enemy fire during the night. Admiral de Robeck had therefore three ships sunk, three put out of action and in need of dockyard repairs, and numerous other units temporarily out of action.[33]

The damage sustained by the forts was relatively modest. Hamidieh II had both guns knocked out and its barracks destroyed, while Rumili had one gun temporarily out of action. At Namazieh one gun was destroyed and its barracks were burnt, and at Chemenlik the magazine had been destroyed. Clearly greater accuracy was required for destroying the guns. Perhaps greater success might have been achieved if all of the fleet's firepower could have been brought to bear on one fort only at the moment when the overwhelming confluence of destruction might have overcome the lack of accuracy; but spotting for so many ships would have become a serious problem.

At 9.30 a.m. on Friday 19 March, Admiral de Robeck held a conference with his captains to review the events of the day before. It was decided to persevere with the naval bombardment. Mine-sweeping was now of greater concern than ever, and a decision was made to fit eight Beagle class destroyers with sweeps, and six River class destroyers and four torpedo boats with light sweeps to locate mines.[34] A flotilla of picket boats, fifty British and a dozen French trawlers would also be added, to clear the straits of any mines. To prevent the enemy from laying new mines, nets would be set on the night before the bombardment, after the straits had been cleared. All these planned activities would require several days of rehearsal.

Some days earlier, *Implacable*, *Queen*, *London* and *Prince of Wales* had left England for the Dardanelles, while the French replaced *Bouvet* with *Henri IV*. On 21 March, de Robeck cabled the Admiralty to the effect that he considered the Turkish forts and batteries could be sufficiently dominated to allow the mine-sweepers to clear the Kephez minefield. On 22 March, General Hamilton and Lieutenant General Birdwood met Admiral de Robeck and informed him that the army would be ready by 14 April. Commodore Keyes also informed the admiral that the new and more powerful sweeper force would not be ready until 4 April.

It was at this time that de Robeck realized that, without the army ensuring the forts were silenced, the lines of communication could not be kept open for the navy to reach and hold the Sea of Marmara. He had hoped that the army would land at Bulair on the neck of the peninsula, to cut off the Turkish army. There would then be no threat to the fleet as it steamed in and out of the Dardanelles; but Hamilton informed him that the landing couldn't be done. It may also have become apparent to the admiral that Hamilton's force was more than just an occupying force, to be landed once the forts had been overcome. It was planned instead to be a force capable of a seaborne invasion, which moved the navy into having a supporting role rather than being the primary weapon in the operation. This provided him with an excuse not to attack with the navy alone; it also saved him from being solely responsible for any possible adverse outcome. The army and the sweeper force were now expected also to be ready at about the same time, therefore Admiral de Robeck changed his mind and decided to delay the attack until the army was ready.

His chief of staff, Commodore Keyes, was still in favour of an immediate bombardment and tried to convince him to go ahead with it. Churchill, too, wanted to order de Robeck to attack as soon as possible, but the War Office refused to support him, and the Admiralty would not interfere with the admiral in command. Churchill tried to convince de Robeck, but had to avoid giving the impression that he was ordering him. On 24 March, Churchill as First Lord wrote to de Robeck:

It is clear that the Army should at once prepare for attack on Kilid Bahr Plateau at earliest opportunity, and Lord Kitchener hopes April 14th can be antedated. This is a matter for the War Office. But the question now to be decided by the Admiralty is whether time has come to abandon the naval plans of forcing Dardanelles without the aid of a large army. It may be necessary to accept check of the 18th instant as decisive, and to admit that it is beyond our power, and if you think this you should not fail to say so. But, before deciding, certain facts must be weighed: 1st. The delay and consequent danger of submarines coming and ruining all; 2nd, the heavy losses, at least 5,000, which the Army would suffer; 3rd, the possibility of a check in the land operations far more serious than the loss of a few old surplus ships; 4th, the fact that even when Kilid Bahr Plateau has been taken by the Army and the Kilid Bahr group of forts rendered untenable, the Asiatic forts will still be effective, and most of the mine danger which is now your principal difficulty will menace you in the long reach above the Narrows.

These must be balanced against risks and hopes of purely naval under-takings. You must not under-rate supreme moral effect of a British Fleet with sufficient fuel and ammunition entering the Marmora, provided it is strong enough to destroy Turco-German vessels. Gallipoli Peninsula would be completely cut off if our ships were on both sides of Bulair Isthmus. It seems very probable that as soon as it is apparent that forts at the Narrows are not going to stop the Fleet, a general evacuation of the Peninsula will take place; but anyhow, all troops remaining upon it would be doomed to starvation or surrender. Besides this there is the political effect of the arrival of the Fleet before Constantinople, which is incalculable, and may well be absolutely decisive.

Assuming only the minimum good results follow the successful passage of the Fleet into the Marmora, viz., that the Turkish Army on Gallipoli continues to hold out, and with forts and field guns close up the Straits, and that no revolution occurs at Constantinople, then perhaps in the last resort the Army would have to storm Kilid Bahr Plateau, and secure a permanent reopening of the Straits. It would be possible with the ships left behind at the entrance, and with those in Egypt, to give the necessary support to the military operations, so that at the worst the Army would only have to do, after you had got through, what they will have to do anyhow if your telegram is accepted; while, on the other hand, the probability is that your getting through would decide everything in our favour. Further, once through the Dardanelles the current would be with you in any return attack on the forts, and the mining danger would be practically over. Therefore, danger to your line of communications is not serious or incurable.

What has happened since the 21st to make you alter your intentions of renewing the attack as soon as the weather is favourable? We have never contemplated a reckless rush over minefields and past undamaged primary guns. But the original Admiralty instructions and telegram No. 109 prescribe a careful and deliberate method of advance, and I should like to know what are the reasons which, in your opinion, render this no longer possible, in spite of your new aircraft and improved methods of mine-sweeping. We know the forts are short of ammunition. It is probable that they have not got many mines. You should be able to feel your way while at the same time pressing hard.

I cannot understand why, as a preliminary step, forts like 7 and 8 should not be demolished by heavy gunfire, first at long range, afterwards at short range, now that you have good aeroplane observation. I wish to hear further from you before any official reply is sent. You may discuss this telegram with General Hamilton if he is with you, and then telegraph fully. Admiralty will then give you their decision. You must of course understand that this telegram is not an executive order, but is sent because it is most important that there should be no misunderstanding.[35]

De Robeck's mind was made up, and nothing was going to change it, as his response clearly showed:

I do not hold check on 18th decisive, but, having met General Hamilton on 22nd and heard his proposals, I now consider a combined operation essential to obtain great results and object of campaign. Therefore my considered opinion is that Fleet should prepare way and indicate in my 268. To attack Narrows now with Fleet would be a mistake, as it would jeopardize the execution of a better and bigger scheme. A full appreciation of the situation in the Dardanelles is being prepared and will be wired.[36]

Communications between the First Lord and de Robeck were to continue for some time, with Churchill doing his best to convince the admiral with perhaps one of his strongest arguments: the matter of what would happen if the army failed in its endeavours. The admiral's only response was: there was only one objective, and that was to win. So much of the campaign success now depended on the upcoming land battles.

A lot has been written about the plight of the Turkish defenders and the acute shortage of munitions, particularly large calibre, after the engagement on 18 March. The German account read:

Most of the Turkish ammunition had been expended. The medium howitzers and minefield batteries had fired half their supply . . . for the five 35.5 cm guns there were only 271 rounds, say 50 each; for the eleven 23 cm between 30 to 50 rounds per gun. . . . Particularly serious was the fact that the long-range H. E. shells, which alone were effective against armour, were nearly all used up. Fort Hamidieh had only 17 of them; Kilid Bahr but 10. Also there was no reserve of mines. What, then, was to happen if the battle was renewed on the 19th and following days with undiminished violence?[37]

The Turkish account indicated that nearly 2,000 shells had been fired and that, out of 176 guns, only eight had been hit. They had suffered forty men killed and seventy wounded. Manufacture of ammunition in Turkey was poor, and at that stage the Balkan States prevented the easy overland passage of ammunition from Germany.[38] Although bullets for the large calibre guns were dangerously low, there were still ample supplies for the howitzers. The Turkish forces were under orders to fight to the last round before deserting their guns. The question is perhaps not whether another naval attack could have silenced the guns and broken through to the Sea of Marmara, though, given the plight of the Turkish forces, such action may well have succeeded. Rather, the question which might well be asked is: if the lines of communication could have been kept open, what would the naval forces have done once they broke through? A naval attack on Constantinople, with the aim of pressuring Turkey to sue for peace, would be obvious. However, with no territory conquered, the likelihood of such a tactic being successful is always questionable.

Von Sanders was acutely aware of the situation, but also realized that the failure of the Anglo–French naval forces to break through the Dardanelles meant that they would now have to employ ground forces. On 26 March he took over the command of all the Turkish forces in Gallipoli and moved his command from Constantinople to the former French consular agent's house in the harbour town of Gallipoli. With news coming from Greece of the build-up of British and French forces, defensive preparations were sped up. The most significant change he introduced was to concentrate inland his force of five divisions. These had previously been scattered along the whole coast as frontier guards, to provide limited resistance at any landing point. By concentrating his forces, von Sanders would be able to provide reserves to defend against, and to counter-attack, any landing.

On the Anglo–French side, preparations were also being made to assemble both the army and sufficient numbers of small vessels (barges and lighters), to land the men. Additional and better aeroplanes arrived to increase the extent of surveillance, which in fact provided evidence that the previous bombardments had actually done little to destroy the enemy's guns. The navy maintained its vigilance, with two battleships patrolling the straits every forty-eight hours, while repairs to the damaged ships were undertaken. Mine-sweeping trawlers continued to enter the straits in an attempt to remove mines but were met, as previously, with considerable fire from the shore batteries. Rear Admiral Thursby, who now commanded the mine-sweepers, went himself to assess the situation. He came to the conclusion that the risks were too great for the crews, and therefore all sweeping finished on 7 April. This now confirmed that a naval breakthrough on its own was out of the question. New surveys of the Gallipoli coastline were also undertaken, which would prove most valuable in the coming invasion. The navy continued the indirect bombardment of forts and strategic targets as it awaited the invasion date.

Submarine activity, April 1915

In March 1915, the Allied submarine squadron was based at Malta and consisted of 5 B class submarines, including *B11*, *AE2*, an Australian submarine[39] under the command of Lieutenant Commander H. D. G. Stoker (of whom we will hear more later) and three French submarines. Holbrook's report from B11 suggested that the chances of a submarine penetrating the Narrows were not high. However, the E class,[40] with its internal gyrocompass and much larger battery capacity, was better equipped for the job. On 7 March, after completion of AE2's patrol, Stoker headed for Mudros, with a typed memorandum to the commander-in-chief of his proposal to break through the Dardanelles.

> It outlined his method of making the most of his battery, gave details of distances and proposed courses, depths and speeds, and ended by submitting that 'given skilful navigation the passage is feasible'.[41]

Due to an unfortunate accident,[42] AE2 was forced to return to Malta for repairs, which denied Stoker his chance to be the first to attempt to negotiate the passage, although, as the fates would have it, he was to play a pivotal role in the future.

On 9 April, two E class submarines – E14, under the command of Lieutenant Commander E. C. Boyle, and E15, under the command of Lieutenant Commander T. S. Brodie – arrived at Mudros with their tender Adamant. E11 had also been sent from England with the other two submarines, but stopped off at Malta for some needed repairs. Commodore Keyes had asked Lieutenant Commander C. G. Brodie,[43] on the arrival of the E boats, to produce all available information on the feasibility of a passage up the straits. His research showed that, while the British were still in Constantinople, little intelligence had been produced other than some admiralty charts and sailing instructions. The French liaison officer did provide a copy of a memorandum from Krupps, which in 1913 suggested to the Greeks – who were fighting the Turks at that time – that a submarine could reach Nagara. Their calculations were based on a U-boat which, they claimed, had a battery endurance of 13 hours at a submerged speed of 4.5 knots, giving about 60 miles range when submerged. They allowed for a current of 4 knots in the Narrows and 1 knot in the wider sections, recommending a diving depth of 20 to 25 metres. Thus for the 20 miles from Kum Kale to Nagara, Krupps had allowed for the U-boat

> to do 3 miles at seven knots (at thrice the cost of 4½), and 17 miles at 4½ knots. That is, one hour at 7, five at 4½, costing a total of eight hours' endurance, leaving a margin of five hours for attacking above Nagara and return downstream.[44]

The difficulty for the E boats was their lower economical submerged speed, of only 3 knots, which, depending on the true speed of the currents within the straits, might not be sufficient to make much progress up the Narrows and would result in a rapid depletion of stored battery power.

On 14 April, on board *Queen Elizabeth*, Commodore Keyes with his assistant, C. G. Brodie, met the E boat commanders and others for a briefing on how an attempt might be made to get through the Dardanelles. Stoker's original plan called for a night surface run of 6 to 7 miles, from the centre of the entrance to the bend in the strait, from which a straight course to the Narrows could be plotted. Aeroplanes or surface craft might also be employed to divert the enemy's attention. C. G. Brodie had previously gone out at night with mine-sweepers, during which time his experience had been that the enemy did not fire on ships going up the straits, but rather waited till they turned and then fired at minimum range. He had also found that the searchlights had difficulty spotting a small craft. The lights would usually sweep slowly through their arcs, never lingering on a target. It was therefore hoped that a submarine could reach a point within 3 or 4 miles off Kephez on her diesel engines. At early dawn, she would dive straight to 90 feet and proceed for an hour on the same course, directly for Chanak. The submarine would then come to periscope depth and could expect to be somewhere abreast of Kephez. There she would be able to get an accurate fix on her position and so estimate the strength of the current for the previous hour. Once she reached the Narrows, the submarine would need to get a few good fixes and then would immediately attempt to round the two difficult bends of the Narrows at high speed. It would be necessary to continue the high-speed run until well past Nagara. From that point on, there would be a relatively simple leg of 17 miles to the town of Gallipoli.

The chances of survival would depend very much on the endurance of the batteries, the various speeds of the currents and Turkish counter-measures, for instance minefields and nets. In addition, other issues relevant to the problem were also discussed. These included the diversionary tactics to be employed by destroyers and surface craft and the use of aircraft during the day – the latter, particularly, for reconnaissance to determine where the submarine might be located. However, most of the discussion centred on the navigational leading marks and their visibility and on the ease of recognition through the periscope, designed to help to get a quick and accurate fix. A lot was also said about the speed of the currents, battery endurance and relative speed over the ground. One aspect which was not discussed was the effect of fresh water getting mixed with salt-water, the relative differences in their densities and the consequences these might have on a boat's trim. Finally Keyes asked: 'Do you think a boat can make it?' Sommerville, the captain of the *Adamant* submarine flotilla, answered 'No', and Pownall, the commander of the Malta submarine flotilla, agreed. C. G. Brodie and Boyle also answered 'No', but T. S. Brodie (C. G. Brodie's twin brother), shy but confident, said 'Yes'; at which point Keyes jumped to his feet and said: 'Well it's got to be tried, and you shall do it.'[45]

Preparations started immediately, with plans to send *E14* after *E15* if she was successful. The ships' captains, Brodie (*E15*) and Boyle (*E14*), were sent to Tenedos to take a flight over the Dardanelles, so that they would become more familiar with the landmarks. Brodie was the only one to make the flight on 12 April with Commander Samson,[46] at low altitude beyond Kephez Point; he was concerned that the enemy might become more active if a second flight were undertaken. *E15* was ordered to leave for Tenedos on 15 April. Before departure the engineers worked all through the night to repair one of *E15*'s diving rudders. At 3 a.m. on 17 April, *E15* left Tenedos for the straits. At 8.30 a.m. C. G. Brodie took off as an observer in a two-seater Farman seaplane piloted by Lieutenant Collett, to check on the submarine's progress. The plane carried a 200-pound bomb, designed to be dropped on Chanak as a distraction. They encountered some flak, but at 6,000 feet and some miles south of Kephez C. G. Brodie spotted the outline of his brother's submarine, *E15*, on a white sandy beach, next to a Turkish torpedo boat, with oily smoke coming from the conning tower.

It was now important to destroy the submarine, so that the enemy could not use it. *B6* under the command of Lieutenant Macarthur proceeded up the Dardanelles that day, submerging at 10.40 a.m., with orders from *Swiftsure* to destroy *E15* or any vessels engaged in salvaging her. For the next four hours the small submarine fought the currents, with Macarthur working the boat every few minutes between its cruising depth of 60 feet and periscope depth of 14 feet, to observe his position. The compass had become useless as it fogged up, which imposed the need for continuous sightings shortly after 1 p.m.; this resulted in the boat coming under heavy fire from both shores each time it raised its periscope. At 2.38 p.m. a vessel was sighted in Kephez Bay on the starboard bow; a torpedo was fired a few minutes later, at an optimistic range of between 1,200 and 1,300 yards. The submarine then turned for home, surfacing at the entrance to the Dardanelles at 4.39 p.m.

Vengeance, which was in the straits, subsequently reported the sinking of a tug, which it thought was the result of the torpedo attack. However, at sunset the destroyer *Scorpion* recovered the fired torpedo as it floated out of the entrance to the straits. The next attempt was for the battleships to fire at long range that afternoon and the following morning, but all attempts proved unsuccessful. Meanwhile two Turkish tugs, the *Maltepe* and the *Sana*, had been sent from Chanak to aid in the salvage of the enemy submarine. Aircraft then attempted to bomb the submarine, but this proved futile due to heavy anti-aircraft fire. That evening, *Scorpion* and *Grampus* made an attempt to reach *E15* by creeping up the Asiatic side, but by the time they were abreast of *E15* they were blinded by the searchlights, which prevented them from seeing the submarine. The next morning, Sunday 18 April, Holbrook in *B11* tried, but was defeated by the morning mist, and with batteries depleted he returned to base. At 1 p.m. that afternoon, *Triumph* and *Majestic* were ordered to enter the straits – but not to venture beyond the mine-swept areas – and to fire at the submarine. The submarine itself could not be seen, but the nearby tug was visible and was therefore used as a marker; nevertheless, the bombardment again proved unsuccessful.

C. G. Brodie arranged to go with *B6* on the following morning, to make another attempt. However, that evening he learnt that Keyes had ordered a torpedo attack by picket boats from *Triumph* and *Majestic*.[47] The command of the operations was given to Lieutenant Commander E. G. Robinson, who had been awarded the Victoria Cross for his previous exploits in leading the demolition parties against the fort at Kum Kale. At 10 p.m. these 56-foot long boats set off on a dark and moonless night. Travelling at a speed of approximately 8 knots, with Robinson leading in *Triumph*'s boat and Lieutenant Goodwin in *Majestic*'s boat 800 yards astern, they travelled the 12 miles to their target, hugging the northern shore. As the boats turned from the northern shore to steam across towards Kephez on the opposite side, they were spotted by enemy searchlights and came under fire at 11.45 p.m. They sighted a dark object, which was not illuminated by the searchlight, and *Triumph*'s boat fired one of its two torpedoes, although no explosion was heard. It was now the turn of *Majestic*'s boat, but, as she came up behind her leader, a beam of light suddenly fell right on the *E15*, 200 yards away. Goodwin then fired a torpedo, but he appeared to miss the target. At that moment his boat was hit below the water-line and began to sink. He turned his boat again towards the submarine, drifted a little closer and fired his remaining torpedo, which struck the *E15* just ahead of her conning tower. As *Triumph*'s boat returned to make its second attack, they saw that *Majestic*'s boat was in trouble. Armourer Tom Hooper had been badly wounded, and *Triumph*'s boat took four complete circles of *Majestic*'s sinking boat before he and the rest of the crew could be retrieved. This was accomplished despite *Majestic*'s boat swinging wildly out of control, as enemy fire fell all around both boats. Fortunately, *Triumph*'s boat managed to get clear without being hit, but Hooper died of his wounds on the way back to base.

The following morning, at 12.45 a.m., *B6* headed for the straits with C. G. Brodie aboard, and under destroyer escort. She submerged south of Kephez at 3.07 a.m., still undetected. Again, the submarine was worked between a cruising depth (this time of 30 feet) and periscope depth. She kept rising occasionally to check her position, achieving a speed of 2 knots across the ground. After travelling for an hour and a half she rose to periscope depth, when an indistinct object was observed about one and half miles off the starboard beam, in Kephez Bay. The submarine's course was altered 50 degrees, and she then submerged to 30 feet. Ten minutes later, at 5.07 a.m., when the submarine rose to periscope depth, the object was still indistinct, although it was thought likely to be *E15*. They continued for another twenty minutes before rising once again to periscope depth, and then, as they waited for the periscope to break the surface, the keel suddenly hit the sandy bottom and the submarine ran up to the surface.

B6 was now in a similar situation to *E15*, with the conning tower and forward structure above water. The order was given to speed up, to blow the main ballast tanks so as to lighten the boat, and to turn to starboard to reach deeper water. *B6* was shorter and tubbier than *E15*, and emptying the tanks[48] had made the boat lighter; hence she was able to swing around more quickly. She made slow headway, but within five minutes had made her way into deep water, where the main ballast was flooded, and she dived to periscope depth. Meantime, as *B6* manoeuvred to deeper water, observations were made through one of the tiny windows in the conning tower. On the port beam, less than a hundred yards away, *E15* was lying on her starboard side, heeled over beyond the horizontal, showing only her bottom and saddle tank. Goodwin's attack had been successful in making her of no use to the enemy.[49] At this stage, the sound of taps was heard as the enemy opened fire. This continued intermittently for the next two hours, but the submarine had already reached the protection of deeper water and continued down the straits and safely back to Tenedos.

It was not until much later that details emerged as to the events leading to the loss of *E15*. Diving deep to get under the minefield at Kephez, most likely while allowing for a current down the straits, T. S. Brodie encountered an undercurrent that took him upstream much faster, but also across to Kephez Point. Later on, Brodie's brother too observed a current of 2 knots in *B6* compared with an estimated speed of 1 knot. T. S. Brodie tried to get his boat off the sandbank by emptying his tanks and going full speed astern. He had just asked if the hull had been hit by fire coming from Fort 8 (Dardanos), when he was killed by a shell which hit the conning tower. Almost immediately, a second shell hit the batteries, producing chlorine gas as the sulphuric acid mixed with seawater and asphyxiating six members of the crew.[50] While shells continued to hit and to penetrate the boat, Lieutenants Edward J. Price and G. Fitzgerald,[51] with the aid of the crew, destroyed charts and confidential documents. The remaining crew, which included the former British vice-consul at Chanak, Mr Palmer (who was now an intelligence officer on de

Robeck's staff and had begged to go on the mission),[52] then abandoned ship. They were picked up by the Turks and made prisoners of war.

AE2 arrived back from Malta on 21 April, and on 23 April Stoker was summoned to the flagship. (The delay may have been due to the preparations that were underway for the troop landings.) Stoker told Admiral de Robeck that it was still possible to get through the Narrows, although the admiral found it difficult to believe this after the loss of *E15*. If *AE2* was going to be successful, other boats would follow, and this had the potential to disrupt Turkish supply lines significantly. Finally, de Robeck agreed with the plan and wished Stoker luck, concluding: 'If you succeed there is no calculating the result it will cause, and it may well be that you will have done more to finish the war than any other act accomplished.'[53]

Two hours after the meeting with the admiral the submarine slipped from *Adamant* and by 2 p.m. moored close to *Queen Elizabeth*, while one of the ship's wireless officers checked her wireless equipment. *AE2* then proceeded to Tenedos, arriving there at 6.30 p.m. Taking on additional supplies from *Swiftsure*, at 1.30 a.m. on the morning of 24 April she headed for the entrance to the Dardanelles. Stoker hugged the European shore and reached Suan Dere, on the other side of the straits from Kephez Point, 6 miles inside the entrance. Having succeeded in progressing so far up the straits without being detected, *AE2* then attempted to dive, only to discover that the foremost hydroplane coupling had broken. Diving being now impossible, the boat had no alternative but to make a run for home before day-break. They arrived at Tenedos at 8 a.m., where the coupling was repaired by noon and a test dive performed. Admiral de Robeck called for Stoker again that night for a report, and gave permission for *AE2* to try again in the morning, commenting: 'It was very bad luck. You did well to get so far. Try again to-morrow. If you succeed in getting through there is nothing we will not do for you.'[54]

However, there was an important change in *AE2*'s orders, so that, instead of attempting to pass Chanak and proceed through the Narrows without being seen by the enemy, she was to attack or sink, if possible, any mine-laying ships found near the Narrows. De Robeck was concerned at the possible risk posed by floating mines to his capital ships. These ships would be supporting the army landing, planned for the next day. Some information had been gathered that the Turks had had a mine-laying ship made ready. Keyes made the comment to Stoker that he was to 'generally run amok at Chanak'. Brodie saw this verbal command as adding one more burden to what was already a difficult mission. He wrote:

Operational orders in those days were sometimes verbal, and the written order often a vague and comprehensive sort of blank cheque produced by a not always fully informed secretary, rather than precise directions. Not having seen the orders one should not pronounce judgment, but this afterthought seems to ignore the dangers of Chanak, and it nearly caused the loss of *AE2*. Orders should surely have made it clear that her objective was to reach the Marmara, and that targets at Chanak were only to be attacked if the former objective was not risked.[55]

With these revised and somewhat uncertain orders *AE2* again departed from *Swiftsure* for the Dardanelles, at 2 a.m. on 25 April 1915.

3

The Gallipoli Landings

Hurried plans

As previously mentioned, on 22 March Admiral de Robeck decided to wait for the army landings, scheduled for 14 April, before recommencing any major naval action. In the meantime, as the training of troops and the gathering of transports in preparation for the landing went forward, supporting orders were being issued by the admiral. These covered matters such as gunfire control in support of the army; mine-sweeping; torpedo and mine defences; and conduct of units in the event of a submarine attack. Additionally, arrangements were made for signals, both visual and wireless, for communication between the army, the navy and the several hundreds of other vessels involved in the landing.

The enemy's only attempt to intercede in these activities came from the torpedo boat *Demir Hissar*, which attacked the transport *Manitou* (6,849 tons/ 1898) off Smyrna on 16 April, as she transported troops northwards through the Aegean Sea to Gallipoli. The torpedo boat approached the transport, whose captain thought it was a British torpedo boat, and came to a stop. The German officer in command Kapitänleutnant von Freigs, ordered the ship to be abandoned in three minutes, but after a protest from *Manitou*'s captain he extended this interval to ten minutes. The *Manitou* had lifeboats sufficient for only one third of the men on board, so panic broke out, boats were overloaded and many men had to take to the water. During this melée the enemy fired two torpedoes, both of which passed underneath the target. The trumpeter of the 97 Battery, D. N. Meneaud Lissenburg, describes thus the events and the lack of discipline that were to unfold:

> I saw the first torpedo plop into the sea and begin its journey directly under me as the gunboat was only twenty or thirty yards away. Nothing happened. We raced to look over the starboard side and there it was skimming away

with its bow well out of the water like a speedboat. I hurried to the orderly room and asked the R.S.M. what I was to do. I expected to have to sound the 'Stand-to' but instead I was told that the order was every man for himself, scuttle away and find a boat. I was going below to get my lifebelt when at the stairs I was astonished to see the panic-stricken crush of men trying to get up, fighting against those trying to get down. There was chaos on the boat deck too. We had never had boat drill nor been allotted to a particular boat. Lieutenant Beckett was however using his formidable figure to secure calm as he grasped the muzzle end of a rifle and threatened anyone who rushed at the particular boat he was supervising. I removed my boots and puttees, got into an overcrowded boat which, badly handled by our own men, capsized as it was lowered and we were all thrown into the water. Fortunately I was a good swimmer and got away from the side of the ship. The crew of the Turkish gunboat were laughing at us. Our ginger-haired doctor organized us into providing help for the non-swimmers, as did the steward, who had already survived the *Titanic* disaster. We were quite a while in the water before a warship, the *Prince George*, approached us and lowered her lifeboats to pick us up.[1]

The *Demir Hissar* then headed for the unarmed dispatch boat *Osiris* and, when she proved to be too fast, returned and fired her third and last torpedo at the *Manitou*; but she missed once again. By this time the alarm had been sounded, and the destroyers *Kennet*, *Jed*, *Dartmouth*, *Doris* and *Wear* were on their way. By 3 p.m., the *Kennet* had come within range of the *Demir Hissar*, near Kalamuti Bay on the Greek island of Khios. With the *Wear* approaching from the other direction and no chance of escape, she beached herself in the bay, where the crew were taken prisoner and interned in Greece.

Meanwhile, General Hamilton's general staff officers worked on the preparation of plans for the landing until 11 April, when Hamilton's administrative staff finally arrived in Alexandria. Hamilton then discovered that, apart from having no personal knowledge either of his enemy or of Gallipoli, he had his forces scattered around the Mediterranean and often ill-equipped for the mission ahead of them.

To their [Kitchener's and de Robeck's] eyes we seem to be dallying amidst the fleshpots of Egypt whereas, really, we are struggling like drowning mariners in a sea of chaos; chaos in the offices; chaos on the ships; chaos in the camps; chaos along the wharves; chaos half seas over rolling down the Seven Sisters Road.[2]

His efforts to improve the situation were also hampered by matters over which he had no control. One instance was the discovery that the armoured landing craft capable of holding 500 men and built for the Baltic would not be made available for his forces. Artillery and ammunition were well below the level laid down by the War Office, and there were no engineers, no head-quarters signal company, no trench stores and no construction materials for piers and jetties. Transports arriving at Mudros had been loaded for peacetime conditions and therefore had to proceed to Alexandria, where facilities were available for reloading. All these measures ultimately required time, which allowed the enemy to prepare their defences better. Great reliance was being placed on the firepower to be provided by the navy, but no adequate fire control, identification or communication had been established. Requests for aircraft in sufficient numbers to dominate the skies over Gallipoli were refused by Kitchener, so the provision of aircraft for the campaign also became a navy responsibility.

All these issues had to be rectified as best they could in four weeks – an unrealistic time frame. Secrecy had also been breached, with Egyptian news-papers reporting the arrival of troops together with the speculation that their likely landing would be the Dardanelles. From 11 April, Turkish aircraft flew almost daily over Mudros harbour to observe the naval build-up. Hamilton also faced some hostility and uninterest from General Maxwell (commander of army forces in Egypt), who was concerned about a Turkish attack on the Suez Canal.[3]

Intelligence with regard to the Gallipoli Peninsula was also modest. Hamilton's staff had a General Staff War Office publication called the *Handbook of the Turkish Army*, which was a detailed and well organized source of basic information.[4] Two additional guide-books were available, although little is known of their value. He also possessed the official handbooks comprising the 1909 *Report on the Defences of Constantinople*, the 1913 *Manual of Combined Naval and Military Operations* and an admiralty report entitled *Turkey Coast Defences May 1908*. A one inch to the mile map of the peninsula, Gallipoli and Asiatic shore of the Dardanelles was made available, which was based on a reduction of a 1854 French 1:50,000 map. Information was also provided on the Greek General Staff's plan of attack on the Dardanelles. There has been some debate over how well prepared Hamilton was, given the level of intelligence with which he was provided. Chasseaud[5] argues that the 1909 *Report* gave a clear idea of the terrain to be encountered, including information on beaches, water supply and roads, and therefore Hamilton was not deprived of meaningful information when he left for the Dardanelles.

Surprisingly, reports by Lieutenant Colonel Cunliffe-Owen, the British military attaché to Constantinople, were not made available, although it is possible that Hamilton was made aware of their contents. These reports contained detailed information on the Dardanelles defences, as well as information provided by the French military attaché at Constantinople, Colonel Maucorps, and were passed on to Kitchener in February 1915. Probably the failure to make this information available was a result of the unworkable level of secrecy maintained by Kitchener, which left his subordinates unaware of its existence. However, the possibility also exists that this is another instance of the reasoning which made Admiral Limpus ineligible for the command of British naval forces on account of the knowledge he had gained during his time at Constantinople, before Britain was at war with Turkey. It was perhaps felt, in a similar way, that the information gained by Cunliffe-Owen and Maucorps should not be made available because it, too, was acquired confidentially during a time of peace. Later, intelligence would be provided daily by offshore naval patrols, through aerial reconnaissance (which increased steadily over time) and, after landing, it would be acquired onshore, from the interrogation of Turkish prisoners of war and through the capture of more accurate and detailed maps.

Meanwhile, on 19 April, Kitchener telegraphed Hamilton to tell him of the tough resistance of the Turks against the British in Mesopotamia. By this stage Hamilton was most concerned about getting his troops ashore, and he became convinced that he had to 'fling' the whole of his troops rapidly ashore at one time rather than piecemeal. He chose therefore to land on the foot of the peninsula, where the territory would be more lightly defended and an attack would achieve greater surprise. The likely disadvantage of his plan was that, after landing, the troops would have a hard slog up mountainous terrain and that, once the surprise effect was lost, the enemy could reinforce its entrenched defenders.

The plan of attack was based on the assumption that the Turkish forces consisted of 80,000 men on the Gallipoli Peninsula; 30,000 on the Asiatic side; and another 60,000 in reserve. Given the size of the anticipated expeditionary force, it would be necessary to rely heavily on the use of naval firepower, since Hamilton's four 'British' divisions only had a third of the artillery pieces usually attached to a force of that size. The general staff had little information about the supply of water or the state of the roads. Therefore every effort was made to provide as many containers of fresh water as possible. It was assumed that some water would be found on shore,[6] but little could be done to provide adequate numbers of horses for transport and fodder to feed the horses for at least twenty-four hours after the landing. This would prove to be a serious problem. The French had favoured a landing on the Asiatic side or at Bulair, but this plan was rejected in view of the strong defences there and the incapacity to surprise the enemy completely. In any case, Kitchener had forbidden a landing on the Asiatic side. The landing therefore had to be made on the peninsula, which had very few beaches suitable for this apart from Suvla Bay to the north and the southern end of the peninsula, near Cape Helles.

The main features of the peninsula are small beaches (which is where an army would have to land), and a line of hills which runs through it like a backbone. An invading army would need to get to the top of the hills as quickly as possible in order to control the heights overlooking the beaches and the Dardanelles. The important high points were: Tekke Tepe ridge, which creates a semicircle around Suvla Bay together with Kavak Tepe and Kiretch Tepe Ridges; the 1,000 feet high Sari Bair chain, north-east of Ari Burnu; and the 709 feet high hill of Achi Baba, 6 miles north of Cape Helles. Hamilton's preference was to land all his forces as one, like a 'hammer stroke', closest to his main objective – the Kilid Bahr Plateau to the north of Achi Baba; but, due to lack of suitable landing craft and to the small beaches, this was not feasible. It is interesting to note that, between 1900 and 1907, Lieutenant Woods undertook intelligence work for the British military attaché in Constantinople. During his walks he determined that many of the important forts were located near Kilid Bahr; that they were open at the rear; and that an attacking force should be landed only five miles to the west. The beaches near Gaba Tepe offered the best approach, preferably what was to be known as Brighton Beach, the planned landing spot for the Anzacs, with the valleys which ran east–west to the north of Maidos providing a rapid approach to the forts.[7]

Hamilton's three senior commanders, Lieutenant General Birdwood (Anzac, two divisions of 30,000 men), Major General Hunter-Weston (29 Division, of 18,000 men) and Major General Paris (Royal Naval Division, of 8,500 men), all strongly disapproved of the proposal. However, the War Office and the Admiralty supported a landing on the peninsula. Hamilton also understood from a telegram he received from Admiral de Robeck on 29 April that, once his army had landed, the fleet would renew its attack on the Narrows. This would give the Turks an aggressive double assault against which to defend themselves. Hamilton and his staff had also expected the fleet to be very active in the lead-up to the landings, especially given that it was now stronger that ever. The force had been strengthened with thirty-eight new sweepers manned by survivors from the lost capital ships and twenty-four destroyers, which had been converted for sweeping. The lost ships had been replaced and a new naval aerodrome had been established at Tenedos. Other than the limited submarine activity and some sweeping support, little had happened between the attack of 18 March and the landing of the army now scheduled for 25 April.

It was decided by Hamilton that his strongest division, the 29, would land at Helles on three tiny beaches named X, W and V, but because of the shortage of small craft it was expected that the landing would take at least two and a half

Map 3.1   Gallipoli Peninsula objectives

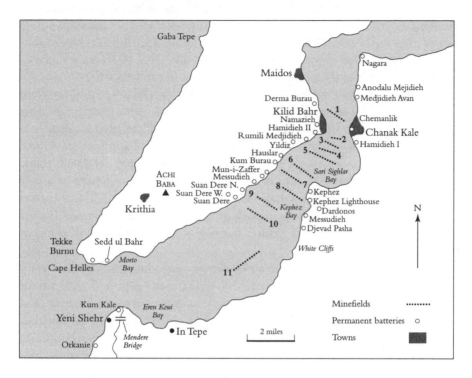

days to complete. Under these circumstances it was obvious that the invasion would have a much better chance of success if the Turks were prevented from concentrating their whole defensive effort on this one small area. It was therefore decided that the Anzacs would land south of Fisherman's Hut (on Z Beach), about a mile to the north of Gaba Tepe. The area was thought to be lightly defended, although it was known that Gaba Tepe itself was wired and entrenched. The Anzacs were to secure the Sari Bair heights (Chunuk Bair, Hill Q and Hill 971) and to push across the peninsula 3.5 miles to Mal Tepe, north-west of Maidos (where the Persian King Xerxes was supposed to have sat in 480 BC and watched his fleet at the Hellespont, on his way to Athens). Hamilton's plan for the Anzacs was: 'firstly, to keep open the door leading to the vitals of the Turkish position; secondly, to hold up as large a body as possible of the enemy in front of them, so as to lessen the strain at Cape Helles'.[8]

It was hoped that, after the first day, 29 Division would occupy Achi Baba Ridge and, with the Anzacs to the north, surround the defenders of Kilid Bahr. Meanwhile the Royal Naval Division was to carry out a diversion off Bulair at Saros Bay, which was aimed at delaying the movement of Turkish reinforcements to the south for at least forty-eight hours. As another feint, the French were to land at Kum Kale on the Asiatic side. It had also been decided to land the covering forces, not from merchantmen, but from warships a mile away from the beaches. The men were to be put into the ships' cutters or into lighters (small open rowing boats), towed by tugs (that is, steam pinnaces), in groups or in line, then finally they were to cut free to row ashore.

Once the high ground had been secured, the main forces would arrive in transports and be ferried ashore in cutters. To allow for a stronger landing force on the heavily defended V Beach, it was decided later that a collier – in this case, the *River Clyde* – would act as a Trojan Horse and pretend to run aground. Once grounded, she would immediately discharge her 2,000 troops onto the beach. Hamilton also decided to land 2,000 more troops at a new location, Y Beach, further up the coast on the western side, which was known to be undefended. This was an important landing place as it offered the only easy approach to the town of Krithia and would threaten communications of the Turkish forces at Helles.

To achieve this plan, Hamilton's 75,000 men (including the French division of 18,000 men) had to be transported 700 miles from Egypt to the islands off Gallipoli. The logistical problems were endless. Tows, barges and lighters had to be assembled and midshipmen needed to be trained in piloting the launches to shore. In addition to the landing of troops, water, food and ammunition, artillery and horses had also to be landed on the beaches. Provision, too, needed to be made for the disembarkation of the wounded into hospital ships, their subsequent transfer to hospitals on the nearby islands and Egypt and eventually – where necessary – to Britain. Fire support from the navy had to be coordinated and a communication network of radios and underwater telegraphs to be established. This was the first major amphibious landing in modern warfare, still studied in war academies today; and, perhaps surprisingly, no serious problems were encountered prior to the landings.

A major aim of landing in two separate areas and then feinting to the north was to prevent von Sanders from knowing where the centre of gravity of the attack was. This, it was hoped, would prevent him from committing his reserves for forty-eight hours – long enough for the ground forces to move inland and gain the upper hand. The difficulty lay in the failure of the general staff to inform the field commanding officers about their objectives once they were ashore; they rather concerned themselves with trivial details about what was seen to be the major difficulty: that of getting on shore in the first place.[9]

In the meantime, von Sanders had committed two of his divisions, 3 and 11, to the Asiatic side near Kum Kale and further south at Besika Bay, which he felt was the most likely landing place, as it was the closest point to Tenedos. Another two divisions, 5 and 7, were located at Bulair, situated at the northern end and in the narrowest part of the peninsula. This was a strategic position which, if captured by the Allies, could allow for the closure of communications to his forces on the peninsula. Of his remaining two divisions, 9 was located at the southern end of the peninsula, at Cape Helles, while 19 was held in reserve near the town of Bokali, near Maidos, to prevent any landing at Gaba Tepe from advancing across to the Dardanelles. Lieutenant Colonel Mustafa Kemal, who was to become the inaugural president of modern Turkey, commanded this division, which was to play a vital role. One other major aspect was von Sanders' decision to concentrate his forces and to scatter only a small proportion of them along the coast, in order to defend the principal beaches and to patrol those areas where landings would be difficult. The major concentration was further inland, which did not sit well with many of his commanders. The opportunity to drive the enemy from the few landing points early in the engagement had thus been lost. However, as Colonel Hans Kannengiesser, who commanded the 9 Division for von Sanders, noted: 'he who covers all, covers nothing' (1926, p. 197). Obviously Hamilton's staff was not aware of the situation, otherwise they might have been less concerned over the mechanics of the landing itself and have concentrated instead on the rapid follow-through which was required before the arrival of Turkish reinforcements. As James states:

> ... the conspicuous feature of the plans of von Sanders and Hamilton was that whereas von Sanders' were essentially flexible, Hamilton's were rigid. The Turks knew that they would have to fight at a place chosen by their opponents, and would have to rely heavily on the initiative of individual commanders; the British plans – except, perhaps at Anzac, where Birdwood proposed to hurl his fiery Anzacs ashore and impressed on all the vital importance of speed and enterprise – left no room for initiative.[10]

On 21 April, Admiral Wemyss summoned a meeting of the naval captains responsible for the landing of troops. It had already been decided that some of the transport steamers were to leave Mudros two days before 25 April and anchor on the north side of Tenedos, while others were to leave Mudros early on 24 April, at ten minute intervals, to proceed to their rendezvous points. Off Tenedos, the former group would each load lighters with supplies for the landing force, including beach equipment. Officers and men intended for the landing were to assemble on board transports allotted to their respective beaches. Commodore Phillimore, the former captain of the *Inflexible*, was given responsibility as principal beach master. By the evening of 24 April, over 200 ships had moved through the Aegean carrying the expeditionary force. With the fall of darkness the ships moved into position; at this time the weather still seemed to be unsettled, but it soon cleared to a bright moonlight and flat seas. Between 1 a.m. and 2 a.m. on the morning of Sunday 25 April, the ships with a covering force had reached their battle stations and had stopped in calm seas. The troops were awakened, given a hot meal, and the first of the troops embarked onto their boats.

The essence of any seaborne attack is the element of surprise, which keeps the defenders uncertain as to where or when the attack will be launched. If the invasion had been undertaken in secrecy and troops transferred, say, to Serbia from Egypt had suddenly landed on Gallipoli instead, the outcome might have been quite different. As it was, the Allies had effectively done everything in their power to forewarn the Turks. As soon as Turkey entered the war, the Dardanelles were bombarded; three and a half months later a major naval attack was undertaken. This was followed by the landing of several small forces, without opposition, and a short time later other landings were attempted, which were easily repulsed because the defenders had been fore-warned. Finally the army began to assemble at Lemnos seven weeks before the invasion, then was transferred to Alexandria, then reassembled back at Lemnos one week before the invasion. The only chance of success now lay in the rapid taking of key objectives by the invading forces, before von Sanders' reserves could be brought into action. Although Hamilton never had the strategic advantage, he did hold the tactical advantage and needed to keep von Sanders off guard for as long as possible.

On the Turkish side, the attack of 18 March was expected to continue the next day, and Kiazim Bey, von Sanders' chief of staff, was of the opinion that it would have succeeded. When it was not continued, the Turkish staff figured that next time it would probably be launched with the assistance of the army. By the end of March, agents informed the Turks that tens of thousands of Australian, New Zealand and French troops were assembling at Mudros, but they had no knowledge of when or where the landing(s) would take place. The Turkish staff felt that the landings could be either feints or full blown landings, and could happen at any of the following places: the foot of the peninsula, Gaba Tepe, Bulair or the Asiatic side of the Dardanelles. Von Sanders thought the Allies would either land on the Asiatic side, to take the In Tepe hills overlooking the forts of the Dardanelles, or at Bulair.

Anzac landings

The first landing was carried out by the Anzacs, with the planned landing approximately 1 mile north of Gaba Tepe. The naval squadron in support of the troops was under the command of Rear Admiral Thursby and included the five battleships *Queen*, *London*, *Prince of Wales*, *Triumph* and *Majestic*, plus

Map 3.2   Anzac Cove

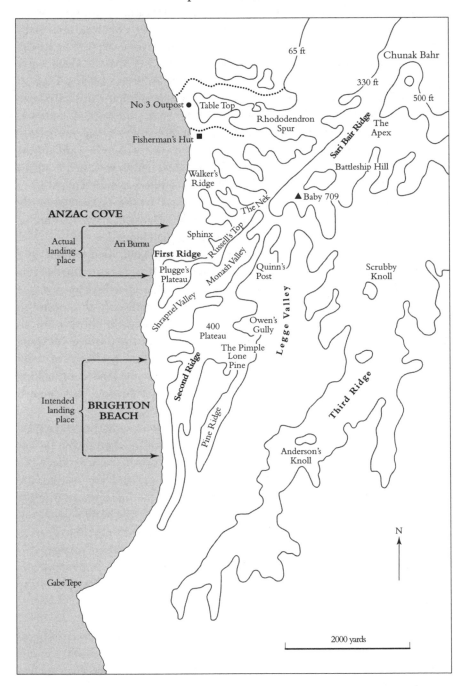

65 ft

Chunak Bahr

330 ft

500 ft

No 3 Outpost ●   Table Top

Rhododendron
Spur

Sari Bair Ridge

The
Apex

Fisherman's Hut ■

Battleship Hill

Walker's
Ridge

The Nek

▲ Baby 709

ANZAC COVE

Sphinx

Russell's Top

Actual
landing
place

Ari Burnu

First Ridge

Scrubby
Knoll

Plugge's
Plateau

Monash Valley

Quinn's
Post

Legge Valley

Shrapnel Valley

400
Plateau

Owen's
Gully

Second Ridge

The Pimple
Lone
Pine

Third Ridge

Intended
landing
place

**BRIGHTON
BEACH**

Pine Ridge

N

Anderson's
Knoll

Gabe Tepe

2000 yards

the cruiser *Bacchante*, eight destroyers and fifteen trawlers. *Triumph*, *Majestic* and *Bacchante* were responsible for covering the landing by gunfire,[11] while *Queen*, *London* and *Prince of Wales* were entrusted with the task of actually landing the initial covering force of 1,500 men. These troops were to be landed in thirty-six unprotected boats, towed by twelve picket boats. A further five destroyers carried 500 troops each. Some five miles west of Gaba Tepe, at 1 a.m., 1,500 officers and men climbed over the side of their ships and down the Jacob's ladders into the landing craft. By 3.30 a.m., the landing craft and their escorts had proceeded to a position within three miles of the shore, from where the picket boats finally towed the landing craft within 50 yards of the shore. From that point on, four seamen in each boat had to row their craft the rest of the way to land. The initial force finally landed at 4.20 a.m., while a further 2,500 men were landed from lifeboats towed by the destroyers shortly after. The remaining 4,000 men of the Australian 1 Division arrived at sunrise (4.50 a.m.) and, by 7.20 a.m., nearly 8,000 troops had landed.

The original plan called for the covering force of 4,000 men to land on a broad front of 2,000 yards, the southernmost point being approximately one mile north of Gaba Tepe. The troops were then to fan out in three groups: one towards the summit of Chunuk Bair to the north-north-east; the second to Scrubby Knoll on the third inland ridge to the east; and the third south, to Gaba Tepe. The battleship *Triumph*'s role was to mark the position off Gaba Tepe, while *Queen*, *London* and *Prince of Wales* landed the first wave of 1,500 men. At sunrise it became clear that, instead of having landed on a long sandbank, the troops were confronting a sheer, scrub covered cliff, located 1,000 yards further to the north of the planned landing place.

During the landing, Lieutenant Commander Waterlow had mistaken Ari Burnu for Gaba Tepe and, thinking he was too far south when in fact he was too far north, he steered his southern side tow to the north. Commander C. C. Dix, who was in charge of landing the covering force and was leading the northern side tow, realized the mistake being made by the southern or right wing. To save as much ground as possible, he took his northerly wing at full speed, moved under the stern of the other wing and called to them to keep to starboard or steer on a more southerly course. The result of these manoeuvres was a clustering of the forces around Ari Burnu. There is still some debate as to the reason why these forces were too far north in the first place; the hypotheses proposed include the following:

- The tows were pushed off course by an unexpected northerly current, at which point Lieutenant Commander Waterlow made his mistake in not recognizing his location, although there is no evidence that such a current exists.[12] This is the official account.

- General Birdwood and Admiral Thursby, together on the *Queen* that night, may have made a last-minute change of plan. This seems unlikely, although there had been a minor change to the original landing place: its location was moved slightly further to the south by about 200 yards.
- The three battleships had anchored to the north-west of the landing beach, while ordering the tows to head directly east, which had them heading north of their intended position.
- A British marker buoy may have been dropped the day before and then moved by Turkish soldiers. There is no record of any such marker buoy, while the task of marking the rendezvous point was the particular responsibility of *Triumph*, which had been given specific orders as to the location where it was to anchor.

Another explanation is offered by the comments of Midshipman John Metcalf, in charge of the No. 2 picket boat from the *Triumph*, who stated:

At the first light of dawn I realized we were heading for the beach just north of Gaba Tepe [the correct one], which I knew to be well fortified, as we in the *Triumph* had often been close to it and, from my action station in the spotting top, I had seen the headland time and time again. My immediate thoughts were that we were too far south. The troops and the boat would be lost by a murderous enfilading fire as we passed, so I hauled away from it to the northward [*sic*] as much as I dared, without crossing the bows of No. 3 tow. A few minutes later when the other tows to port had conformed, it appeared to me that we were still going too near Gaba Tepe, and again I altered course away from it. Eventually we landed south of Ari Burnu, with No. 3 tow only a few yards away on my port side.[13]

Although this story may have been made up to fit the historical events, it was a bold statement and does have some credibility. Eric Bush who was one of the other midshipmen commanding a picket boat (in this case, No. 8), observed in his own log: '4.20 a.m. land sighted, flotilla altered course two points to port'. Commander Dix, in charge in picket boat No. 12, also observed that the right wing steered across the bows of the centre group.

The likely answer is perhaps that the mistake was due to one or more contributing factors: the confusion that often surrounds landings which are planned in moderate haste; the difficulty of twelve steam picket boats steering by magnetic compass and towing boats, at night, to a featureless coast; and the inaccurate maps and modest inaccuracy of the navigation of the day, which resulted in the battleships releasing the tows too far to the north to begin with.[14]

Once ashore on what was to become known as Anzac Cove, the men moved very quickly, following the explicit instructions of their commander, to reach the high ground as rapidly as possible. By 6 a.m. they were in complete possession of the First Ridge, some were already moving across the Second Ridge, and on their left flank the Turks were falling back in disorder. At that time, the covering force of 4,000 Anzacs was probably only facing 700 Turks. By 7 a.m., small parties of Anzacs had crossed Legge Valley and had reached the Third Ridge, from where they could see the waters of the Narrows only 3 miles away. Once firing had been heard, the remainder of the Turkish Regiment 27, which was based at Maidos, went into action, moving across to Ari Burnu. The small Anzac forces, which had reached the Third Ridge, were forced to withdraw following the arrival of superior Turkish forces, led by Kemal.

By 10 a.m. a major battle had developed. A Turkish battery behind Gaba Tepe, having fired its first shot at 4.45 a.m., began to shell the landing area at Anzac Cove. The Turkish battery fired shrapnel, that is, a shell loaded with pellets, which exploded in the air, maiming or killing unprotected soldiers. The small landing area made it very difficult for the main Anzac forces to land, causing a major bottleneck and limiting the follow-up of the covering force. On shore, there was almost complete disarray and confusion over what was happening: maps were proving worthless, groups of men were going into battle in an uncoordinated way, with numerous stragglers, and there were no suitable locations to deploy artillery. Although the first of the Indian Mountain batteries arrived at 10.30 a.m. and commenced firing at noon, they were forced to withdraw by 2.30 p.m., when the Turkish artillery fired shrapnel above their heads. Various artillery pieces were to arrive piecemeal during that evening and throughout the following day, some being removed not long after they arrived. This highlighted the poor staff work and the conflicts between the commander of the Australian 1 Division, Major General Bridges (who was concerned over the vagueness of the front and proper location of artillery), and the artillery commanders.[15] Meanwhile, the navy was unable to tell friend from foe and was therefore also unable to provide fire support. It was not until 5 p.m. that the first naval bombardment of a located Turkish battery was underway.

By 2 p.m., 12,000 Anzacs were facing 4,000 Turks; but they were unable to bring their superior forces to bear because of confusion, lack of communication and very difficult terrain. By 5 p.m., the Turks were counter-attacking along the whole front, the greatest threat to the Anzacs coming from their left or northern flank. Initially, on landing, it was thought that the right-hand flank would be at greatest risk, which resulted in a failure to secure the heights to the north-east. The situation had reversed from the early hours of dawn, and the Anzacs were now fighting for their lives. With inexperienced troops in very difficult and confusing terrain, under fire from artillery and snipers, with many of their officers dead or wounded, the morale and organization of increasingly separated groups of men deteriorated rapidly. As the war correspondent Ashmead-Bartlett, who landed from a pinnace at 9.30 p.m., was later to comment:

No army has ever found itself dumped in a more impossible or ludicrous position, shut in on all sides by hills, and having no point from which it can debouch for an attack, except by climbing up them.[16]

Hamilton was to excuse the mistake in the landing to the north by stating:

Although this accident increased the initial difficulty of driving the enemy off the heights inland, it has since proved itself to have been a blessing in disguise, inasmuch as the actual base of the force of occupation has been much better defiladed from shell fire.[17]

Ironically, Birdwood had considered landing the troops further to the north if the defensive fire against the landing ships had been too heavy, although he felt that the country near Fisherman's Hut was so difficult and broken that it was impossible to attempt a landing during the dark.[18]

Southern landings

To the south along the Helles coast, the soldiers of 29 Division prepared to go ashore shortly after the landings at Anzac Cove. They were opposed by only 1,000 Turks of the 3rd Battalion, 26 Regiment. Admiral Wemyss was in charge of the naval squadron, which consisted of seven battleships – *Swiftsure*, *Implacable*, *Cornwallis*, *Albion*, *Vengeance*, *Lord Nelson* and *Prince George* – as well as four cruisers – *Euryalus*, *Talbot*, *Minerva* and *Dublin*. Additionally, there were six fleet sweepers and fourteen trawlers.

At Y Beach, 2,000 troops were brought within 4 miles off-shore of their landing point, 3 miles north of Tekke Burnu, in two light cruisers, *Amethyst* and *Sapphire*, and two transports, *Southland* and *Braemar Castle*, supported by the battleship *Goliath*. At this point, they were transferred to trawlers and boats lowered from the transports. The trawlers departed at 4 a.m. and arrived at Y Beach an hour later. The beach was largely undefended and there was no immediate opposition. However, there was some confusion as to who was in command of the forces on the beach and what their objectives were. A party of marines went inland and made contact with only four surprised Turks,

Map 3.3   Helles landings at the end of the first day

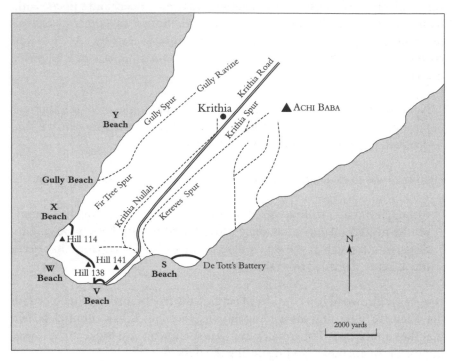

while two companies of Scottish Borderers had penetrated about a mile south, towards X Beach. Lieutenant Colonel Matthews in command of the marines, one of the two senior officers in the landing, walked across to an area within 500 yards of the deserted village of Krithia before returning to the camp. Lieutenant Colonel Koe of the Scottish Borderers, who was initially under the impression that he was in command (no one had informed him that he was subordinate to Matthews), appealed to divisional headquarters for information and advice but received no reply. The landing had been reported to the Turkish divisional commander, who ordered the 25 Regiment to march south, with the 3rd Battalion reaching Krithia at about 2.30 p.m. These men were ordered to attack Y Beach, while the other two battalions were ordered to march on to the Helles area and arrived there around 9 p.m. The British at Y Beach had decided to entrench at 3 p.m., but by 6 p.m. the Turkish forces had attacked and by nightfall the Y Beach force was appealing for reinforcements; again, they received no reply, as Hunter-Weston ignored their requests. At dawn on the next day still no replies were received to the urgent requests for troops and ammunition. Signals were being sent via *Goliath*, stationed off-shore, and even her captain, in desperation, sent a signal for help; but no reply was received. Ironically, when the troops landed on Y Beach they were equal in numbers to the whole of the Turkish forces on the tip of the peninsula; they probably could have pressed forward, encircled them all and opened the way for an advance to Achi Baba.

At X Beach, there was better coordination between navy and army, with a prolonged bombardment maintained until just before the landing. *Implacable*, under the command of Captain 'Tubby' Lockyer, had proceeded to a place within 1,800 yards of the shore, and at 5.30 a.m., using her 6-inch guns, had commenced bombardment of the shoreline. At this point, the boats were sent in with men of 86 Brigade, while the ship used her small calibre guns to fire on the ridges until the troops had landed. Finally, using her anchor, *Implacable* was brought up to within 450 yards of the shore, to offload the remaining troops. *Implacable* had fired 10 rounds from her 12-inch guns, 179 rounds from her 6-inch guns and 154 rounds from her 12-pounders. Thanks to Lockyer's foresight in using 800 sandbags to protect the personnel on the bridge, no injuries were suffered as the ship drew fire away from the landing parties. Only twelve Turks were defending the beach, as that was not expected to be a landing place, and these offered little resistance under the massive bombardment. So it was that, on the flank of the major landings at V and W Beaches, the troops from the two successful landings at X and Y Beaches sat idly by, when they were more than strong enough to rout the facing enemy, had decisive action been taken.

At S Beach, which was located in Morto Bay, the navy performed a similar coordinated attack. However, there were additional concerns, as the bay was reported to be mined and there was the ever present threat from the batteries on the Asiatic side of the straits. *Prince George* entered the straits to counter the batteries, while *Agamemnon* covered the eight destroyers and five mine-sweepers which had entered the bay beforehand, to sweep for mines and then net the bay. At 4 a.m., troops from the South Wales Borderers of the 87 Brigade, which had been brought from Tenedos in *Cornwallis*, embarked outside the straits into four trawlers, each towing six boats, and then started a slow journey to their landing beach. Casting off 400 yards from the beach at the tip of Morto Bay, the troops were ashore by 7.30 a.m., being covered by *Lord Nelson* and *Cornwallis*. They landed under erratic fire from the Turks, with *Cornwallis* protecting them as best she could, shelling both the Asiatic and European shores. To ensure that all that could be done was done, the captain of the *Cornwallis*, A. P. Davidson, who had been asked by Admiral Wemyss to stay and support the troops until they had effected a landing, took his orders literally and went ashore with a party of his own seamen. By 8.30 a.m., de Tott's Battery and the ridge above had been captured and Captain Davidson remained on the beach, waiting to assist in the evacuation of the wounded, until he was finally recalled to his ship. This delayed the departure of *Cornwallis*, which was to have proceeded earlier to support the landings at V Beach; thus these troops were deprived of badly needed assistance. The troops on S Beach now dug in, as they awaited British forces to their south to link up.

At W Beach, the three platoons of Turkish defenders, having survived a major naval bombardment by *Euryalus* and *Swiftsure* at 5.22 a.m., had resolved to defend their positions. The Lancashire Fusiliers, who had embarked on the two ships, commenced landing at 6 a.m. The barbed wire covering the beach, as well as the Turkish trenches and Maxim machine-guns, were still intact. The defenders held their fire until the landing force was within 100 metres of their trenches; then they commenced firing, causing a considerable number of casualties. Eventually the Lancastrians broke through the wire and flooded over the beach.[19] Brigadier General Hare, in charge of the landing force, spotted a reasonable landing site to the left of the beach, to which he directed his second landing party. These troops, under the cover of a cliff and sheltered from the fire of the defenders, scrambled to the summit, attacking the enemy's left flank. Slowly, the Turkish defenders were forced to fall back, but only after they had inflicted over 600 casualties on the 957 officers and men who had made the original landing. At this time, the Turkish battalion commander had no reserves left to support his remaining W Beach contingent, so Hill 138, a vital strategic position, was virtually open for the taking. At this critical point General Hare was wounded and the operations on W Beach became extremely confused through the loss of vital equipment. This included maps, the absence of which made it more difficult to determine the location of Hill 138.

At V Beach, the first troops to come ashore were the Dublin Fusiliers, in cutters towed by naval steamboats while the rest of the covering force, comprising the Munster Fusiliers and the Hampshire Regiment, landed by means of the collier *River Clyde*. The landing site was in a bay that formed a natural amphitheatre, with the Sedd el Bahr fort on one side and a lighthouse on the other. The first landings were made at 6.20 a.m., with no opposition from the three platoons and four old machine-guns which made up the defences at V Beach. The defenders waited until the boats had grounded, and then opened fire, causing great carnage amongst the landing force. Troops in the cutters were shot to pieces as they endeavoured to reach the beach. The *River Clyde* was also under heavy fire. During all this time Commander Unwin,[20] with several others, struggled in the water, under fire from shore, to hold in place a bridge of lighters from the collier to the beach, so that the troops could disembark. The motor hopper *Argyle*, which should have performed this operation, had become immobilized.

A graphic description is given by one of the men in the boats of the No. 4 tow from the *Cornwallis*:

Suddenly a terrific fire was opened on them – the bullets were flying like a storm of hailstones, and the boat's side was riddled. Directly she touched the beach the bowman, Taylor, jumped out with the painter, and he was instantly shot, dying later in Malta Hospital. The few untouched soldiers jumped into the water, and of the thirty-two originally in the boat only three got ashore, a Major, Captain and Lieutenant being killed or wounded with their men.

By this time there were only two left at the oars – Skitmore, A. B., and Boy Darling, with Leading-Seaman Ford at the tiller. Cragie, A. B., and Roy Runacres were in the bottom of the boat dressing the wounded. Lynn, A. B. had been hit in the leg by a bullet which had first passed through the boat's side, and though he could not move he dressed the wounded who were within reach. Boy Darling was shot next, and Ford left the tiller and took his oar.

'Cheer up, my son; it will soon be over,' he said; and almost immediately a bullet found a billet in his shoulder. He continued to row with one hand, and he and Skitmore between them backed the boat out.[21]

By this stage the Turkish fire was concentrated on *River Clyde*. No naval covering fire was provided, as the navy was unaware of the difficult situation that confronted the landing troops and *Cornwallis* was delayed because of the foolish action of her captain at S Beach. As soon as Admiral de Robeck discovered that there had been no advance, *Queen Elizabeth* opened fire. Despite this, as soon as the trapped men on the beach tried to move, machine-gun fire from the Turks would commence once again. Additional forces that were to land at V Beach were now diverted to W Beach because the cutters that were to be used after the initial landing were holed, drifting, and filled with dead soldiers, sailors and sixteen-year-old midshipmen. This was the same beach the marines had walked on in safety two months earlier. The carnage was so great that, while patrolling from the air, Commander Samson was to write: '[t]he sea for a distance of about 50 yards from the beach was absolutely red with blood, a horrible sight to see.'[22]

Meanwhile, the 1,000 remaining troops in the *River Clyde* stayed below decks, where the steel hull protected them from the enemy's fire. On deck, the ship's machine-guns continued to provide covering fire for the less than 200 soldiers who made it on shore and were now doing their utmost to survive until dark.[23] The success of the Turkish defence was attributable to the local commander, Sergeant Yahya of Ezine, and to his sixty-three soldiers, all of whom were eventually killed.

As the morning progressed, men and equipment were being steadily deployed ashore at the main Beaches X and W. By 11.30 a.m. the Turkish commander in the area had no reserves, had effectively been outflanked and was outnumbered by over 10 to 1. Not until after 3 p.m. did the British at last capture Hill 138, and not until after dark had the X and W Beach forces linked up. Meanwhile, the commanding officer of the British landings, Major General Hunter-Weston,[24] ordered his men to entrench and consolidate the positions they had occupied without change since 11 a.m. It was not until 9 p.m. that units of the Turkish 25th Regiment reached the Helles area, by which time the two battalions of 26th Regiment had been almost totally destroyed. Had the British forces been given the opportunity to be as aggressive as the Anzacs in moving forward, the battle may have been won that day. But the uncertainty over the strength of the enemy, who had proved to be better organized and disciplined than expected, caused a fateful hesitation.

On the Asiatic side, the French squadron comprising *Jaureguiberry*, *Henri IV*, *Jeanne d'Arc* and the Russian cruiser *Askold* bombarded Kum Kale. However, it was 10.15 a.m. before any of the French troops actually got ashore, as more powerful tows had to be arranged to overcome the swift currents. Kum Kale was only defended by one platoon of Turkish infantry (the remaining defenders were concentrated at the ruins of ancient Troy, 3 miles inland), which retreated as the French landed. The Turkish commander of 3 Division, Colonel Nicolai, was so overwhelmed that counter-attacks by Turkish forces were uncoordinated and uninspired in the early stages. All in all, 3,000 French troops landed, without much opposition, to occupy the village of Kum Kale. At 5.30 p.m., the French were ready to begin a move in the general direction of Yeni Shehr, but, as night fell, Turkish resistance increased and the French were halted roughly halfway between the two towns. Increasingly, Turkish resolve strengthened and bitter fighting developed on the outskirts of Kum Kale.

At 5 a.m. on 25 April, von Sanders awoke to be told of the Allied landings at Gaba Tepe, Sedd el Bahr, Tekke Burnu and Morto Bay, and that more landings seemed to be imminent at Kum Kale, Besika Bay and Bulair. On hearing the news he immediately ordered the troops stationed at his headquarters near the town of Gallipoli to march north to Bulair. Riding to the high ground above the Gulf of Saros, von Sanders had an excellent view of the diversion which was being undertaken by the Royal Naval Division at Bulair. Von Sanders watched as the naval activity unfolded, where previously at 4.30 a.m. the *Canopus*, *Doris* and *Dartmouth* had bombarded the lines at Bulair, with trawlers simultaneously sweeping for mines while eleven transports moored off-shore beyond the range of shore batteries. The bombardment continued throughout the day and then towards evening of the 25th, the troops boarded the cutters of their transports, formed groups of eight towed by a trawler, and headed for shore. However, before landing darkness fell and they were able to return to the transports without being seen. That evening, Lieutenant Commander Freyberg, after rowing to within a mile of the shore, swam the rest of the way and, once on shore, lit three flares in an attempt to give the impression that troops had landed. After hearing and seeing no enemy activity he swam back off-shore, where, totally exhausted, he was fortunate enough to be picked up. On the morning of the 26th the Royal Naval Division was ordered back south.

Von Sanders had became suspicious and, realizing that the landing at Bulair was only a diversion, ordered his two battalions coming from the town of Gallipoli to turn back south to Maidos. The reports von Sanders received from his field commanders were not good; it was clear that the enemy had landed on a number of fronts and that all his reserves had been committed. The reported presence of a British submarine in the straits also meant that any plans for ferrying troops over from the Asiatic side had to be abandoned.

Maintaining a foothold

By nightfall on 25 April the Allied commanders faced the following situation:

- At Bulair to the north, a brave attempt was being made to light flares on the beaches to convince the Turks that something was afoot.
- On the Asiatic side, the French had established themselves at Kum Kale.
- At Y Beach, a frantic battle was raging.
- At X and W Beaches, where the two landing forces had made contact with each other, the men were digging in.
- At V Beach, *Queen Elizabeth* pounded the Turkish defenders, who ran short of ammunition. With the fall of darkness the men could move about, and 1,000 troops on the *River Clyde* were landed. Attempts to remove the many wounded were disrupted once the moon rose and the firing recommenced.
- At Anzac Cove, the situation was somewhat desperate, with a cold drizzle falling. The sea was rising and the men had the air of a defeated army.

Although the landings at Helles had the potential to take the high ground at Achi Baba, the lack of clear orders and the loss through casualties of significant numbers of officers required to carry out what orders and strategy were known greatly hampered any sensible advance. The failure of the divisional headquarters to maintain control was partly exacerbated by difficulties of communications, although wireless and visual signals between ships and shore provided some level of contact. The other difficulty that became more evident was the reluctance of senior commanders to interfere with those charged with the execution of specific orders. Hamilton would not interfere with Hunter-Weston and de Robeck would not interfere with Wemyss, an attitude instilled by staff college training prior to the First World War.

The difficulties at Anzac Cove were so great that Birdwood was asked by his two divisional commanders, Bridges and Major General Godley commanding the New Zealanders, to join them on shore. Both commanders were emphatic about the fact that they wanted to evacuate their forces. Eventually Birdwood conceded to it, but thought fit that the decision should be Hamilton's. A message was sent, some have suggested, through the war correspondent Ashmead-Bartlett, who, having landed at 9.30 p.m., was initially arrested as a spy but was soon released after being identified by a boatswain from a pinnace. The message, written on a signal form by Godley but not addressed, was delivered to Admiral Thursby on *Queen* by Captain Vyvyan, the naval beach-master, by 11 p.m. Thursby thought the message was for him and he was planning to go to Anzac to discuss it, when the *Queen Elizabeth* arrived; so he decided to take the following message to Hamilton, who was awoken from his sleep:

> Both my divisional generals and brigadiers have represented to me that they fear their men are thoroughly demoralised by shrapnel fire to which they have been subjected all day after exhaustion and gallant work in morning. Numbers have dribbled back from firing line and cannot be collected in this difficult country. Even New Zealand Brigade, which has been only recently engaged lost heavily and is to some extent demoralized. If troops are subjected to shellfire again to-morrow morning there is likely to be a fiasco, as I have no fresh troops with which to replace those in firing line. I know my representation is most serious, but if we are to re-embark it must be at once.[25]

Hamilton, Robeck, Thursby, Keyes and Major General Braithwaite, Hamilton's chief of staff, met on the *Queen Elizabeth* to discuss the request. Thursby, supported by Keyes, made a recommendation against the evacu-ation. At that time Brodie interrupted Keyes, to provide him with a message that had just been received about the progress of *AE2*. Hamilton was informed and penned the following message to Birdwood:

> Your news is indeed serious. But there is nothing for it but to dig yourselves right in and stick it out. It would take at least two days to re-embark you, as Admiral Thursby will explain to you. Meanwhile the Australian submarine has got up through the Narrows, and has torpedoed a gunboat at Chunuk

[*sic*]. Hunter-Weston despite his heavy losses, will be advancing tomorrow which should divert pressure from you. Make a personal appeal to your men and Godley's to make a supreme effort to hold their ground,

Ian Hamilton.

P.S. – You have got through the difficult business, now you have only to dig, dig, dig, until you are safe. Ian H.[26]

In one of those coincidences of war, on the day the Anzacs landed at Gallipoli, which is celebrated as a major national holiday in Australia, the Australian submarine *AE2* was the first naval vessel to penetrate the Narrows and enter the Sea of Marmara.

Admiral Thursby went ashore at Anzac Cove to deliver the message to Birdwood, but by that stage the Anzacs had already decided to dig in and await the next morning's onslaught, as did the British and French troops at the other landing spots.

4

Breaking into the Sea of Marmara

The initial Allied submarine activity was focused on attacking enemy shipping below the Narrows and on intercepting any enemy forces attempting to run through the Dardanelles. With the enemy's capital ships withdrawn above Nagara and the bulk of supplies for Turkish troops coming across the Sea of Marmara, the submarine campaign had to move to the next stage: attacking within the land-locked sea.

To get there, Allied submarines had to proceed up the Dardanelles submerged for most of the way, using dead reckoning for their position, and come to periscope depth for a quick sighting as infrequently as possible. This meant that the journey had to be made during daylight hours, which in turn meant that a submarine could come under attack by shore guns or enemy patrol craft, if its periscope was sighted. Added to a commander's concerns was the presence of minefields; it was proposed to avoid them by diving deep enough to pass underneath. The disadvantage of this manoeuvre was the ever present possibility of snagging a mine anchor cable and dragging the mine down onto the submarine, with possible disastrous results. Once they were past the minefields, any submarine nets encountered had to be negotiated. This was to be achieved by ramming them at full speed, with the aim of using the submarine's momentum to tear a hole, without getting fouled and caught in the net. Commanders also had to hope that remnants of the net would not get caught on the submarine and be dragged along with it, which could interfere with its trim or give away its position.

With limited battery endurance, the submarine had to negotiate the length of the Dardanelles submerged, while fighting a current which passed down and out of the straits into the Mediterranean (at greater depths, there is a denser salt-water layer which moves slowly up the straits). Once she had negotiated all these obstacles, with a nearly exhausted battery, the submarine had to surface to ventilate the boat and recharge its batteries. Because it was now in enemy waters, there was always the possibility of harassment by enemy

Map 4.1 The Sea of Marmara

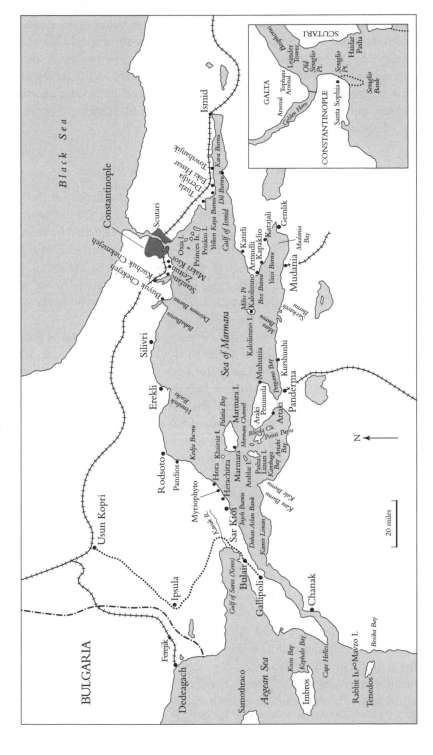

surface craft, while these essential operations were being carried out. It was under these difficult conditions that the submarine force would have to battle its way into the Sea of Marmara, and, after having caused as much damage to enemy assets as possible, overcome the same obstacles on the return journey. This generally proved to be uneventful, given the prevailing downstream current and the fact that the submarine would ultimately be surfacing in friendly seas.

AE2's first war patrol – 25 April to 30 April

We left *AE2* as it proceeded from Mudros to 'run' the straits for the second time in the early hours of 25 April. Stoker remained at the entrance to the Dardanelles until about 2.30 a.m., when the moon set, and then he entered the straits at about 8 knots. The weather was calm and clear and searchlights were sweeping the straits. The impact of the modification to Stoker's orders is apparent from his official report, made in 1919, which stated: 'As the order to run amok in the Narrows precluded all possibility of making the passage unseen, I decided to hold on the surface as far as possible.'[1]

The searchlights off White Cliffs, sweeping the lower reaches of the straits, forced him to edge towards the northern shore. At about 4.30 a.m., when he was not quite abreast of the Suan Dere, a gun opened fire from the northern shore at a range of 1.5 miles, forcing him to dive. He immediately dived to a depth of 70 to 80 feet and proceeded through the minefield. For the next half hour or so, the hull was heard scraping against the wires that anchored the floating mines and on two occasions something was caught up forward, but then worked loose and scraped all the way to the aft of the boat.

> All British submarines were fitted with 'jumping wires' to slide a mooring wire over projections, and they were efficient, but one also had a suspicion that the Turkish moored mines were not easily detonated, many boats surviving the ominous knockings and scrapings.[2]

On two occasions Stoker rose to periscope depth to determine his position and, although the possibility of striking the shallow mines was greatly increased, it was necessary to ensure that he didn't run aground, as *B6* and *E15* had done previously. On the third occasion, at around 6 a.m., he raised his periscope and found that he was in good position over to the northern side of the straits, with about two miles to go to the Narrows. Stoker had made good progress in reaching the Narrows thanks to a strong counter-current that ran underneath the main outflow of fresh water down the straits. He had travelled at greater depth than either *E15* or *B6* had done previously, perhaps at the suggestion of C. G. Brodie that stable water could be encountered at a depth of around 90 feet.[3]

Stoker remained at periscope depth to observe the situation near the Narrows, but the periscope was immediately sighted and heavy fire from both sides of the Narrows made observation difficult.

In order to comply with the revised order to attack mine-droppers it was necessary to keep the periscope up for a considerable time to take stock of the situation; the surface of the water was an absolute flat and oily calm, therefore the periscope was immediately sighted, and a heavy fire opened from the forts on either side. The shock of projectiles striking the water overhead caused subdued thuds in the submarine, whilst sounds as of hailstones were presumably caused by shrapnel bullets falling through the water on the boat's deck.[4]

However, Stoker observed a hulk anchored off Chanak, on the starboard side of the Narrows, as well as several destroyers and some small craft further upstream. Considering that the hulk might be responsible for dropping mines, he decided to attack it and moved to starboard for that purpose. A small cruiser was now observed coming from behind the hulk and, believing that this was more likely to be laying mines, Stoker decided to attack it at a range of 300 to 400 yards. He fired the bow torpedo, immediately ordering a dive to 70 feet, to avoid a destroyer which was attempting to ram him on the port side. The destroyer passed overhead as the torpedo was heard to hit.[5]

Fearing that the cruiser might be sinking ahead of his submarine, Stoker altered course one point to starboard, believing at the time that he was in the centre of the straits. Some four minutes later he altered course back to his original track and ordered the submarine to rise to a periscope depth of 20 feet. As the boat was rising, she hit bottom and slid up onto a bank, at a depth of 10 feet; this resulted in a large part of the conning tower being exposed above the water-line.[6] Through the periscope he observed that his position was immediately under Fort Anedola Medjidieh.[7] The situation was not all that different from that of B6, with both submarines so close to the forts that the large guns could not be depressed low enough to fire directly at them. As one of the guns fired, Stoker observed the flash of the gun almost reaching the top of his periscope, which he promptly lowered. For the next four minutes the boat was under continuous attack from various guns. Stoker adjusted the trim and, by going full astern, as Macarthur had done in B6, he was successful in re-floating AE2; she slid back down the bank to a depth of 70 feet, with the bow pointing down the straits.

Once AE2 was off the bank Stoker turned to starboard, to turn the boat's bow quickly towards the centre of the straits. The vessel again struck bottom and slid up a bank to a depth of 8 feet, though this time it was on the European side of the straits.[8] Through the periscope, Stoker judged that his position was immediately under the fort at Derma Burnu. He also observed two destroyers, a gunboat and several small craft nearby in the straits which had him under heavy fire, and a cluster of small boats which, he assumed, were picking up survivors from the cruiser he had previously sunk. He remained in this position for some five minutes. The submarine was inclined downwards by the bow, from which Stoker assumed that he had risen up and over the obstacle, and therefore he went at full speed ahead. Shortly afterwards the submarine started to move down the bank, gave a slight bump, increased the speed and then bumped heavily again. However, she continued to descend, and at 80 feet dived off the bank. Stoker believed that the last bump may have seriously damaged his submarine; but, believing that the primary purpose of his mission was to prove that a passage through the straits was possible, he decided to continue his course.

Shortly afterwards he rose again to 20 feet, and through his periscope observed that the submarine was approaching Nagara Point, but with destroyers, gunboats and numerous other pursuing craft surrounding him on all sides. When these craft saw the periscope, the destroyers, again, attempted to ram, and he dived to 70 feet.[9] With so many pursuing craft nearby, Stoker decided to round the point without making any further observations, and he dived to 90 feet. Some time later he rose again to periscope depth and found himself in the centre of the strait, heading for the Sea of Marmara, with Nagara Point on the starboard quarter. The pursuing craft were still searching for him below Nagara Point, but once his periscope was spotted they opened fire and resumed the chase. Forced to dive to 90 feet, AE2 remained at that depth for half an hour. Rising to 20 feet, Stoker observed that the pursuing craft were again close by on every side. Just ahead, two tugs had a wire stretched between them which aimed to capture him, or at least to establish his whereabouts. He immediately dived to 90 feet and, given the enemy's continued presence, he considered the possibility that his submarine was marking its own position, perhaps by dragging some drift net or other floating marker. He therefore decided to run up to the Asiatic side and await developments. His batteries were losing power and what remained was not sufficient to allow him to get far enough out into the Sea of Marmara to have any chance of evading his pursuers. He altered course to starboard and then ran aground intentionally, at about 8.30 a.m., lying at a depth of 80 feet so as to conserve battery power. As it was a Sunday, prayers were read and then the crew went to their diving stations.

Around 9 a.m., a vessel passed overhead and something she was towing (possibly a chain) hit the boat's side and jumped over. Other vessels continued to pass overhead at frequent intervals. As *AE2*'s position was outside the usual shipping channels, Stoker decided that these ships must be searching for him; therefore at 11 a.m. he moved to a safer location. Minor leaks from the last 'bump' had caused some water to collect in the motor bilges which was impossible to pump out, as oil mixed with the water would float to the surface and immediately give away their position. The water was therefore carried forward and emptied into the beam torpedo tube well. When Stoker attempted to move *AE2*, it was discovered that the boat's trim had been lost and all efforts to regain it without the risk of breaking the surface proved futile. Each time the boat simply slid down the mud, beyond its maximum 100 feet depth limit. He therefore had little option but to haul it back onto the bank and wait until darkness to rise to the surface and adjust the trim tanks.

At 9 p.m., the submarine rose to the surface on a bright moonlit night. Fortunately there were no ships in sight, so *AE2*'s diesel engines could be started in order to commence the all-important recharging of her batteries. After sixteen hours spent below the surface, conditions for the crew must have been quite foul, so they were allowed to take turns on the conning tower to get some fresh air. The boat's position was about half a mile from the Asiatic shore, in the sweep of a bay just above Nagara Point. Inland was a marshy swamp devoid of habitation, which helped to ensure that the boat would not be observed from the shoreline. Now that the diesel motors had been restarted it was an important moment to send a message, informing Admiral de Robeck that *AE2* had been successful in its penetration of the straits. The damp aerial wire threw off blue sparks as the call sign was flashed. No return signal was received from the admiral; this was a disappointment to Stoker, as he had no way of knowing if his signal had been received. However, as previously mentioned, the message was received, and it played an important part in boosting the morale of the Allied forces. In other respects, the presence of *AE2* impacted on von Sanders' ability to move troops across from the Asiatic shore and was, in effect, the 'starting order' for submarine warfare in the Sea of Marmara. Within hours of the receipt of the message, Lieutenant Commander Boyle of *E14* was ordered to report to the flagship, was briefed, and several days later also headed off to penetrate the straits.

Towards 11 p.m. on Sunday 25 April 1915, cloud cover from the east shaded the moon, and by midnight rain began to fall, so that *AE2* was hidden from any nearby passing vessel. This allowed her to finish charging her batteries. By 3 a.m. on the following day the weather had cleared and the moon had passed behind the horizon. Half an hour later the trim of the submarine had been adjusted and she was ready to continue her passage into the Sea of Marmara. Just before dawn, Stoker sighted two ships and decided to dive and attack. He observed through the periscope two approaching warships, the smaller one leading a larger ship further astern. Because the sea was very calm, he could only use his periscope intermittently, to avoid the enemy detecting his presence from the surface plume created by the moving periscope. He therefore had to use dead reckoning to steer a course parallel and opposite to that of the enemy. When he was ready to attack, he raised the periscope again, observed a ship in line of sight off his port beam and immediately fired a torpedo from his port side tube. At that moment the ship, which was 500 yards away, altered course and the torpedo missed its target. Stoker discovered that he had fired at the leading ship and found it impossible to alter his submarine's course in time to bring the other tube to bear on the second ship, which he believed to be a battleship of the Barbaros class.[10] Stoker attributed his failure to the state of the sea and to his personal error in 'overdoing an unseen attack'.[11]

He continued on course through the straits, and on the way examined the town of Gallipoli's anchorage but found no targets worth attacking. He proceeded on to the Sea of Marmara, entering it at about 9 a.m. Stoker's primary duty was to prevent the passage of enemy troops and supplies to the Gallipoli Peninsula; however, the submarine carried no gun (an innovation incorporated on later submarines) and had only torpedoes, which in any case were not of the most modern type in use at the time. With the presumed failure of his wireless, he was also unsure as to whether other submarines would join him and therefore as to how he could best fulfil his duty. He decided that great care should be exercised in the expenditure of his torpedoes and that he should frighten as much as possible any ships he did not fire on – in other words, let the Turks know that an enemy submarine was in the Sea of Marmara. Around 9.30 a.m. he sighted four ships ahead, approaching on separate zigzag courses and, as Stoker relates: 'I had no intelligence as to the nature of ship likely to be met with, and the ships flew no flag.'[12] He therefore decided not to fire unless he was certain that troops were on board the enemy ships, and so he came up close to the leading ship, a tramp steamer of about 2,000 tons. Passing about 200 yards abeam of her he saw no sign of troops or ammunition, but, as he passed her stern, she ran up her battle colours and opened with rifle fire at his periscope. He then dived over to the next ship and at 400 yards fired a starboard beam torpedo, which failed to hit the target. He was unable to get into range of the other two ships, so he rose to the surface half an hour later, spending the remainder of the day charging his batteries and making good any defects on the boat. He also examined some fishing boats, hoisting the White Ensign and steaming up close, to frighten 'the hell out of them'.

Shortly after dark on 26 April, while still on the surface, *AE2* again attempted to establish wireless communication with the fleet, but a steam launch came within sight and, with the aid of a full moon, fired upon *AE2*, forcing her to dive. Throughout the night, whenever the submarine surfaced, it was forced to dive again within minutes, as the area was full of pursuing craft. Stoker was to learn later that six surface craft had been assigned the task of hunting him down. On one occasion, while he attempted to submerge after having been sighted, the conning tower hatch would not close properly and it was necessary to show a light while repairs were made. This greatly increased the risks, and one round of enemy fire came close to hitting its mark.

At daylight on 27 April, a ship was seen to be approaching from the east. *AE2* dived and steered to intercept her. The ship, which proved to be of about 1,500 tons, was apparently of some importance to the enemy, as she was escorted by two destroyers, one ahead of her and the other on her starboard beam. Stoker brought his submarine past the first destroyer and then across the bows of the second, to a distance within 300 yards of the target. He fired a bow torpedo for a beam shot at a range of 200 yards but was dismayed to see that, once the torpedo had left the tube, its engine failed to start and it rose to the surface with compressed air bubbling out of its stern. A destroyer[13] immediately turned, in an attempt to ram the submarine, and *AE2* was forced to descend quickly to 70 feet in order to escape. For the remainder of the day no ships were sighted.[14] After the tiring efforts of the previous two days, Stoker decided to give his men a rest and spent six hours lying on the bottom of Artaki Bay, at 60 feet.

On the morning of 28 April, in calm weather, *AE2* attacked a small convoy of ships guarded by two destroyers. Stoker fired the starboard beam torpedo at a range of 300 yards, and again failed to hit the target. A second shot was not possible, as one of the destroyer escorts[15] altered course and attempted to ram the submarine. At dusk, two men-of-war were sighted approaching at high speed from the west. Stoker dived to attack, but by the time they should have been within range it was too dark to make them out. Judging that they were relatively near, and obviously becoming frustrated at his lack of success, he fired a blind shot from the port torpedo tube, which failed to hit the target. *AE2* then proceeded towards the town of Gallipoli, to reach the point nearest to the receiving ship in the Gulf of Saros and try once again to make radio contact.[16]

At dawn on 29 April, *AE2*, while submerged, observed a gunboat patrolling off Eski Farnan Burnu at the head of the straits. In an aggressive approach, Stoker dived under the gunboat, travelled down the straits and then returned back up, this time showing his periscope. In doing this, he hoped to give the impression that another submarine had succeeded in coming through the Narrows, unaware that *E14* had already done so. Destroyers and torpedo boats came out to assist the gunboat in the pursuit of *AE2*. Stoker then doubled back to scrutinize the anchorage at Gallipoli, but found nothing worth attacking. He moved back out towards the Sea of Marmara, then half an hour later rose to periscope depth and observed the gunboat crossing his stern tube's line of fire. As the submarine was low on battery power, he decided to fire at the gunboat in an effort to bring the pursuit to an end, and at a range of 700 yards fired his stern torpedo. The gunboat altered course and, as Stoker was to learn later, the torpedo missed its bow by no more than a yard, while the gunboat gave up on its pursuit.[17]

Stoker then proceeded to a pre-arranged rendezvous point, 5 nautical miles north of Kara Burnu. After he had travelled on the surface for several hours, just when he was about to reach the rendezvous, a submarine surfaced on the port bow. This proved to be *E14*. The contact with *E14* was a great morale booster, the more especially because of the isolation caused by *AE2*'s failed wireless. The two submarines closed and exchanged greetings and information through megaphones for about fifteen minutes. Boyle, the commander of *E14*, was the senior officer and, on asking Stoker what his plans were, was told that he intended to go to Constantinople. Boyle suggested that they meet at the same location at 10 a.m. the next morning, by which time he would have made contact with the admiral and would be able to relay his orders for future operations. *AE2* proceeded to a bay north of Marmara Island and rested on the bottom for the night.

At daylight on 30 April, it was discovered that an exhaust-tank valve (that is, a muffler box) was not watertight, and it was refitted. *AE2* proceeded to its rendezvous with *E14* and at 10 a.m. sighted a torpedo boat approaching from the west. While the submarine was diving to avoid the torpedo boat, smoke was seen in the direction of Artaki Bay, so Stoker headed south to investigate.[18] At about 10.30 a.m., the boat's bow suddenly rose and the submarine started to head for the surface from a depth of 50 feet. Stoker ordered ballast to be transferred to the forward trim tanks and called for full speed ahead and for the hydroplanes to be put to full dive. The submarine continued to rise and partially broke surface at approximately 1 mile from the torpedo boat. Stoker immediately ordered the forward tanks to be flooded; the submarine's bow now dipped downwards and she started to slip rapidly below the surface, but at such a steep angle that the crew was unable to stand. In the meantime, the torpedo boat commenced firing, as did another gunboat from Artaki Bay, about 3 miles away.

Once the submarine started to descend, Stoker stopped the flooding of the forward tank and the transfer of water to the forward trim tank, in an attempt to arrest the descent and level *AE2* off at 50 feet. But, with the significant addition of weight to the front of the submarine, she went out of control and plunged towards the bottom. Although water was pumped out of the forward tanks as quickly as possible, the submarine continued to sink, reaching the 100-foot limit of its pressure gauges. Stoker had to take emergency action, so he ordered full astern on both motors and blew the main ballast. At last the submarine started to rise. However, the combined effect of these two emergency measures over-compensated, causing her to break surface again by the stern.

The torpedo boat *Sultan Hissar*, under the command of Captain Riza,[19] opened fire as soon as they saw the stern come to the surface, and immediately holed the submarine in three places near the engine room.[20] With the bow down at an angle and the pressure hull pierced from enemy fire, Stoker was in the unenviable position of being unable to submerge and of having no surface armaments or an effective torpedo tube to fight the enemy. Because of the significant inclination of the boat, it was impossible for Stoker to use his periscope and it was useless to attempt a ramming of the torpedo boat. Water was entering *AE2* through the holes, so Stoker ordered the blowing of the main ballast, to lift the crew above the water-line; he also ordered all hands on deck.[21] Petty Officer Bray took charge of the crew's evacuation off the submarine's casing. *Sultan Hissar* ceased firing once it was evident that the crew was abandoning ship and she circled the submarine, blowing her siren to prevent other boats from firing. Those who could swim went into the water and headed for the torpedo boat, while those who could not waited for the small dingy that was lowered by *Sultan Hissar*.[22] Meanwhile, Stoker was assisted by Lieutenant Haggard (who was not, however, in favour of scuttling the boat but advised fighting on) in flooding the main ballast tanks and thus scuttling the submarine.[23] The third officer, Lieutenant Carey, remained on the bridge, to give them warning on the rising level of the water. Stoker sent Haggard up to the bridge and made a last check inside the boat, noting how dishevelled it looked and, as he was warned that she was going down, he recalled: 'In the wardroom my eye was caught by my private dispatch-case, which contained, I remembered, some money. That was bound to be useful – I ran and picked it up, and darted up the conning tower.'[24]

By the time Stoker reached the bridge, the water was about 2 feet from the top of the conning tower, with half a dozen men still left on the stern. At approximately 10.45 a.m. on 30 April 1915, in 70 fathoms of water, *AE2* slowly sank into the Sea of Marmara, approximately 4 miles north of Kara Burnu.[25] All three officers and twenty-nine crewmen were picked up safely.[26]

Stoker was unable to provide an explanation for the sudden rise of the bow which had led to the loss of *AE2*. In his opinion, the possible leaks caused by the final bump when they were grounded at the Narrows were not a cause for the loss of trim. He did refer to a similar incident experienced by Lieutenant

Commander Nasmith in *E11*, but fortunately that other event had occurred in shallow water and, when back in port, an inspection revealed no defects.[27] Wheat suggests that the main ballast tank was full of water, but, with the submarine submerged, this was the way it should have been.[28] (See Appendix I on operating a submarine.) However, as mentioned above, there existed a denser layer of salt water below the outflowing fresh water in the Narrows, which was also the case in the Sea of Marmara. As Brodie commented:

> The salt water cushion at about 90 feet seems to have been sufficiently widespread and uniform for our submarines to use it later with confidence. But the strong currents through the Marmara, and the conformation of the bottom must cause irregularities, as also might the effect of wind on a sea a hundred miles across. The reason *AE2* suddenly rose must surely have been her running from the normal fresh surface water into an area of salt.[29]

Brodie's conclusion appears to be based on the reasoning that, when the bows of the submarine penetrated the denser salt-water layer, the bow rose; this may have been a transient event, but the rapid over-corrections exacerbated the situation, ultimately leading to the submarine's rising to the surface and so to her eventual loss.

Given the large number of enemy targets that presented themselves to Stoker during his short patrol, it is surprising that he had such little success. Although he was reasonably aggressive in his attempts, poor-quality torpedoes and his lack of experience played a part in limiting his success, but, perhaps most importantly, he didn't have the 'good luck' that other commanders were to have in the Sea of Marmara.

Bernoulli and *Joule*[30]

On the same day that *AE2* was lost, the French submarine *Bernoulli*, under the command of Lieutenant de Vaisseau Defforges, was sent up the straits to attack Turkish shipping below the Narrows. The submarine was smaller by 10 feet and lighter by 250 tons than the E class submarine and carried 6 torpedoes external to her hull (and one internal). However, after she got into the vicinity of Nagara, the currents of the straits and an exhausted battery proved too much for the submarine, and she was forced to return to her base without having sighted the enemy.[31]

The following day, 1 May, her sister ship the *Joule*, captained by Lieutenant de Vaisseau du Petit-Thouars, departed for the Sea of Marmara. Keyes provided her captain with an obsolete and compromised signal book, which contained a day-to-day transposition table for encrypting her wireless signals when she made contact with her assigned destroyer, once she had entered the Sea of Marmara. Prophetically, as it turned out, the compromised signal book was provided should the submarine be sunk in shallow water, where the book could be recovered by the enemy. A few hours after the *Joule* departed, a part of one of her torpedoes, an air vessel, floated down the straits and was recovered by a patrolling destroyer. It was presumed, and later confirmed by the Turks, that she was blown up by one of the mines off Kephez Point and that all her crew were lost.

E14's first war patrol – 27 April to 18 May

Once word had reached Admiral de Robeck of *AE2*'s successful passage through the straits, Lieutenant Commander E. Courtney Boyle of *E14*, who was the senior submarine officer, was finally allowed to follow suit. *E14* departed at 1.40 a.m. on 27 April. Prior to departing, the battery had been brought up to 100 per cent charge and was 'fizzing', then it was ventilated and kept topped up until half an hour before submerging, to give the boat the best chance of getting through the Dardanelles. At the mouth of the straits, the canvas bridge screen was removed (there was no permanent metal screen). All but one of the stanchions that held up the cover were also removed. The remaining one was left as a hand-hold for the captain, who was the only one to stay on the bridge.[32] The submarine proceeded on the surface under one engine, in a calm sea and dark night. The sounds of gunfire could be heard from the nearby shore, with French battleships occasionally firing from behind. The bright searchlights streaming down from the Narrows eventually illuminated *E14* and forced her to submerge at 4 p.m. After getting past the minefields and avoiding fire from the nearby forts at Chanak, Boyle sighted a torpedo gunboat[33] and fired a torpedo at a range of 1,600 yards, with little likelihood of success. The following account by Boyle mentions one of the earlier methods of 'anti-submarine warfare':

> There were a lot of small ships and steamboats patrolling, and I saw one torpedo gunboat, 'Berki-Satvet' class which I fired at range about 1,600 yards. I just had time to see a large column of water as high as her mast rise from her quarter, where she was presumably hit, when I had to dip again as the men in the small steam boat were leaning over trying to catch hold of the top of my periscope.[34]

Two torpedoes were actually fired[35] at the gunboat (somewhat extravagantly, given the size of the target), both of which were the Mk V11 type. These were disliked and mistrusted by the crew: they preferred the more reliable Mk

V type, which were later used in the Sea of Marmara. The crew heard the muffled noise of a possible explosion but it sounded as if there had been incomplete detonation of the charge, a characteristic of that type of torpedo.[36]

The submarine continued travelling near the European shore and, when it was estimated that she should be abreast of Kephez Point, a quick fix was taken through the periscope. Already at this stage it was apparent that the currents were not as strong at greater depths, which would help in extending the battery endurance. Numerous fixes were taken as the submarine made the appropriate course changes to pass by Kilid Bahr. At 6.15 a.m., Boyle observed through his periscope a tramp steamer dismasted, aground, and half submerged on her side off Nagara Point. By 6.30 a.m., E14 rounded the point and dived to 90 feet, with still another 20 miles to go to the Sea of Marmara. The batteries at this stage started to show a declining density (charge), which necessitated the shutting off of all heaters and unnecessary lights. The boat went over to hand steering, which also reduced the drain on the batteries, and then to half speed, which reduced the battery discharge by a further 158 amps. Each time Boyle came up to periscope depth to make an observation, patrol boats covered the area.

After six hours and a quarter, E14 passed the town of Gallipoli at 10.15 a.m. A number of authors of the period[37] have suggested that E14 travelled the critical stage between Chanak and Nagara on the surface or with the top part of the conning tower exposed, so that the diesel engines could be used for maximum speed. It has also been suggested that, although fired upon by the forts, E14 was not hit. This was not the case, and Brodie suggests that some authors must have relied on the graphic and fictionalized account provided by Rudyard Kipling.[38] There is no question that destroyers and torpedo boats continually pursued E14. Observations made while she was submerged were recorded for 7 a.m., when three pairs of small patrol boats were observed; for 8.30 a.m., when more boats were observed sweeping the area; and for 9 a.m., when a ship that might have been the Muin-I Zaffer was sighted a quarter mile astern, going towards Nagara. Boyle could not get a shot away in time, but observed many small steamboats patrolling the area. Lieutenant Stanley, the executive officer, mentions the changing density of the currents, which required continuous pumping in order to trim the boat and keep her at a constant depth.

On entering the Sea of Marmara, further enemy craft were observed. Boyle managed to surface at 3.40 p.m. to ventilate and recharge, but within twenty minutes he was forced to dive. Each time E14 attempted to surface and recharge the batteries, she was quickly sighted and compelled to submerge, unable to get a full charge. At 7.50 p.m., E14 surfaced again, with a critically low battery recording an electrolyte specific gravity of 1,140, compared with a full battery of 1,240. On this occasion *E14* was able to recharge for fifty-four minutes before being once more forced under. The navigating officer, Lieutenant R. W. Lawrence, later wrote:

> We were all very happy and everyone started congratulating everyone else. We now had our first meal at 8 p.m. and after the excitement of the day, it was a hearty one.[39]

The submarine again surfaced at 9.18 p.m., but at 10.50 p.m. she was once again forced to dive by 4 destroyers. This pattern of quick surface recharges until the patrolling ships compelled her to submerge was to go on for several days. Finally, Boyle was forced to travel to the centre of the Sea of Marmara, to find a lonely place to recharge his desperately low batteries. He was so concerned about being surprised at night that he preferred to charge by daylight. He felt that in this way the enemy could be seen coming and thus could be avoided. This tactic would not have worked had there been enemy submarines in the area, or regularly patrolling aircraft. On 28 April, *E14* had to dive on four occasions, with her longest period on the surface being of about three hours. At 7.30 p.m., she surfaced north-east of Marmara Island, but was sighted by a destroyer at 1 a.m. on the following day and fired on. Again, she had to dive, but, in the early hours of 29 April, Boyle finally got his chance to recharge, as he reports:

> Surface at 5-0 a.m. and charged till 8-0 a.m. The motors were then so hot, having run continuously for over 50 hours that I had to stop.[40]

Of the first 48 hours of her trip since submerging in the straits, *E14* had been submerged for a total of nearly 40. By 9.30 a.m., Boyle was forced to dive again, when he saw smoke approaching from the east. By 12.30 p.m. the smoke proved to come from two destroyers and two torpedo boats heading towards Constantinople. At 1.15 a.m., more smoke was sighted and, eventually, Boyle saw two troop transports escorted by three destroyers. The range was extreme but he manoeuvred closer. The sea was calm and he feared that his periscope would be noticed (Boyle only had the use of one periscope as the other had had its upper window-pane broken by a lucky shot the day before). Eventually he was sighted and fired upon by one of the destroyers, which headed straight for him. At 2.23 p.m. Boyle therefore decided to fire one torpedo from his starboard bow tube at one of the transports, at a range of 1,500 yards. Given the lack of any mechanical computer aids in those days and the reliance of commanders on trigonometry and on a 'feel' for the required offset for the aiming of a torpedo, this was a relatively long range to fire. On firing, the torpedo was sighted but the nearby destroyer (most likely the *Muavent-i Milliye*) attempted to ram, so *E14* dived beneath her.[41] Although the explosion was not seen, it was heard by those on board *E14*, confirming a hit. Boyle remained deep for half an hour and then went to periscope depth, where he observed that the three destroyers were now escorting only one troop ship. The other transport, trailing clouds of yellow smoke, was making for the shore at Sar Kioi, in the hope of beaching herself on the shoreline so that she would not sink in deeper water.[42]

That afternoon, *E14* surfaced at 5 p.m. and commenced to charge batteries; twenty minutes later, as previously mentioned, she met with *AE2*. Boyle states:

> Sighted *AE2* and spoke to her. She told me that they had had bad luck with their torpedoes, had sunk one Gunboat (name not known) and had one torpedo left. I arranged to meet her again the next day after I had communicated with the Vice Admiral by W.T. We sighted her early the next morning, but before we could communicate we had to dive, and I did not see her again.[43]

At the meeting the next morning, Boyle intended to inform Stoker of the admiral's orders. *AE2* was seen astern at 9.50 a.m. the next day, but, as described above, was lost that day and the meeting did not take place.

The transportation of troops to Gallipoli was a crucial issue for the Turkish army. By sea it was a distance of 130 miles from Constantinople, while by rail it was a distance of 160 miles, followed by a 100-mile march. The presence of Allied submarines had resulted in reduced sailings, which in turn limited the opportunities available to *E14*. On 30 April, at 12.45 p.m., *E14* gave chase to a tug towing three sailing vessels off Sar Kioi, to check if they were carrying ammunition. Leading Stoker Haskins and Able Seaman Barker were ordered on deck by Boyle, where they fired two rounds from their rifles at a range of 900 yards, hitting the side of the tug. This was enough, in the early part of the campaign, to bring it to a halt. The sailing ships proved to be empty and were sent on their way back to Constantinople, as a newly arrived gunboat started firing at *E14*, forcing her to submerge. The tubes were made ready for a possible attack, but the gunboat made off before *E14* could engage her. That night Boyle tried again to communicate by wireless, but at 9.40 p.m. was forced by a destroyer to dive and then spent the night submerged off Karabuga Bay, at a depth of 85 feet. The following day, due to the lack of suitable targets, Boyle wrote: 'As I had not sighted any transports lately, I decided to sink a patrol ship as they were always firing at me. . . .'[44] At 10.12 a.m., *E14* observed an enemy gunboat, *Nur-ul Bahir*, near Myriophysto, and at 10.42 a.m. she fired the starboard beam torpedo, at a range of 600 yards. Boyle was able to observe two seaman at the stern of the enemy boat cleaning a gun, until they themselves saw the torpedo approaching and ran for the ship's bridge, attempting to warn their captain. The gunboat, which had an unusually shaped sloping stern and looked as if it had been fitted as a minelayer, was hit and sank with the loss of four officers and thirty-two crew members. A second gunboat, the *Zuhaf*, which came quickly to the scene, rescued twenty-nine men.[45] Boyle then closed in on the rescue ship and at 12.09 a.m. fired his starboard bow torpedo, which was followed fifteen minutes later by a second torpedo from the port beam tube. Both ran erratically and missed the target.[46]

For the following two days, 2 and 3 May, destroyers and torpedo boats unsuccessfully hunted *E14*. On a number of occasions, when the submarine was sighted from land, the Turks would light fires to signal the presence of a submarine to any nearby patrol boats. Between the 4 and 7 May, *E14* cruised primarily between Sar Kioi and Marmara Island. Her next major engagement was on 5 May, when *E14* sighted a transport escorted by a destroyer. The transport was taking essential reinforcements to Gallipoli, the Turks being prepared to take the risk because of the pressure which was brought to bear on their land forces. The transport, coming from the direction of Constantinople, was behind her zigzagging escort destroyer. Once again, Boyle showed his excellent judgement and reached a perfect firing position only 600 yards ahead of his target, at a point where the destroyer was on the other leg of her zigzag, behind the transport. Boyle fired but no explosion came, even though the torpedo had run straight and true. It was believed to have hit the transport amidships but to have failed to explode. The following day at 2 p.m., a large transport was again sighted between Marmara Island and the southern shore, coming from Constantinople. *E14* dived and prepared to attack, but before she could get into position, the transport, which must have received warning of the submarine's presence, turned around while still out of range of the torpedoes and headed back to Constantinople.

During these days, *E14* made her presence known in the Sea of Marmara so as to cause as much consternation amongst the Turks as possible and to give the impression that more than one submarine was operating in the area. For example, on 8 May at around midday, *E14* stopped the steamers *Tecilli* and *Hayrullah*, which were on a voyage between Rodosto and Panderma, carrying expelled Greeks.[47] The ships were duly allowed to proceed. Later that day, Boyle chased a steamer into Rodosto and approached to a distance of within 1,200 yards, until he was hit by rifle fire. Seeing no troops on board the steamer *E14* withdrew. That evening they tried to reach the fleet by wireless, but were unsuccessful. Early during the following day they tried once again, and this time made contact, to be told that the land battle was going well.

The next major action occurred on 10 May, when the Turkish army was forced once again to send reinforcements by sea. That afternoon, the crew was taking a swim alongside the submarine when an enemy destroyer was sighted. In spite of the confusion that resulted as they scrambled aboard to their diving stations, *E14* still submerged without mishap at 5.30 p.m. The destroyer passed over her and by 6.05 p.m., off Constantinople, Boyle sighted two large transports escorted by a destroyer. They were still 10 miles to the east, near Imali Ada, on their way towards Gallipoli. *E14* fired its port bow torpedo at 7.23 p.m., but this did not run straight and passed astern of the *Patmos*. However, the starboard bow torpedo, fired five minutes later, hit the *Gulcemal*.[48]

There is some confusion between Turkish and British records over this incident. The British believed the ship had been sunk, as Boyle had reported that she 'was much down by the stern', but it got too dark and windy to see whether or not she finally sank. As to the level of damage and the number of men aboard, Turkish accounts record that the escort *Gayret-i Vataniye* with Captain Cemil Ali Bey, remained with the damaged transport, which had over 1,600 men on board. *Gulcemal* was not seriously damaged, and two ferries from the Bosphorus, No. 26 and No. 46, arrived later to take her to Constantinople. On examination, it was discovered that the bow had been completely broken through.[49] English reports suggest that *Gulcemal* was carrying 6,000 troops and a battery of guns, which never reached their destination, Gallipoli, and that she was so badly damaged that she had to be beached.[50] Whatever the truth of the matter, *E14* had, nevertheless, once again succeeded in delaying important reinforcements to Gallipoli. She now had only one torpedo left but it had a broken main air-pipe, which, despite repeated attempts, it was not possible to repair. *E14* therefore spent the next week roaming the Sea of Marmara, causing as much disruption as she could with her only remaining offensive weapons – a few rifles that she carried on board. However, to add to the enemy's concern and confusion, Boyle had a dummy gun rigged on deck, using a pipe, an oil drum and some canvas.[51]

Between 11 and 12 May, *E14* sighted no targets, but on the 13th she chased the steamer *Dogan* and forced it to ground near Pandios, where an exchange of rifle fire ensued. It was a bitter time for Boyle, as he observed a number of targets which he was unable to attack. *E14* also learnt at this time, by wireless, that the crew of *AE2* were now prisoners in Constantinople. *E14*'s captain and crew were also congratulated by the vice-admiral on their efforts, and assured that their presence in the Sea of Marmara was invaluable.[52]

On 14 May at 10.50 a.m., Boyle chased and then stopped a tug, towing a lighter loaded with balks of timber, but had to let her proceed when he was approached by a torpedo boat. At night, when on the surface, Boyle reports that it was not unusual to discover an enemy torpedo boat close by, without any action being taken against him. By day, the appearance of the submarine was greeted with the lighting of signal fires, so that the enemy was generally aware of her location. By 16 May, the supply of fresh water was running so low that the crew was rationed to one pint of water per day as they waited, expecting to be resupplied by *E11*. Finally, on 17 May, *E14* received a wireless message ordering her home. Again, while preparing to return home, *E14* sighted a destroyer and two transports but was unable to attack. At 8 p.m., north of the Island of Marmara, *E14* dived and headed, submerged, towards Gallipoli.

E14 was now preparing to do what no other submarine had previously attempted – return through the straits safely. At 4.35 a.m., the following day she surfaced to recharge her batteries, but by 4.57 a.m. she was forced to dive when fired on by a gunboat. At 6.55 a.m., *E14* tried again to travel on the surface while recharging her batteries, but was forced to dive at 7.50 a.m., when a gunboat, later joined by a torpedo boat and tug, came too close. The three vessels then shepherded the submarine to Gallipoli, perhaps expecting her to get entangled in the nets. At 9.45 a.m., 2 miles north-east of Gallipoli, *E14* descended to the greater depth of 97 feet, and proceeded for one and a quarter hours without noticing any net obstructions. Boyle then came up to 22 feet, to make a periscope observation off Karakova, where he observed a gunboat off the port quarter and a tramp steamer in the Gallipoli town harbour. Boyle took the submarine back to 95 feet for another half an hour, when he again rose to periscope depth. This time he observed a tramp steamer in Indji Liman and another gunboat off Bergaz Bank, before diving again to 95 feet. At noon he made further observations and spotted a large yacht off Moussa Bank, and, by Khelia Liman, what he believed to be the battleship *Torgud Reis*;[53] also, half a dozen tramp steamers in Ak Bashi Liman. By 12.30 p.m., the *Torgud Reis* was sighted 400 yards off *E14*'s port beam, 1 mile north of Nagara. With no useable torpedoes, Boyle was once more unable to do anything but observe, on what had proved to be one occasion during the campaign which offered great opportunities for a submariner.

Now making observations every ten minutes, *E14* altered course around Nagara at 1.20 p.m. and sighted a lonely torpedo boat in Dardan Bay at Chanak. The submarine was then kept at a depth of between 22 and 40 feet until she rounded Kilid Bahr; when she was south of the point, *E14* was fired upon from Chanak. At 1.40 p.m., Boyle took the submarine to 95 feet, to clear the minefield, and by 2.30 p.m., when he was a mile south of Suan Dere, he observed friendly ships off the entrance. *E14* had proceeded at 5.5 knots, making a speed across the ground of 4 knots while she went up the straits, and, aided by the fast moving current, made better time down the straits, with a speed of 7 knots across the ground. Boyle also noticed that there were tides set into all the bays, and a particularly strong one into Sari Siglar Bay. He was also to observe how useful a small deck gun would have been. At 3.40 p.m., *E14* rose to the surface off Cape Helles, near a French battleship of St Louis class, after being submerged for six hours.

Lieutenant Commander Boyle was awarded the Victoria Cross for his outstanding achievements during the three-week patrol.[54] He was also specially promoted to the rank of commander. His officers, Lieutenant Edward Stanley and Acting Lieutenant R. W. Laurence, RNR, both received the Distinguished Service Cross (DSC), and the remaining crew received the Distinguished Service Order (DSO). *E14* returned to Mudros to rest and refit. The French Admiral Guépratte, who was to become renowned for his courage and audacity, steamed around the submarine in his flagship, with the band playing 'God Save the King' and 'Tipperary', and later referred to the submarine's crew as 'beautiful boys'. General Sir Ian Hamilton generously commented that *E14* had been worth an army corps of 50,000 men. The patrol had had the desired effect on the enemy, with sea transportation of troops and materials almost brought to a stop. Only shallow draft boats would proceed, hugging the shallow shoreline.

It was important to maintain the pressure and *E14* was recalled after *E11* had undergone repairs[55] and was ready to take her place. Admiral de Robeck felt it important that Boyle should brief Lieutenant Commander Nasmith, the captain of *E11*, so they had dinner with the admiral and Commodore Keyes on the evening of Boyle's return. At the meeting before dinner, the two commanders discussed details, mostly of leading marks and enemy measures in the Sea of Marmara, and Brodie commented on being surprised

> . . . at the small total of information that seemed capable of being passed on. Boyle was tired, but quietly elated. Nasmith, whose few questions showed how thoroughly he had already laid his own plans, was his serene friendly self, sharing our congratulatory mood.[56]

Like Brodie, Nasmith had flown over the straits in a two-seater Farman seaplane, with pilot Lieutenant Bell-Davis, to get a 'feel' for the geography. He was unable to observe any lines of mines, but it seemed that there were no nets in position, and he was able to spot the lighthouses, which he would use as marker points when submerged in the straits. At 1.10 a.m. on 19 May, after prayers on the boat's casing, *E11* set off from Mudros.

5

Gallipoli Action

Opportunities lost

On the day following the landings of 25 April, the onshore results were mixed. At Helles the fighting during the night had been heavy, but the British forces held their positions. With daylight on the 26th, the warships again pounded Sedd el Bahr, but the troops on the beach were so exhausted that it was difficult to get them back into action. The bombardment was initially directed at the village rather than at the fort, but the troops eventually grouped on the right of the beach and advanced on the fort, which was cleared quite quickly. In the village, however, fierce hand-to-hand fighting developed and it was only through the efforts of additional troops from the beach, who came in support, that ultimately the village was taken. It was not until 3 p.m. that the last Turkish resistance in the village was overcome, and the British forces were able to stream north across the plain which lay beyond the coast, towards the olive groves on the lower slopes of Achi Baba. There were few Turkish troops remaining between the British and Achi Baba. However, the British made no effort to advance further, as they had no idea that the Turks had been routed. Intelligence reports had suggested that there was another division, apart from the troops which had been fighting the British, waiting to defend Achi Baba. The accurate reports of Turkish dispositions from Anzac were discounted. The British troops were exhausted and badly shaken by the Turkish resistance, with high casualties among officers and men, while the problem of landing food, water and ammunition was becoming acute.

The commanders of both armies regarded Cape Helles as the key sector. Accordingly, most of their attention was focused there. The Anzac Cove area was considered less dangerous as any rapid advance was virtually impossible in such rugged terrain. . . . It was a day when both armies regarded survival as victory.[1]

Most appalling was the evacuation of the wounded, which had become a major problem, while at Anzac the situation was even worse. Originally, General Headquarters (GHQ) had informed Birdwood that he would have one hospital ship, the *Gascon*, for up to 300 seriously wounded, plus one transport, which was later increased to two, for the lightly wounded. Less than two days before the landing, an additional two transports were to be provided, which would be equipped to take 100 serious cases and 1,000 lightly wounded men. In spite of the increase, the level of hospital and medical service still proved to be grossly inadequate.

There were isolated cases of merchant ships refusing to accept injured men. One open boat with several hundred wounded people, was found at 3 a.m. on the morning of 26 April, drifting in an ugly swell after having been turned away by seven transports.[2] The pity of all this was that well-equipped hospital ships and base hospitals were available, but coordination had been very poor. One assumption was that hospitals would be installed on the beaches, but at this early stage it was impossible to do that. Even so, the casualties were too many, too fast, and transport ships too ill-equipped to handle the wounded. Peter Hall, on 2 May, on board the transport *Seang Choon* in Alexandria harbour, wrote this graphic description of his impressions and experiences:

I shall not easily forget that first feeling of awe that came over me as I looked over the side of the ship, down on these boatloads of mangled human beings. As [our] infantry had not left the ship the blankets had not been sterilized – three English doctors and fifteen men none of whom had been trained for anything but general duties in a hospital trying to attend 659 wounded men, the majority of them in an awful state – it was a matter of difficulty to walk anywhere on the decks so closely were they packed. Some of these men with arms and legs all smashed up lay squeezed up against others with half their faces blown away. Men sat all night and well into the next day with congealed blood hanging from mouths unable to speak, but with an awful appeal in their eyes imploring you to bring the doctor. The doctors were doing their best but it was an impossible task to attend to so many. One man begged of me to take five sovereigns he had, just to bring the doctor to him for one minute. [One] man sat there while the doctor cut away the loose pieces of flesh and removed the shattered teeth and bone. Men [were] going for days without having broken limbs set – [there were] no proper splints.[3]

By 7 a.m., news was received that the situation at Y Beach was desperate. Hunter-Weston, who was never as enthusiastic as Hamilton as to the merits of a landing at this more isolated beach, was so preoccupied with the battles at

Helles that he passed the message on to Hamilton, adding that there were no reserves to spare. However, at 7.45 a.m. he ordered six battalions of French infantry to land at W Beach. Hamilton was reluctant to interfere with the operations under the command of Hunter-Weston, but by 9.30 a.m., on his own initiative, he ordered a French brigade to Y Beach. When Hamilton arrived off Y Beach on the *Queen Elizabeth*,[4] he observed that the *Sapphire*, *Dublin* and *Goliath* were lying close inshore, that men were coming down from the steep cliffs, and that parties of these men were being ferried to *Goliath*. He assumed that they were wounded, but also noted that no soldiers were going up the cliffs, though many troops were standing idle on the beach.

What Hamilton was unaware of was that, due to a misunderstanding, an unauthorized evacuation of Y Beach forces was under way. The Turks, though heavily outnumbered, had pushed hard throughout the night and the British had suffered heavy casualties, including the loss of Colonel Koe. The men had also run desperately short of ammunition and, when some came back to the shore seeking assistance, the navy mistakenly embarked them. This created the illusion that a withdrawal had been ordered, so other officers and men were ordered to evacuate. By 7 a.m., several hundred men were waiting to be ferried off. Meanwhile, on the cliffs the remainder of the force fought off the last of the Turkish attack. However, the word was spreading about disembarkation and the apprehension increasing.

By the time the Turks had been defeated on the cliff tops, Colonel Matthews, who had been in command during the attack, on seeing so many men heading back to the beach, assumed that the order for evacuation had come from headquarters. He therefore allowed the evacuation, which was not intended and for which no authority had been given. The contingent therefore embarked without any intervention from the Turks, but left behind most of their equipment and ammunition. Lieutenant Commander Adrian Keyes, the brother of Commodore Keyes, climbed the cliff to see if anyone had been left behind and walked about the battlefield for an hour without a single shot being fired by the enemy, who had withdrawn to avoid the naval shelling. It was not until well after the evacuation that the Turks realized what had occurred; their forces were then redeployed to Krithia, to help in the battle developing at Helles. Although the evacuation was well conceived and initially well executed, the failure of all members of the divisional staff to travel the twenty minutes it would have taken to see the situation for themselves was inexcusable, as was the fact that they left the harassed local commander without instructions for twenty-nine hours.

At Anzac Cove the troops dug in as best they could. On the morning of 26 April, British warships shelled the Turkish troops whenever they spotted them, forcing them to abandon their plans for a counter-attack that morning and giving the Anzacs more time to fortify their positions. They were continuously under rifle fire from the Turks, and any plans for an Anzac advance towards Maidos were also abandoned. Over the next few days, the Turkish commander Kemal used the eighteen battalions hastily assembled in the area to launch a series of attacks. These were repulsed at great loss of life, as the Anzacs, with little or no cover, fought to maintain their foothold.

Between 26 and 27 April, except for the occasional rifle fire, little occurred in the Helles area. The 29 Division was ordered by Hunter-Weston to dig in and make preparations to repel the expected Turkish counter-attack. There were now over 20,000 British troops in the Helles area, opposed by 6,300 Turks, and, although the British had few of these opposing them directly, there was an initial reluctance by senior officers to take advantage of the situation. Hunter-Weston was concerned that the troops were tired and low on ammunition and perhaps felt that a great deal had been achieved in making a successful landing in the first place; unfortunately he hesitated rather than capitalizing on his initial success. Meanwhile, on the evening of 26 April the French forces withdrew from Kum Kale, having suffered 778 casualties and having captured 450 Turkish prisoners. The Turks had suffered the loss of 1,730 officers and men, including 500 missing. The feint at Kum Kale had held the Turkish 3 Division, but had only momentarily delayed the departure of the Turkish 11 Division to Helles. However, by 27 April the British and French forces were ready to advance, with the French on the right flank, 88 Brigade in the centre, 87 Brigade on the left and 86 Brigade in reserve. The troops set out in the early afternoon and moved forwards until sunset, by which time the units had made contact with one another and a front had been established across the peninsula.

On the 28 April, they were again ordered to advance, but by this time the supply situation was becoming a matter of concern, with few horses or mules available to move guns and supplies. This placed further pressure on the already tired troops, forcing them to carry their own supplies. There was also little artillery available at this time (28 pieces) and many machine-guns had been lost during the landing. The advance commenced at 8 a.m. and the troops met little opposition. By 9 a.m. it seemed that the capture of Krithia was imminent, and by 11 a.m. the Turkish commander had ordered the withdrawal of his forces to the top of Achi Baba Ridge, behind Krithia. However, by midday, the Allied advance had lost its momentum and the centre of the advance had become disorganized. Some elements did reach Krithia, but they were forced to fall back when the battle was broken off at 6 p.m. The Allies had suffered 3,000 casualties out of a force of 14,000. The front line had moved forward and now stretched from just south of Y Beach, south-east across the peninsula, to the south of Kereves Dere. Morale was now at a low ebb, with tired men once again digging in and burying their dead.

Coordination with the navy was still not well established, but improving, and the trajectory of their gun-fire still created problems, as is described below by one of the pilots spotting in the aircraft used to observe the fall of shot:

> For the rest of the month we were constantly spotting for ships' gun-fire. Accuracy increased with practice, but ships varied very much in their readiness to accept the air reports of fall of shot. The old battleships of the Magnificent class were particularly good. Their guns had a lower muzzle velocity and consequently higher trajectory than the more modern guns. The procedure for directing a ship's guns on to a target was complicated by the fact that the maps originally provided were inaccurate. The aircraft passed the map square number of the target to the ship. The ship laid off the compass bearing by the map and then selected a point of aim on that bearing on the shore by eye. The rough range was taken from the map and set on the sights.
>
> The first shot might be anything up to half a mile off the target. The aircraft first corrected for line and, when that was right, for range. If the line was very badly out it usually meant that the ship had to select a new point of aim, which delayed matters. New maps were eventually made from our photographs but that took some time.[5]

The Turks also had better artillery support when it mattered, especially from the Asiatic side. Turkish reinforcements were being rushed to the peninsula, with two more divisions sent by sea from Constantinople, together with one of the Asiatic divisions, for a total of 75 battalions against Hamilton's 57. These numbers were to increase further during May, with divisions withdrawn from the Caucasus as the threat from Russia diminished. Meanwhile Hamilton had hoped that he would not have to ask for reinforcements before the taking of Achi Baba; but now, tentatively and supported by Kitchener, he requested the deployment of the 42nd East Lancashire Division from Egypt, from a protesting General Maxwell. The French also decided to commit another division. Crucially, it would be some weeks before these forces arrived, and all the while the Turkish forces held the high ground.

At 10 p.m. on the evening of 1 May 1915, Turkish artillery opened up and the Turkish counter-offensive at Helles began. Enver had ordered von Sanders to 'drive the invaders into the sea'. With limited supplies of ammunition and under threat of a massive bombardment by the Allied naval guns, a night-time assault was the only option available. The Turkish soldiers attacked en masse and, in spite of the confusion which resulted from the difficulty of launching an attack on a dark night, they managed to break the Allied lines at two points. These breaches were held, nevertheless, and by 10 a.m. on the morning of 2 May, the Allied forces commenced an advance of their own along their whole line. Although the Turks had suffered significant casualties in their frontal attacks, they had enough time to regroup and managed to repel most of their attackers. During the nights of 3 and 4 May, the Turks once again attacked the southern portion of the front held by French troops. Again, no major success was achieved, and the Turks returned to their trenches at daybreak after having sustained terrible losses. At this stage von Sanders ordered a halt to the disastrous attacks. He told the new commander at Helles, General Weber, who had taken command after von Sodenstern had been wounded, to defend and not to retreat northward to a widening peninsula, as fewer men were required to defend the currently shorter line of trenches.

Meanwhile fire from Turkish ships in the straits had proved so accurate that it was suspected they had spotters at either Nibrunesi Point or Gaba Tepe. On the evening of 30 April, the destroyer *Harpy* landed a small number of sailors at Nebrunesi Point who climbed to the top of Lala Baba; there they destroyed a telephone wire found in a small trench at the summit. On 2 May, *Colne* and *Usk* landed a party of fifty men of the New Zealand Division, who surprised seventeen men sleeping in a Turkish trench. Two were killed and an officer and twelve men were taken prisoner, the remaining two escaping. At dawn on 4 May, after the peninsula had been bombarded by *Bacchante* and *Dartmouth*, 120 soldiers were landed at Gaba Tepe from the *Colne*, *Chelmer*, *Ribble* and *Usk*. On landing, the troops came under heavy enemy fire and could only manage to advance 15 to 20 yards. They then sought cover under a ledge and remained there for about an hour, while the six ships hammered the enemy's positions. The troops were then disembarked while still under fire, although the Turks held their fire while the wounded were carried away. Three or four were left on the beach, presumably dead. However, one of these was seen to move occasionally, so a steamboat with a Red Cross flag towed a dinghy ashore, where the wounded soldier was recovered with no interference from the Turks. While they were transferring the wounded soldier back to a ship, a party of Turkish soldiers appeared on the beach, faced the ships, presented arms, grounded them and then buried the English dead. They then fell in again, presented arms once more and marched away.[6]

Hamilton decided that a major offensive would be made in the Helles sector on 6 May. He considered that the Anzac line was secure and therefore instructed Birdwood to abstain from any major offensive action and to send two infantry brigades and twenty Australian field guns, together with their crews, to Helles. With additional reinforcements from Egypt, this brought the total Allied army at Helles to about 25,000 men. Hamilton wanted to attack before dawn, to minimize casualties while crossing no-man's-land, and then to hit the enemy at first light. Hunter-Weston was concerned about the previous loss of officers, which at that stage had been proportionately much higher than the loss of troops, and therefore opposed an advance in the dark. Once again Hamilton gave in. Additionally, Hamilton and his staff were too far away from the battlefields to appreciate fully what was happening minute by minute, and with no single commander of both navy and army coordination of the two forces was still a major problem.

Hunter-Weston's orders for the advance of the Allied line punctually at 11 a.m. on 6 May were, as usual, vague, and also delivered with insufficient time for field commanders to prepare for action. Reinforcements such as the Anzacs were not provided with adequate details of their role, their orders having been issued only seven hours before the assault was due to begin. The second battle of Krithia, as it was to be known, lasted for three days and resulted in a gain of only some 600 yards along the whole front. During this period the Allies suffered over 6,000 casualties – nearly 30 per cent of the troops engaged in the action. On each of the three mornings, following an ineffectual bombardment, the battle started in brilliant sunshine at about the same time and in much the same way, so that the Turkish defenders were given ample warning of the impending attack. However, even under these difficult conditions, the British troops, with a numerical superiority of about 5,000 men, very nearly achieved a decisive victory. At one stage, under the tremendous bombardment of the navy's guns, which surrounded the penin-sula on three sides, and with the continued aggression of the British troops, the Turkish commanders lost their nerve and implored the German commander Weber to withdraw behind the Achi Baba ridge. Von Sanders would not allow a withdrawal and told them to establish their trenches as closely as possible to the enemy, to avoid the artillery fire.

From the Allies' point of view, the artillery bombardments appeared to have little effect: once they ceased and the infantry commenced their advance, enemy machine-guns started firing again. The numerous gullies that traversed the area provided defensive positions for the Turks and allowed commu-nications to flow between their lines without detection by the Allied troops or bombardment by the fleet. The Turks held much of the high ground, while the Allied soldiers had difficulty in making progress, as they suffered from exhaustion and at the same time were inadequately supplied with the types of weapon best suited to the terrain, such as hand grenades. On 7 May no advance was made, and the orders for 8 May, which were not sent out until just before the attack began, were again unrealistic. Four battalions of New Zealanders were to capture Krithia, which was defended by nine battalions, while 29 Division was to advance straight up Fir Tree Spur and the French were to try once again to capture Kereves Dere.

One colonel told his company commanders: 'The battalion will attack from the front-line trenches at 10.30 a.m. precisely; 12th Company will lead. And I am sorry, gentlemen, that I cannot give you any further information.[7]

By 3.30 p.m. the attack had failed, with the New Zealanders, Australians and British returning to their trenches after suffering heavy casualties, while the French had been unable to move from theirs.

Around this time Hamilton received information from the War Office which made it clear that the additional ammunition requested might not be forthcoming as a prolonged occupation of the peninsula had not been planned. Therefore at 4 p.m. he gave orders for the whole line, reinforced by the Australians, to attack again at 5.30 p.m., with bayonets fixed, while the navy was to give unrestricted fire support. It was one last effort, as only 1,000 rounds of high explosive and 10,000 rounds of shrapnel were left, and these had to be kept in reserve for defence. The heaviest barrage on the peninsula thus far commenced at 5.15 p.m., and shortly afterwards the British and New Zealand troops rose from their trenches to launch the attack. As happened so many times before, machine-gun and rifle fire from the Turkish defences mowed down the advancing forces, so that, within a short time, the attack had been brought to a halt and no ground had been gained. During this first lull in the battle, the Australians moved up quickly to attack the Krithia Spur, which no one had previously attempted. The Australians came under heavy bombardment as they made their way up to the British lines and, having reached there, continued on towards their objective. In an act of great valour, they succeeded in advancing 500 yards up the spur, for the loss of one third of the 3,000 men who made the attack.

That evening, two companies of British troops came up to relieve them and to consolidate their position, without a shot being fired at them. At six o'clock the French charged across Kereves Spur and initially seemed to have overrun the enemy trenches. At this point the Turks opened fire with high explosive shells and within a short time had decimated the French forces, which fell back to their old trenches. Another attack was ordered, and again the French went forward, capturing some ground. At seven o'clock the order was given to all Allied troops to dig in as best they could. With both armies spent, the next few days were used to patch up their lines, bury the dead, attend to the wounded and reorganize the units. Between 26 April and 10 May, 10,000 casualties from 29 Division had been evacuated, and over a similar period the French suffered 12,610 casualties out of a total strength of 22,450.

Neither side delivered a major attack from 8 May to 4 June. As the Turkish bombardment intensified and improved in accuracy, the Allies were forced to dig ever deeper. Meanwhile, the Turkish defenders were given time to consolidate their own trench networks and to extend them gradually across the peninsula. It was becoming apparent that the Turkish defenders did not expose themselves directly to fire from the ships and, as long as their trenches remained close to the Allied trenches, naval support was suspended through fear of hitting their own troops.

Turkish counter-attacks at Anzac

At Anzac Cove, the fighting had been continuous for the first week after the landing. Kemal wanted to dislodge the invaders and continued to throw his troops into battle. As Anzac casualties mounted and Turkish reinforcements arrived, by the evening of 27 April the numerical superiority of the Anzacs was lost. Numerous battles developed on various fronts in an uncoordinated fashion as both sides attempted to gain the advantage in the very rugged and difficult terrain. Kemal continued to throw his forces into action piecemeal, as smaller units, rather than as a major coordinated push. On the south-eastern edge of 400 Plateau, the Australians had actually won and occupied the high ground, but reinforcements failed to arrive and by 28 April this crucial area was lost. On this day, Kemal launched a coordinated attack on the whole Anzac line, but because of poor weather conditions and bad ground it developed into a number of sporadic attacks, which were beaten off with heavy losses. These losses were in large measure due to naval bombardment, which had such a significant impact that the Turks never again attempted a daylight action on any ground exposed to fire from the navy.

Ever since the landings, rifle fire against the Anzacs had been almost continuous, with very little safe cover. On the 29th, relief finally came in the form of two battalions of Royal Marines, one of which, the Deal Battalion, relieved most of the Australians at the 400 Plateau. During the previous six days, the Australian and New Zealand army corps had suffered 6,554 casualties, of which 1,252 had been killed. The Turkish casualties were even greater. In the period from 25 April to 4 May, the Turkish general staff estimated the Turkish casualties at Anzac to be 14,000, of whom many were killed or had died of their wounds.

On 1 May, Kemal again hurled his troops at the Anzac lines, in one final headlong attack. The Turks were mowed down by the defenders, and after twenty-four hours of fighting Kemal gave the order for the attack to stop. He was ordered by his superiors not to undertake any further frontal attacks for the time being. Birdwood made his last attack of the period on the night of 2 May, in an attempt to capture the hill named Baby 700. However, there was congestion in the valleys leading up to the objective, and due to the darkness many of the troops arrived late. Some ground was taken, but in the morning the positions gained proved to be untenable, and even more so with naval 6-inch shells falling on the captured trenches.[8] So, by noon of 3 May, the Australian troops had returned to Monash Valley. By that time their casualties had increased to over 8,000, of which 2,300 had been killed. In the fighting on the night of 3 May alone, they suffered over 2,000 casualties, of which half were killed. The remaining troops were exhausted; it was now just a matter of holding on to their positions and forcing the Turkish defenders to stay put. On 9 May, Hamilton discussed with Birdwood the possibility of an evacuation, but Birdwood was confident that his men could hold their present lines. The Anzacs now dug in like never before.

General Essad Bey, commander of the central and northern portions of the peninsula, and Kemal still believed that they could push the Anzacs back into the sea; so another attack was planned for 3.30 a.m. on the morning of 19 May. A force of 40,000 Turks was assembled and, to increase the element of surprise, it was decided not to have any preliminary bombardment. Kemal wanted to concentrate his attack at The Neck and the head of Monash Valley, but this plan was rejected by von Sanders in favour of an attack along the whole front. Reports were received from aircraft and from the *Triumph* that Turkish reinforcements were moving from Maidos to Krithia. Reduction in rifle fire on the night of 18 May also alerted the Anzacs. As the Turkish troops assembled in Legge Valley, Australian outposts spotted the glistening of their bayonets in the moonlight at 3 a.m. and commenced firing. With the element of surprise lost, the Turks proceeded to attack. The Turkish troops were mown down at point-blank range, as they advanced all along 400 Plateau. The advancing troops were given no covering fire, so the Australians were able to sit on their parapets, shooting as fast as they could. Misled by reports of an advance, Kemal ordered further attacks until noon, when the operation was finally called off.

The Turkish casualties were over 10,000, of which 3,000 lay dead or wounded in a no-man's-land between the lines of trenches. Had Kemal been able to attack as he had originally intended, it is quite likely that the 17,000 defenders could have been overrun. Once the Turkish assault had failed, no major advance was made by the Anzacs to take advantage of the situation. A short truce was arranged that evening, so that the Turkish wounded could be collected. A nine-hour armistice had to be called on 24 May, to make it possible to bury the rotting dead. By this stage it had become apparent to the Turks that they would not be able to dislodge the Anzacs and that, in turn, their own trenches could not be breached. The number of Turkish troops at Anzac was therefore reduced accordingly, and the surplus troops sent to Helles. As the Turkish War Office was to state after the war:

After May 19 it was realized that the British defence at Anzac was too strong to enable us to effect anything against it without heavy artillery with plenty of ammunition, and since our own position was also very strong in defence, two weak divisions were left in the trenches and the other two were withdrawn.[9]

Both sides were desperately short of ammunition; in particular, the Allies had few howitzers or, even more importantly, trench mortars, while hand-grenades were made out of old jam tins. Hamilton asked Kitchener for more ammunition, to 'hammer' and thus demoralize the enemy, as well as for another two divisions, so that the trench warfare that was developing might be avoided. On 14 May, under instructions from the War Council, Kitchener asked Hamilton how many additional troops would be required. The latter's response was that a further four divisions would be needed. No word was heard back for the next three weeks, however, and in the meantime the submarine and naval campaigns continued.

Turkish naval efforts

After the Allied landings, the Turkish navy initially supported the Turkish ground forces. However, the Turkish defenders were in a much better position than the Allies to use their land-based artillery more effectively in providing close support. As already mentioned, the naval assistance started at 4.15 a.m. on the morning of 27 April, with what was to be known as the 'morning hate'.[10] Indirect fire came from either the *Goeben* or the *Torgud Reis*, from their firing position opposite Kilid Bahr. The fire was relatively accurate, as an observation post had been established at Nebrunesi Point; this was the southernmost arm of Suvla Bay, 7 miles north of Gaba Tepe. Hidden behind a hill called Lala Baba, the observation post was connected by telephone to the ships.

The Turkish fire succeeded in forcing a number of British ships to move out to sea. On 29 April, *Triumph*, with a seaplane spotting for her, attempted to bombard the enemy ship, but it was eventually discovered that the Turks were sending false and misleading signals, so the attempt was abandoned. The next day a more concentrated and detailed method was employed, which eventually forced the Turkish ship to retreat. *Goeben* also got involved in the morning shoot, but her involvement was very limited after a kite-balloon from the *Manica*, spotting for the *Queen Elizabeth*, forced her to move for cover at 9 a.m. on 27 April and prevented her from carrying out any further firing on the Anzacs. A greater contribution was the deployment of crews from *Goeben* and *Breslau*, with twenty-four machine-guns, to support the Turkish ground forces. Neither the *Goeben* nor the *Breslau* ever ventured below Kephez into the Dardanelles until 1918.

Both off Helles and off Anzac Cove, divisions of British destroyers, some-times numbering up to ten, would sweep the areas two and three times a day for mines. Support was provided by a battleship that suppressed enemy fire from the shore. In the straits, the destroyers also strafed the enemy positions in support of the French forces holding the eastern end of the Allies' line on the peninsula. On the evening of 12 May, the battleship *Goliath*, with *Cornwallis* to seaward of her, was anchored in Morto Bay and by 8 p.m. was in support of a line of five destroyers further up the strait. It was a dark night with some fog in which the Turkish ship *Muavent-i Milliye*,[11] one of four German-built 30-knot destroyers, under the command of German Korvettenkapitän Rudolf Firle and Turkish Binbasi Achmed Effendi, hugging the shoreline, passed the British destroyers unobserved. Previously, in early May, Admiral Usedom had planned a torpedo attack against the British battleships which were inflicting heavy casualties on the Turkish forces. The *Muavent* had been sent to Chanak on 10 May and was prepared for action, with the fitting of three Mark A/08 Schwarzkopf torpedoes, set to run at 6 feet and 1,300 yards.[12] The destroyer came up to *Goliath*'s bow at right angles, was challenged with the Morse code letter 'O' and replied with the same. On being challenged a second time, she once again replied with the letter 'O', and at 1.17 a.m. on 13 May, while confusion still existed on the *Goliath*, she fired three torpedoes at a range of 300 yards, which struck the ship's starboard side. *Goliath* got off a few rounds without effect, and the ship then heeled over to starboard and sank.

Since 11 May, with the news that a German submarine might be in the area, *Goliath*, like the other battleships, had deployed steel torpedo nets. These nets were a cumbersome affair, being arranged along each side of the ship and suspended some 30 feet out, with the aim of causing torpedoes to explode harmlessly before striking the ship. The bowshot by the destroyer avoided the nets, which were strung along her sides. Of a total complement of 750, only 21 officers and 162 men were saved. Many others were swept down the straits, to drown from cold and exhaustion, while those who were still alive thought that the rescue ships were steaming right through them.[13] The *Muavent* then proceeded back the way she had come and, as she reached the Narrows, sent off a wireless signal of her success, which was heard by other British ships in the area. No further ventures by Turkish ships were made into the Mediterranean after this successful attack.

The impact of this sinking on the British was immediate. The risk of losing the *Queen Elizabeth* was considered too great, so she was sent back behind the anti-torpedo boom at Mudros, and subsequently back to England. Admiral de Robeck transferred his staff to the *Lord Nelson* on 14 May and, a few days later, to the steam yacht *Triad*. Two 14-inch monitors, two battleships, *Exmouth* and *Venerable*, and two cruisers, *Cornwall* and *Chatham*, replaced *Queen Elizabeth*. This in turn was initially offset early in May by the transfer of four battleships, *Queen*, *London*, *Implacable* and *Prince of Wales*, plus four cruisers, *Amethyst*, *Sapphire*, *Dublin* and *Dartmouth*, to the Adriatic, until the date of Italy's decision to declare war on Austria on 23 May. Not only had the effective firepower been reduced, but also the battleships were no longer able to use their searchlights at night and thus were forced to support the army only by day, lying with their nets out. From then on, troops and supplies would be transferred to the Dardanelles primarily at night, through the use of fleet sweepers and trawlers.

6

German Submarine Activity

Desperate measures

In the early part of 1915, Admiral Souchon felt that the Turkish navy should have submarines to defend the Dardanelles. He set a message to the Austrian commander-in-chief, Admiral Anton Haus, asking for some to be sent from Austria. However, at the start of the war, the Austrians only had six small submarines and subsequently acquired only two more: one, a private experimental vessel which was requisitioned, and the other, the captured French submarine *Curie*.

The Austrian navy had ordered five additional larger U-boats from Germany, which were being constructed in Kiel. However, with the outbreak of war, these were sold back to Germany, becoming *U66* to *U70*. Admiral Haus therefore refused Souchon's request for submarines, stating that only two were fully ready for action. One of these, *UIV*, had a battery of only half capacity, while the second, *UXII*, had a limited range, from the Straits of Otranto to the Dardanelles, and then only under the most favourable conditions. The entire trip would have to be made on the surface, a requirement which meant that enemy warships had to be avoided, while the weather needed to be completely calm.[1]

These submarines used gasoline as fuel and carried only four torpedoes. Haus also claimed that the submarines were required in the Adriatic, to help defend the Austrian bases at Pola and Cattaro (now Kotor in Montenegro). Souchon therefore sent a request to Berlin for new boats to be sent to the Dardanelles. This request was fully supported by both the Turkish government and the German ambassador to Constantinople. Tirpitz, state secretary of the Reichsmarineamt, was keener to see the Austrian U-boats in action at the Dardanelles. Tirpitz therefore offered two smaller U-boats to Austria in exchange for their larger U-boats. However, if the Austrian U-boats were not forthcoming (which proved to be the case), the two smaller submarines, crewed by Germans, would make the trip to the Dardanelles.[2]

There were two ways in which the Germans could send the submarines to Turkey. One was to order one of the newer and larger U-boats from Germany through the Straits of Gibraltar. This was, however, a very long trip, and given that the British Admiralty was sure to anticipate such a move, would be extremely hazardous. The approach which was initially adopted was to dispatch a number of the smaller-type submarines. These could be broken up into sections and then transported by rail to Pola, where they would be reassembled. The submarines would then complete their journey to Turkey by sea, down the Aegean through the Mediterranean and then through the Dardanelles. Coincidently, designs for two new smaller submarines had been completed on 19 October 1914. They were, basically, coastal submarines known as the UB type and coastal minelayers of the UC type.

The UB boats, which were called 'tin tadpoles' by the crews, had a surface displacement of only 127 tons and a length of less than 100 feet (see Appendix I). The original design only allowed for a petrol motor, with no additional power, which was not only antiquated but also inherently dangerous. However, in the end an additional 60 horsepower diesel engine was added and this provided a surface speed of about 6½ knots. Submerged, they could do 5 knots for about one hour's duration. The armament consisted of two 18-inch torpedo tubes with no reloads. The UC boats were only slightly larger, carrying mines in twelve external mine chutes, and were unable to carry any torpedo armament.

Each of the submarines was made up of three main sections, which were loaded onto railway wagons and shipped to Pola, with other wagons carrying the conning tower, engines, batteries and various other parts of the casing and equipment. At Pola, the submarines were reassembled in approximately fourteen days. At one stage it was planned to send two submarines directly to Constantinople, if rail transport through Bulgaria became possible, but this never occurred. Components for the first boat (UB8) arrived in Pola on 26 March 1915 (an amazingly short time to build the submarines, given the completion date of the design). When assembled the only water tightness test that could be applied was with compressed air, at a very low positive pressure of 1 pound per square inch.[3] Within a month, Oberleutnant zur See Ernst von Voigt had completed UB8's sea trials and was ready to take the small craft to Turkey.

UB8

The Austrian cruiser Novara was initially used to tow UB8 for the first leg of her journey, and commenced their trip at 2.10 p.m. on 4 May. However, by about three o'clock in the afternoon, with the submarine being towed at 9½ knots, the bow suddenly dipped. Petty Officer Döhler, who was the officer of the watch, was unable to cut the tow quickly enough, but managed to close the conning tower hatch just before the submarine went under. Water poured through the partially open hatch as the submarine descended to 18 metres with a 20 degree down angle, while Döhler and Seaman Rausch, now in the sea, fought for their lives. The *Novara* stopped at once, and the submarine rose back to the surface and was able to use its electric motors to turn and pick up Döhler. Rausch, who couldn't swim, was not found after torpedo destroyers searched the area for another two hours. *UB8* was forced to return to Palazzo harbour on the Isle of Curzola for repairs, to refuel and replace the lost sailor.

UB8 departed again the following day at 1 a.m., towed by *Novara*, which was camouflaged to simulate a transport steamer by stretching a large piece of linen between its funnels and some wire netting above it. The camouflage proved important since, after *UB8* and her escort passed through the Straits of Otranto and while they were still 100 nautical miles from Cape Matapan, French warships came over the horizon. The *Novara* turned towards Patras, leading the enemy forces away from *UB8*, which submerged to 20 metres at 10.50 a.m. on 6 May, without being sighted. When *UB8* was thought to be safe, *Novara* removed her camouflage, hoisted her ensign and succeeded in escaping from the pursuing French ships.[4]

Three days later, *UB8* was hit by a force eight gale causing the submarine to roll so badly that von Voigt feared that the battery acid would spill. The submarine was forced to heave to, but from a rolling motion it then turned into a vicious pitching motion. Fearing further damage to his craft, von Voigt took the boat down to 20 metres, to a still unpleasant but more manageable pitching motion.

By 11 May, *UB8* had arrived at the island of Orak near Bodrum on the Gulf of Kos, 230 miles south of the Dardanelles and 100 miles south of Smyrna and while attempting to enter the harbour as it surfaced, it ran into a small island, approximately 4 nautical miles from the entrance. There was no change in pressure aboard the submarine, which suggested there were no leaks and no damage to the torpedo tubes, although the bow was slightly pressed in. As von Voigt moved further out to sea to surface and inspect the damage, a two-funnelled English warship was sighted. Believing the enemy ship had seen him, he spent the next hour and a quarter submerged, before he raised his periscope to discover that the surface vessel had departed. That afternoon he headed back to Orak and after observing that no flags were flying on the two posts situated on either side of the entrance – which signalled that no enemy was present – he finally proceeded into the harbour.

Heading off on the 13 May, after *UB8* had refuelled and taken on further provisions, the submarine ran into further difficulties, with a leak of 10 to 12 kilograms of air each day from one of its torpedoes. Her compressor was also causing problems, proving capable of providing only 140 kilograms of air before its bearings overheated. To add to these difficulties even further, on 15 May the gyrocompass, which had caused problems initially, when the submarine left on its mission, was once again faulty so that it became necessary to use the less reliable magnetic compass. That evening the sea conditions became so heavy and the small submarine rolled so much that she had to head into the swell and eventually submerge. On 16 May, faced with continuing difficulties with the compressor and the gyrocompass, von Voigt was finally forced to head for Smyrna for repairs. The next day, as *UB8* approached Smyrna, several English destroyers were seen; but by 8.45 a.m. *UB8* was only half a nautical mile from land, and surfaced to take on board a Turkish pilot who helped navigate it past the minefield. At this time von Voigt observed a submarine at a great distance, followed by a destroyer. By 11 a.m. *UB8* was safely past the fort and moored, with camouflage netting to protect it from enemy aircraft.

Around the same time *B11*, in company with *Wear*, was patrolling off Smyrna guarding a line of mines, and on the lookout for enemy submarines. At 10 a.m. on 17 May, Holbrook reported sighting a U-boat (almost certainly *UB8*):

10 a.m. Sighted hostile submarine, apparently on motors, bearing about S. W. four miles from me proceeding towards Smyrna and very close inshore. She looked very much like one of our later 'E' boats, with a straight bow and more superstructure forward than aft, and had a conical shaped conning tower. I dived immediately to attack her. 10.30 a.m. I came to the surface, and discovered she was under way full speed on her engines with a large bow wave, but on sighting me she dived immediately. I never saw her again.[5]

This was the first confirmation of a new class of U-boat in the eastern Mediterranean.

By 30 May, *UB8* was submerged off Mudros harbour looking for the enemy, when, at 9.25 a.m., von Voigt sighted a Goliath class battleship, but was unable to get within firing distance. A little later, a destroyer was spotted heading for the submarine. After twenty minutes von Voigt raised his periscope, only to find the destroyer still heading his way. This made him believe that an aeroplane might be in the air, looking for the telltale signs of a raised periscope. Turning to the east and heading for the Gallipoli Peninsula, von Voigt raised his periscope some twenty minutes later, to discover that he was at last clear of the destroyer. He surfaced at 2 p.m. and headed back towards Mudros.

At 5.30 p.m., after having seen no transports, he sighted a passenger ship, a cargo vessel and a tug making their way out of Mudros in a south-westerly direction; but again, von Voigt was unable to get within range. Then at 7 p.m. he sighted what he believed to be a warship heading towards Mudros, zigzagging every fifteen minutes, and in the twilight he saw what looked like two guns on the back of a very wide and slow moving ship. Von Voigt then tried unsuccessfully to identify the ship from the German navy's pocket-book of ship silhouettes (next day he determined, from a supplementary book, that it was a Tiger class battlecruiser). At 8.15 p.m., after the range had closed to 400 metres, von Voigt fired his torpedo, and thirty to forty seconds later a big detonation was heard. On raising his periscope he observed parts of the ship's deck flying around. Another torpedo was prepared as the target was still moving, although it looked as if it was heavier in the stern and had a small list. By this time the range had increased to 2,000 metres, the light was failing and destroyers were arriving, so he decided to abandon his attack. Von Voigt had torpedoed and sunk the British steamer *Merion*, with the loss of four out of a total crew of 117. The ship was part of the Special Services Squadron and had been altered to look like the battlecruiser *Tiger*.[6]

The following day, a small old cruiser was spotted coming from Mudros and heading in a westerly direction; but, again, it was too far to attack. At this stage the charge on the battery had became of concern to von Voigt, as he planned to go through the Dardanelles within the next few days. Surfacing and avoiding contact with enemy ships, he spent the remainder of that day, as well as the next, charging his batteries. At 1 a.m. on 2 June, as *UB8* approached Cape Helles on the surface, a destroyer was sighted within only 500 metres, and the submarine crash-dived just as the destroyer turned to ram. Remaining submerged, von Voigt observed several steamships anchored at Helles, as well as small ships and a number of destroyers patrolling the entrance to the straits. By 2.45 a.m. he was in front of the destroyers near Morto Bay, and forty-five minutes later he had passed under them undetected. At 4.22 a.m., with no compressed air left, he was forced to surface and run on his electric motors to remain quiet, as he observed seven destroyers patrolling the entrance. He also found that his submarine was 1 nautical mile further down the strait, and hence closer to the destroyers than he had expected. Finally, at 4.50 a.m., he sighted the Turkish motorboat, which was waiting to escort him through the minefields; he started his diesel engine for the trip to Chanak and arrived safely at 6.25 a.m. By 10 a.m. *UB8* was under tow by the *Basra*, and by 9.45 a.m. on the following day *UB8* tied up at the Arsenal in Constantinople.[7] After several weeks of maintenance, *UB8* left Constantinople on 14 July and, while in the

Marmara, was sighted by *E7*. Von Voigt undertook two unsuccessful attacks and, when the smell of chlorine gas became evident, after rough weather he was forced to return to Constantinople.

UB7

The next boat to depart was *UB7*, under the command of Oberleutnant zur See S. Werner; she left Pola at midday on 11 May. The U-boat was successfully towed through the Straits of Otranto on the night of 15 May by the destroyer *Triglav*, arriving at Orak without incident on 20 May. *UB7* then headed to the Aegean; during this time it had engine trouble, which required the crew to set up a makeshift sail on the 22nd to help it to return to port. By the 23rd, as the submarine approached Lemnos, the number of enemy sightings increased; these included a cruiser of the Indomitable class, which Werner wanted to attack. He eventually decided that this was not possible, as the attempt would have to be made using batteries that would be exhausted before he could get close. Instead, he headed south-west, around the island of Skyros, in the hope of intercepting the target on its return in the evening. With fully charged batteries and compressed air bottles, Werner waited with *UB7* partially submerged, but no ships were sighted, so he continued his journey around Lemnos towards Gallipoli.

By 8 p.m. on the evening of 24 May the problems with the motor worsened, but some makeshift repairs made it possible to run the motor to recharge the batteries, if only at a modest 100 amps. Engaging the clutch to drive the propeller resulted in stalling the engine. So the only alternative was to charge the batteries at night while they were stationary, and then during the day to use the electric motors to propel the boat and to set sail when it was safe to do so, with the right wind conditions. In desperation Werner contacted the Turkish pilot at the nearby Bay of Saros, only to be informed that there was consider-able hostile activity in the area. Werner proposed that *UB7* should remain submerged in the bay by day doing repairs and surface at night to take on supplies. He also requested that mechanics be made available.

On 25 May progress was very slow, due to winds and currents which reduced the boat's speed to only 0.5 knots. Water was in such short supply that water had to be drained from one of the torpedoes and added into the drinking-water tank. Electric power had to be conserved as much as possible, but, whenever the submarine had to dive, more power was consumed in keeping it moving to maintain depth (see Appendix I). To avoid her having to move while submerged, an ingenious idea was employed: an empty innocuous-looking 40-litre drum was attached to the top of the conning tower by a 3-metre length of rope. When the submarine submerged, the drum remained on the surface, literally holding the submarine from sinking further than 3 metres below the surface while it was stationary. The periscope was still usable in this position, allowing any enemy movements to be observed.

At 9 p.m. on that evening the main problem with the motor was finally diagnosed. By 6 a.m. on the 26th, three of the four cylinders were fixed, with the fourth cylinder eventually being repaired too. After losing two days and a half drifting at sea, with a half empty battery, in sight of the enemy-controlled island of Lemnos, Werner's laconic observation in his log was: 'This is, from the point of view of a submarine commander, a very unpleasant situation.'[8]

On 27 May, *UB7* then headed for Imbros, in the hope of attacking British warships. At 6.30 a.m., smoke and masts were visible in Kephalos harbour on the eastern shore of Imbros Island, although because of condensation on the periscope's magnifying lens it was not till an hour later that a small cruiser, the battleship *Queen Elizabeth* and several destroyers were observed. Some twelve to fifteen steamers were moored in front of the warships to protect them. Werner manoeuvred *UB7*, trying to get further into the harbour and position for an attack, but a high-running sea, shallow water, patrolling craft and low battery power made the task too difficult, and he was forced to withdraw.

Heading for Gallipoli, Werner noticed guard ships and balloon ships at the southern end of the peninsula and made the observation that the major ships were being kept back in port, perhaps due to possible submarine activity, as in the North Sea. He was, at the time, unaware of the recent successes of *U21*. The next two days were spent travelling to Smyrna to undertake crucial repairs. At midday on 30 May, *UB7* surfaced in the gulf to the south of Midilli Island and sighted an English destroyer. Diving, Werner went into attack and fired a torpedo, but the destroyer quickly manoeuvred out of the way and spent the rest of the day searching for the submarine. At 8 p.m., *UB7* once again surfaced, exchanged recognition signals, was advised by the pilot to sail towards the mine barrier gap and, with the help of a tug, finally anchored at 1.15 a.m. the next morning.

Repair work on the submarine started immediately, with engineers from Constantinople giving her an extensive overhaul. On hearing of the success of *U21*, Werner felt that the modest offensive quality of his small submarine could have been compensated for by the element of surprise but that this had not been possible on account of its mechanical problems.

UB7 departed from Smyrna on 13 June and headed for the Dardanelles. By the 14th, a French Duplex class armoured cruiser was sighted south of Lemnos, heading in the direction of the island of Skyros. On the following day numerous steamers were seen without escort between Lemnos and Tenedos. Werner's plan was to head for Gaba Tepe to attack vessels around Helles; but, at a speed of 2 knots, battery endurance would not allow him to travel submerged for the six required hours and return beyond the cordon of guard ships, without having to surface. He was therefore forced to delay his attack till the following day.

At 5.30 a.m. the next day, *UB7* was at Gaba Tepe and Werner observed three separate groups of twin destroyers patrolling the area, two hospital ships and a number of steamers behind the destroyer screen. By 10.12 a.m. he was in position to attack a transport steamer and fired his first torpedo at a distance of 250 to 300 metres. This was observed to head for the target, but there was no explosion. Werner then headed behind the steamer and again, at a distance of 250 to 300 metres, fired a second torpedo, which also appeared to head for the target but, again, failed to explode.[9] By this time two French destroyers had appeared on the scene and *UB7* was forced to withdraw.

On the following day, 19 June, near Gaba Tepe again, Werner manoeuvred *UB7* though a screen of five English destroyers, to get close to a coal steamer. The steamer was protected by two torpedo boats; with a smooth sea, it was not long before the submarine's periscope was spotted and fired upon. Werner considered the conditions too difficult, once again gave up, departed from the area and, later on that day, headed into the Dardanelles. Early on the 20th, *UB7* was met by the Turkish torpedo boat *Muavent* and by 9.30 a.m. was under tow and taken through the minefields, eventually arriving at Constantinople on 21 June, to tie up alongside *U21*.

The third boat to depart from Pola on 23 May was *UB3*, under the command of Leutnant zur See S. Schmidt. She was due to arrive at Smyrna between 28 and 29 May, but, when she was 80 miles from her destination an incomplete radio transmission was received from her. This was the last that was ever heard from *UB3*. It was assumed that she disappeared due to technical difficulties, as there was no report of enemy action and no minefields in the area.[10]

British counter-measures

For some time the British had been receiving information that the Germans were establishing a base at Bodrum. It was therefore decided to send Allied submarines to keep watch. The task was allocated to the older B class submarines and to the French boats. The first of these patrols was carried out from 16 April to 5 May by *B10*, under the command of Lieutenant S. M. G. Gravener, in the company of the converted mine sweeper *Gazelle*, previously an ex-railway ferry.

The submarine left, in the company of *Gazelle*, at 4 p.m. on 16 April and 24 hours later arrived off the western end of Kos island, which became the overnight billet location for the two vessels. *B10* proceeded on in the early morning of 18 April, diving within 2 miles of Bodrum and inspecting the harbour while submerged, to discover only one small sailing vessel. *B10* and its escort kept up these patrols for three fruitless weeks, with the submarine laying alongside *Gazelle* overnight if the weather was bad, or otherwise close by, before proceeding to her daytime position an hour before daylight. As night fell, prior to returning to her billet, *B10* would proceed to Bodrum, entering the harbour by the south-east entrance and leaving by the north-west entrance, with occasional visits to Kos harbour.

On 21 April, Gravener observed that Kara Island (just outside of Bodrum) was uninhabited, except for two farms on the north-eastern side, so he decided to place small moorings 600 yards from shore in a position that provided a good look-out for the various channel approaches between Kos, Bodrum and the mainland. This allowed the submarine to tie up to these moorings during daylight hours. Occasionally the boat's first officer, Lieutenant North, and sometimes Gravener himself would land on Kara Island and climb to the island's summit, a position from which Bodrum harbour could be observed. On 2 May, when Lieutenant North and two other crewmen reached the summit, they were fired upon, so patrolling the island was undertaken to see if any boats had landed, but none was found. By this time *Gazelle* had returned to Mudros, and *B10* remained on the moorings except when it went to patrol Bodrum harbour. On 4 May, two locals approached by land until they came facing the submarine at its mooring. They were carrying a white flag, a large cheese and a live goat! Gravener rowed ashore, where he found that the locals insisted on giving him the goods without payment, perhaps as a result of the unintentional shooting several days before. *Gazelle* returned to the mooring on the evening of 5 May and departed for Tenedos in company with *B10*, arriving there on 7 May.[11]

As it became apparent that the Germans were not establishing a new base at Bodrum, activity for the B class boats continued to be a relatively boring succession of defensive patrols. On 11 May *B10*, in company with the mine-sweeper *Hythe*, proceeded to patrol the Doro Channel between Andros Island to the south and Euboea Island to the west. Gravener decided that during the night *B10* would patrol slowly, without lights, while *Hythe*, under the command of Lieutenant Commander Rogers, would patrol across the mouth of the channel, 4 miles to the south. During the day *Hythe* moored close to the eastern shore, landing an observation party, while *B10* moored near a small island in the channel, where another observation party was landed. From the evening of 12 May, Gravener altered the night-time arrangements, with *B10* patrolling the western shore and *Hythe* the eastern shore, on the assumption that any enemy submarine would stay close inshore when passing through the channel on the surface at night.

At 7.45 a.m. on 15 May, the shore party reported the sighting of a possible submarine to the south and Lieutenant North was sent ashore to verify the sighting – but without success. The submarine had indeed been sighted from *B10*, but was difficult to see properly. The shore party and Gravener were certain that the submarine they had seen was not German, but French. *B10* proceeded to the eastern shore to confirm the sighting, accepting that the risk of an accidental attack by the French or of an intended attack by the Germans was always a possibility. Having failed to find the submarine, *B10* closed on *Hythe*, reported the sighting, and ordered her to proceed round the south-east of Andros Island and check every bay. When this proved unsuccessful, Gravener assumed that the French submarine was returning from her night-time patrol area at Steno Pass. By 19 May, *B10* was recalled and ordered to rendezvous at Steno Pass at 4 p.m. with *B7*, two French submarines, *Coulomb* and *Bernoulli*, which arrived late, and a French trawler. *B10* returned safely to Mudros at 7.30 p.m. on 20 May.

UB14

On 15 July *UB14* under its new commander, Oberleutnant zur See Heino von Heimburg, departed for Gallipoli, towed by the Austrian destroyer *Triglav* until she was some 70 miles south of Cattaro. Von Heimburg, while in command of *UB15*, had made a name for himself, which was to continue under his new command. Arriving at Orak on 24 July, *UB14* underwent a complete overhaul, although due to the difficult conditions the engine reinstallation was not completed till 12 August. As the fitter to repair the secondary compressor was not expected until 17 July, it was decided to depart on the 13th for a short patrol, covering the transport route between Alexandria and the Dardanelles.

In the very early hours of 13 August, von Heimburg spotted, at a distance of 4 nautical miles, a hospital ship, which he let pass. Later in the morning he sighted another large vessel and headed off at high speed to intercept her. Though not getting close enough to attack, he realized that the target was another hospital ship, the P & O liner *Soudan*. However, a little later, another larger steamer was seen heading from the south and at 9.15 a.m., at a distance of 1,000 metres, von Heimburg fired a torpedo which hit the ship's stern. After about three minutes the stern started to sink and within seconds the bow was upright. A few minutes later she disappeared below the waves.

The torpedoed ship was the transport *Royal Edward* (11,117 tons), sailing unescorted for Madras. Apart from her crew of 220 members, she had on board 31 officers and 1,335 men, mainly reinforcements for 29 Division. Survivors were picked up by the *Soudan*, by French torpedo boats and by some trawlers and steamers which were near the scene, although there was still the unfortunate loss of 900 lives.[12] UB14 did not harass the rescue ships, as von Heimburg 'was concerned about over-extending his boat', whose batteries were becoming depleted, so he returned to Orak the next day at 1 a.m.[13]

After repairs to the secondary compressor, UB14 left for the Dardanelles at 8 a.m. on 18 August. At 9 p.m. on 22 August, within 4 nautical miles from Gaba Tepe, the submarine got caught in a steel net at a depth of 18 metres. After trying to go through the net, the submarine reversed without success, with the net still remaining fastened to the stern. Von Heimburg took the submarine down to 35 metres and then to 45 metres, to ensure that any marker buoys would be dragged underwater and would not give away his position. Several explosions were then heard, indicating that the enemy was aware of his presence. Using full emergency power and risking burning out the motors, he succeeded in tearing the net and the submarine was able to proceed, although she remained at 50 metres depth till dark.

On surfacing, there were no enemy ships in sight, and after one and a half hours of manual effort the submarine was finally free from most of the net that had remained attached from the previous exertions, though some was still wrapped around the propeller shaft. Surprisingly, the fifty or sixty glass balls attached to that netting had still not given away her location. Some damage was suffered, which resulted in the vessel responding poorly to the helm. Without a detailed knowledge of the barriers that might be in place in the Dardanelles and in ignorance of other possible damage done to the boat, von Heimburg took a cautious approach and decided to return to Orak, arriving back on the 25th. Over the next five days all the required repairs were undertaken.

On the evening of 30 August, UB14 started for Constantinople once more, but this time with Sub-Lieutenant Mellenthin as pilot officer. The next day, due to heavy seas and strong winds, the submarine was forced to shelter behind Strati Island. In the early hours of 2 September, while still to the south of the island, a steamer was sighted coming from the south. UB14 dived to attack but the steamer passed at too great a distance. A short time later, a second steamer approached from the same direction. On this occasion, von Heimburg was able to get UB14 into position at a range of 1,300 metres and at an angle of 90 degrees, and fired a torpedo at 9.46 a.m. After firing the torpedo the submarine rose, with the conning tower breaching the surface. Then she went deeper by way of compensating for this, and von Heimburg was unable to see the torpedo hit its target. When next he raised his periscope, the steamer had stopped and UB14 passed by its stern, where von Heimburg observed that all the lifeboats were being lowered. Remaining in the area for a further two hours, he concluded that the ship must have been hit in the bow, as this was now half a metre lower than the stern. Fifty lifeboats were into the sea and a number of ships were coming to the rescue, so von Heimburg decided to leave the scene.

The ship von Heimburg had torpedoed was the transport *Southland*,[14] which didn't sink, and was later salvaged from shallow waters in Mudros Bay. On board were Australian troops of 2 Division which, in the process of abandoning ship, lost 44 soldiers, including 4 officers, while 26 sailors also lost their lives. The nearby hospital ships *Neuralia* and *Massena*, as well as a number of torpedo boats, rescued 166 men from the sea.

At around 3 a.m. on 4 September, after observing a streamer with obscured lights to the north, *UB14* surfaced 4 nautical miles to the south-west of Cape Helles. At 5.20 a.m., a steamer was sighted in front and a destroyer behind his submarine, so von Heimburg was forced to submerge just off Helles. A little later, after having surfaced again, *UB14* was forced down by two destroyers at the entrance to the straits, near Sedd el Bahr. Several detonations were heard, which sounded like shells impacting on the surface; this suggested that they had been sighted. Shortly after 11 a.m., *UB14* surfaced just to the north of Monto Bay, off Eski Hissarlik and, with the Turkish pilot on board, went through the minefields and anchored at Chanak. Their return was marked by a visit from Leutnant Prinz Heinrich Reuss, who came aboard to congratulate the crew. Departing on the morning of 5 September and towed by tugboat *MC13*, *UB14* finally reached Constantinople that evening.

UB14 was to play one more significant role in her action against the British efforts at the Dardanelles. As described elsewhere in this book (see Chapter 11) the French submarine *Turquoise* was captured by the Turks and information was recovered which gave the time and location of a rendezvous with other Allied submarines. On receiving this information, Admiral Souchon sent the following order to *UB14* on 4 November:

Very Secret
O. Matter
U – Boat task No 13.

Task: Attack hostile submarine in the Marmara Sea

Information from enemy

    1.) a hostile submarine on 3. and 4. November in front of Mudania. Possibly as noted by 'Turquoise' presence of E12, E20 and H1 in Marmara Sea.

    2.) meeting point of hostile submarines from 9 till 10 am and 4 – 5pm at 28° 10′ 0, 40° 45′ N.

Mission: U14 to sail from Bosporus on 4.11 at 12 midnight escorted by gunboat. During the day stay near the hostile meeting point.

Transport of 'Turquoise' is expected on 5.11 from Palatia to Constantinople.

Transmission of news: Gem. F.T. U-Boats command No. 2

Return: At 12 midnight on 7.11 stop 2 nautical miles east of Proti Island where a gunboat will be waiting to escort. Light-signal B will answer with a white star.

Souchon

On 5 November, von Heimburg set out from Constantinople, to become involved in sinking a second submarine. At 5.45 a.m. he stopped and ventilated his boat 10 to 15 nautical miles from the rendezvous site. Submerging and heading south 5 nautical miles from the rendezvous, at 4 p.m. he sighted the conning tower of a submarine, which he thought initially was moving; then he realized she was stationary. He decided to approach from the west, so that the sun was behind him and in the eyes of the target. The sea was very smooth, so he used the periscope sparingly and carefully while reducing speed, to minimize the periscope's 'feather effect' on the surface.

A further difficulty arose as the periscope's magnifier was faulty; but, at a range of 2,000 metres and a bearing of 160 degrees, UB14 steered for the other submarine. The torpedo was made ready and von Heimburg quickly checked his progress at a range of 1,200 metres. At 5.10 p.m., at a distance of 500 metres and travelling at half speed, he fired the torpedo and UB14's conning tower broke the surface. At 5.16 p.m., the torpedo was seen to hit the target, which was immediately covered by smoke and by a water column, followed by the sound of a weak explosion. By the time the smoke and water had cleared there was no sign of E20 (see p. 244 below).

At 5.20 p.m., UB14 surfaced and rescued two officers including E20's captain, Warren, and six of her crew. On board the U-boat, Warren commented on how small UB14 was, although there was enough room to keep the prisoners below so that normal operations could continue. He also mentioned to von Heimburg that he had been in the Sea of Marmara for four weeks and that he had intended to remain there longer. Initially Warren thought that a friendly submarine was surfacing when UB14's conning tower broke surface as it fired the torpedo and, on seeing the torpedo heading for his submarine, he did attempt to restart the engines. He also asked how the U-boats were getting past the Allies' net blockade, indicating to von Heimburg that the Allies believed that the U-boats were readily moving in and out of the Dardanelles.

Due to the relatively small size of the UB class, it was decided that they would be better suited for Black Sea operations and they took no further part in actions against the Anglo–French forces. *UB8* was handed over to the Bulgarians, while on 27 October *UB7* torpedoed the Russian battleship *Panteleimon* off Varna on the Black Sea, and was herself lost in September 1916, possibly destroyed by a mine.[15] Despite all of the difficulties encountered by the submarines of the UB class, they performed well. But they did show, in their offensive capacity, insufficient speed underwater and a too small radius of action, which was not good enough for the area of operation near the Dardanelles.

On 29 July *UC14*, under the command of Oberleutnant zur See Caesar Bauer and the first of the UC class boats, was to arrive via Orak. She was quickly followed by *UC15* on the 18 August, under the command of Oberleutnant zur See Albrecht von Dewitz. Both of these boats were assembled at Pola, and then used to transport 8 tons of materials to Constantinople. Two pressure-proof containers were fitted into each of their mine chutes, and each also carried four torpedoes as cargo, as well as vital materials.[16] To help them on their way, Austrian destroyers took them 50 miles south of Cattaro. In late September *UC14* was sent back to the Adriatic,[17] and *UC15* remained in the Black Sea until November 1916, when she departed from Constantinople to lay mines off Sulina, at the mouth of the Danube; then she disappeared without trace.

UC13, under the command of Oberleutnant zur See Johann Kirchner, was the last of the submarines to join the Black Sea flotilla. She was assembled in Pola and fitted with a special purpose container, which could carry 30 tons of supplies. She departed from Pola on 17 August and reached Orak on 26 August; there she sank the Italian steamer *Sahina Noria*, travelling under the Turkish flag. Three days later she departed for Constantinople, arrived on 6 September and was the first German boat to reach the Black Sea on 25 September. *UC13* operated in the Black Sea until she suffered a compass failure and was driven onto the Kerphen Reef, 55 miles east of the Bosphorus, by a storm on 29 November, then blown up by her crew.

Ocean going submarines – *U21* arrives

The possibility of sending a larger, ocean-going submarine directly to the eastern Mediterranean was considered in Germany at a meeting held on 17 March and attended by Konteradmiral Paul Behncke, who represented the chief of the Admiralstab, and by Kapitänleutnant Otto Hersing.[18] Hersing, an experienced submarine officer, commanded *U21*, which was considered the most appropriate choice for the mission.[19] He was the first submariner to sink a warship in the First World War – namely the cruiser *Pathfinder*, off St Abb's Head in the Firth of Forth, on 5 September 1914. His torpedo struck the magazine, sinking the ship in three and a half minutes, with only eleven survivors out of a crew of 350. The following month he stopped, boarded and sank by gunfire, in the English Channel, the transports *Malachite* and *Primo*. In January 1915, he also succeeded in entering the Irish Sea through St George's Channel, in attacking shipping near Liverpool and in setting a new submarine distance record of 1,600 miles.[20]

The meeting discussed various issues, including the possibility of using a northern Spanish harbour for refuelling and repairs. It was suggested that a small steamer could be chartered, to work out of Barcelona, which could meet and re-supply the submarine. The German naval attaché in Madrid, Captain Hans von Krohn, had already been ordered to arrange for fuel and provisions and had left for Barcelona. There he located a number of Austrian and German sympathizers, who were willing to pay the necessary fee of 67,000 pesetas to acquire a suitable steamer and pay the crew.[21] A Greek harbour rendezvous was considered less favourable, due to communication difficulties and the possibility of being captured. It was decided that, if the submarine commander had insufficient fuel for the entire trip and missed his rendezvous, he could go to Italy, if she were still neutral, or, failing that, to a Spanish harbour, or possibly to Cattero in Austria.

After considering all the available boats, it was decided that *U21* should attempt the trip and that preparations should commence immediately. The Kaiser approved the sending of *U21* on 30 March. An additional difficulty was the supply of the torpedoes. There were torpedoes on the *Goeben* and *Breslau*, but they were not suitable for *U21*, although the smaller UB boats could use them. If torpedoes could not be surreptitiously brought to the Mediterranean under a false flag, then it would be necessary for *U21* to return to Pola for replenishment. It was also decided, by reason of the Turks' low level of security, not to inform them of the movements of the submarine.

Hersing's departure from Wilhelmshaven on the morning of 25 April, at the start of his historic journey, was somewhat delayed. Room 40 of British Naval Intelligence at once detected *U21*'s departure but did not know its destination. By this stage, the English Channel was covered by mines and nets, which made it very dangerous for U-boats. Hersing therefore chose the long route via Scotland and the northern tip of the Orkney Islands – a trip of over 4,000 miles – with the aim of avoiding all enemy patrols and with the intention of passing up on any targets of opportunity which might present themselves.

When he was north of the Orkneys and while on the surface in thick fog, Hersing discovered himself among a group of patrol boats, just as the fog suddenly cleared. The nearest patrol boat signalled him to heave to before he could dive. Fortunately for him, the British were not certain it wasn't one of their own submarines, and then the fog closed in again and Hersing sped off at full speed, evading the patrol.

A week after leaving Wilhelmshaven, *U21* was off the north-western coast of Spain, approaching Cape Finisterre. On 2 May Hersing observed a large cruiser heading to the west, and although he did not want to make his presence known, such a large target was too valuable to let go. The cruiser was, however, too far aft of his location to allow him to get into an attacking position. Not long afterwards, the supply ship *Marzala* was sighted. When close enough, they engaged in signals and *Marzala* turned towards the coast. *U21* submerged and followed the supply ship into Corcubíon Bay, where she made fast to her in the early morning of 3 May, surprising both the steamer's captain and the crew, who had thought that the *Marzala* was on a smuggling mission. That night *U21* took on board large supplies of food and, by 5.15 a.m. the next morning, 12.5 tons of fuel oil and 1.9 tons of lubricating grease. Both of these were contained in barrels, which had to be emptied out into her tanks – an agonizingly slow process. During loading, the First Officer informed Captain von Krohn[22] that the specific gravity of the oil was too high, at a specific gravity of over 0.95. Krohn suggested only that he mix it with remaining good oil. Hersing and Krohn arranged a rendezvous with the supply ship at 8 p.m. that evening further down the Spanish coast, in nearby Arosa Bay, to complete transfer of the fuel.

U21 left Corcubíon Bay and headed south on one engine, but it was quickly discovered that the fuel oil received from *Marzala* refused to burn in her diesel engines, as it had the wrong flash point. Mixing of the fuels was also not possible because of their different specific densities. Hersing was now in a difficult position, one option being to return to base. However, he had used up 30.5 tons of oil and had only 26 tons of good fuel oil left for the long trip back around the north of Scotland. Even without additional hazards such as bad weather or having to dive to avoid regular patrols, the remaining fuel was barely sufficient. A second option was to seek a passage through the well-defended and risky English Channel. This was certainly not an attractive alternative.

The third option was to continue towards the Dardanelles. This was a longer distance by 200 miles (the first port of call would be Cattaro), yet Hersing hoped the sailing conditions would be much more favourable, as he would not have to dive as often. He calculated that, if he was able to remain on the surface, travelling at his most economical speed of 9 knots, the trip would require 23.3 tons and he might just make it. It was important not to have to submerge too often to avoid enemy patrol boats, as this would result in greater use of fuel oil. As Hersing was to recall:

I was called upon to make a decision that, although I did not suspect it, had perhaps some influence on the course of the World War. Should I turn back toward Wilhelmshaven or go on to Cattaro? Neither alternative was pleasant.[23]

As his inclination was to take the bolder approach, he decided to head for Cattaro. A second steamer, which had been chartered in Barcelona, was being hindered from leaving by Spanish authorities. Therefore, when at 7.30 p.m. he met again with *Marzala*, Hersing dismissed the supply ship without taking on further fuel, and asked Krohn to give a message to the ambassador about his intentions.

U21 travelled along the surface and kept as far away as possible from the shipping lanes. Whenever they sighted smoke on the horizon, they would alter course to avoid contact. The run from Cape Finisterre to Gibraltar took four sunny days in calm seas, and *U21* did not have to submerge once.

However, when *U21* was 36 miles to the north-west of the Burling Islands situated to the north of Lisbon, the transport *Teiresias* spotted her. On reaching Gibraltar on 6 May, *U21* hugged the African coast, keeping as far as possible from the British ships and guns across the narrow strip of water and hoping that his boat's silhouette would be hidden by the yellow sand dunes. No patrol boats were observed, and Hersing assumed that the British had not thought of keeping on the look-out for U-boats. However, in the afternoon, two small British torpedo boats appeared, No. 92 and No. 96, and headed towards *U21*, which immediately crash-dived. The torpedo boat to make contact was No. 92, under the command of Lieutenant Commander W. Ward Hunt of the Gibraltar Patrol. (At the end of April, the patrol had received news that a German submarine was on the way and expected to have rendezvous with a supply vessel at Alboran Island, situated 125 miles east of Gibraltar.)

The submarine was sighted at 3.10 p.m. 40 miles west of the island. With a fresh easterly wind blowing at the time and the submarine steaming into the seas, the heavy spray she threw up made her conspicuous. The distance between the vessels was about 7 miles. The torpedo boat went to full speed and gave chase. The following passage gives Hunt's view of events:

After an interval of a few minutes, when I deemed we had reached the spot at which she might be, I saw her periscope come up suddenly, about 200 yards on our starboard bow. I immediately put the helm hard aport, with hopes that she would expose her hull and give us a chance to ram her. But she had evidently sighted us, for she dived, and a few seconds later, when we had passed over her hull (which was plainly visible in the clear water) she had reached a depth which brought her conning tower well below our keel.

We did, however, probably damage her periscope, since it deeply scored the bottom, as we subsequently found on docking. *U21*, in the meanwhile, had fired a torpedo at us, which we saw running away on the surface. These were the days before depth-charges, and our means of offence against a submarine were practically nil, unless she was caught on the surface. I had, however, still hopes of further encounter, as I had two other patrol vessels stationed just in sight of Alboran Island, and we in TB 92 followed the course she might be assumed to take for the island.[24]

Hersing's patrol report states only that, after he had dived to 20 metres, the patrol boats apparently sailed away, as the noise of their propellers had faded by 3.40 p.m. By 3.50 p.m. Hersing saw through his periscope that the patrol boats seemed to be protecting a steamer, and they headed off on a southerly course. At 4.10 p.m. *U21* surfaced and resumed its journey.

The response by the British to this confirmed sighting was the introduction of anti-submarine measures in the area of the Dardanelles. The anticipated arrival of the enemy submarine was around the time of the sinking of *Goliath*, which added to their concerns and resulted in the removal of *Queen Elizabeth*. Hersing was able to avoid the patrol boats, but the news was now out that an enemy submarine had, for the first time, entered the Mediterranean.

Hersing's concern was the number of times he might have to submerge to avoid contacts and thus waste precious fuel oil. It took one week to reach the Adriatic, during which time he was forced to submerge for three French destroyers off the northern coast of Tunisia. On 11 May, while heading due west near Cape Passero, Sicily, *U21* was forced to submerge at 7.10 a.m. for two French destroyers, one of which, after having passed, suddenly turned, gave a signal and then fired at the submarine's periscope, at a range of 700 metres. Hersing surfaced at 9.30 a.m., but at 10.10 a.m. a large passenger ship, most likely from the Cunard Line, forced *U21* to submerge again, although had the opportunity presented itself, Hersing would have attacked. During that day, *U21* had to dive a further five times to elude the dogged destroyers; this caused the fuel to drop to a critical 5.6 tons.[25] *U21* passed Malta to the north, rounded to the south of Sicily and then headed over to the eastern side of the Adriatic.

At 8 a.m. on 13 May, Hersing sent a signal to base to the effect that, at 11.30 a.m. that day, *U21* would be waiting for a pilot to take her into Cattaro. At 3.30 p.m., eighteen days after having left Wilhelmshaven, *U21* tied alongside the tender *Gäa*, previously the steamer *Fürst Bismark*, in the middle of Cattaro harbour, to cheers from sailors on the nearby ships. *U21* had only 1.8 tons of fuel oil remaining in its tanks, enough for eighteen more hours of cruising.

As Hersing was to recount later in life, he might forget numbers such as those related to his birthday and his age, but the figure of 1.8 was indelibly fixed in his mind. On arrival at Cattaro, with his submarine renumbered 'U51' to add to the enemy's confusion, he received news of the landings at Gallipoli and of the excellent opportunities to attack the relatively undefended British capital ships supporting the land forces. The Admiralstab also informed Hersing of the disposition of the British battleships bombarding Gallipoli on 19 May, which was intercepted by Room 40 and passed on to Admiral de Robeck.[26]

U21 remained in Cattaro for a week while repairs were carried out and she took on supplies. At 6.50 p.m. on 20 May, led through the nearby minefields by the destroyer *Pandur*, she headed off down the coast, around the Greek archipelago and across the Aegean, to the peninsula of Gallipoli. To avoid the anticipated minefields laid by the British, U21 hugged the shallow waters near the coast.

Numerous events were now to unfold which heightened Allied tension around the Dardanelles. On Thursday 20 May, a floating mine was sighted by the *Majestic*; *Majestic* destroyed it by gunfire. The following day *Majestic* was hit by a 6-inch shell which caused some damage. On the 22 May at 10.30 a.m., a submarine sighting was reported; this caused ships to zigzag and fire their guns at anything that remotely resembled a submarine's periscope. On Sunday 23 May, the battleship *Albion* went aground at Gaba Tepe during a local fog. Turkish field guns and their battleship in the Narrows opened fire on her, while the *Canopus* tried between 4 a.m. and 10 a.m. to pull her off. The *Lord Nelson*, which arrived with Commodore Keyes on board, was able to suppress the Turkish naval fire, and eventually *Albion* was re-floated and returned to Malta for repairs.

On 24 May, U21 avoided the first of the Allied patrols and discovered the Russian cruiser *Askold* 5 miles off Dedeagach. Although Hersing felt he could have attacked successfully, he decided not to. Instead, he continued to maintain the element of surprise, while seeking larger targets. Travelling south along the Gallipoli Peninsula, Hersing discovered the major portion of the Allied fleet in the harbour at Imbros, but again decided to carry on and launch his attack closer to the straits themselves.

On the morning of the 25th, U21 submerged and at 4 a.m., peering through his periscope, Hersing could make out the first of the British ships anchored off Gaba Tepe. To the rear he could discern the French liner *Suffren*, which passed by; but, once again, he decided not to attack, being intent on sinking a British ship if possible. In calm seas, Hersing raised his periscope in only short bursts, to minimize the chances of being sighted. To the south he could distinguish three large British warships, which he determined were most likely of the Majestic class. The ships that Hersing had sighted were *Majestic*, *Swiftsure* and *Agamemnon*. They were firing at Turkish positions in the nearby hillsides. A hospital ship stood close by, while a number of patrol boats and destroyers surrounded the battleships in a defensive perimeter. At 7.40 a.m., *U21*'s periscope was sighted by *Swiftsure*, which opened fire with its 12-pounders. With the 'confirmed' sighting of a submarine, the more modern *Agamemnon*[27] was ordered to return to the relative protection of Mudros.

Hersing headed back towards Gaba Tepe and intercepted *Vengeance*, which was on its way to Anzac Beach to relieve *Canopus*. At 10.30 a.m., Hersing fired a torpedo at a range of 1,000 metres. The torpedo bubbles were seen by *Vengeance*, which immediately turned to starboard, and the torpedo narrowly missed. Once the alarm was raised, Commodore Keyes immediately boarded the destroyer *Grampus* and headed for Anzac Beach. *Canopus*, which had just been relieved, was returning to Mudros and, as Keyes was closing in on *Vengeance* to enquire about the recent torpedo attack, *Canopus*, 3 miles to seaward, signalled that she had sighted a periscope. *Grampus* altered course and gave chase. However, not all sightings turned out to be of submarines or of their torpedoes. In heading for *Canopus*, as Commodore Keyes later wrote,

. . . half an hour was wasted before we came to the conclusion that the *Canopus* submarine was a porpoise, and we had been drawn away from the danger spot at a critical moment.[28]

Submarine sightings obviously intensified tension amongst the various ships' crews, especially those whose ships had to remain stationary for the bombardment.

Indeed, it was a rare opportunity for a U-boat to come across so many large battleships in stationary positions. Suddenly Hersing saw a destroyer heading in his direction, so he lowered his periscope and ran blind as he laid a course north, from the tip of the peninsula towards Gaba Tepe. Raising the periscope shortly afterwards, he spotted another battleship in front of the Anzac beaches. He determined that the battleship was most likely of the Triumph class, which was protected by a number of patrol craft and escorted by a destroyer (*Chelmer*). Lowering his periscope, Hersing dived to 70 feet and headed towards it, passing below the line of patrol craft. He heard the noise of the propellers as he went underneath, and after having spent some four and a half hours avoiding the enemy and manoeuvring, *U21* finally got into position to torpedo the battleship. Using the periscope sparingly to avoid detection, Hersing waited to get into a firing position.

'Out periscope!' H.M.S. *Triumph* stood in thundering majesty, broadside to us, and only three hundred yards away. Never had an undersea craft such a target. 'Torpedo-fire!' My heart gave a great leap as I called the command.[29]

Hersing remained at periscope depth and watched the telltale streak of the torpedo as it sped away in a straight and true course. Moments later, at around 12.30 p.m., it struck the bow of the *Triumph*,[30] and a huge cloud of smoke leapt out of the sea. In the conning tower, Hersing and his watch keeper first heard a metallic concussion, and then a terrible reverberating explosion. Hersing remained at the periscope, somewhat fascinated, to see the events unfold. However, he realized that to delay too long might cost the lives of his crew; for, once the torpedo had been sighted, the destroyers would make for his position.[31] *U21* dived rapidly, as the sound of propellers was heard from above. Hersing now regretted that he had not dived immediately after the torpedo was fired, as those few seconds of delay greatly increased the chances of being rammed by one of the pursuing destroyers. Hersing called for full speed ahead, and followed the course of the torpedo straight towards the *Triumph*. It was a risky decision, but he decided to go deep and proceed under the sinking battleship to avoid his pursuers.

Meanwhile on the *Triumph*, when the periscope was sighted, one of her officers reported:

> The anti-torpedo attack armament was manned, and about half-past twelve we saw the periscope off our starboard beam, followed almost immediately by the track of a torpedo. Instead of exploding on the nets, as we expected, the torpedo passed right through them as if they were not there, striking us amidships. The *Triumph* immediately took a list of 20 degrees to starboard, making it impossible to get the boom boats out.
>
> Our list rapidly became worse and, after a few minutes, it was recognized that nothing could save the ship, so the order came to abandon her. A destroyer came alongside the port quarter and took off a large number of men. The remainder jumped overboard, but the net defense made things more difficult as it was impossible to get clear on the port side, except off the forecastle and quarter-deck. I, personally, jumped in off the former, and swam well clear of the ship. Within ten minutes of the torpedo striking, she turned turtle and remained for some time on the surface, bottom up, finally disappearing slowly.[32]

The battleship listed to port for about eight minutes, then turned turtle for about another twenty minutes, before she sank. The Anzacs and Turks rose from their trenches and watched, as the great hulk slowly rolled to her death. The Turkish batteries opened fire at around 1 p.m., having allowed sufficient time for the crews to be removed. The casualties were 3 officers and 53 men lost. At 3.30 p.m., after having observed the sinking of *Triumph*, Rear Admiral Stuart Nicholson transferred his flag, well-stocked wine cellar and large quantities of luxury tinned foods from the *Swiftsure* to the *Majestic*, which was renowned for its comfortable quarters.[33] The war correspondent Ashmead-Bartlett also accepted an invitation from the admiral to transfer to the *Majestic*, and saw his belongings thrown pell-mell into the trawler with the admiral's belongings, for a quick transfer. That evening, at a meeting between Nicholson and de Robeck, he observed how things had changed over a short period of a month. Of the mighty armada that had sailed from Mudros, all that now remained was the *Majestic* surrounded by torpedo nets and the little yacht *Triad*, which transferred de Robeck from one scene to the next. The remainder of the fleet had been recalled to Mudros or Kephalos.

Given the intense surface activity, Hersing chose to remain submerged and continued to move away from the area, until his batteries were spent at around midnight. *U21* had been under water for a total of 28 hours, at which point the oxygen level had become so low within the submarine that the crew grew drowsy and had great difficulty moving about. She finally surfaced, lay there for the rest of the night and recharged her batteries. On the following morning *U21* made a wide circle and attempted to find the Russian cruiser *Askold* (nicknamed the 'packet of Woodbines' because of her five tall funnels), which had previously been sighted on the way across the Aegean to Gallipoli. Hersing covered the route taken the previous day, but made no sighting of the *Askold*. When night came on the 26th, Hersing steered south again, and under the cover of darkness *U21* returned to the scene where she had sunk the *Triumph*.

When day broke on the 27th, the sea was running and, although there was a large number of sundry craft, no battleships were sighted. Hersing therefore headed further south towards Cape Helles, where he eventually discerned a great deal of activity on one of the beaches and nearby waters. He observed that several large transports near the beach were landing troops, while 500 yards from the shore was one battleship of the Majestic class, which was covering the landing. The battleship was surrounded by an almost impenetrable number of patrol boats of all kinds, which made it difficult to get in close; in addition, there was the possibility that these small boats would cut across the path of any torpedo track. Due to the choppy waves, the periscope was not so obvious, which made Hersing's task a little easier.

Travelling first in a westerly course, then turning to the east, Hersing manoeuvred to get himself into a firing position. At a range of 600 to 700 yards he decided that that was the best he could do, and waited for the annoying surface craft to move out of the way, and for an opportunity to present itself to fire the torpedo. When the chance arrived at 5.38 a.m., he fired one torpedo between two steamers, at an angle of 120 degrees, and dropped his periscope. A little while later there was an audible detonation. After diving to 20 metres and waiting ten minutes for the destroyers to pass, Hersing was able to observe, between the two steamers, the capsized hull of a ship above the water-line. This time it was not difficult to avoid his pursuers, though half a mile away a flotilla of destroyers and patrol boats was systematically searching the water and working its way in his direction. *U21* crept away as fast as she could, but passing Cape Helles the boat suddenly got caught in a swirling current. Fortunately for Hershing, the submarine was quickly brought under control and was able to pass underneath the line of the destroyers, as loud explosions were heard nearby.

The battleship that Hersing had struck was the *Majestic*[34] herself, the British navy's oldest capital ship, to which Admiral Nicholson, as mentioned, had only transferred his flag a few days before. *Majestic* had departed from Kephalos at 8 a.m. on Wednesday 26 May, zigzagging her way across to Cape Helles, and anchored as close in to W Beach as possible, to support the ground forces. She anchored in water with a depth of 9 fathoms (54 feet), her nets were rigged for protection against torpedo attack, and a cordon of transports was anchored around her, to provide added protection. This was now the only battleship not tucked behind the safety of a boom. The Turkish forces shelled one of the transports, forcing her to leave the area and thus withdrawing some of *Majestic*'s cover.

On the morning of the 27th, Admiral Nicholson had given orders for *Majestic*'s steam barge to be made ready for his use as the *Exmouth* was expected at any moment. Accordingly, crew members were standing by to move the port side nets aft, to allow the barge to be dropped into the water. Many of the men were already on the port side making preparations for this move, when, 350 yards off the port beam, a whitish coloured patch, marked by the absence of a ripple on the water, started to emerge.[35] A line of bubbles extended rapidly in the direction of the ship. There was little time to raise the alarm, but the crew of a 12-pounder (that is, an artillery piece which fired a 12-pound shell and had a calibre of 3 inches), seeing the torpedo, fired two rounds – one where the submarine was, and the other at the torpedo, hoping to deflect it. As the torpedo got closer, the men rushed over to the starboard side, to get clear of the explosion when it came. The torpedo struck under the port engine room, blowing away a large potion of her bilge. The ship began to list immediately to port and, within five minutes of being torpedoed, turned bottom up and sank. Ships quickly clustered around the battleship to take survivors on board. The loss of life from the sinking was surprisingly low – only forty-three men. For months afterwards, the whole length of *Majestic*'s hull could be seen below the waves and her bows stood erect above the water-line.[36] As Petty Officer Cowie dived off the ship before she sank, his last recollection was of seeing Ashmead-Bartlett standing on the bridge, 'coolly looking at his watch to time the occurrence of the disaster'.[37] Ashmead-Barlett would later recall:

A voice replied from somewhere, 'There's a torpedo coming.' I just had time to scramble to my feet when there came a dull heavy explosion about fifteen feet forward of the shelter deck on the port side. The hit must have been very low down, as there was no shock from it felt on deck. The old *Majestic* immediately gave a jerk towards port, and remained with a heavy list; then there came a sound as if the contents of every pantry in the world had fallen at the same moment, a clattering such as I had never heard, as everything loose in her tumbled about. I could tell at once that she had been mortally wounded somewhere in her vitals, and felt instinctively she would not long stay afloat.

As I had been prepared for days for just such an emergency, the actual realisation came as no great shock. Having mapped out my programme in advance, I proceeded to carry it through. I stooped down to pick up my life-belt, and then, to my intense disgust I discovered it was not blown out. Thus the first part of my plan, namely, not to take to the water unless encircled by a good belt, was at once knocked on the head. I decided not to lose any time over it now, but to get off the ship at once, as she listed more and more and seemed likely to turn turtle at any moment. I was swept down the ladder to the main deck by the crowd rushing by me, and from there made my way aft to the quarter-deck, which was crowded with men, some wearing lifebelts, some without, who were climbing up the side and jumping into the sea, determined to get clear before she went down. The explosion was followed by a cloud of black smoke which got down my throat and in my eyes, so that all this time I seemed to be in semi-darkness. I looked over the side, and saw that I was clear of the torpedo-nets, and then climbed over, intending to slide down a stanchion into the water and swim clear. But again my programme was upset by unforeseen events, for, just as I had both legs over the rail, there came a rush from behind, and I was pushed over the side, falling with considerable force on to the net-shelf, where the nets are stored when not out. I made no long stay on the net-shelf, but at once rebounded into the sea and went under. I came up at once still holding my useless belt, and, having got some of the water out of my eyes, took a look round. The sea was crowded with men swimming about and calling for assistance. I think that many of these old reservists, who formed the majority of the crew, had forgotten how to swim, or else had lost all faith in their own powers. A few yards from me I saw a boat, towards which everyone in the water seemed to be making.[38]

For two days *U21* sailed around the peninsula looking for more battleships. But she had done her job; the British had withdrawn their large capital ships to the harbour they had established at Mudros. On 29 May, Hersing took *U21* into Kephalos harbour; there his submarine caught itself on a net which was suspended under a number of floating buoys. Fearing that movement of the buoys might be sighted by the surface patrols, Hersing tried to back the submarine away from the net, but without success. He therefore decided to go forward with the nets attached, and slowly headed out to sea. Early that evening *U21* surfaced and the crew spent an hour removing the mess that entangled the boat. With no suitable targets, *U21* turned and proceeded to the port of Bodrum for a day's rest. Hersing returned to Gallipoli on 2 June, hoping to find some battleships, but after surveying the 10 miles of beaches through his periscope he failed once again to see any appropriate targets.

On 4 June, *U21* turned into the Dardanelles to head for Constantinople. At the entrance to the straits, the boat dived to a depth of 42 metres and went ahead, uncertain what the currents were like at this depth. When the submarine surfaced at 1 p.m., after hearing a number of explosions while submerged, Hersing discovered that he had travelled further up the straits than he had anticipated, and was therefore further from the British screen of destroyers, at the opening to the straits. He also observed that the French cruiser *Briux* was firing towards the shore, and concluded that the explosions he had heard were probably those of the Turkish return fire. *U21* had surfaced in front of the Turkish mines and nets at Kephez, so at 1.20 p.m. he took on a pilot to guide him through an opening left for the submarine. Prince Reuss also came aboard at that time. By 2.15 p.m., *U21* was moored alongside the gunboat *Zohatt* at Chanak, where Admiral Merton came on board to congratulate Hersing and his crew. By 5.10 p.m. *U21* was once again on its way, under the escort of the destroyer *Yarhisar*, and proceeded to the Sea of Marmara. On 5 June, forty days after having left Wilhelmshaven, she arrived at Constantinople, this time with only half a ton of oil left in her tanks. Hersing had managed to cause considerable disruption to the Allies' ability to support their troops with heavy naval gunfire (although destroyer support was maintained), as well as creating further disruptions to communications and the transport of supplies.

For the next month the submarine was repaired and made ready to return through the Dardanelles. *U21* departed from Constantinople on 3 July under the escort of the *Yarhisar*, and by 4 July was off the Gallipoli Peninsula, where Hersing sighted a French liner. The current conditions were unfavourable for an attack, so he elected not to, but moved instead towards the French transport *Carthage* (5,600 ton), which had just unloaded her cargo of ammunition. After some careful manoeuvring, Hersing fired a torpedo at a distance of 800 metres, which hit the stern of the ship. The bow rose out of the water until the stern hit the shallow bottom. When she was lying suspended in this position for short a while, belching smoke from her funnels, there was another heavy explosion, followed by blowing of steam, and she then sank below the water. Given the increased activity of destroyers in the area and a weakening battery, Hersing decided not to attack other steamers in the area.

No further opportunities presented themselves over the next two days, but by 7.50 a.m. on 6 July *U21* was near Gaba Tepe, where several small transport ships were observed, together with one large transport and next to it another, just unloading its cargo. Two trawlers were in front of the targets and, in the smooth sea conditions, *U21*'s periscope was observed. Immediately, one of the trawlers charged at the submarine from a distance of 4,000 metres. The trawler's siren was heard as it raised the red and white U-boat alarm flag. *U21* dived to 20 metres, and then to 30 metres, and then the sound of the trawler's propeller increased, as it got nearer. Suddenly at 8.03 a.m., one minute after diving and at a depth of 22 metres, there was a strong detonation behind and close to the submarine, which broke all the instruments in the control room and threw loose objects about. The force of the explosion caused the internal central hatch to close itself, and glass lamps, amp meters, water-level glasses and the like were broken, while water was coming in from loosened external hatches. All the lights went out, but after a quick check all compartments reported that they were watertight. However, the diving planes were not working properly, and at best the submarine could only be maintained at periscope depth while submerged. *U21* immediately limped back to Constantinople, arriving safely on the 11th.

It took six weeks to complete the needed repairs. *U21* then left Constantinople on 28 August and headed for Suvla Bay, but found that the nets and patrols were too efficient for attacking any ships. Hersing then headed off to the Gulf of Salonika, but no targets were present there and so he decided to head back to Mudros, where on 9 September he fired at a transport at long range but missed. He then discovered that his return journey up the Dradanelles was blocked by the nets that nearly caught *UB14*; so he decided to head for Cattaro, where he arrived on the 21st, and then to Pola for a major refit.

Having done such a good job of forcing capital ships away from the Dardanelles, *U21* was engaged in attacking Allied merchant shipping in the Mediterranean for the next two years, returning to Germany in March 1917. The Kaiser awarded the Iron Cross to all the crew of *U21*, while Hersing was

awarded Germany's highest honour, the *Pour le Mérite*; he was the first
German submariner to win this award. At the end of the war, Hersing had to
turn over the *U21*, but while under tow by a British ship, it sprang a
'mysterious' leak and sank.[39]

Hersing's work had been done, as the Allied naval war ships would now be
bottled up in their ports. To counter the perceived submarine threat, the
British introduced more indicator nets, which were light-weight nets designed
to detect, and warn of, the presence of submarines, and stronger anti-
submarine nets, to prevent the entry of submarines into sheltered harbours.
Bulges were placed on some ships such as the monitors and certain cruisers
(*Theseus, Endymion, Grafton* and *Edgar*). These were a second outer skin,
which in theory would cause the torpedo to explode without causing harm to
the ship's inner main hull. Importantly, instead of small craft ferrying supplies
to shore from ocean-going ships moored off the Dardanelles, they would now
have to travel 60 miles on each trip, from Mudros.

7

The Next Land Phase

Further dithering

The land forces struggled on, while the navy's submarine force started to achieve results in the Sea of Marmara. The navy's capital ships, however, had done little to force the Dardanelles, while their support of ground forces had been severely weakened by the enemy's U-boat successes and by their forced withdrawal back to Mudros. Back in London, the animosity between Fisher and Churchill continued to grow. Fisher was concerned that Churchill was interfering in his role and undermining his position. Churchill favoured further attempts by the fleet to break through the Dardanelles; this plan was championed by Keyes, who kept up his requests for another naval attack on the Dardanelles. On 9 May, a conference of admirals was held on *Queen Elizabeth*, where Keyes put forward a new plan of attack, with mine-sweepers and new battleships. The admirals were convinced, and de Robeck sent a slightly cautious message to the Admiralty asking for permission.

Fisher, on the other hand, was against the idea, believing that the opportunity for success was gone. He was concerned about the risk of Turkish gunfire at point-blank range; about the inability to sweep for mines adequately; about the risk of enemy submarines; and about the logistics of maintaining a fleet in the Sea of Marmara. The sinking of *Goliath* and the resulting withdrawal of *Queen Elizabeth* angered Kitchener, who had been dubious about naval bombardment from the beginning. He had, in fact, only agreed to a land campaign on the basis of the statements made about the power and abilities of *Queen Elizabeth*, which at this critical stage were being withdrawn. Kitchener's anger only annoyed Fisher still further.

On 11 May, Fisher received a telegram from de Robeck suggesting that the land battle had failed, and asking if he should free the straits using his ships. Churchill wanted to send a telegram giving de Robeck the option to undertake the action, but Fisher fervently disagreed, which resulted in a major argument with Churchill. Fisher threatened to resign if such an action was approved, so the Prime Minister was forced to overrule Churchill. Although Churchill and Fisher tried to overcome their differences, Churchill's lack of tact, particularly with a plan drafted without consultation to send additional naval forces to Gallipoli, ultimately led to Fisher's resignation.

Then, on 14 May, *The Times* attacked the British government for an alleged shortage of shells on the western front. With the coalition government under increasing pressure Churchill was forced to resign on 17 May, his place being taken by Arthur Balfour while Sir Henry Jackson replaced Fisher. Although any control of the navy had been removed from Churchill, he still remained on the War Council. With the collapse of the Asquith Liberal government in late May and the formation of a new coalition, it was not until 7 June that Kitchener once again considered Hamilton's request for a further three divisions. He persuaded the newly formed Dardanelles Committee (consisting of nine ministers) to authorize further attacks at Gallipoli during the second week of July and, in addition, to approve the sending of more troops. It was also decided to send two supplementary cruisers (fitted with bulges to protect them from torpedoes), six submarines and fourteen shallow draft monitors[1] with large calibre weapons and no secondary armaments, which could get close inshore and thus avoid submarine attacks better; these would remove the risks attendant on the use of the larger crewed battleships.

This three-week delay proved costly as it gave the Turks additional time to send reinforcements and to dig in. At this point, Kitchener was still hoping for the army to advance steadily up the peninsula rather than try to cut off the Turkish garrison through a landing at Bulair. In his eyes, starving the Turkish defenders into submission depended on submarines being able to restrict their supplies. As he said to Ashmead-Bartlett on 12 June:

> You probably know that the Turks made a great accumulation of stores and supplies in Asia Minor for the invasion of Egypt, and that they have been transferring this stuff up north by railroad as far as the railhead, and from there by camels and carts to Chanak, or the neighbourhood. Our submarines cannot prevent them landing supplies in Gallipoli from Chanak, as they run them across in sailing boats, or in those 'penny' steamers from Constantinople. We do not think they bring much via Bulair, except food for horses, and cattle, and anything they are able to collect locally in Thrace. We might be able to obtain the same result if, instead of seizing Bulair, we sent more submarines into the Marmora, thus closing the sea route from Constantinople and Rodosto.[2]

In the trenches, the month of May dragged on as the heat intensified and morale weakened. A labyrinth of trenches developed, which with their narrow width only made the heat more unbearable. There was no continuous frontline, because the ravines and gullies cut the line trenches at different places. Bombardments by the Turks from the Asiatic shore intensified and became more accurate. The lack of experienced officers and combat hardened men added to the difficulties. However, throughout May, steady pressure had been applied by the Allies along the Helles front, with the lines being in some places pushed forward by up to half a mile. On 24 May, after all his failures, Hunter-Weston was promoted to Lieutenant General and made a corps commander. Towards the end of May, the Allied forces on the Helles front consisted of three British and two French divisions, the arrival of 52 (Lowland) Division being expected in the first week of June.

Third battle for Krithia

With Kitchener pressing for another attack, Hamilton agreed on 31 May that a third battle for Krithia should take place on 4 June, before the arrival of 52 Division. In early May Hamilton had considered Birdwood's proposal of gaining important tactical positions which the enemy would be forced to attack, so as to cause maximum casualties amongst the Turks; but this was rejected as being too slow.[3] Operational orders were issued on 2 June for a plan of attack along a broad front, and also to provide sufficient time for the plan to be studied by field commanders. The plan called for all troops to show their bayonets above the trenches after the initial artillery barrage, in the hope of drawing the Turkish reserves to the front line. At that point, the artillery would again resume its barrage. Two waves of attack would then follow, with the first to take control of the enemy's first trench line. Fifteen minutes later, the second wave would pass through the first wave and take the second line of trenches. Next, engineers would follow, to prepare the captured Turkish trenches for any counter-attack by the enemy.

Communication trenches were to be constructed, back to the Allied trenches. Grenades were in limited supply, with only eight per platoon, while marksmen were detailed to shoot snipers. On the track from Cape Helles to Krithia, an armoured car squadron was to be deployed, to bring their Maxim guns to bear.[4] Only seventy-eight field guns were available to the British, although some assistance would be available from the French, and two battle-ships, the *Albion* and the *Implacable*, would zigzag up and down the coast to provide added support, a clear indication of the effect *U21* had had on reducing the navy's supporting role.[5]

An advance of 800 yards was expected, with an assaulting force of 20,000 in the first wave and a further 10,000 men in the second wave. The Helles line consisted of the French Corps (two divisions) on the right, then the Royal Naval Division, the 42nd Territorial Division, 88 Brigade of 29 Division and the 14 Sikhs Regiment on the left, at Gully Ravine. It was a generally accepted maxim that the attacking force should outnumber the enemy by at least three to one. What the Allies were not aware of was that a Turkish force of 28,000 was facing them. Additionally, many of the enemy's lines were protected by barbed wire, with strong-points concealing machine-guns – some, as noted earlier, manned by men from the *Breslau* and the *Goeben* – which were providing supporting crossfire. More importantly, as in Europe, trench warfare had now evolved to the point where, as a matter of routine and survival, the defenders dug a series of parallel trenches anywhere from 100 to 250 yards apart. If one line of trenches was overrun, there was another one the defenders could retreat to.

Early on the morning of 4 June, the artillery barrage started, with fire from the French artillery across the British front seeming to have the most powerful effect. At 11.20 a.m. the artillery stopped, and all the troops raised their bayonets. Shortly afterwards, the barrage recommenced and continued until noon, when the Allied troops went over the top, all along the front. Within fifteen minutes, the French advance (which was to secure the high ground over Kereves Dere), an advance of 450 to 600 yards, had completely failed, with heavy casualties due to the entrenched enemy machine-gun nests which mowed them down. On the left flank of the French, the Royal Naval Division, although suffering heavy casualties, succeeded in taking the first line of enemy trenches. The second wave now took on the assault and succeeded in taking the second line of trenches, only to come under fire from machine-guns on their right flank, which was exposed as a result of the failure of the French to advance. By 1 p.m., the survivors were forced back to the lines from which they had started one hour earlier.

The 2nd Naval Brigade had lost 60 of its 70 officers and 1,000 of the 1,700 men who had started the attack. On their left flank, 42 Division, through determined effort, had managed to break through not only the first and second lines of trenches; one company had even advanced to the fourth trench line, at the lower slopes of Achi Baba. By then the advance had lost its momentum, although the Turkish and German officers believed that the British were near victory. At this crucial point it was time to call up the reserves to exploit the situation, but Hunter-Weston and General Gouraud, who commanded the French troops, decided to use the reserves to launch an attack at 4 p.m., along the unbroken enemy lines on each flank of 42 Division's breakthrough. A golden opportunity had been lost, with the French finally deciding not to go on with the new attack that evening. To the left of 42 Division, 88 Brigade faced strong fire from machine-guns which had not been destroyed by the bombardment, but it made good progress until communications failed; they were eventually pushed back to their original lines. On the extreme left, the 14 Sikhs, who were to advance along the cliff tops astride Gully Ravine, were also decimated by machine-gun fire, with virtually no advance made. Meanwhile the armoured cars provided little support, as they became bogged down in the mud. By 1 p.m. the battle had practically come to an end, with 42 Division left out alone in Turkish territory, with both flanks under threat. Exhausted, with little ammunition or water, they were eventually forced to retreat back to their own trenches.

At 5.30 p.m., Hunter-Weston ordered all troops to dig in and hold their positions against the expected Turkish counter-attack. This did not materialize as the Turks had suffered 9,000 casualties of their own that day. British casualties totalled 4,500 and French a further 2,500. Had the Allies been able to launch another attack, it is quite likely that they would have succeeded in overrunning the Turkish positions;[6] but, as had happened in the past and would happen again in the future, they were unable to bring the battle to a successful conclusion. This, tragically from a British viewpoint, was a continuing story in the whole Gallipoli campaign, with the Allies never being able to take full advantage of initial successes. During the battle, some 400 men and 11 officers were taken prisoner, including five Germans – the remainder of the volunteer machine-gun detachment from the *Goeben*. As Churchill was to write after the war,

> A week lost was about the same as a division. Three divisions in February could have occupied the Gallipoli Peninsula with little fighting. Five could have captured it after March 18. Seven were insufficient at the end of April, but nine might just have done it. Eleven might have sufficed at the beginning of July. Fourteen were to prove insufficient on August 7. Moreover, one delay breeds another.[7]

By mid-June, a new plan of attack for a major offensive on the Gallipoli Peninsula was evolving. Two important events had occurred, which proved the catalyst for Hamilton to plan his most aggressive venture to date. Firstly, in mid-May, a New Zealand patrol had discovered that it was possible to traverse the difficult terrain and reach the high point at Chunuk Bair to the east of Anzac Cove; and, further, that there were few enemy troops in the area, and none apparently at Chunuk Bair itself. Turkish deserters also confirmed that the areas around the northern end of Sari Bair and Suvla were lightly defended. Reconnaissance of Suvla Plain, and the capture of a map of the area, further confirmed the lack of enemy defences. Birdwood formulated in May a plan for the capture of Chunuk Bair by a surprise night-time march. Once that was in the Allies' possession, it would be a simple matter to drive the Turks off Battleship Hill to the south-west and advance across the peninsula. By mid-June, although somewhat compromised by the enemy's retaking of an outpost that lay in the path of any future advance, the plan was accepted by Hamilton as part of the overall operation.

The second event occurred on 7 June, when the newly created Dardanelles Committee met for the first time in London to consider possible options for the campaign. Kitchener favoured replacing Hamilton's losses, and then allowing him to do the best he could under the circumstances. Churchill, as always, was strongly in favour of a substantial increase in military support for Hamilton's efforts. Importantly, public opinion was turning in favour of the Allies' efforts in Gallipoli; it was somewhat spurred on by the enthusiasm of Australian and New Zealand efforts to raise volunteer troops for the campaign, but also by the lack of success in France. On 9 June, therefore, the government decided to send three additional divisions, the 10, 11 and 13, designed to arrive by the second week of July, together with additional navy forces including six submarines. By 17 June Kitchener had offered, and Hamilton had accepted, a further two divisions, the 53 and 54, to arrive by the middle of August. However, artillery shells continued to remain in short supply, but Hamilton was not forceful enough with Kitchener to overcome the problem.

The navy did occasionally lend support, as on 20 June when the *Lord Nelson* shelled the town of Gallipoli and the nearby docks, firing a total of 127 rounds. To help in this indirect bombardment, a kite-balloon was used to spot the fall of shot. Hamilton also persisted with offensives at Helles during June and July, to keep the pressure on the Turks, and perhaps to mislead them over his planned major offensive for August. Another offensive was planned for 21 June, after the arrival of 52 Division, with the objective of taking the Haricot Redoubt and the Quadrilateral – strong points in the enemy lines, which were heavily defended by machine-guns and barbed wire. The artillery and naval fire commenced at 5.15 a.m. and continued for forty-five minutes, until the assault started at 6 a.m. The Haricot was quickly taken, but the attack on the Quadrilateral failed. On the right, the 6th Colonial Regiment, which had suffered significant casualties, including the loss of their commander, proved unfit to attack again, but the French troops did manage to take control of a small part of the Turkish defences. Another attack was therefore planned for 28 June in the Gully Ravine area.

Again, due to the lack of ammunition for the British artillery, French guns had to be moved into position to provide adequate support. Major General de Lisle was in command of the attack along a 700-yard front. The artillery support was concentrated on the centre and left flanks, as it was believed that

1 One of the major contributing factors to events in the Dardanelles was the sale to Turkey of the German battlecruiser *Goeben* and her escort *Breslau*, seen here in action.

2 A North Sea trawler loaded with troops for landing. Trawlers were also used as mine-sweepers and for anti submarine patrols. Transport and landing vessels for troops and supplies were always an issue for the Allies.

3 View from *River Clyde* a few hours after she was run aground on V Beach as a failed Trojan Horse, with Sedd el Bahr castle in the background. In the foreground are the many injured in the lighters. Six Victoria Crosses were awarded to seamen that valiantly tried to help the soldiers get ashore.

4 *Rescue* was a converted tug off Gallipoli with a spherical army observation balloon previously used in the Boer War. Spotting for the fall of shot from the battleships was crucial given the rugged terrain on shore and was partially accomplished through the increased use of aircraft.

5 Anzac Cove with the makeshift piers, lighters and barges bringing supplies to be stockpiled on shore. Although under constant threat from enemy artillery fire, soldiers still braved the water for a refreshing and cleansing swim.

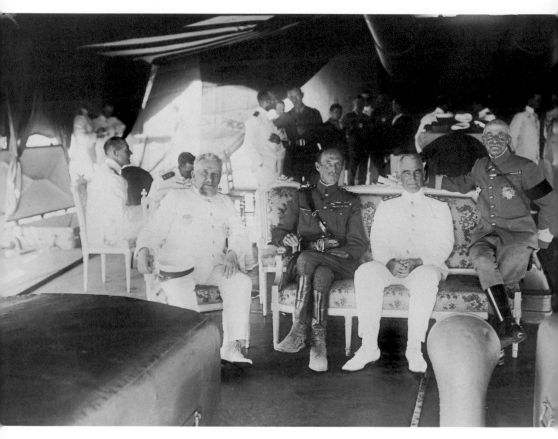

6 Four Commanders-in-chief, rather than one supreme commander, was always going to be controversial. Seated on board ship (*from left to right*) are Vice Admiral de Lapeyrere (French navy), General Hamilton (British army), Vice Admiral de Robeck (British navy) and General Bailloud (French army).

7 Lieutenant Holbrook on board *Adamant* with *B11* in the background. Holbrook was to win the first submariner Victoria Cross for the sinking of the Turkish battleship *Mesudiye*.

8 Lieutenant Commander Boyle, the second submariner to win the Victoria Cross, on board *E14*. This submarine has the unique distinction of having two captains both of whom received the Victoria Cross; the second was Lieutenant Commander White, killed in action at the mouth of the Dardanelles three years later.

9 *E11* trimmed down with Lieutenant Commander Nasmith sitting on the gun and enjoying a cigar after lunch. Nasmith was the most successful of the Allied submarine commanders in the Sea of Marmara, also wining the Victoria Cross.

10 After being torpedoed, the Turkish gunboat *Peleng-i Derya* was able to fire from its 6-pound gun as she was sinking, and amazingly the first round hit *E11*'s conning tower; this was later removed and Nasmith forced to use the secondary periscope.

11 *E11* lashed to the side of a captured Turkish dhow with only the conning tower above water. The dhow was ordered to set sail in the hope that the submarine was less likely to be observed from the shore as it continued its patrol.

12 *E20* at Malta with 6-inch howitzer and ammunition lined up for re-stowing prior to her first patrol of the Sea of Marmara. Unfortunately, the impact of this large calibre weapon was never truly tested due to the sinking of the submarine by the German U-boat *UB14*.

13 Forlorn Turkish prisoners sitting on the stern of *E11* as she is underway. The sinking of small craft that often didn't have their own life rafts necessitated taking prisoners onboard until another vessel was found for their transfer.

14 *H1* interior showing Fressenden switchboard with headphones which was used to communicate underwater with *E20* over a distance of 30 miles thanks to the stable density layers of the inland Sea of Marmara.

15 German U-boat *U21* at Cattaro preparing for the final run to the Dardanelles where she was to sink the battleships *Triumph* and *Majestic*. More importantly for the Turks their loss resulted in the withdrawal of most of the Allied fleet to safe harbours.

16 The busy Allied port of Mudros, the main supply hub for the Gallipoli operations. Protected by submarine nets, Allied ships were safe, but later in the campaign rarely ventured out for fear of German and Austrian submarines.

'Turkey's going to get
it's Constanti—nose pulled,
on it's Dardane"-LL"s.

17 A postcard image of the time, highlighting the unrealistic expectations of the Allies, who initially thought that the Turks would be easily defeated.

Map 7.1   Helles battle lines

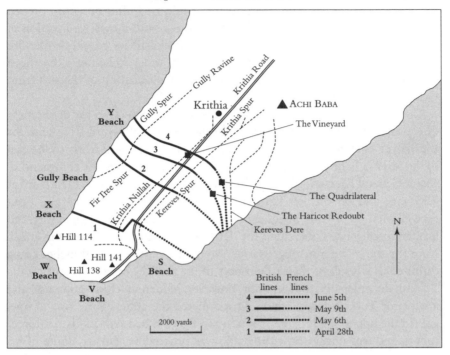

the Turkish trenches on the right were lightly defended. The initial bombardment of the trenches by howitzers began at 9 a.m., followed by lighter field
guns at 10.20 a.m., to destroy the enemy wire. At 10.45 a.m. the bombardment
ceased and the right flank started its attack followed by the centre and left
flanks fifteen minutes later. The Royal Scots, on the right flank, met intense
fire from stronger than expected Turkish defenders, and were halted. The only
success was on the left flank, where an advance of three quarters of a mile was
made, while two days later the French finally succeeded in taking the
Quadrilateral.

   It must be remembered that it was necessary throughout this period to
continue to bring men and supplies to the beaches and to remove the
wounded on a regular basis. Due to the long lines of supply, inevitable problems arose, and the already chaotic arrangements for the discharge, stock-
piling and distribution of stores were not improved when ships arrived
without manifests. Many stores ended up on the wrong beaches at the wrong
time. In making deliveries on shore, small trawlers such as the *Lord Wimborne*
were often under fire. An example of the difficulties encountered occurred on
the evening of 4–5 July, when seven attempts had to be made over an eight-
hour period to come alongside the beached *River Clyde*, while it was under fire

and illuminated by enemy searchlights. The supply of water was critical, and the estimate of the amount of water that could be found on shore proved inaccurate. With the high summer temperatures, with a massive invasion of flies (which were more hated than the occasional artillery round or rifle fire from the enemy) and with a shortage of clean water, dysenteric diarrhoea eventually affected everyone. This resulted in an evacuation of the sick from Gallipoli at a rate of over 1,000 per week.

The next attack was planned for 12 July with the objective, for the French, of consolidating their gains on the right flank over a 700-yard front and, for the British, of seizing the Turkish trenches over a 1,000-yard front, to the east of the Sedd el Bahr to Krithia road. The 52 Division, under the command of Major General Egerton, launched its attack on the right flank of their front at 7.35 a.m. and on the left flank at 4.50 p.m., after the artillery had been repositioned to provide adequate support. Once again, poor planning and limited intelligence concerning the Turkish dispositions doomed the attack from the start. The morning attack started off well, the front trenches being captured as a result of the earlier effect of the artillery bombardment on the Turkish defenders. Within an hour, however, hidden machine-gun nests and a superior Turkish force, which outnumbered the attackers by two to one, gained the upper hand. By early afternoon Egerton had sent in his reinforcements, and was unsure how the battle was proceeding. Earlier, some of his units had quickly overrun the Turkish trenches, but their lack of discipline resulted in units going beyond the Turkish defences, some almost reaching the foot of Achi Baba. Having failed to finish off the Turkish defenders and fired upon by their own artillery, the British forces were steadily being wiped out.

Egerton then received orders from Hunter-Weston to commence the afternoon attack. This attack succeeded in overrunning the first two lines of defence and in capturing the third line of trenches, which proved to be shallow. The British fought off a Turkish counter-attack, and prepared themselves for the coming night. The Turkish trenches had been taken, but at huge cost, and so the marines were sent in to relieve what little was left of the attacking force. At 4.30 p.m. on the following day, Hunter-Weston ordered the depleted Royal Naval Division to attack the Turkish trenches on the right flank, which had still not been taken. The Turkish artillery was waiting with shrapnel and, when the attack commenced, quickly wiped out the attackers. One battalion succeeded in taking one of the forward trenches, only to discover that it was held by British forces from the previous day's fighting. At this point, Major General Shaw temporarily relieved Egerton of his command and discovered that the casualties had been much higher than expected – 3,000 were dead – and that the troops were on the verge of collapse. Over the next twenty-four hours, the tired Royal Naval Division took over from 52 Division, but there were no additional forces to capitalize on the gains made. The Turkish force was also spent, and was unable to repel the attackers. At this time, the Turkish Second Army was arriving in the Krithia area, which spelled the end to any Allied victory. Hunter-Weston also felt the strain, and suffering from sunstroke and physical exhaustion, left Gallipoli for the last time.

Allied efforts were once again close to success but short of victory, as von Sanders commented:

> Just as the troops at Seddulbar [Sedd el Bahr] were being relieved by those of the Second Army on July 13, a heavy Anglo-French attack materialized which was repulsed with difficulty and not without the use of the last reserves. It was fortunate for us that the British attacks never lasted more than one day, and were punctuated by pauses of several days. Otherwise it would have been impossible to replenish our artillery ammunition.[8]

For the months of June and July, the territory, won or lost, and the casualties on both sides can be summarized as follows:

Table 7.1   *Helles casualties*

Date	Allied casualties	Turkish casualties
4 June	200–500 yards for 6,500 casualties	9,000 casualties
21 June	200 yards for 2,500 casualties	6,000 casualties
28 June	1,000 yards for 3,800 casualties	unknown casualties
5 July	minimal casualties	0 yards for 16,000 casualties
12 July	400 yards for 6,000 casualties	9,000 casualties

Source: Aspinall-Oglander, 1992

8

Submarines Take Control of the Sea of Marmara

The importance of disrupting Turkish supplies, particularly through the Sea of Marmara, and of thereby forcing the Turks to use the long and tortuous overland route, was not lost on the Allies. From mid-May till the end of the Gallipoli campaign, a total of eight submarines, two of which were lost, undertook thirteen patrols, and at one stage three submarines were on patrol at the same time in the Sea of Marmara. The effectiveness of the submarine campaign can be debated: the submariners were exposed to great risks, as the Turks increasingly strengthened the net and mine defences in the Dardanelles in an attempt to trap or destroy the enemy on their way to the Sea of Marmara. At no other time have submarine captains been forced to run such a narrow expanse of water, against swift flowing currents, to meet the enemy, and then, at the end of their patrol, to return through the same obstacles.

If there was a turning point, and if any one submarine commander was most responsible for taking the initiative away from the Turks in the Sea of Marmara, then that officer was Lieutenant Commander Nasmith. From his first patrol in *E11*, he showed that he always had the ability to create his own luck and achieve the greatest victories during the campaign.

E11's first war patrol – 19 May to 7 June

As mentioned previously (see p. 104), on 19 May *E11*, under the command of 32-year-old Lieutenant Commander Martin Eric Nasmith,[1] proceeded into the straits, escorted by the destroyer *Grasshopper*. While still 10 miles away from the Dardanelles, they could see the searchlights of Kum Kale and also gun flashes, as Turkish artillery fired from the Asiatic shore against targets on the Gallipoli Peninsula. Nasmith slowed his submarine's speed to 7 knots, to reduce the size of the boat's wake, so that it would be less visible to the Turks. At 2.45 a.m., still following *Grasshopper*, they passed between Cape Helles and

Kum Kale. After passing Sedd el Bahr, by 3.10 a.m. they reached a line of British trawlers patrolling across the straits to provide warning of any sortie by enemy destroyers. A further 4 miles up, they passed between two destroyers, and *Grasshopper* turned 180 degrees and headed back towards the entrance.

It was important for *E11* to continue on the surface, as far up the straits as possible, to save her batteries. Nasmith was concerned about being spotted, and at about 3.50 a.m. he decided to dive a little sooner than Boyle had done, particularly as the beam of the powerful searchlight at Kephez, some 5 miles away, started to come close to *E11*. As he entered the control room, he told his third officer, Lieutenant Brown,[2] to plot a course about a mile off the European shore.

The submarine's trim was adjusted and she was taken down to 22 feet, where Nasmith raised the periscope, had a quick look around, and then ordered the submarine to be taken to 80 feet. The submarine proceeded at a slow but steady 3 knots, when suddenly there was a metallic clanging forward, as the first of the mine mooring cables started to scrape along the outside of the boat's hull. Nasmith ordered the port engine to be stopped to prevent fouling the propeller with the cable. More wires ran along the hull and each time the port or starboard propeller would be stopped to prevent fouling and the possible dragging of the mine down to the submarine's hull. About ten minutes after the scraping had stopped, Nasmith decided to go to periscope depth. Although there was some risk that they might still be in a minefield, the risks of running aground were even greater, and it was therefore important to get a sighting and to plot *E11*'s position in the straits.

At 4.50 p.m., Nasmith gave the order to rise to periscope depth, but the submarine refused to go above 63 feet. Water was pumped from the auxiliary tank but nothing seemed to be happening. Nasmith was reluctant to blow the main ballast tanks for fear of breaking the surface. However, at one point the boat overshot the 22 feet mark and looked as if would break the surface, but control was maintained, and she finally levelled off. The periscope was raised, and Nasmith was blinded by the light from the nearby lighthouse. He brought the periscope down immediately and ordered the submarine to be taken to 70 feet. He realized that *E11* was opposite Kephez, and he was astonished that they had travelled so far in such short time. Nasmith concluded that there was little, if any, current at 70 feet and, as they had proceeded so rapidly up the straits, he now felt that it would not be necessary to recharge the batteries while still in the straits.

As *E11* was only located half a mile from the searchlight, a course of 48 degrees was taken to clear Kilid Bahr. At 5.16 a.m., she bumped into the point at Kilid Bahr at a depth of 50 feet, slid around and then into deeper water, directly south of Nagara Point. At 5.30 a.m., at first light, Nasmith took his submarine to 22 feet and raised the periscope. At this point she was immediately fired upon by several destroyers, but Nasmith saw beyond them two battleships moving in the direction of Nagara. He lowered the periscope and ordered the bow torpedo tubes to be made ready, guessing that the enemy battleships some 2 miles away were *Torgud Reis* and *Barbaros Hayreddin*.

There was no way he could attack them on the spot, but at least he could follow them through the straits. The destroyers anticipated this move and were standing off Nagara Point, hoping to intercept the submarine as she negotiated the right-angle bend through the narrowest and swiftest flowing part of the Dardanelles. *E11* went right over to the European side before turning east, and at 6.10 a.m., when Nasmith next raised the periscope, he discovered that the battleships had doubled back and were disappearing behind Nagara Point on their way back down the straits. Once again *E11*'s periscope was fired upon, but it was quickly retracted and the submarine headed further upstream.

It was now 6.40 a.m., at which point Nasmith took *E11* down to 70 feet, and reduced speed to save the batteries, while the torpedo tubes were closed and drained of water. It was now a fairly straight run up the remainder of the straits as long as the batteries held out. These were frequently tested by Nasmith's 29-year-old executive officer Lieutenant D'Oyly-Hughes. The tests indicated that the chase of the battleships had exhausted the batteries alarmingly. Every few miles, Nasmith was coming up to periscope depth, to check his position and his rate of advance.

At 9.30 a.m. Nasmith observed the town of Gallipoli and took *E11* down to 90 feet. At 1.30 p.m., reducing speed to 2 knots and having estimated that they should be at the end of the straits, he brought the submarine up to 50 feet, and listened for any enemy craft. Hearing none, he went to periscope depth and saw that they were past the straits and well into the Sea of Marmara, 5 miles from the Asiatic shore, with no enemy boats in sight. The European shore was 3 miles away and he headed in that direction, until the water was shallow enough for the boat to be rested on the bottom.[3] The men were given their daily tot of rum and slept as best they could in the foul conditions which existed on the boat.

At 9 p.m., 18 hours after having first submerged, *E11* surfaced and started charging her batteries immediately with the port engine, while the starboard engine was used to get under way. The wireless masts and aerial were rigged, so that a signal could be sent to the destroyer *Jed*, which was stationed off Bulair, in the Gulf of Saros, 15 miles away – at about half the transmission-operating range of the submarine's wireless set.

Almost immediately the look-outs reported that a destroyer was bearing down on them from the north, and diving stations were sounded. The engines were shut down, but the boat still did not have sufficient forward momentum to maintain control, so the submarine sank back to the bottom with a thud. The sound of the destroyer's propellers was heard to pass and then fade in the distance, which suggested that the submarine had either not been seen or that the destroyer was not willing to risk waiting about. Some fifteen minutes later, *E11* came to the surface again and continued to recharge her batteries. At 0.30 a.m., another destroyer was sighted, heading from the west, and the submarine was forced to submerge once more, but the destroyer passed harmlessly by, and ten minutes later *E11* was back on the surface. Throughout the night they continued to make unsuccessful attempts to contact *Jed*.[4] By 4 a.m. the batteries were fully recharged and Nasmith decided to dive to periscope depth and observe the western end of the Sea of Marmara.

At 5 a.m. towards the east he sighted Marmara Island and then began to patrol between this island and Kodja Burnu on the European shore, 20 miles away. He observed no shipping but he did see a column of smoke rising from the shore, which, he assumed from Boyle's comments, was a signal warning of the presence of a submarine in the area. Nasmith also observed a column of smoke on Marmara Island. Without sighting any enemy ships, he abandoned his patrol line and headed to the port town of Rodosto, 8 miles beyond Kodja Burnu. Through his periscope he could clearly see the village and the fact that there was no ship at anchorage. However, a large column of infantry was on the road out of town, as well as artillery and heavily laden mules. It was one out of many occasions when Nasmith and his crew wished they had a gun to fire at the enemy; but their presence in the Sea of Marmara was obviously having the desired effect of preventing the movement of troops by sea. Nasmith then took *E11* 12 miles off-shore, to recharge her batteries. In groups of three, the men were now allowed to bathe in the sea for ten minutes at a time. It was at this time, when the officers were relaxing in the wardroom, that D'Oyly suggested going ashore and blowing up a viaduct or ammunition dump – a proposal which Nasmith immediately dismissed.

At 11.30 a.m. on 21 May, with a surface visibility of only about 2 miles, a relatively large sailing vessel, which looked deeply laden and could possibly be carrying military stores, was sighted heading in the direction of Gallipoli. *E11* increased speed to head her off, and Nasmith shouted through a megaphone, for her to heave to. D'Oyly, with an armed boarding party, went on board the vessel and inspected her for contraband. When none was discovered, Nasmith decided that he would tie the submarine to the sailing boat, trim her down so that only the conning tower was above water, and send a man up to the top of the mast as a look-out.

He ordered the sailing boat to set sail and then proceeded to the east, hoping that, disguised in this manner, he was less likely to be observed from the shore.

While the two boats were shrouded in mist, Nasmith boarded the sailing vessel himself, so as to survey her; by this time D'Oyly had discovered some chickens and eighty eggs,[5] which were confiscated (although one shilling was offered as payment – refused by the skipper). In the afternoon the mist dispersed somewhat, and they were able to study the coastline more clearly. The two vessels now altered course and headed out to sea. By 8 p.m. the fog had lifted altogether, at which time Nasmith decided to cast off from the sailing vessel, letting the captain know that he was free to continue his voyage.

During the day the wireless set had been overhauled and as no faults had been found, *E11* again headed west. By 3 a.m. on the morning of 22 May they came within range, and for three hours attempted, unsuccessfully, to make contact. Nasmith then headed east to continue his patrol right up to Constantinople, with the aim of surveying the harbour and observing the route taken by Turkish ships. From this information he hoped to get some idea of where the minefields had been laid and then to decide if *E11* could also make the hazardous entry into the harbour. There were reports that mines could be fired electronically and that, as part of the other defences, torpedoes could be set to circle around the harbour. At 4 p.m. *E11* surfaced but was forced to crash-dive immediately, as a destroyer attacked her. After the coast was clear, *E11* surfaced again and continued east while charging her batteries.

At 3 a.m. on Sunday 23 May, *E11* approached Oxia Island, where she captured a small sailing vessel, and then noticed an empty transport returning to Constantinople. Nasmith therefore altered course to the north and, as the sun rose, headed for Constantinople, which could be made out in the distance. Another sailing ship was stopped with the intention of boarding, when a look-out reported a steamer approaching from the west. *E11* immediately headed for her, but she turned and ran back into harbour for shelter. *E11* returned to the sailing ship, but, while D'Oyly and a boarding party were examining her for contraband, a torpedo boat was observed at the entrance to the harbour. The boarding party returned and *E11* dived to 30 feet and headed for the torpedo boat, to the northeast. The torpedo tubes were made ready, while Nasmith observed, at 5.50 a.m., that the torpedo boat had dropped her anchor and was showing no sign of activity. *E11* closed the distance and at 6.30 a.m., when she was some 300 metres from the target, fired the port torpedo. She lurched as the torpedo left the tube, but the coxswain managed to maintain her depth. Thirty seconds later there was the sound of an explosion and cheers on *E11*, as the crew celebrated the success of their first hit.

Nasmith remained at the periscope and observed the torpedo strike the gunboat amidships on the starboard side. As she began to sink, he observed members of the crew running to the gun deck, man a 6-pound gun, and fire it in his direction. The shot was immediately followed by the sound of metallic clanging as shrapnel fell on the deck of his boat, below water. Amazingly, the first round fired had hit the periscope! Nasmith ordered 'down periscope' but nothing happened, as it was jammed. *E11* was taken to 30 feet, so that, even in its raised position, the periscope would descend below the surface. Using his second periscope, Nasmith took another look at the gunboat, and saw her sink by the bows five minutes later.[6]

Nasmith turned *E11* away from Constantinople and headed back out to sea. When he thought that they were at a safe distance, *E11* was brought up to the surface and the periscope inspected. It was discovered that a 6-pounder shell had passed clear through the upper tube of the forward periscope and practically severed it.[7] *E11* anchored in 10 fathoms to the north of Kalolimno Island, on the southern side of the Sea of Marmara, while repairs were undertaken. The damaged 4.5-foot section of periscope was, with some difficulty (using a heat from a flame to loosen it), unscrewed from its base. Once removed, the hole in the periscope was filled with a wooden plug and covered with canvas and a rubber solution. The boat was inspected and the batteries recharged. Nasmith had vowed not to drink or smoke until he sank an enemy warship, so his officers now provided him with a beer and a box of cigars.

The rest of Sunday was spent by the crew in physical exercise and bathing. Meanwhile, D'Oyly and a couple of seamen constructed a raft from old timbers and paint drums, which he had designed to carry a cargo of gun-cotton and a firing pistol. He planned to carry this ashore at night, so that, if the opportunity arose, he could attempt to blow up a railway line. Suddenly, at 2.30 p.m. a sailing ship was sighted, so the men scrambled back on deck, the anchor was raised and the submarine submerged. *E11* surfaced an hour later, to discover that not only had the sailing ship disappeared, but also the raft that D'Oyly had built.

E11 now headed once again to the western end of the Sea of Marmara, to try to get in touch with the destroyer *Jed*. Nasmith was keen to send a signal reporting the damage done to his periscope, so that a new periscope top could be sent out from England and be available when he got back to Tenedos.[8] That night, with batteries fully charged, *E11* used her electric motors and proceeded partially submerged, so that a rapid dive could be achieved if they encountered enemy ships. At 2 a.m. on 24 May, they were once again in range of *Jed*, and this time they finally made wireless contact, after having discovered the fault. This turned out to be a break in the contact between the radio and the aerial, which resulted from failure to fill an oil cup where the aerial came through the deck. The first message sent mentioned the need for a new periscope; it was followed by a report of activities, after which messages from the *Jed* were accepted. Several signals came from the *Jed*, the most serious being that *B11*, while patrolling off Smyrna, had sighted a U-boat. When asked about news of land operations, *Jed* replied 'heavy fighting continues'. At 5 a.m. they dismantled the wireless mast and got under way, heading to the north-east.

Nasmith now decided on a more aggressive policy and patrolled on the surface. He was determined to let no ships get through to Gallipoli and, if none were encountered, he would proceed again to Constantinople. At 10.30 a.m. on 24 May, they sighted the small steamer, *Nara*,[9] coming directly towards them from the east, and *E11* dived so that Nasmith could study the target through the second periscope. Observing that the steamer was heavy with cargo and did not appear to be armed, *E11* surfaced on her port quarter and ordered her to stop. The steamer ignored the order and altered course away from the submarine. At this point, Nasmith called for a rifle and fired several rounds at her bridge, whereupon she slowed down, and Nasmith ordered her crew to abandon ship. Much has been written about the following events, and embellished particularly by Shakland's book *Dardanelles Patrol*.

In essence, pandemonium broke out as the crew ran to the lifeboats, and in the ensuing panic some were capsized. Fortunately they could be righted and all survivors rescued. Standing on the deck of the steamer after having acted as a translator for the ship's captain was the American war correspondent Raymond Swing, often referred to as Silas Q. Swing,[10] of the *Chicago Daily News*, who had previously observed the naval bombardment in March. He and a number of correspondents had been offered the opportunity to visit the fighting at Gallipoli and, while the other journalists chose a torpedo boat for their journey, Swing was concerned about possible submarine activity and unfortunately chose the steamer.[11] After speaking to Nasmith, the American walked over to the third lifeboat, swung out on a davit and lowered himself into the boat. Nasmith's laconic report of the above events reads as follows:

> An American gentleman appeared on the upper deck who informed us that his name was Silas Q. Swing of the Chicago Sun and that he was pleased to make our acquaintance. He then informed us that the steamer was proceeding to Chanak with Turkish marines and that he was not sure if there were any stores on board. Ran up alongside and put Lieutenant D'Oyly-Hughes on board with demolition party. He discovered a 6-inch gun lashed across the top of the fore-hatch, the fore-hold containing one large 6-inch gun mounting and several smaller 12-pounder pedestals, the guns for which were probably at the bottom of the hold. The after hold was full of 6-inch projectiles, and on top of this were resting about fifty large white-metal cartridge cases marked Krupp. The demolition charge was then placed against the ship's side in the after hold, well tamped with 6-inch shells and cartridges. All hands returned to the boat and the charge was fired. The vessel exploded with a loud report and a large column of flame

and smoke shot up. Her bow lifted into the air and she sank a few moments later.[12]

Raymond Swing's view of events was somewhat curter, perhaps coloured by the loss of his belongings. In conversation with his fellow war correspondent George Schreiner,[13] he stated that the following exchange took place:

'Who are you?'
'I am Mr. Swing, war correspondent of the Chicago Daily News,' I shouted.
'I don't want to know who you are. What I want to know is what ship that is,' said the officer.
'Then why didn't you say so?' I remarked.
'Never been spoken to at sea, I suppose,' returned the officer, sort of fresh.
'Not in that manner,' says I.
'Well, what bloomin' ship is it you are on?' he asked.
'Don't know,' I replied. 'Her name's on her bow in red letters. But I can't read it. Maybe you can.'
'What sort of cargo does the ship carry?' asked the officer next.
'Don't know,' I said. I knew that she had several guns and a bunch of ammunition aboard. But that wasn't my business. Was it?
'Are those sailors from the Turkish navy or are they merchantmen?' was the next question.
'Merchantmen,' I replied, without knowing whether this was so or not. I didn't want to go to the bottom of the Marmara without making a bid for getting ashore somewhere.
'What are they wearing those red hats for?' asked the officer.
'All Turks wear red hats,' I answered. 'Those things are fezzes.'
'I see,' remarked the officer. 'Tell the captain that he and his men will have ten minutes in which to get off the boat. I am going to sink her.'

E11 then headed off for another steamer, whose smoke had been spotted while the previous vessel was sinking. Nasmith dived to attack but, having sensed danger, the steamer increased speed and headed north for Rodosto. *E11* surfaced and headed at full speed for the steamer, *Hünkar İskelesi*,[14] which was heavily laden with packing cases, and slowly closed the distance. The steamer made it to the pier at Rodosto first; the crew jumped off the ship and dashed along the pier to the town. Nasmith reduced speed to 2 knots, submerged *E11* in the shallow water (6 fathoms) and made the torpedo tubes ready to fire. *E11* touched bottom, and he slowly took her along the sand, to get as close possible to the steamer and make sure of hitting his target. At 12.35 p.m., at a distance of 2,000 yards, he ordered the bow torpedo to be fired.

Nasmith saw the torpedo hit the ship and explode. The ship then disintegrated, killing two crewmen and taking the end of the pier with it. Rifle fire
broke out at the now exposed periscope, which could not be retracted any
further and Nasmith ordered slow astern (that is, reverse) on both engines as
E11 scraped along the bottom, gradually finding deeper water. When out of
range, *E11* surfaced to inspect the periscope at a place where previously the
sound of a hit had been heard. It was then discovered that, amazingly, a bullet
had lodged in the lower section of the periscope! After removal of the bullet
the periscope moved freely up and down, which, given that the other
periscope had already been destroyed, was very fortunate.

Nasmith now headed for Constantinople, but shortly after he got under
way he observed smoke and submerged to approach what turned out to be a
paddle steamer, the *Kismet*, heading towards Rodosto. *E11* surfaced on her
quarter and called on her to stop, which she did immediately. The ferry was
carrying a few horses and had her decks heaped with rolls of barbed wire.
Using a megaphone, Nasmith ordered the steamer's crew to abandon ship
and told D'Oyly to stand by to board her. At that moment, the steamer went
ahead on one paddle and astern on the other, swinging around rapidly until
it faced the submarine, then came straight for her. Nasmith sounded the
klaxon, ordered full ahead on both engines, and *E11* drew away just in time
to avoid a collision. She was forced to turn and pursue the paddle steamer
which was racing for the shore. Nasmith called a firing party on deck and
ordered them to fire at the wheelhouse, forcing the helmsman to leave his
post. As a result of this, *Kismet* swung off course, presenting its full length
to *E11*. As D'Oyly prepared to board, the helmsman returned and swung
the steamer away from the submarine once more. Again, the firing party
directed fire at her and again the helmsman abandoned his post so that she
swung away. As *E11* closed on her once more, she turned to ram and headed
straight for the submarine, requiring Nasmith to take avoiding action for the
second time.

Eventually the steamer reached the coastline and ran straight up on to the
beach under some cliffs, where her crew leapt overboard. Nasmith blew *E11*'s
ballast tanks to lighten her and ran up behind the steamer to land a boarding
party. At that point, a detachment of Turkish cavalry arrived along the hill-
top. Nasmith ordered his firing party to fire at the cavalry, which dismounted
and returned fire. Nasmith had no choice now but to order his crew below
deck and, on his way down the hatch, a bullet hit his uniform cap. *E11* then
pulled away from the shore, but owing to the shallow water it was some time
before she could submerge. Nasmith was concerned about the barbed wire
reaching the trenches, so, at long range, he fired a torpedo from the stern tube
at the beached steamer's stern. The torpedo missed its target and exploded on

the beach, with Nasmith commenting: 'Probably frightened the horses. Sole effect of a torpedo worth a thousand quid.'[15]

At 6 a.m. on 25 May, approaching Oxia Island with Constantinople in sight, *E11* dived to periscope depth. Through the periscope Nasmith could make out the bright outline of the city on either side of the Bosphorus, but no ships were entering or leaving the harbour.[16] By noon *E11* was 1 mile south of Marmara Tower and then followed the sea walls on the European side, at a distance of 1 mile, for 3 miles towards Seraglio Point. *E11* then followed the path taken by a steamer they had observed previously on the 23rd, and, after passing Seraglio Bank, headed north towards the dome of St Sophia, then around Seraglio Point and into the Bosphorus. With only 1 mile separating the European and Asiatic shores, *E11* turned to port around Old Seraglio Point into Constantinople harbour.

Nasmith raised his periscope in quick bursts, as he discovered the harbour cluttered with small vessels moving about. Nasmith then sighted a cruiser, USS *Scorpion*, and was about to fire a torpedo, when he realized that she was carrying an American flag.[17] Continuing the search, at 12.30 p.m. he spotted a large transport, *Stambou*,[18] in company with a smaller vessel, lying at the quay in front of the main Turkish barracks at Tophane Arsenal. Nasmith thought he might get them both, and when he was in position at 12.35 p.m. he fired the port torpedo, which failed to run, and then the starboard torpedo. He was unable to observe what happened, as the cross tide was pushing the submarine ashore and he was busy observing what he thought was an enemy Brennan torpedo in the water. It was likely that this was his own port torpedo, which had probably blown out its tail plug and so was running with a capsized gyrocompass.

Nasmith was then forced to take evasive action by diving to 75 feet, as the defective port torpedo turned and headed for *E11*. The torpedo missed and continued its erratic path, exploding somewhere near the Galata Bridge, which protected the naval harbour. A moment later the starboard torpedo was heard to explode, but Nasmith didn't dare to look through the periscope, now that the Turks were alerted to the presence of a submarine.[19]

E11 now headed out of the harbour, but she suddenly grounded heavily at 70 feet and bounced up to 40 feet. Nasmith ordered corrective action, with both engines full astern and flooding of the internal tanks. The rise was caught when the boat swung to starboard and then went down. Correcting action was ordered again, with the stopping of the port engine until she swung to port. At this point the starboard engine was stopped, the auxiliary blown and the hydroplanes set hard up. The roller-coaster ride continued, Nasmith trying to keep *E11* on the right course out of the harbour and at the same time trying not to break the surface or to go too deep. Explosions could be heard on the surface, as the enemy fired at random into the water. At 60 feet, the submarine suddenly struck the bottom and the current drove her up towards the shore. Nasmith reversed engines and flooded the main ballast, bringing *E11* to a stop on the bottom at 40 feet.

Not knowing exactly where they were, he was in a difficult position. *E11*'s ballast would have to be blown and her depth controlled, but at the same time he had to turn her in the right direction to get out of the harbour. As they rested on the bottom, the boat began to swing in an anti-clockwise direction, from south-south-east through east and north around to west, as the current grabbed the boat. This meant that the current was strongest on the westerly side, which in turn meant that the *E11* was nearer to Leander Tower on the Asiatic side of the entrance to the Bosphorus.[20] Nasmith ordered the blowing of the ballast tanks until *E11* lifted just enough to clear the bottom. He then ordered the hydroplanes hard down in order to keep *E11* bumping along the bottom, while she went full ahead on both engines in a southerly direction. A little time later she reached deeper water in the middle of the channel and, keeping her at 85 feet, they headed south out of harm's way, returning to the surface some twenty minutes later. During *E11*'s time in Constantinople harbour, Nasmith had taken the first wartime photograph through a periscope.

The next morning, 26 May, while *E11* was surfaced and stationary, the remaining torpedo's gyroscopes were overhauled while the men rested. Torpedoes were designed to sink once their motors ran out of compressed air without hitting a target. Nasmith decided to bend the rules, and set the sinking valve so that the torpedo would float. That evening at 7.30 p.m., *E11* headed for the signalling billet, to communicate with *Jed* and to send a long and historic message of the attacks undertaken and of the successful venture into Constantinople harbour.

At 1.30 a.m. on 27 May, after having sent her signal, *E11* headed off eastward. Ten minutes later a ship's outline was sighted at close range. Nasmith manoeuvred into a parallel course, and submerged until little more than the conning tower was above the water. He could make out two destroyers, the *Drac* and the *Yarhisar*,[21] escorting what initially looked like a large transport but eventually turned out to be the battleship *Barbaros*, coming through the Marmara Channel en route to Gallipoli. Nasmith manoeuvred *E11* between the starboard destroyer and *Barbaros*, allowing the big ship to close the gap. As he was getting ready to fire, the destroyer changed course and headed straight towards *E11*. She was forced to go deep, thus missing any chance of completing the attack, and once again *Barbaros* escaped.

During the day, in the middle of the Sea of Marmara, they continued with maintenance of the torpedoes, and sighted no other ships until 5 p.m. that afternoon. What they saw then was only a small steamer, the *Iskenderun*,[22] which had the appearance of a yacht. Nasmith had decided to board her, but they were fired on by the steamer's small gun. *E11* immediately submerged, as a second shot rang out from the steamer.

At 8 a.m., *E11* returned to the signalling billet, where they had broken off contact early that morning, and reported their unsuccessful attack on the *Barbaros* and the attack on them by the Q ship. The signal from *Jed* mentioned that neutral sources had confirmed the confusion caused in Constantinople as a result of the attack. The signal also included a report that enemy troop reinforcements were now being sent from Constantinople by train to Panderma, via Smyrna, to shorten the sea passage to Gallipoli.

At 1.20 a.m. on Friday 28 May, they broke off wireless contact with *Jed* and headed eastward on the surface. At 6.30 a.m., smoke was seen on the horizon to the north-east; this turned out to come from five merchant vessels, escorted by a destroyer zigzagging ahead of them. *E11* submerged to 30 feet, to escape detection. At 7.15 a.m., *E11* dived under the destroyer and rose to 20 feet, moving slowly towards the convoy of one large ship and four smaller ones, so that the periscope would not give away their position. At 7.30 Nasmith fired the port beam tube and made a hit on the larger ship, on the port after side.[23] He saw the torpedo impact, the ship settle by the stern and then, within a minute, heel over to starboard and sink. The smaller boats continued on, and the destroyer, sighting *E11*'s periscope, made for it. Nasmith ordered *E11* to 80 feet, but, once again, the boat could not be taken below 70 feet. The destroyer's activities precluded *E11* from pursuing the other boats, so Nasmith decided to head back to Constantinople, as this seemed to be the direction from which the convoy had come.

At 11.30 a.m., *E11* was in a position to observe Constantinople from the surface. By 12.30 p.m. she was submerged and stalking a ship which had left the harbour, believed to be carrying troops. At 1.45 p.m. *E11* was in a firing position, and a torpedo was fired from the starboard beam tube. No explosion was heard, but the ship did stop; then, a short time later, she proceeded on her course. As she got closer Nasmith saw that there were no troops on the decks, only civilians, including women and children.[24]

It had been a lucky escape on both sides, but it was now time to recover the torpedo, which had been set to remain on the surface[25] if it failed to hit the target. *E11* cruised around until they found the torpedo, and, as they had no small boat, Nasmith stripped off and dived into the sea. When he got to the torpedo, he discovered that it had apparently grazed the top of its head against the bottom of the target vessel and that the firing pin had moved and was now barely one sixteenth of an inch away from the fulminate of mercury in the detonator.[26] With great care, he unscrewed the firing pistol to make the torpedo safe to handle. He then moved along to the side of it and pushed the starting lever, to ensure that there was no compressed air left in the engine, before swimming back to the submarine, with the firing pistol. In the meantime, a derrick had been placed over the forehatch, which was specifically designed to handle torpedoes during loading. With some careful manoeuvring E11 was brought alongside the 17-foot long torpedo, where a sling was passed under it, to lift it on board and to lower it through the forehatch. Once it was below deck, examination showed that the head had been crushed, which suggested that the torpedo had struck the vessel low down and had continued underneath her.[27] Some hours later, the torpedo had been restored to a state of readiness and placed in the starboard beam torpedo tube.

That afternoon, at 4.30 p.m., they stopped a small sailing vessel, which carried no contraband but did provide some fresh fruit (five oranges) for the crew's evening meal and some tobacco.[28] After the meal, Nasmith suggested to D'Oyly that, on future occasions, spent torpedoes could possibly be brought back on board through an empty torpedo tube; this was better than risking opening the forehatch, which would make it impossible to submerge should the enemy surprise them. That evening they communicated with *Jed*, and received advice of possible activity by enemy ships in the entrance to the Sea of Marmara. During the night the battery was recharged, and at 4 a.m. they dived and turned west, heading for the Narrows.

While submerged, at 7 a.m. on 29 May, a laden steamer was sighted coming from the east. As the submarine came into a firing position it unexpectedly dipped, and the periscope went under the water. The coxswain had lost control and, in over-correcting, caused the submarine to break surface in full view of the steamer, which immediately altered course to get away. While the submarine was on the surface the trim was adjusted, and Nasmith took her down to 20 feet, but unfortunately the opportunity to attack the steamer had been lost. They continued their patrol all day and sighted no further worthwhile targets.

It was apparent from their trip through the Narrows that E11's average speed had been greater over the ground than through the water, and therefore that, instead of having a current flowing against them of from 1 to 4 knots, there was at depth a following or assisting current of 1 knot. It was clear from this that the heavier seawater was constantly flowing up into the Sea of Marmara (at varying depths), while the lighter fresh water was flowing above and out to the Mediterranean. It was possible, and even probable, that over the whole of the Sea of Marmara the less salty water was on the surface, floating above the heavier seawater.

Nasmith decided after the experiences of that morning that he would carry out an experiment to see if his observations were correct. That evening when it grew dark he made for an area where they had had difficulty in diving below

70 feet. Once there, Nasmith took *E11* down in a gradual dive to 70 feet, and then gave orders for her to go deeper, but the coxswain reported that she wouldn't go any lower, although the boat was going ahead with the hydroplanes hard down. Nasmith ordered the auxiliaries to be flooded, letting in 3 tons of sea-water ballast, which also had no effect. He let in another 3, and then another 3 tons, but still the submarine would go no deeper. Then he ordered the coxswain to raise the boat with the hydroplanes full up, but with the 9 tons of extra ballast there was no way that this could be achieved. As the submarine could not go up, and at the same time would not go down, the engine was stopped, the boat slowed and gradually lost headway.

It was probably the first time a submarine had ever lain suspended in the water, at the depth of 70 feet, with 200 feet below it; but *E11* was locked in this unusual position. Nasmith had discovered that, rather than a gradual change in the water density,[29] which would normally necessitate that a submarine maintain forward motion to keep its required depth, there was a rigid line of demarcation between salt water and fresh water. This phenomenon allowed the men to relax in safety and comfort as the submarine could be safely suspended, rather than to attempt to find one of the few places in the Sea of Marmara – which were often patrolled by enemy boats – where it might have been shallow enough to lie on the seabed.

The following day was a Sunday, and at 8 p.m. that evening *E11* took up station at the eastern end of the channel, between the southern shores of Marmara Island and the Kapu Dagh. This placed it on the shortest route from Panderma to Gallipoli. No ships were sighted that evening, and so at dawn on Monday 31 May Nasmith headed for Panderma. On arrival he sighted a single large ship at anchorage off the town. At 9.20 a.m. he got within range of the target, which had been identified by Brown as one of the latest ships of the German Rickmers Line, and fired the port bow torpedo at a range of 1,000 yards. The torpedo struck the liner amidships on the port side, which resulted in an exceptionally large explosion. The ship listed to port and a tug immediately came out from Panderma and got a line aboard. The ship slipped her anchors and the tug began to tow her towards a beach as she sank lower and lower in the water. At this time Nasmith only had three torpedoes left and was reluctant to waste another one, given that substantial damage to the ship had already been achieved.[30]

That evening *E11* headed towards the long and narrow Gulf of Ismid, situated at the north-eastern end of the Sea of Marmara, to find out if the port of Ismid, which was at the head of the gulf, was being used to embark troops, as had been suggested by previous signals received from *Jed*. At dusk, *E11* went to periscope depth, slipped into the entrance of the gulf, but sighted no enemy ships. Nasmith went close to the northern shore, where the main railway line comes close to the sea and follows the coastline for 27 miles. It was this section that D'Oyly had selected as the most suitable place for a shore raid he was planning. *E11* surfaced 400 yards off a beach, at a point 30 miles by rail from Scutari (on the Asiatic side of Constantinople), and nearly 600 miles off from Panderma via Smyrna, but only 90 miles away from Panderma by sea. It was night-time and they could hear numerous sounds, including that of a train making its way along the railway.

At 4 a.m. on the following morning, *E11* was brought back up to periscope depth, and D'Oyly, looking through the periscope, drew a sketch of the viaduct that the train had crossed the previous evening. Then they left the gulf, patrolled until nightfall, recharged batteries and headed back to their signalling billet, making contact with *Jed* at 4 a.m. on the morning of 2 June. Nasmith continued the patrol to the north-east, along the northern traffic route. At 8.10 a.m. smoke was again observed on the horizon and Nasmith steered to intercept it, but he soon realized that the ship was a destroyer travelling at high speed. As he was about to leave, smoke was seen towards the east, coming from a large supply ship, and the two vessels were approaching each other from opposite directions. He therefore steered *E11* towards the supply ship.

At 9 a.m. *E11* surfaced, with the destroyer nearly out of sight, but the supply ship now only 3 miles away. *E11* went to full power on its diesels, to close the distance. Diving to 20 feet and manoeuvring herself into a firing position, she fired a torpedo from the starboard bow tube at 9.40 a.m. The torpedo struck the ship on her port side just ahead of the bridge, with a violent explosion appearing to lift the upper deck and throw it overboard; this suggested that the ship had been loaded with munitions. After the smoke had cleared, her bows were under the water and within three minutes she had completely disappeared.[31]

At 10.15 a.m., a small steamer was sighted close inshore and the submarine altered course towards her. The target quickly disappeared into a bay, but ten minutes later she reappeared around the headland, cautiously following close to the coastline. At 10.50 a.m., Nasmith fired a torpedo from the port beam tube but missed the ship, which had seen the torpedo track and immediately turned and made for the shore. Nasmith brought *E11* to the surface and tried to head her off as she made for a small beach and, just before beaching, let go her anchor.[32] The crew abandoned ship and headed for shore. Nasmith decided that he would put a demolition party aboard, but, as soon as he approached the ship, he came under rifle fire from the nearby village. He therefore left the ship alone and cruised around, looking unsuccessfully for the floating torpedo. At that stage he realized that his impetuous attack on the small steamer had wasted one of his two remaining torpedoes.

By 12.20 p.m. they were back at sea, when smoke was again sighted. It turned out to be from one small two-funnelled ship, of the type used for carrying dispatches, and escorted by two destroyers. At 3,000 yards, Nasmith, in calm seas, lowered the periscope and then used dead reckoning and the sound of the enemy's propellers to get into an attacking position. When he thought he was there, he raised his periscope and discovered he was only 600 yards away from the target. He immediately fired his last torpedo at 2.15 p.m., which ran straight but missed the target, probably passing underneath, due to the very shallow draught of the vessel.

Once the convoy had disappeared, *E11* surfaced and found the floating torpedo. D'Oyly dived overboard and removed the firing pistol, and then the new method of recovery was tried. *E11* was trimmed down so that the stern torpedo tube was just awash. While the inner door of the tube was kept closed, the outer door was opened after the torpedo tube had been flooded. Six seamen dived into the water and guided the front of the torpedo into the torpedo tube. The tube was pumped dry, sucking the torpedo in completely, and then the outer door was closed. The tube was pumped out, the inner door opened and the torpedo removed. As it was obviously facing in the wrong direction, it was manhandled using an overhead rail system through the submarine to the port bow tube, so that it now faced the right way. The torpedo was then examined and tested.

On 3 June, *E11* proceeded, on the surface, to a position south of Oxia Island, with the aim of intercepting any ships which might take an alternative route, along the southern shore of the Sea of Marmara, on their way from Constantinople to Gallipoli. At 2 p.m., *E11* dived and patrolled westward, when smoke was sighted on the horizon to the north-east. After approaching the target for ten minutes, and with no apparent improvement in the distance that separated them, Nasmith ordered *E11* to surface and headed for the target at full speed. By 3 p.m. they were close enough to make out the small target, when suddenly the distance between the two ships reduced rapidly and it became apparent that the yacht had reversed course and was heading directly for the submarine.

At 3,000 yards, Nasmith ordered a rapid dive, and he closed the conning tower hatch only at the last possible moment. Unfortunately, the diving muffler valve to the diesel engines had not been shut quickly enough, and the diesels were flooded. The dive had been achieved in record time, although Nasmith was annoyed that no one had realized until the last moment that the ship had turned and was attempting to ram them. At 3.45 p.m., after the ship had departed, *E11* was brought to the surface, and the stokers had the laborious task of turning the main engines by hand, in order to eject the water before they could be started again. Half an hour later they saw a destroyer zigzagging at high speed, obviously looking for them.

That evening they proceeded to their signalling post and reported to *Jed* at 3 a.m. on 4 June. *E11* then headed eastward and patrolled off Oxia Island, where several destroyers were observed, possibly looking for her; but each time *E11* avoided them by submerging. Of greater concern on the following day was the discovery, by the electricians, that the insulation on the armature of the port motor was shorting seriously; this meant that the armature could not be used without risking a flash or a fire, which could completely destroy the motor. As Nasmith noted in his log:

Discovered a full brilliancy earth on the Port Main Motor Armature. In view of this and of the fact that the starboard intermediate shaft was cracked it was considered advisable to return.[33]

The defect, already discovered, in the intermediate shaft between the engine and the electric motor meant that it was now possible for the shaft to break when the diesels were used, if it was put under too much strain. It was impossible to repair either of these defects while on patrol, and so on the following day, 6 June, the batteries were recharged and the boat prepared for the return journey through the Narrows. *E11* returned to the signalling billet, and at 9.30 p.m. sent a signal that they should be expected off Cape Helles at noon the following day. She departed for Gallipoli at 10 p.m. By 3.40 a.m., as day was breaking, they had still not received any acknowledgement from *Jed*. Nasmith therefore removed the wireless masts, dived to 20 feet, and headed for the entrance to the straits.

At 6.30 a.m. on 7 June, *E11* passed the town of Gallipoli, from where Nasmith regularly went to periscope depth, in search of a suitable target for his last torpedo as he proceeded down the straits. On the Asiatic side he only saw small steamers, so he moved over to the European side and examined the anchorage at Karakova, which proved to be empty. As they approached Moussa Bank, he saw a large liner lying at anchor, an easy target which he was tempted to attack. However, he still hoped that his last and twice recovered torpedo could be used to sink the *Barbaros* further downstream. As *E11* approached Nagara Point, Nasmith moved well over to the European side to get a clear view, through the periscope, of the whole of the next reach to Chanak; but there was no sight of any battleship.

Nasmith took *E11* to 50 feet, flooded the auxiliaries to pass through the critical level between the different water densities, reached the upflowing seawater, turned 180 degrees and headed back up the straits again. By noon he was within striking distance of the transport off Moussa Bank. At a distance of 300 yards he fired the port bow torpedo, which ran true and struck the ship on the port side towards the bow. She immediately heeled over to port and began to settle by the bow.[34] Nasmith continued his turn to starboard and headed down the straits, leaving the transport sinking behind him.

E11 safely negotiated Nagara Point at 1.40 p.m., giving it a fairly wide berth, but, as she reached Kilid Bahr at 2 p.m., her trim became quite abnormal. An unknown force was trying to bring *E11* to the surface, which was countered by flooding the forward trim and then the internal ballast tanks, allowing a total of 8 tons of water to take *E11* to 70 feet. While heading for the European shore and still in deep water, a scraping sound was heard, as if *E11* had hit the bottom. With some difficulty the submarine was taken to periscope depth, where Nasmith raised the periscope, only to get the fright of his life. Ahead of them, 20 feet from the periscope, was a large horned mine. *E11*'s port hydroplane had fouled the mine's moorings.

There was now a risk not only of detonating the mine, but also of betraying their presence. It was 3 p.m. and they were off Chanak. Nasmith didn't tell his crew of the danger, but ordered a course of 220 degrees and a depth of 30 feet. Nasmith then opened the lower conning tower hatch, climbed into the conning tower, opened one of the deadlights and peered through the thick glass scuttle. He could see that the mine's cable was fouled around the port hydroplane, with the mine above and its sinker, hanging beneath, in equilibrium. Fortunately the cable had not twisted around the hydroplane, but was held in position by the boat's forward motion. The mine was only 10 feet from the scuttle from which he was looking, and he could see six horns protruding from it. Each horn was made of lead which covered a glass tube, so that, if the horn made contact with the hull of the submarine, the soft-leaded horn would crumble, breaking the glass tube beneath. This would then release an electrolyte, closing the electric circuit and detonating the 80-pound charge. Nasmith went back below and ordered that the submarine be kept at 30 feet.

They were approaching the Kephez minefield, and he needed to take the submarine down to 80 feet to go below it, so he gave orders that the dive was to be undertaken in a very steady and regular manner. As they continued through the minefield, the sounds of scraping wires were heard, but only Nasmith had the additional pressure of knowing that the captured mine could easily detonate at any time. Finally Brown announced that they were now through, at which point Nasmith reluctantly ordered the submarine up to 30 feet, to get the benefits of a stronger current. At 3.50 p.m. they were opposite the front-line trenches, and they altered course to make for Cape Helles. Eventually they could hear the sound of destroyer propellers patrolling up and down, so Nasmith ordered *E11* to periscope depth, and raised the periscope. He saw that the cliffs of Cape Helles were half a mile to starboard, and a destroyer, which he identified as *Grampus*, was half a mile to port. He was unsure whether *Grampus*, which by now was turning in his direction, was aware of their presence, and, if so, whether they would assume it was an enemy submarine. He decided that it was necessary to surface and identify *E11* immediately.

A crew member got ready to go into the conning tower with the White Ensign, so that it could be quickly hoisted. Nasmith then announced to the crew that they had fouled a mine forward and that he was going to get rid of it by going full astern, while blowing the after tanks to keep the bow submerged. After this action had been taken, the stern rose as the reversing screws checked *E11*'s way and started to move the submarine backwards. The mooring wire slipped off the hydroplane, and the mine was dragged down by its sinker and disappeared. They continued to go astern to get clear, blew the main ballast so that the submarine surfaced, quickly hoisted the White Ensign and signalled to *Grampus* that they had cleared a mine, which had fallen in the sea ahead of them.[35] The crew on the deck of *Grampus* gave three cheers for *E11*, whose exploits were already known, and left a marker at the spot where the mine had been released. *Grampus* turned and led *E11* towards Kephalos. For this daring mission Nasmith was awarded the Victoria Cross and promoted to the rank of commander; D'Oyly was awarded the Distinguished Service Order.

E14's second war patrol – 10 June to 3 July

On 10 June at 12.40 a.m., *E14* weighed anchor and, under the command of Lieutenant Commander E.C. Boyle, proceeded on the surface, under escort by *Jed* until they reached de Tott's Battery; there they parted company. When about 2 miles south-west of the Suan Dere searchlight, the submarine was illuminated by another searchlight 2 miles south of Kephez Point, so the order was given to flood all external tanks and the No. 2 auxiliary tank, and *E14* submerged at 2.55 a.m. At 4.20 a.m., the submarine altered course when she was abeam of Kilid Bahr, to go through the Narrows, with Chanak half a mile ahead. By 5.30 a.m. she had rounded Nagara, but Boyle sighted nothing of importance in the Narrows, except one small steamer and two torpedo boats. The tide was strong, and Boyle had to keep his submarine at 95 feet as long as possible, passing the town of Gallipoli at 10.30 a.m. *E14* finally surfaced at 12.29 p.m., 3 miles south of the Dohan Aslan Bank. Although sighting a strange object astern, possibly a buoy, the submarine continued on the surface to Sar Kioi, recharging her batteries. This was significantly different from Boyle's first mission up the Dardanelles, when he suffered continual harassment by enemy patrols. Another important difference was that *E14* had since been fitted with a new, though small, 6-pounder deck gun.

On 11 June, after submerging to avoid an enemy destroyer, *E14* later stopped a brigantine at 9 a.m., about 5 miles north-west of Kara Burnu, heading towards Gallipoli. A rifle shot was fired across her bows, she lowered sails, and the crew got into their lifeboat, cursing the submariners. Due to the rough seas, Lieutenant R.W. Lawrence swam across to her and found that she carried loose straw; but, given that she was heavy in the water, he suspected there was another cargo below. Lawrence therefore set her alight with the aid of paraffin oil, burning her to the water-line. At 11 a.m., a small funnelled gunboat, seen off Sar Kioi, fired on the submarine. Boyle dived and then attempted to attack by torpedo, but was unable to get within range.

On the following day, after spending the night to the north of Marmara Island, *E14* headed for the harbour at Panderma, where a steamer was sighted close inshore near a pier, apparently transferring her cargo to four dhows. At 1.11 p.m., Boyle fired the port bow torpedo, which appeared to hit the target, but at that moment *E14* dipped and, when the periscope broke the surface again, Boyle could see that the steamer was still there. However, on her starboard side where the dhows had been, there was now only a brown stain on the water. Small guns and rifles fired at the submarine's periscope from the shore; but, undaunted, Boyle came around to attack once again. At 2.50 p.m. the starboard bow torpedo was fired, with another hit recorded, while shore fire again forced Boyle to lower his periscope. Surprisingly, a few minutes later a big explosion was felt and badly shook the boat, while it was at a depth of 30 feet. Boyle suggests in his report that, while turning, the stern of the submarine may have caught the moorings of a mine, exploding it, rather than the explosion being the result of a large shell bursting overhead. If this was the case, then the submarine was indeed very lucky. Boyle must have concluded that he did not successfully sink the steamer, as he goes on to suggest that it was grounded and may have been the one *E11* had previously torpedoed.[36]

Over the next few days *E14* patrolled the waters around Marmara Island without success, although several empty dhows were intercepted; but Boyle allowed them to go, as they had no lifeboats. However, this didn't mean that the days were without danger or uneventful.

In the early afternoon of Sunday 13 June, *E14* chased a small steamer towards Artaki Peninsula after it had turned away and was running for the shore, as others had done in the past. When Boyle got to within 2,000 yards at around 1.50 p.m., he became suspicious and ordered that the gun and casing be secured. At this moment, the steamer suddenly turned and opened fire with two 6-pound guns. *E14* dived immediately, realizing that the enemy target was a gunboat. It managed to fire about two dozen rounds, some of them falling within 20 yards of *E14*. An important lesson had been learnt. In the early morning of 15 June, *E14* was in pursuit of another steamer of similar size (700 tons), 10 miles from Rodosto, but when he was within 3 miles range, Boyle once again became suspicious and gave up the chase.

On 17 June, near Sar Kioi, at 5.30 a.m., *E14* was intercepted by the *Samsun* and the *Yarhisar* as they raced out from under the cover of land; then they fired at her. She quickly dived and succeeded in evading them without any difficulty. Boyle then proceeded to an area within 15 miles of Constantinople, to the south-west, but found only a few sailing dhows, which were not worth sinking.

The following day at 9.45 a.m., Boyle sighted a destroyer[37] coming from the direction of Princes Islands; at this point *E14* dived and manoeuvred until 10.17 a.m., when Boyle fired the port bow torpedo; it narrowly missed the target's stern. Later that evening, he tried again to attack the same ship, but was unable to get *E14* into a firing position. At 8.45 p.m., flames from a ship's funnel were sighted, but this and other sightings that night proved to be enemy torpedo boats and destroyers, which *E14* successfully avoided.

On 19 June, inspection of the ports at Silivri and Panderma produced no targets, but during the next day three small sailing vessels were stopped and destroyed by incendiaries and explosive charges. Boyle was reluctant to sink small sailing vessels unless the safety of their crews could be assured. As few of the vessels had lifeboats, he was again reduced to finding other, more suitable craft to sink. For example, on 20 June, *E14* stopped, boarded and sank three sailing dhows carrying grain, one by setting alight and the other two with 2.25 pound gun-cotton explosive charges. Boyle then towed the crews ashore some 8 miles away.

E14 then met up with *E12* on 21 June at 5.20 p.m., after having unsuccessfully tried to attack a destroyer in the morning. They remained tied alongside for three hours and arranged to meet up again on 25 June, to the west of Marmara Island.

While *E14* was in Mudania Bay the next day, a few sails were sighted and an empty sailing ship was sunk. Boyle then intercepted a small steamship, which he chased inshore by Yassi Burnu, until she hoisted a signal saying she was a 'passenger ship', and then quickly waved an Italian flag from the bridge. Her decks were filled with men and women, so Boyle chose to let her go rather than board and inspect her. The following day several empty sailing dhows were sunk, and in one case the crew of two dhows looked so miserable that Boyle allowed one to go free, taking both crews to safety. On 24 June near Rodosto, *E14* intercepted two large sailing dhows loaded with paraffin, grain and other provisions, which were duly blown up. Another deserted dhow was sighted about a mile off, which Boyle had decided to leave, when he suddenly saw two men in the water, a further half mile from the deserted dhow. They had jumped overboard with fright, after having seen what had happened to the other two dhows. Boyle now felt obliged to pick them up, and after feeding them, placed them back onto their dhow. [38]

The following day at 6 a.m., *E14* made wireless contact with *Jed* and proceeded to the east of the Sea of Marmara; she also attempted without success to contact *E12* and to send her back to base. The next day, after trying again, unsuccessfully, to contact *E12*, Boyle kept cruising about until he spotted her at 5.30 p.m. coming from the Mudania Bay. He closed up on her, passed on her orders and cast off again at 7.10 p.m.

Relatively few targets were found for the remainder of the patrol. On 27 June, *E14* fired on a brigantine at 1,600 yards, forcing her to drop sail. After transferring her crew and their belongings to a rowboat, Boyle attempted to sink her with gunfire, but, although she was loaded with granite blocks, he finally had to come alongside and sink her with an explosive charge. At that time a small gunboat was sighted, so *E14* submerged, but was unable to get into a firing position so as to use her torpedoes.

On 29 June at 1.30 p.m., Boyle sighted a torpedo boat near Erekli, towing four dhows. Remaining on the surface, he tried to cut them off, until the torpedo boat slipped its tow, forcing him to submerge. The dhows proceeded under sail, until some time later they were once again picked up by the torpedo boat. At 3.45 p.m., *E14* finally reached a firing position and, in what appears to be some frustration, Boyle fired two bow torpedoes. Both of them missed, passing behind the torpedo boat[39] and in front of the dhows. The estimation of the target's speed of 8 knots proved to be too low.

On 1 July, after unsuccessfully looking for *E7* at the rendezvous point, Boyle proceeded to Rodosto, where he allowed the hospital ships *Gülnihal* and *Rember* to pass. While preparing to attack the Bosphorus ferry *Intizam*,[40] which was travelling at 13 knots, Boyle abandoned the attempt when he became confused over the signal flags flown. The ferry was flying a white flag, with what looked like a small red pattern in the centre, which suggested to him that it might also have been a hospital ship. That evening, at 7.45 p.m., *E7* was finally sighted and her captain came aboard *E14*.

On the following day, *E14* sighted a destroyer in Palatia Bay, on the north coast of Marmara Island, and at 1.20 p.m. Boyle fired the starboard bow torpedo at a range of only 1,300 yards. The torpedo broke surface twice and Boyle immediately took *E14* deep, in case the torpedo turned back on him; but it eventually struck the bottom and exploded nearby. The shock wave caused the after hatch to lift and allow water to enter the submarine, but no serious damage was done. Boyle then immediately turned to bring his submarine back into a firing position, but by this time the destroyer had moved out of range. After avoiding several more destroyers that evening, *E14* advised *Jed* by radio, at 10.30 p.m., that she was heading for Gallipoli and then returning to base the following day.

On 3 July, at 5.30 a.m., *E14* commenced her return passage down the Dardanelles, diving south of Dohan Aslan Bank. The following provides a typical chronology of manoeuvres, with a variation between a periscope depth of 22 feet, used to make the observations, and the remainder at differing depths, used to avoid minefields and nets.

Table 8.1 *Chronology of manoeuvres*

Time	Location	Depth in feet
6.40 a.m.	3 miles north-east of Gallipoli	90
7.50	1 mile south of Galata Burnu	70
8.12	half a mile east of Karakova Burnu	70
9.02	three quarters of a mile south-east of Uzun Burnu	70
9.45	half a mile east of Ak Bashi Liman	95
10.20	south-east of Khelia Liman	70
10.27	east by south of Maidos	60
10.35	one third of a mile north-north-east of Derma Burnu	40
10.45	1 mile east of Kilid Bahr	40
10.55	1 mile south-south-west of Kilid Bahr	90
11.45	south of Suan Dere	90
12.30 p.m.	1 mile south-east of Cape Helles	Surfaced

Boyle sighted little in the Dardanelles, except for a steamship in Ak Bashi Liman and a small steamship or gunboat near Kilid Bahr, heading in the opposite direction. While travelling from Gallipoli to Nagara, *E14* was effectively escorted by a small steamship, which also proceeded down the straits. This fortuitous escort, however, just added to Boyle's difficulties when he came to periscope depth to take sightings while trying to remain unseen. Off Bokali Kalessi, a loud bang was heard as *E14* passed through some obstruction, but this didn't slow her down. Of all of the risks of the mission, perhaps the greatest occurred while *E14* was anchored off Cape Helles, awaiting her escort, and was fired upon by a 4.1-inch gun from the Asiatic shore. One of the four rounds fired only missed the submarine by 4 yards, whereupon *E14* quickly weighed anchor and left for Kephalos.

Loss of *Mariotte*

Departing on 26 July under the command of Lieutenant de Vaisseau Fabre, the French submarine *Mariotte*[41] passed under the minefields but then ran into difficulties, with her starboard propeller becoming stuck in some obstruction, most likely a mine cable and its sinker. She ran aground at 80 feet in the Narrows off Chanak and, while attempting to get free, broke surface and was fired upon by shore batteries at Chemenlik, under the command of Lieutenant Serif. After the conning tower was hit, Fabre ordered the boat to be abandoned and flooded the ballast tanks. Turkish forces attempted to secure the submarine with cables from the shore, but she sank and was salvaged twenty years later.[42]

E12's first war patrol – 19 June to 28 June

E12, under the command of Lieutenant Commander K. Bruce, left Mudros for Kephalos Bay in the afternoon of 19 June and at midnight headed for the Dardanelles. At 2.30 a.m. on 20 June, *E12* was forced to dive when she was fired on by shore batteries. She rounded Kilid Bahr at 5.15 a.m., and then arrived at Nagara Point at 5.55 p.m.

Prior to the naval operations in the Dardanelles, the Turkish anti-submarine net consisted of fishing nets supported by floating empty mine cases. This proved entirely ineffective and was destroyed by British naval action. In June 1915, a steel net was placed between Nagara and Bokali Kalessi. The net was in 60 to 70 metre sections, and provided coverage up to a maximum depth of 70 metres.[43]

E12 was probably the first submarine to get entangled in the new nets while attempting to travel under the minefields. Bruce tried to reverse out of the net without success, and had to go ahead at full speed until part of the net gave way. He then reversed once more and charged the net again and again, finally tearing a hole big enough to let *E12* through.[44]

By 10.15 a.m. on the following day, *E12* was off the town of Gallipoli, and Bruce discovered that he had problems with his electric motors, probably as a result of the intense load put on them in breaking through the nets. By the time he reached the Sea of Marmara, they were exceedingly hot. Bruce therefore decided to give his motors a rest, and took his submarine to the bottom in 11 fathoms of water, about 30 nautical miles north-east of Gallipoli. Nine hours later he surfaced, to run on his diesels and charge his batteries, as *E12* headed eastward.

At 6.30 p.m. on 21June, *E12* had a rendezvous with *E14* and made plans to meet for a combined patrol at a later date. In the meantime, *E12* was ordered to cruise the western half of the Sea of Marmara and went on her way at 8 p.m. The electrical motors continued to remain a problem, and on 22 June, while she was heading towards Rodosto, the port main motor armature burnt out. At 3.10 p.m. that day, the torpedo cruiser *Peyk-i Sevket* was sighted off

Rodosto, but *E12* was unable to manoeuvre into a suitable firing position because she was only running on her starboard main motor. To make matters worse, this motor also developed small defects and ran hot, producing a very slow speed. An important target had been lost as the torpedo cruiser was on her way to Chanak, carrying munitions for the front.[45] It therefore became necessary for *E12* to lie on the bottom later that afternoon to undertake repairs on the motors. The repairs continued throughout the following day, but problems still persisted with the port main motor. *E12* and *E14* met again at 9 a.m. on 24 June, before *E12* continued into the eastern part of the Sea of Marmara, where at 3.30 p.m. she stopped and sank a sailing vessel loaded with sulphur.

More dramatic events unfolded on the following day, when, near Mudania Bay, *E12* sighted a small steamer towing two sailing vessels, and then another small steamer with three boats in tow.[46] *E12* surfaced ahead of the first steamer and cruised around her, observing that she was carrying a lot of stores and that the crew were on deck in their life vests as she had no lifeboat. After concluding that she carried no gun, she was ordered to stop. *E12* came alongside and Bruce sent on board his First Lieutenant, Tristram Fox, and two seamen, to open her seacocks and sink her. *E12*'s gun was loaded, and Bruce had several crewmen on deck with rifles as the boarding party stepped aboard the steamer. Suddenly, an object believed to be a bomb was thrown onto the deck of the submarine, but failed to explode. At the same time some of the Turkish crew opened fire with rifles and with a small concealed gun of about 1-inch calibre.

With his men trapped on board, Bruce desperately fired his deck gun at the steamer, at a range of 10 yards, with the coxswain, Charles Case, acting as the ammunition hoist to keep the gun firing, while the gun crew[47] was under fire from about twelve rifles. During the engagement the small sailing vessels came in on *E12*'s other flank, also subjecting her to rifle fire while they tried to foul her propellers. Bruce now concentrated his fire on the sailing vessels, driving them off, and then he silenced the gun on the steamer before quickly withdrawing his boarding party. *E12* then opened fire, sinking the ship after hitting her from bow to stern with ten rounds; one round caused a large explosion forward, a fact which suggests that she was carrying ammunition. The steamer sank in about fifteen minutes. *E12* then sank the sailing vessels, with only two members of the Turkish crew saved. Amazingly, only one member of *E12*'s crew was wounded, as a result of a splinter from the explosion on board the steamer.

Due to the continuing problem with the starboard main motor, it took some time to get clear of the first steamer; but Bruce then turned his attention to the other steamer, which was making for shore. He opened fire at 2,000 yards and got to within 1,500 yards, hitting her three times before he was forced to withdraw because of fire from the coastal batteries on Kalolimno Island, which had been alerted by the gunfire. The steamer, although damaged below the water-line, was able to beach herself and was later recovered.[48]

On the afternoon of 26 June, *E12* chased several steamers, forcing the nearest one, the paddle steamer ferry *Intizam*, aground. Although she was acting as transport, Bruce thought she was not carrying anything of military value, so he decided not to open fire for fear of setting alight the wooden houses in the nearby town – one of the many acts of chivalry of the time. Bruce attempted to locate the other steamer without success, and at 4 p.m. *E12* and *E14* met once again. At this meeting, Bruce was informed that he had been ordered to return to base at once.

During the following morning, *E12* passed a large steamer marked with a red cross and confirmed that she did have wounded on board. At 3.30 p.m., a gunboat was sighted and Bruce gave chase and opened fire, but an hour later he broke off the engagement. That evening they tried to contact *Jed*, but were unsuccessful, and so they proceeded to the town of Gallipoli, settling on the bottom at midnight, 12 miles away. At 2 a.m. *E12* surfaced and again tried to raise *Jed* without success, so she carried on towards the Dardanelles at a slow pace, to keep the motors cool.

Diving at 3.30 a.m., *E12* rounded Nagara at 1.15 p.m. and passed Chanak at 2.20 p.m. She encountered some difficult currents, which forced her to the starboard side of the straits, and on rising to 20 feet she was turned towards Kephez Point. It became necessary to take an extra 5 tons of water on board to keep the boat down and under control. *E12* finally reached Kephalos at 8 p.m.

E7's first war patrol – 30 June to 24 July

Leaving in the very early hours of 30 June, *E7*, under the command of Lieutenant Commander Archibald D. Cochrane, submerged at 3.50 a.m., off Achi Baba, and then travelled at a depth of 80 feet, occasionally coming to periscope depth to fix her position. By 6.30 a.m. the boat had become heavy, making depth control more difficult, and Cochrane's order for the partial blowing of only the Number 4 tank exacerbated the situation by causing a list in the boat. He also became increasingly offensive to his second in command, Lieutenant Oswald E. Hallifax, and, when the submarine was submerged, he spent much of his time seated with his eyes closed.[49] It was not until the next day that Cochrane told Hallifax that he had felt so sick the previous morning he was barely able to see through the periscope. Hallifax too had been feeling ill at this time. Indeed, Cochrane and his crew were to suffer from high fevers and dysentery throughout the whole voyage, which made the cramped submarine conditions even more difficult. Cochrane's report, although failing to mention his own discomfort, stated: 'As both the available officers and several of the crew were suffering from constant diarrhoea very little work was done.'[50]

Due to his illness, Cochrane was in the throes of deciding whether or not to return to base, when E7 rounded Nagara at 7.20 a.m. and five minutes later hit the bottom at 80 feet, listing heavily. Cochrane then put both motors to full power, to regain control, drawing 1,000 ohms, and the port motor blew up. (It was this distraction that caused Cochrane to forget his thoughts of returning home.) The submarine, however, was able to proceed, and by noon E7 passed Gallipoli, submerging to the bottom till dark, to allow the crew to rest. Surfacing at 8.30 p.m., she was immediately confronted by a torpedo boat only 400 yards away, and was again forced to submerge.[51] Later that night, at 11.45 p.m., E7 was able to surface, charge her batteries and try, unsuccessfully, to communicate with Jed.

On the first day of July, in the early morning, the hospital ship Gülnihal was sighted and allowed to proceed. At 8 a.m. the deck gun was mounted, and, after setting trim, E7 patrolled near the Dardanelles, but sighted nothing of value before meeting up with E14 that evening, off Kalolimno Island. Cochrane transferred to E14 to meet Boyle, while Lieutenant Stanley came across to visit Lieutenant Hallifax on E7.

At sunrise the next day, a hospital ship was sighted, and then at 9.30 a.m. one steamer and five sailing vessels were sighted off the grain store in Rodosto Bay. As the submarine approached the steamer on the surface, rifle fire was directed at her from on shore, though the bullets only just made it to the submarine. The deck gun was readied for action, and E7 came alongside the steamer, where Hallifax and Able Seaman Matthew went on board with a tin of petrol to set her alight. Once on board, they went below decks and poured the petrol around. They took their time, unaware of the volatility of petrol when mixed with sufficient air, particularly in a confined space. When a match was struck to light the petrol, there was an immediate explosion, but fortunately both men managed to struggle back on deck. Matthew was burnt on the face, neck, forearms and hands, while Hallifax's right forearm was burnt raw as well as his feet and legs, which were blistered up to the thickest part of his calves as he had taken off his shoes and rolled up his pants before going aboard the steamer.[52]

Meanwhile, a 16.25-pound charge was placed aboard one of the sailing vessels which was blown up. Hallifax and Matthew where picked up and several rounds fired into the burning steamer below the water-line, to make sure of her sinking.[53] Not long afterwards the hospital ship Gülnihal was sighted, but suddenly, at 12.25 p.m. the gunboat *Aydin Reis* reappeared, forcing *E7* to crash-dive in order to escape the scene. Near Marmara Island on 3 July, a small brigantine loaded with charcoal and firewood and manned by a Greek crew, but commanded by a Turk, was sunk by gunfire, before *E7* was forced to leave the area, due to the presence of an enemy destroyer.

Over the next two days, while Matthew and Hallifax recuperated from their burns, further repairs were undertaken to the previously damaged electric motors, including the replacement of a bent connecting rod in the port engine. By 6 July the general health of the crew was much better, except for telegraphist Albert Parodi, who was still suffering from dysentery. Just after noon, 10 miles off Bos Burnu, *E7* sank by gunfire a large dhow of 200 tons, loaded with charcoal. She then proceeded to tow the crew towards Kalolimno Island, and continued on the way to the Mudania Bay. At 4.30 p.m., a large steamer was sighted alongside the Mudania Pier, but she managed to escape before Cochrane could get within range – a manoeuvre made all the more difficult by the setting sun. Another steamer[54] was then sighted alongside the pier. The starboard beam torpedo was set for long range and slow speed; it fired but missed, running up a sand bank instead, with no damage to the steamer.

Later that evening, a large empty brigantine was stopped and sunk by explosive charges. On the next day, *E7* sighted two small steamers off Venedeck Rocks, one of which was a small tug, which ran on to the rocks and was destroyed by gunfire. The other was a ferry, which ran up onto the nearby beach, receiving support from about thirty soldiers, who ran out and commenced firing at the submarine. At a range of 2,000 yards, *E7* fired ten rounds into the ferry,[55] which was holed on the water-line and settled by the stern.

E7 then returned to the east of Marmara Island and that afternoon, around 2.25 p.m., sighted a steamer towing a dhow. Somewhat suspicious, Cochrane fired a shot across her bows at 3,000 yards, at which the steamer returned fire from her small 2- or 3-pounder guns and continued to do so until she was out of range. Once this happened, the steamer slipped her tow and made off, but due to a steering fault *E7*'s firing was off target and produced only one hit on the steamer's upper works. Cochrane now concentrated his fire on the dhow; but when he was at short range he came under fire from a ship lying under the cliffs of Marmara Island. This forced *E7* to withdraw, and soon afterwards she was chased by a destroyer. Later that day, at 7.15 p.m., *E7* forced the ferry steamer *Intizam* aground near Kale Burnu, before several rounds were fired at her hull.[56]

The next day, 8 July, *E7* attacked a convoy of two tugs, eight dhows and four destroyers, off Hora Burnu. The port beam torpedo was fired, but missed its target and hit one of the nearby cliffs. Later that evening, Cochrane intercepted the *Intizam*, which he thought he had already sunk; hence he proceeded to finish the job. A number of other steamers (which subsequently proved to be hospital ships) were sighted, as well as patrol boats and destroyers, these latter forcing *E7* to submerge several times. By 8.15 p.m., *E7* was able to surface and, as on the previous night, she tried to communicate with *Jed* and send her patrol reports, but no reply was received.

On the afternoon of the following day, a smart looking sailing vessel, filled with firewood as well as a number of chickens, was sunk off Baba Burnu, after four rounds were fired into her. However, due to the arrival of a torpedo boat, the chickens unfortunately could not be confiscated before *E7* was forced to submerge. Greater success was achieved on 10 July, when once again *E7* attacked the *Biga* at Mudania, at around 9 a.m. She was loading desperately needed ammunition and additional protection was provided by mooring several sailing ships across the pier. However, *Biga*'s stern had been left exposed, so *E7* dived and fired a torpedo at a range of 1,500 yards hitting the target in the stern abreast the main mast. This resulted in a heavy explosion, with a column of water shooting 300 yards up into the air, after which *Biga* broke in two and sank in shallow water.

On the 11th, after surfacing at 8.50 a.m., the engines were started and, after a loud explosion, they stopped functioning. It was found that water had got into the No. 3 port and had burst the cylinder liner, the piston and the connecting rod. *E7* made its way out to the middle of the Sea of Marmara and, while the engine was repaired, the crew had an unscheduled opportunity to rest. *E7* was back in action on the afternoon of 13 July, when, submerged, she followed a large gunboat into Karabuga Bay. Cochrane attempted to get into a firing position with the bow tube, but, while the target was swinging around to the northeast, *E7* suddenly got stuck in soft mud.[57] An attempt was then made to fire a stern torpedo, but the crew had forgotten to open the outer door, and by the time this was accomplished the gunboat had departed, escorting two steamers out of the bay. Seeing that there were still two small steamers by the pier, Cochrane fired a torpedo at them, but, although there was an explosion, the resulting damage was unknown.[58]

That evening a ship was sighted anchored inshore and, while checking her out through the periscope, Cochrane noticed what looked like wounded crowding her decks. Bringing the conning tower just above the surface, he was able to get a better look, and saw that there were indeed wounded disembarking from the ship. *E7* therefore left the area, but it was not long before a tug and four dhows were sighted at Sar Kioi; they were also crammed with wounded who were being discharged into the town, which was filled with field tents being put into use as temporary hospitals. These wounded troops were casualties from the 12 July offensive by the Allies, which had attempted to take the right flank of the peninsula.

On 14 July, at 1 p.m., when he was about 10 miles to the east of Marmara Island, Cochrane observed a U-boat, under tow by a destroyer, proceeding at about 6 knots; but he was unable to attack. He then proceeded at full speed for the northern coast, while being screened by the sun, hoping to get ahead of them. Unfortunately, when he was off Myriophysto village, at about 400 yards off the destroyer's quarter, heavy rifle fire from the village gave away his position, forcing E7 to submerge. However, the incident did highlight a new danger in the Sea of Marmara – the presence of a U-boat, so E7 headed off to report it by wireless, but again received no reply.

Cochrane then decided to make for Constantinople, and at noon on 15 July E7 dived off Oxia Island and proceeded towards Seraglio Point, where four destroyers towing dhows were observed. The submarine touched bottom at 60 feet off Demir Kapu and, after altering course to starboard, grounded ten minutes later, on the shoals off Leander Tower. The scum on the surface was so thick that it took only a few seconds to obscure any periscope observation, which required Cochrane to dip the periscope continually below the surface to clean the lens. At 3.22 p.m., Cochrane fired a bow torpedo at the arsenal, but this ran ashore and exploded. E7 then proceeded, submerged, towards the Zeitun powder factory,[59] and at 10.30 p.m. surfaced, with only the conning tower exposed. Cochrane and the gun layer Hooper searched the horizon looking for the factory on a clear but dark night. About an hour later a train that ran behind it silhouetted the target, and so at 11.30 p.m. E7 opened fire with her deck gun, at a range of 2,000 yards. After the first round, E7's crew lost their night vision and so only twelve rounds were fired, before a small craft was observed underway inshore, bringing the engagement to a quick end.

The next day, while they were south-west of Oxia Island, considerable firing was heard coming from Constantinople, but due to a thick fog they were unable to make out the cause. Later on, a dhow loaded with charcoal was sunk, Cochrane experimenting by attempting to chop a hole in her hull to sink her. This proved unsuccessful, so a 2.5-pound charge was exploded in the aft section of the dhow, blowing the stern completely off. However, the bow had an air pocket, so it persisted in floating with the bow pointing into the air. Next, E7 rammed her twice, but she still refused to sink quickly and took her own good time to disappear. The crew, who had been taken off, were in their lifeboat and protested that they were Greek and not Turkish, so Cochrane took them in tow towards the Princes Islands. Later he discovered that they could communicate in Spanish, so they were given a supply of water and sent on their way, with Constantinople in the distance. The following day, E7 surfaced at 7 a.m. and intercepted a single-masted sailing vessel; it was much larger than usual, which suggested that she normally sailed in the Black Sea. She was sunk with a 2.5-pound charge, but not before some chickens and eggs had been confiscated.

At around 9.30 a.m., *E7* fired on a railway cutting 1 mile west of Kava Burnu, and succeeded in blocking the line to Ismid. After diving to pass Dil Burnu, *E7* proceeded on the surface up the Gulf of Ismid, finding the shipyard at Deridja, until Cochrane sighted a heavy troop train and decided to give chase on the surface at full speed; he was hoping to catch her at the section of line which had previously been blocked. About twenty minutes later, the train was seen heading back eastwards, and finally stopped in a group of trees near Yarandji station, which afforded it some cover. *E7* opened fire with her deck gun, firing twenty rounds at the target, with three ammunition cars seen to be destroyed. Later another train was shelled near Kava Burnu, with several cars being hit.

On Sunday 18 July, *E7* patrolled off Mudania and, after seeing nothing of interest inshore, moved out and intercepted a large brigantine loaded with timber. When a shot was fired across her bow, the brigantine stopped and was abandoned by her crew, who took to their lifeboat. The brigantine was described by Hallifax as a 'superior vessel' from which a number of collectables were retrieved, including a shotgun, and was photographed by Cochrane before she was set on fire. As they proceeded to Gemlik, at around 8.30 a.m., two steamers, each of several hundred tons, were sighted at the beach and, as *E7* approached on the surface, she suddenly came under rifle fire from the town, at around 1,000 yards. After getting out of rifle range, *E7* fired at the steamers, hitting one, and then fired ten rounds into the town from which the rifle fire had been coming. One of the small sheds on the beach exploded when it was hit by *E7*'s return fire.

Because of his diminishing supply of shells, Cochrane decided it was not worth shelling the Mudania railway station and he proceeded to investigate a small bay near Boz Burnu, where ten small dhows were sighted. After firing a round to silence rifle fire coming from the shore, inspection of the dhows showed them to be too small for him to worry about. The following day, two dhows were set alight off Erekli Point, and at 11.30 a.m. a steamer was sighted at anchor, near the Herachitza village. On closer inspection, Cochrane discovered that the ship was full of refugees. Not long after, at around 1 p.m., a gunboat was sighted in the vicinity, and a submerged torpedo attack was made, but, because of shallow water, *E7* got no closer than 750 yards from the target, which spotted the torpedo and managed to avoid it. Later that afternoon, two more sailing ships were sunk. Cochrane believed these had previously been observed carrying ammunition to the front under tow, and were now returning empty, under sail.

On the night of the 21st, after having sunk a sailing vessel that afternoon, *E7* dived into the entrance to the Gulf of Ismid and once again tried her hand at attacking trains. On the following morning at 7.30 a.m., she sighted a train rounding Kava Burnu and, coming to the surface, she fired three rounds which burst over the train but caused no damage – luckily, as it transpired that the train was carrying the captured crew of *AE2*.[60] Cochrane went on firing at a stone railway bridge, at a range of 3,400 yards, but only a few of the 6-pound rounds hit, causing little damage.[61]

E7 then went on to meet *E14* at 6.55 p.m., with Boyle and Stanley coming aboard *E7*, so that Cochrane could be informed of the increase in defences, including the new nets in the straits. He was also advised that all of *E7*'s wireless signals had been received, so it became clear that the submarine's problem was with receiving signals. On the next day, as on so many others before, *E7* rose from the bottom at 5.15 a.m., came to periscope depth, and then drifted along until 6.15 a.m., after ensuring that it was safe to surface. Once surfaced, the diesel engines were used until 9 a.m. to recharge her batteries, as she cruised between Erekli Point and Hora Burnu. That afternoon the deck gun was stowed, and preparations were made to leave the Sea of Marmara the next day. In the evening wireless signals were transmitted, and *E7* spent the night on the bottom of Dohan Aslan Bank.

At 4 a.m. on 24 July, *E7* set off and passed Gallipoli at 6.30 a.m., missing the chance to sink a destroyer, which passed too close to fire on. The boom north-west of Nagara Point had apparently been dragged from its position, so *E7* found plenty of room to pass between it and the shore. Cochrane then observed a line of large buoys stretching between a position 1 mile north of Maidos village and a small steamer moored in Nagara Harbour. *E7* dived to 90 feet, about 200 yards in front of the buoys, and passed beneath without any difficulties.

Chanak was observed to be empty, except for one small torpedo boat, but at 11.05 a.m., when *E7* was about a mile south-west of Kilid Bahr, she caught on a mine-mooring cable forward. This swung the boat around to port, with her bow pointing upstream; but of even greater concern was the fact that it also caused the submarine to rise. The X and Z compensating tanks were filled, and she stayed down with both motors stopped. The helm was reversed, the port motor put ahead, the starboard motor put astern, and then she quickly turned around. It was not possible to tell on which side the mooring cable had fouled, but it took another twenty minutes of further manoeuvring before control was regained. A little while later, at around noon, the same thing happened again. It took a further twenty-five minutes of twisting and turning before the mooring cable slipped and *E7* could again proceed.

Battery power was extremely low, so that only emergency lighting could be afforded; but even with the restricted use of power the submarine was in darkness by 2 p.m., except for two small lamps in the fore compartment. At 3.30 p.m., *E7* came to the surface off Eski Hissarlik, having been submerged for a total of eleven hours, and then continued to a hero's welcome at Mudros. Later, Cochrane was to receive a Distinguished Service Order for the patrol, and Lieutenant Twymanthe and Petty Officer Wedsdale, who assisted while Hallifax was incapacitated, each received the Distinguished Service Cross.

E14's third war patrol – 21 July to 12 August

In the early morning of 21 July at 12.35 a.m., in the company of *Grampus*, *E14* left Tenedos under the command of Lieutenant Commander Boyle. At 3.36 a.m., while she was proceeding up the Dardanelles and still on the surface, a searchlight, which Boyle assumed must have been mounted on another ship, forced *E14* to dive, well short of Suan Dere. Immediately after diving, about a mile south of Kilid Bahr, the submarine fouled something on the forward hydroplane, which momentarily jammed it and threw her off course. A little time later there was a scraping along the sides, but she was quickly clear of the obstruction. Later it was discovered that the forward guard wire had been almost severed. (The incident occurred at about the same place where *E14* had been caught on a previous mission.) By 5.15 a.m. *E14* had passed Chanak, and, while nearing Nagara, Boyle saw a net, indicated by a line of lighters halfway across the channel, and a small steamship in the vicinity. With the sun at a low angle it was not possible for Boyle to see much, so submerging to 80 feet, *E14* passed through the gate in the net, reaching the town of Gallipoli at 10.40 a.m. At 12.20 p.m. *E14* surfaced and stayed to the west of the Island of Marmara until wireless contact had been established; then she proceeded to the east.

In the early hours of the following day, after avoiding a torpedo boat, *E14* dived to investigate a two-funnelled target in Rodosto Bay, which proved to be a hospital ship. Boyle then sighted *E7* at 5.10 p.m. and got under the cover of land, to be free from the prevailing wind and allow the two submarines to come alongside and make fast. Later that evening they continued on their separate ways, and on 23 July *E14* moved around to Mudania Bay, observing small sailing vessels and the ship that had previously been sunk by *E7*, with only her superstructure above water.

The next day Boyle sighted a hospital ship off Silivri, en route to Constantinople, followed by another hospital ship soon afterwards.[62] *E14* proceeded towards Stefano Point, where at 4.55 p.m. she intercepted and sank a sailing dhow loaded with fruit. Another sailing boat was fired at and hit with two shots before she ran ashore. At sunset, a motorboat was sighted and also fired at, but she was out of range and managed to escape due to her higher speed. Over the next two days numerous small targets were intercepted, as the Turkish authorities limited the movement of major shipping during daylight hours. A brigantine loaded with charcoal was sunk north of Boz Burnu, and later on a dozen small sailing vessels of the size of dinghies, and loaded with dried plums, were intercepted and forced to turn back towards the Mudania Bay. Three empty two-masted topsail dhows were sunk off Rodosto Bay, followed later by two smaller dhows – one loaded with lime and the other with wine, barrels of fish, oil and charcoal.

At 6.30 p.m. on the 26th, 4 miles north-east of Khairsiz Ada and heading to the south-west, *E14* was surprised by a destroyer (Samsun class), which, due to the low sun and the surrounding landscape, had approached undetected. While *E14* was submerging to mount an attack, the destroyer fired at her but narrowly missed. Boyle, however, had time to note that she was towing what looked like a submarine. Unable to get into firing position, Boyle surfaced after they had passed but he was unable to pursue because of their greater speed and the closing darkness. He immediately proceeded to the west and tried unsuccessfully to get off a wireless communication reporting the possible presence of an enemy submarine in the Sea of Marmara.

The following morning Boyle moved to Karabuga Bay, where he observed a steamer by the pier. The water was too shallow to fire a torpedo, so Boyle surfaced but was immediately fired on by two small shore guns. He therefore decided to continue towards Sar Kioi, where again he located a small steamer[63] anchored near the pier, and this time the water was deep enough for a torpedo attack. Proceeding on the surface, Boyle observed the crew abandoning ship, as they anticipated what was about to happen. The starboard torpedo was fired at 4.20 a.m. and, on hitting the ship, caused a bigger than expected explosion, which suggested that the ship may have been carrying ammunition; this would have explained the hasty departure of the crew. Later that evening, after having been fired upon by a small gunboat, *E14* tried to make wireless contact but once again was unsuccessful. The following day, after the avoidance of a close incident with a torpedo boat, some house-keeping chores were undertaken, with the replacement of two exhaust valves. *E14* cruised south from Rodosto, passed two hospital ships, and once again observed various small sailing vessels beached along the shoreline. The submarine came under occasional gun and rifle fire from the shore and sometimes she returned fire, but caused little damage.

At 5.55 a.m. on 29 July, *E14* set fire to a sailing vessel, which was carrying olive oil and thousands of eggs. The crew was taken aboard and, with their lifeboat in tow, carried towards Panderma, while the ship's captain explained that there were plenty of guns and mines in the area. Later on a topsail schooner, which only carried two horses, was blown up north of Mara Burnu.

The following day these events were repeated, with the sinking of a sailing vessel loaded with olive oil, north-west of Kalolimno. The crew was taken to Erekli, and this time the captain of the sunken vessel knew a few words of English. He informed Boyle that Constantinople was short of food and that no flour could be acquired from Romania. There were no men in the city, as all men between 16 and 60 years of age had been called up for active service, although old men could be excused on the payment of a fine of £60. Both Constantinople and Artaki were full of wounded, and hospital ships continued to bring more each day. All new combat troops were sent to Rodosto by rail (there was no rail at Rodosto and he probably meant Usun Kopri) and then marched to Gallipoli, a journey of six hours by train followed by three days of marching. The bombardment in February had resulted in considerable damage, and people were surprised that the British navy had not proceeded through the straits. Most importantly, the captain went on to say, that no steamers were now making the passage across the Sea of Marmara; rather, sailing vessels were moving at night under tow by destroyers.[64] He also confirmed that there was one German submarine at Constantinople, slightly smaller than *E14*, which carried a crew of thirty-three men.

At 4 p.m. that afternoon, after they passed another fully laden hospital ship, an empty sailing vessel was burnt; but it had no life raft, so Boyle spent the remainder of the day trying to find a boat to get rid of the captured crew. It was not until 7.30 p.m. that a small sailing vessel was found and the crew disembarked. The next day *E14* made her way to the Gulf of Ismid, where many sailing craft were sighted. One of the larger ones, full of refugees, was stopped 3 miles south-west of Yelken Kaya Burnu and made to wait while Boyle blew up two other large vessels, each carrying about 300 sheep, and transferred their crews on to the first ship. Three more sailing ships were sunk, the crew being transferred on each occasion on to the remaining vessel. At one stage a tug did try to chase Boyle's submarine, but, once she returned fire, the tug moved quickly out of range. On the following day, *E14* proceeded around Marmara Island to the south, inspecting all the likely anchorages, but saw nothing of interest. That evening, wireless contact was again attempted without success. Boyle was concerned that the previous deep-diving might have resulted in water affecting the contact between the aerial and the wireless at the connection point on the deck. He therefore experimented by running the feeder down the conning tower directly to the wireless, and then had no difficulty in making radio contact just before midnight.

On 2 August, another hospital ship heading west was sighted, and later on a small steamer was discovered alongside a pier at Karabuga Bay, but the water was too shallow to fire a torpedo and the submarine was quickly fired upon by a 6-pound gun from on shore. That afternoon, a sailing boat full of lime was sunk off Marmara Island; this was followed by the sighting of two more hospital ships heading east. The next day Boyle proceeded to the Mudania Bay and sank one empty sailing vessel. On the way into the bay, *E14* had been fired at by shore guns from Kalolimno Island, so he decided to fire at them on the way out. However, fire from several 3-inch guns off Milos Point was not only able to outrange his gun, but proved to be uncomfortably accurate, and Boyle was forced to beat a hasty retreat, leaving the fall of shot in his wake. At 6.30 p.m., a large empty sailing dhow was set on fire and two very old men who could not fit into the small lifeboat were taken aboard the submarine and set ashore near Kurshunhi that evening.

Things should have improved on 4 August, when, at 8.30 a.m. in Silivri Bay, Boyle attacked a convoy of two steamships escorted by a destroyer.[65] He fired only one torpedo at the larger empty steamship, but he missed. After passing another hospital ship that morning, *E14* crossed to the western side of the Sea of Marmara, to send a wireless message. She was forced to submerge at 8.45 p.m., after having been followed for the previous two hours by a destroyer. Boyle assumed that he had been observed from the shore when transmitting from the same location on 1 August. At that time, overcharged aerial arching illuminated his position for all to see. The following day a small one-funnel gunboat was observed, and Boyle made several attempts to attack but failed; at 7.30 p.m., off Herachitza, a torpedo was fired in failing light but, again, missed the target.[66] A gunboat was later seen to be firing, and Boyle suspected correctly that it was engaging *E11*, which was in the area for a rendezvous with *E14*.

On 6 August, after chasing what turned out to be yet another hospital ship, *E14* met with *E11* at 2 p.m. and received new orders. Half an hour later, the torpedo cruiser *Peyk-i Sevket* was sighted and both submarines gave chase. Although *E14* was unable to close on her, she was successfully torpedoed and sunk by *E11*. The submarines then met again, and at 8 p.m. they moved to the west, to take up positions to shell Turkish troops on the coastal road between Bulair and the town of Gallipoli. From 3.30 a.m. next morning, Boyle patrolled about a mile from shore, surfacing a number of times when he thought he had sighted troops on shore, but it was not until 1.30 p.m. that afternoon that he finally saw dust coming from the nearby road. Once surfaced, *E14* began shelling troops as they marched towards Gallipoli. *E11* had also been firing on troops as they passed her location, which was to the north-east of Dohan Aslan. *E11* then moved down to *E14*'s billet and joined in the bombardment for the next hour.[67] As Boyle recorded:

I got off 40 rounds and about six of them burst on the road in the middle of the troops and one in a large building. I had to put full range on the sights and aim at the top of the hill so my firing was not very accurate. E11's 12. Pdr. did much more damage and scattered the troops several times. I think the troops marching along by that road must have been delayed and a good number of them were killed.[68]

The troops under fire from the submarines were no doubt being moved up because of the offensive undertaken by the Allies the day before (see Chapter 9). Later that afternoon, at 5.15 p.m., a torpedo was fired at a small one-funnelled gunboat, but it missed, passing under the stern. Boyle's luck improved on the following morning, 8 August. After remaining in the area of Dohan Aslan Bank for most of the day, in the hope of sighting further troop movements, he saw a steamer at 2.30 p.m., between Dohan Aslan and Injeh Burnu.[69] He fired a torpedo which hit amidships, but the ship managed to beach herself. E11 then returned, having just sunk the *Barbaros Hayreddin*, and, together with E14, shelled the stranded ship, setting her on fire.[70] At around 4 p.m. that day, a small gunboat arrived at a position close to the place where the submarines had been shelling the troops, and patrolled the area to keep them at bay.

On 10 August, the two submarines met in the afternoon, and E14 trans-ferred two torpedoes[71] and a stop valve to E11 and took on board all her empty cartridge cases, before heading back to base. Later on, Boyle took his submarine into Silivri, to try to torpedo a ship of about 1,500 tons, but was thwarted when the bow of the submarine hit bottom at a range too far out to fire. This was not the first occasion on the patrol where the maps of the day proved to be faulty in their estimate of the depth of the bottom. At Injeh Burnu, the submarine hit bottom at 4 fathoms, when the chart showed a depth of 9 fathoms. That evening, Boyle also used Nasmith's technique of floating between the density layers of fresh and salt water at 66 feet. The next day preparations were made to return to base, with the 6-pound gun dismantled and stowed for the return journey. Another hospital ship was sighted carrying wounded, and later that afternoon, at 5.50 p.m., wireless communication with *Jed* was initiated, while yet another hospital ship was sighted.

At 4 a.m. on the following morning, 12 August, further wireless contact was made with *Jed* and, just before the dive for the return journey at 5.20 a.m., an Allied seaplane was sighted flying eastward over the Bulair Lines. Boyle decided to make the return journey along the same track as the one he had taken coming up the straits, in the hope of passing through the same gate in the net off Nagara. However, this time he was not so lucky and hit the net, the submarine being forced up from 80 feet to 45 feet in three seconds and luckily thrown only 15 degrees off course. As Boyle reported:

There was a tremendous noise, scraping, banging, tearing and rumbling and it sounded as if there were two distinct obstructions, as the noise nearly ceased and then came on again and we were apparently checked twice. It took about twenty seconds to get through.[72]

While rounding Kilid Bahr at 11 a.m., *E14* was fired upon by coastal batteries, and then a torpedo fired at her from Chanak and broke surface a few yards astern. The submarine had another lucky escape when she scraped past a mine, a mile south-west of Chanak. Boyle was later to observe that some twin electrical wire had wound around his submarine propellers and that the jumping wires, the top of the periscope standards, the bow and various other parts of the boat were scraped and scored by wires. *E14* successfully passed through the Dardanelles and surfaced off Sedd el Bahr at 1.45 p.m. Boyle and his third officer had been unwell for the first week of the patrol, and his First Lieutenant, E. G. Stanley, had been sick with gastroenteritis for the remainder of the journey, which greatly impeded the submarine's activities. On the completion of this mission, the submarine had travelled 12,000 miles without any major overhaul, for which Boyle gave credit to his engine room artificer, James Hollier Hague; but it was also another testimonial to the overall reliability and versatility of the E class submarines.

9

The August Land Offensive

One last gamble

As mentioned earlier, the commanding officer of the Australian troops Lieutenant General Birdwood formulated in May a plan to take Chunuk Bair at the north-eastern end of the Sari Bair range by a night attack. His proposal rested on the discovery by a patrol of New Zealanders in mid-May that, in spite of the difficult terrain, it was possible to reach the highest point of this objective. Furthermore, it appeared that there were very few Turkish troops in the area and none at Chunuk Bair itself. Although the subsequent retaking, on 29 May, of an outpost (No. 3) by the Turks did pose some problems, the plan had been endorsed by Hamilton. Hamilton also intended now that his next great assault should be made in August, in combination with the attack on Chunuk Bair, after the arrival of the additional divisions promised by Kitchener.

Birdwood's plan called for the attacking troops to move along the reconnoitered route of Table Top and Rhododendron Ridges, which had been shown to be both lightly defended and physically negotiable. This part of the operation was to be called the Right Assaulting Column, and was to be carried out by a New Zealand infantry brigade and the troops of an Indian Mountain battery, under the command of Brigadier General Johnston. In the meantime, No. 3 Outpost was to be subjected to evening bombardment by a destroyer, in the hope that the New Zealanders would take the post by surprise while the enemy was still under cover.

With Hamilton able to provide an additional number of troops (13 Division under the command of Major General Shaw, to be distributed amongst the various forces), Birdwood now expanded the operation to include a second force of 5,000 men, or Left Assaulting Column, which would march 2 miles north along the beach and then head inland to the north of the Right Assaulting Column. At this point, the Left Assaulting Column would separate into two groups, with one, the 29th Indian Brigade, under the command of Major General Cox, climbing the steep ravine at Aghyl Dere to capture Hill Q, on the north-eastern flank of Chunuk Bair. The other group, consisting of 4th Australian Infantry Brigade, under the command of Brigadier General Monash, would move along the Abdul Rahman Spur, to take Hill 971 (Koja Chemen Tepe), still further to the north-east. Neither of these routes had been properly reconnoitred.

Special covering forces were to move out ahead of the right and left assaulting columns, firstly, to clear Turkish observation posts from the intended path of the advance and, secondly, to offer flank support as the attacking force moved forward. The right covering force of 2,000 men was primarily made up of the New Zealand Mounted Rifle Brigade, under the command of Brigadier General Russell, while the left cover force, under Brigadier General Travers, was made up of the Headquarters 14 Brigade. Additionally, Major General Walker was to lead the Australian 1 Division in a diversion against the heavily entrenched Turkish positions at Lone Pine in an attempt to draw the Turkish reinforcements away from the right flank of the Right Assaulting Column. General Walker argued that this would be a futile and wasteful effort, but ultimately he lost his argument.

Hamilton now considered the best way to deploy the other two newly arrived divisions: 10, under the command of Lieutenant General Mahon, and 11, under the command of Major General Hammersley. One approach which was considered was to attack the heavily defended Gaba Tepe, while the other, which was the one eventually chosen, was to land troops at Suvla Plain, to the north of Anzac Cove. This was a large amphitheatre surrounded on three sides by hills: Kiretch Tepe to the north on the left flank, Kavak Tepe and Tekke Tepe ahead and the Sari Bair Range to the south or right flank. It had a desolate salt lake in the middle and was thought to be lightly defended. Hamilton discussed the landing operations with de Robeck and Keyes, who recommended a landing to the south of Nibrunesi Point (the southern tip of the amphitheatre). They wanted to use the newly arrived, 500-man capacity, 4.5-foot draft, bullet-proof motor-lighters, under the command of Commander Unwin. This, they felt, would remove a major concern over the landing of the men, while the newly arrived 1-mile-long torpedo nets could be used to protect the ships from submarine attack. Additionally, a 300-foot pontoon was constructed, to be towed across to the beach (an early version of the Mulberry Harbours of D-Day), and four 500-ton water-lighters were to be delivered by the steamer *Krini*, which held a further 200 tons of water. Once again, great reliance was placed on the fact that natural water sources could be found, once one was ashore.

The two new divisions were formed into the IX Corps, and command was ultimately given to Lieutenant General Stopford, aged 61, who, although initially enthusiastic, was semi-infirm and had little combat experience. He was, effectively, the last choice from among a small group of generals who were senior to Lieutenant General Mahon. Kitchener insisted that Mahon should retain his position, and Stopford was the only one whom both Hamilton and Kitchener could agree on. Stopford was initially given command of VIII Army Corps and arrived at Imbros on 11 July, to gain some combat experience before taking over the IX Corps.

The plan called for the Suvla landings ultimately to support Birdwood's offensive from Anzac Cove to the south. However, Stopford, and in particular his chief-of-staff, Brigadier General Reed, VC (who was obsessed with having artillery support before any move forward could be made), were not happy with Hamilton's plans. So Hamilton once again weakened in the face of complaining commanders, and on 29 July new orders were issued, which made the primary objective the securing of Suvla Bay. Once this had been achieved, the next step was to give assistance to the Anzacs in their attack against Hill 971, but with no specific timetable. So the plan of attack for 6 August was aimed at taking the high ground at Lala Baba and then to the east of the salt lake at W Hills (these were spurs off Teke Tepe) and between Chocolate Hill and Green Hill (to protect the left flank of the Left Assaulting Column coming from Anzac). However, by dawn the plan came to be one of taking Suvla Plain itself, together with some of the nearby hills, which held little strategic value. Hamilton failed to see and rectify the change in Stopford's understanding of his orders. Stopford had no intention of moving forward as quickly as possible to take the high ground surrounding Suvla Bay.

The offensive ultimately called for the attack by 100,000 men at three locations: Suvla, Anzac Cove and, as a diversion only, along the Helles front. A diversionary landing of 300 irregulars on the north shore of the Gulf of Saros, to attack the Turkish railways, turned out to be a dismal failure. Secret landings of reinforcements were also to take place on the three nights before the attack, with an additional 20,000 men to be landed at Anzac Cove on an already cramped area, while at Suvla 30,000 were to be landed on 6 August. The logistics were once again as complex as for the April landings. Artillery support was inadequate and, at Suvla, almost non-existent, while the navy's firepower was limited. Hamilton's staff was not only overwhelmed by the complexity of the operation, but also obsessed with maintaining a high level of secrecy. Given the tight time frame of no more than two months, these factors of speed, complexity and secrecy compounded to produce inevitable mistakes and misunderstandings. The high level of secrecy meant that very few knew what the military objectives were, and those who did find out, did so only just before the landings.

Notwithstanding the importance attached to secrecy, von Sanders had begun to hear rumours in early July, including a report from Germany on 22 July, which suggested that a major attack could be expected in August. At the time, the only area he considered unlikely for a landing was Suvla, where he only stationed three weak battalions of about 1,800 men, with no barbed wire or machine-guns, thus offering the Allies a great opportunity for success.

The Helles diversion

The operation commenced at 2.20 p.m. on 6 August, with the bombardment of the Turkish lines north of Krithia Nullah. The navy also provided artillery support in the form of one cruiser, five monitors and five destroyers. The Turkish forces responded with an artillery barrage of their own against 29 Division, which was to make the attack. At 3.50 p.m., the troops scrambled over the parapets, attacking one of the strongest enemy positions along the whole Helles front. The attackers suffered, and continued to suffer, heavy casualties and, with a breakdown of communications, the assault became very confused, with much of the fighting centred on the Vineyard area.

The following day renewed attacks were made, but an entrenched force of over 40,000 opposed the Allied force of 39,000, and no significant gains were made. Of greater importance was the hope that the attack would draw in Turkish reserves and thus improve the chances at Anzac and Suvla. However, the Turks had already become aware of the assemblage of new troops, ships and transports at the nearby islands of Imbros and Tenedos. Furthermore, they had already started to strengthen their positions around Anzac and, on 7 August, von Sanders ordered the reserve division at Helles to be sent north. Indeed, after the first two hours of the battle on 6 August, von Sanders began sending troops, under the command of Kannengiesser, north from Gaba Tepe, towards where he had decided that the likely centre of the Allied attack would be.[1] The sacrifice of so many men had once again been in vain.

The Lone Pine diversion

At Lone Pine, General Walker and his staff showed some flair in their approach to what was seen as a very difficult assault. For three days prior to 6 August, a steady barrage of artillery was used to destroy the barbed wire defences in front of the Turkish trenches. Tunnels were dug across no-man's-land towards the enemy, so that the first assault wave could unexpectedly emerge from these tunnels using the element of surprise, and also the shorter distance to be covered, to reduce exposure to enemy fire considerably. A tunnel was also dug right up to the trenches, which, immediately after the attack was begun, was converted into a trench, so that reinforcements could travel across no-man's-land, again protected from enemy cross fire.

At 5.30 p.m., the Australians emerged from the tunnels and took the Turkish forces by complete surprise. However, they were unaware that the Turks had covered their trenches with wooden logs, which greatly increased the difficulty of gaining access to the labyrinth of trenches below. Bitter fighting now took place, much of it hand to hand, in a very confined space, with no quarter given by either side. The Australians initially gained the upper hand and had almost succeeded in breaking through, but the arrival of the Turkish 1st Battalion of the 57th Regiment proved to be enough to allow the Turks to hold the last line in their defences. An Arab battalion of the 72nd Regiment had only that day relieved this particular battalion, which meant that they were not only still in the vicinity, but also familiar with the trench system under attack.

Had the Australians been equipped with more bombs (hand grenades), and had the supporting troops been able to get to the weak points more quickly, the attack would probably have succeeded. By nightfall, the Australians had taken the whole Turkish front line and two thirds of the trenches, and resisted the mounting counter-attacks by the Turks. For the next two days fighting continued at Lone Pine, during which time 1,700 Australians and 5,000 Turks died. In three days of fighting, a total of seven Victoria Crosses were awarded.

The Anzac offensive

At 9 p.m. on the 6th, the destroyer *Colne* switched on its searchlight and shelled the No 3 Outpost near Anzac Cove for exactly ten minutes, followed by a ten minute break. Then another ten minutes of shelling would normally follow – a pattern established over the previous three weeks, either by *Colne* or *Chelmer*. During the bombardment, the Right Cover Force of 2,000 New Zealanders crept up to the trenches and, once it stopped, overwhelmed the startled defenders, still waiting under shelter for the regular bombardment to recommence. By 10 p.m., the outpost had been secured by the attacking force. By 1.30 a.m. on 7 August, two hours behind schedule, the Left and Right Cover Forces had overcome nearly all resistance and captured the enemy's outposts in the foothills.

Although somewhat delayed, the assaulting columns were now able to begin their advance on the primary objectives. The Right Assaulting Column advanced rapidly up onto Rhododendron Ridge, although they were delayed for an hour by having to deal with a Turkish picket which had been missed in the earlier sweep by the covering forces. As dawn was breaking they were within 1,000 yards of the deserted summit of Chunuk Bair, but, against strict orders not to wait for other units, the commanding officer, Brigadier Johnston, stopped the column's advance at the Apex, to wait for the Canterbury Battalion, which had lost its way.

The Left Assaulting Group, which was to travel further north before heading inland, also left late, having had difficulty in assembling the men. The column soon encountered sniper fire, which, for troops without previous experience of night fighting, caused some degree of panic and disorganization. The column had difficulty in locating its position at night, and by daybreak was in disarray, still in the foothills and nowhere near its objectives, which were to have been taken four hours earlier. However, the Gurkhas had managed, under their own initiative, to get within 1,000 yards of the summit of Hill Q, where they, too, were ordered to stop their advance and to take up a covering position.

At around 6 a.m., in one of those quirks of fate – as the embellished stories surrounding events at that time would have it – Colonel Kannengiesser, who, as mentioned earlier, had been sent north by von Sanders, walked ahead of his men to the top of the deserted Chunuk Bair and observed the events unfolding at Suvla. At the same time he noticed New Zealand troops advancing to the top of the hill. Unable initially to persuade his own troops to engage the enemy, he personally (as it seems) fired on the New Zealanders, who went to ground and stopped their advance, although they outnumbered the Turks at that time by ten to one.

Kannengiesser paints a more modest picture of the sequence of events. He and his staff were reconnoitring the ridge, while he dictated his reports and orders, which were being translated into Turkish. Suddenly the enemy appeared in single file 500 yards away, looking very tired. Kannengiesser sent an order to his twenty men covering platoon to open fire:

'We can only commence to fire when we receive the order of our battalion commander.'

This was too much for me altogether. I ran to the spot and threw myself among the troops who were lying in a small trench. What I said I cannot recollect, but they began to open fire and almost immediately the English laid down without answering our fire or apparently moving in any other way. They gave me the impression that they were glad to be spared further climbing.

Now I received unexpected reinforcement. From the direction of Dustepe I suddenly saw a Turkish column coming which was about to descend rearwards in the deep valley. It was two companies of the Infantry Regiment 72. My orders to halt immediately and come under my command had to be urgently repeated before they obeyed. At the same time the Commander of the 1st Battalion of Infantry Regiment 14 reached the Kodjadschemendagh, and I took him with his companies under my orders.

Thus I was slowly able to establish a small firing front which I grouped in two wings, as the commanders of the Infantry Regiments 25 and 64 reported to me that their battalions would shortly be arriving. I had been successful in keeping this exceptionally important height in our hands and bringing the forward progress of the enemy to a halt.[2]

This was a critical failure, as the capture of Chunuk Bair was a key part of the next phase of the offensive, which started with an artillery barrage at 4 a.m. on the morning of the 7th, at the head of Monash Valley. At 4.30 a.m. Australian and British forces attacked the Turkish defences at The Nek, Pope's and Quinn's, located along a ridge at the end of Monash Valley, between Lone Pine and Chunuk Bair. The plan called for a simultaneous attack from the captured Chunuk Bair to help suppress the deadly machine-gun fire and, although now this of course would not occur, Birdwood refused to call off the attack. The supporting artillery and naval barrage had stopped seven minutes earlier than scheduled, to reduce the risk of hitting their own men, and to allow for time to switch to other targets. So, fearing that another bombardment might take place, the troops waited, giving the enemy crucial time to regroup and prepare for the attack. As a result, within the space of fifteen minutes, the Australian Light Horse lost nearly 300 men lying dead at The Nek, in an area smaller in size than several tennis courts. The attacks also failed at Quinn's and at Pope's, where the fighting was over by 6 a.m., and the total casualties numbered 650 men.

Another attempt by the New Zealanders to take Chunuk Bair was made at 10.30 a.m., but was repulsed by the growing number of Turkish reinforcements, which were also suffering mounting casualties. It was not until the morning of 8 August that a new offensive was planned. The Gurkhas, still in position on the side of Hill Q, were ordered to attack the summit at dawn, and succeeded in getting within 100 yards of the crest. At Chunuk Bair, the Wellington Battalion attacked at dawn and captured the summit, after the Turkish defenders had been driven off by naval fire. The New Zealanders then occupied the shallow trenches they had captured, but were under constant fire on both flanks from Hill Q and Battleship Hill. Another attempt to take Hill 971 and Hill Q failed, and by 2 p.m. any plans for further attacks that day were abandoned. Eventually, the New Zealanders were driven off the summit of Chunuk Bair, and joined British forces on the slope of the hill. They were now also being fired on from the summit, and had to repel Turkish advances coming along the crest line. The 450 Gurkhas, together with some British troops under the command of Major Allanson, who were located on a crest halfway between Hill Q and Chunuk Bair, were also under constant fire throughout the day.

A quick plan was formulated to recover from a situation that was increasingly falling short of its objectives. Aircraft reported Turkish reinforcements marching from Helles and Bulair; while *E11* reported firing on troops advancing along the shoreline. The attempt to capture Hill 971 was abandoned and a heavy naval bombardment was planned for the morning of 9 August, followed by an attack on Chunuk Bair, along Rhododendron Ridge, by fresh British troops of the 38th Brigade under Brigadier General Baldwin. Baldwin met up with Johnston at The Apex, where Johnston advised him to take the low path and attack along a small plateau known as The Farm. This was, arguably, one of the greatest mistakes of the campaign. During the night march to get to their starting point, the troops became hopelessly lost, the first of them only arriving at The Farm at 6 a.m., and were thus unable to attack when the bombardment finished at 5.20 a.m.

The British and Gurkhas under Allanson had, during the previous night, managed to advance a further 50 yards towards the summit of Hill Q, but in the morning they were pinned down as they came under fire by Turkish artillery. With no bombs of their own and being under constant sniper fire, they remained in their trenches. During the night, the men fired on the Turks, who were illuminated by navy searchlights, so that sleep was impossible. On the morning of 9 August, although tired and with little food and water, the men were again ordered to attack, following a naval bombardment. When the bombardment ceased at 5.20 a.m. (five minutes late, by Allanson's watch), the men charged and fought hand to hand, until they finally overcame the defenders, chasing them down the reverse side of the hill, only to come under friendly artillery fire. (Given that the shells hit the reverse slope, the fire most likely came from shore artillery and was not naval fire, as Allanson was to claim later.) Without support from the right flank by Baldwin's men, who, due to the strong resistance of the Turkish defenders, had dug in at The Farm, Allanson's position was not defensible and he was forced to retire to his original position near Chunuk Bair. The northern flank came under attack by Turkish forces during 9 August, as all available Turkish reinforcements were sent to the area. On the night of 9 August, the exhausted New Zealand troops were relieved by British troops; since 6 August they had sustained losses of 1,871 men killed out of an original force of 4,500.[3] The British and colonial troops had now fought for three days with little rest, as had the Turks, all suffering significant casualties.

Kemal at this point took a major gamble, and decided to mount a surprise frontal attack with his remaining six battalions of reserves, located on the reverse slope of Chunuk Bair. On the morning of 10 August, Turkish troops led by Kemal swept up and over Chunuk Bair, without any prior artillery barrage to warn the defenders at The Pinnacle to the west of Chunuk Bair, and quickly took the British positions. The New Zealand machine-guns at The Apex further to the west, as well as naval guns, fired at the charging troops as they headed north-west towards The Farm. Here a major battle developed, but by 10 a.m. Baldwin and most of his officers had been killed, and the remaining defenders were fleeing into the nearby ravines, where many of them died. At The Farm itself, over 1,000 were dead or dying. What remained of the Turkish troops retreated back to the crest of Chunuk Bair and The Pinnacle. The Gurkhas were recalled from their now more isolated position near Chunuk Bair, the loss of which meant that the August offensive for the heights of Anzac had finally failed.

The Suvla landing

At Suvla, shortly after 9.30 p.m. on 6 August, British Force 'B' consisting of 32 and 33 Brigades and of 11 Division headquarters landed south of Nibrunesi Point, and within half an hour four battalions were ashore with only one casualty. The 7,000 troops were transported to the area by seven destroyers, *Grasshopper, Foxhound, Racoon, Basilisk, Arno, Scourge* and *Mosquito*, each carrying 500 troops and also towing an armoured lighter carrying a further 500 troops. The destroyers came within 50 yards of the shore in line abreast; the lighters then deposited their men on shore before quickly returning to disembark the men off the destroyers. The remaining 3,000 troops followed in later, on board *Endymion, Theseus*, the sloop *Aster* and six trawlers. Naval support for the operation consisted of four 14-inch gun monitors and four cruisers of the Endymion class carrying 9.2-inch and 6-inch guns. All of these ships were considered to be 'proofed' against submarine attack, and by 9 a.m. on 7 August half of Suvla Bay had been netted. Additional support included the *Bacchante*, the *Talbot*, ten small monitors with 9.2-inch guns, two kite balloon ships, *Hector* and *Manica*, and a number of destroyers.

Opposing the landing were three battalions of Turkish troops without machine-guns, a little barbed wire and a few pieces of artillery, all under the command of Major Willmer. His orders were to prevent a landing or an extension of the existing fronts, but there was little he could do except position his men into several strong points along the summits of hills to the east of the salt lake at Suvla and wait.

The first objective, Lala Baba on the coast, was quickly taken, but only after some casualties. The impact of having been on their feet for 17 hours, combined with the after-effect of cholera shots the night before, took its toll on the attacking troops and greatly reduced their effectiveness. The lack of training in night attacks then started to play a part in increasing the state of confusion. Further difficulty arose in reporting positions; this was due to darkness and the landing of some forces south of their intended position. The moonlight was also of more assistance to the defenders than to the attackers, which resulted in high casualty rates amongst British officers and Non-Commissioned Officers (NCOs): these were wearing white armlets which made them more visible and therefore obvious targets. On the shore, as more troops arrived, the state of confusion increased, and Hill 10 was not even located by the arriving force, let alone captured. One battalion of the Manchesters did advance 2 miles inland, and by 3 a.m. had climbed the Kiretch Tepe Ridge.

Force 'A', consisting of three destroyers *Bulldog*, *Beagle* and *Grampus*, plus three lighters, landed 3,000 men of 34 Brigade to the north of Nibrunesi Point,[4] but due to the existence of reefs, of which the attacking force was not fully aware, the men were not landed till 1 a.m. on the following morning, about 1,000 yards south of their intended position. The men were dropped into water when their lighters could go no further, because of shallow water 100 yards from the shore. The original plan had called for all troops to be landed south of Nibrunesi Point, to avoid the problem the navy now encountered; but, once again, Hamilton had agreed to the change in deference to Stopford.

Map 9.1   The Suvla landings

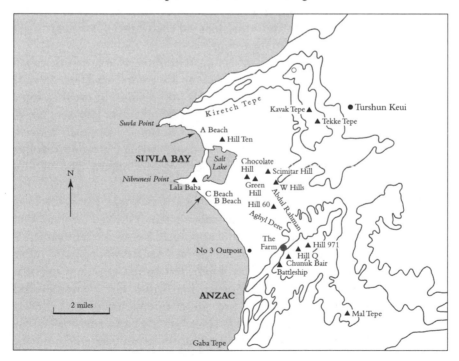

By daybreak on 7 August, the British had not advanced beyond the beaches. Stopford and his chief of staff had remained on board the small sloop *Jonquil*, standing off-shore from Suvla. The lack of direction became evident as the force, 20,000 strong after the later landing of 10 Division, yet disorganized, remained in place under constant sniper fire from the Turks. The enemy positions could have been quickly overrun, but the lack of communication between Stopford's General Headquarters staff, administrative staff and field commanders prevented any such victory. As was later observed by von Sanders:

We all had the feeling that after the various landings beginning August 6th, the British leaders had delayed too long on the shore instead of advancing from the landing place at any cost.[5]

As the day wore on, a greater threat appeared: with the temperature rising, the supply of drinking water was being rapidly exhausted. Although water-supply problems had been anticipated and receptacles provided for 100,000 gallons, together with mules to carry water to the forward lines, distribution had not been planned well. In supporting the landing, water needed to be available quickly, so that a rapid advance was not delayed. In the event, water-lighters had been left at Imbros; the store ship *Prah*, with equipment for digging wells, remained moored off-shore for a week; no artillery was landed on 7 August; and the navy and army blamed each other for failing to get adequate water and supplies to the troops.[6]

At 3.40 a.m. on 7 August, the Turkish 7 Division received orders to march from Bulair, and at 8.30 a.m. the 12th Division also commenced their 30-mile march from Bulair along two roads heading south to Suvla. By evening, some of the nearby British objectives at Chocolate Hill and Green Hill were taken, but 3 battalions of Turkish reinforcements from Bulair had finally arrived. Von Sanders also arrived at Suvla that day and, on hearing that reinforcements were arriving, ordered an attack for the morning of 8 August. The night of 7 August was particularly quiet.

The following morning, the Turkish attack didn't take place: the local commander Feizi Bey claimed that the troops had not arrived on time. Von Sanders immediately dismissed him and appointed Kemal as commander. It was Hamilton's lack of this form of determined leadership, revealed in his allowing incompetent generals such as Stopford to continue in command, that lost the day. During the day of 8 August, the British forces accomplished little, lethargy and confusion still prevailing among troops and officers on the beach. Stopford sent a message to Hamilton at 11 a.m. advising that the beaches had been taken, but that it was time to consolidate and await the arrival of supplies and artillery before any serious advance could be undertaken. The use of artillery before any advance could be made was Stopford's primary reason for delaying any major assault or any assault against an entrenched position. However, Hamilton was aware (although he failed to impress this upon Stopford) that in landing on a hostile shore that order had to be reversed: troops should advance and gain the high ground to cover the landing and to provide artillery positions for the main thrust.

The very existence of the force, its water supply, its facilities for munitions and supplies, its power to reinforce, must absolutely depend on the infantry being able instantly to make good sufficient ground without the aid of the artillery other than can be supplied for the purpose by *floating* batteries.[7]

On 8 August, having received little news, Hamilton sent his general staff officer, Colonel Aspinall, to review the situation at Suvla. Lieutenant Colonel Hankey, who was then on a visit to Gallipoli to assess the situation and report to Cabinet, also accompanied him. Aspinall discovered the troops on the beaches enjoying themselves, and assumed initially that the hills to the east must have been taken, as there was no enemy fire, and that little was going on. He and Hankey were horrified to find that the front line was a two-minute walk from the beach; they hurried to Stopford to suggest that Hamilton would not be pleased by this turn of events. Stopford now planned for an immediate advance; but, on hearing that plans had been made for an attack on the hills the following morning, he dropped the idea.

Meanwhile Hamilton's 11 a.m. departure from Imbros was delayed through a fault on his destroyer *Arno*, and he only arrived at Suvla at 6 p.m., after a one-hour sea journey on board the yacht *Triad*. Out of character and no doubt frustrated at a great opportunity being lost, Hamilton overruled Stopford, went ashore and gave orders for Tekke Tepe to be taken that night. What neither Hamilton nor his regimental commanders knew was that a patrol had climbed half the way up to Tekke Tepe and found it deserted, except for a few sentries. Two battalions of 32 Brigade had advanced on their own initiative, and one of them (6 Yorkshire), was holding Scimitar Hill to the north-east of Chocolate and Green Hills. However, they were now called back to the main force; thus more valuable time and positional advantage were being lost. The Turks quickly re-occupied Scimitar Hill.

Ironically, had Hamilton not intervened when he did, the morning attack of 9 August might have succeeded. Instead, the reorganization of 32 Brigade, together with the time and position lost, meant that they were not ready till dawn in any case. By this time the Turkish reinforcements had arrived and attacked at dawn, overwhelming 32 Brigade as it struggled up the slopes of

Tekke Tepe. At 6 a.m. the British line broke, with all the officers killed, the battalion and brigade headquarters overrun, and the wounded left to die amongst the dry scrub, which had now caught fire from the battle. The fighting continued throughout 9 and 10 August, with the British establishing a line of defence not that much further forward from the position they had held on 7 August.

By 10 August, not a single height objective of any importance at Suvla or Anzac had been obtained, and the battle for the Dardanelles had in effect come to an end. Between 6 August and 10 August, a total of 50,000 men had been involved in the campaign, with casualties of 18,000. By 13 August, 22,000 sick and wounded had been evacuated from the peninsula. The Turkish 8 Division was also brought from the Asiatic shore to reinforce the defenders further. However, at this time 53 and 54 Divisions arrived, and Hamilton was determined that these fresh, though ill-equipped, troops should be used to win Chunuk Bair. The aim was to advance from Suvla round the northern flank of the Sari Bair range, in support of Birdwood's troops, but morale on the Suvla Plain was at a low ebb, with high casualties and overall lethargy.

Stopford, having previously complained that the lack of water, guns and ammunition had prevented any advance, was now not supportive of Hamilton's plans, complaining of the poor preparation of the new troops and, prophetically, that they 'would not secure the hills with any amount of guns, water and ammunition assuming ordinary opposition, as the attacking spirit was absent; chiefly owing to the want of leadership by the Officers'.[8]

On 12 August a badly organized initial attempt was made to take Tekke Tepe, with 163 Brigade moving forward in the afternoon, in preparation for a more general offensive that night. Carried out without any proper recon-naissance and with only vague orders, the advance was easily repulsed by the Turks. It was during this advance that the unsupported 1/5 Norfolk Regiment, consisting of 15 officers and 250 men, disappeared and was never seen alive again.[9] Stopford therefore refused to undertake the planned attack on the following day, and was ordered by Hamilton to consolidate his lines as far forward as possible.

On 15 August, Stopford ordered the exhausted troops from 10 Division to move along the Kiretch Tepe Ridge. This was the ridge that initially was of greatest concern to von Sanders: had it been taken by the British, it would have been impossible for the 5th Army to get reinforcements to this area on 6 or 7 August. By the time the attack was made, however, the Turks had been able to build defensive lines, and the British then quickly suffered 2,000 casualties, although it did require the last of von Sanders' reserves to hold them. At this point, Hamilton with the support of Kitchener dismissed Stopford and a number of other generals. He placed Major General de Lisle in charge of the

IX Corps at Suvla until the arrival of Lieutenant General Byng from France, as well as Major General Stanley Maude and Major General Fanshawe. Although it was by then too late, Kitchener was finally sending younger and more able commanders. On his arrival, de Lisle discovered how bad conditions were, and sent a report on the situation to Hamilton, who in turn was forced to request an additional 45,000 men from Kitchener to bring his existing units up to strength, plus a further 50,000 to bring his total force to 190,000 men.

By 21 August, de Lisle was in a positive mood and ordered an attack for the afternoon, in the hope that the attackers would gain some advantage by having the sun at their backs. The assault was to be carried out by 11 and 29 Divisions, supported by 3,000 men from the Anzac battalions. The objectives were the taking of Scimitar Hill directly in front of Salt Lake, and of Hill 60 to the southeast. This was the largest battle fought during the campaign and, like so many before, it failed right from the start. Effective Turkish artillery decimated the advancing troops and a mist fell over the battlefield, removing any advantage they might have had with the sun at their backs. Although a few troops reached Scimitar Hill, they were driven back by the Turks after suffering casualties of 5,300 from an attacking force of about 14,300. The composite force of the Anzacs and British continued to attack their objective, Hill 60, for another week, suffering further casualties of 2,500, before the action was finally halted.

Table 9.1   *Relative military strength*

	Turkish		British and French, actual		British and French, available*	
Date	Divisions	Rifles	Divisions	Rifles	Divisions	Rifles
18 Feb	nil	5,000	nil	2,000	4	36,000
20 March	3	14,000	4	40,000	5	60,000
25 April	6	42,000	5	50,000	5	60,000
		70,000–				
7 July	10	75,0000	8	52,000	14	150,000
7 August	20	120,000	14	120,000	14	120,000

Source: Churchill 1923, p. 478.

Although the Suvla plan might have been a good one, the commanders on the scene and the raw infantry recruits were not up to the task; this was made even more difficult by the lack of artillery and by the ineffectual naval fire, both of which contributed to the failure. Had the 29 or the Anzac divisions

*i.e. that could be sent within a month of the given date.

and their experienced commanders undertaken the landing at Suvla, and had they, in turn, been replaced by the newly arrived divisions, the battle, perhaps, might have been won. It would also have required less secrecy from Hamilton to ensure that everyone knew the objectives; but the opportunity for success was clearly there. Head-on attacks like those in France achieved little in Gallipoli, particularly given the topography; but surprise actions, carried out correctly, had a much better chance of success. At Anzac, the aims were too ambitious. The Turkish counter-offensive in May was launched from a superior position and carried out with strength and resolve, but nevertheless still failed. This should have indicated to the Allied commanders that an attack launched from an inferior position was fraught with even greater danger and had little chance of success.

As von Sanders was to state:

If on August 15th and 16th the British had taken the Kiretch Tepe they would have outflanked the entire Fifth Army and final success might have fallen to them. The ridge of Kiretch Tepe and its southern slopes dominated the wide Anafarta plain from the north. From its eastern end a decisive attack could easily be pushed through the great depression extending toward Ak Bashi clear across the peninsula.[10]

10

Containing the Austrians

Although the Dardanelles were the centre of activity for British and to some extent French naval forces, containment of the Austrian navy in the Adriatic was still a critical matter. On 26 April 1915, patrols were out covering the Otranto Straits when the 12,351-ton armoured cruiser *Leon Gambetta* had slowed to 6.5 knots, to lower a boat in order to inspect a sailing vessel in bright moonlight. Austrian submarine UV, under the command of Linienschiffsleutnant Georg Ritter von Trapp, who was to become one of Austria's most successful U-boat commanders, shortly after midnight fired two torpedoes which hit and caused the ship to sink, with the loss of 684 lives, including Rear Admiral Sénès. This was the day after the Gallipoli landings and the same day that Italy signed the Treaty of London, joining the Allies and agreeing to declare war on Austria within a month. This provided the Allies with two good bases from which to fight the Austrians at the foot of Italy, one at Taranto and the other at Brindisi on the Adriatic. Italy also possessed its own fleet, comprising five dreadnoughts, five battleships, seven armoured cruisers, light cruisers and an assortment of destroyers, torpedo boats and submarines.

On 10 May a new naval convention was signed in Paris. Under the new agreement Britain was to provide a further four battleships and four cruisers (under the command of Rear Admiral Thursby), to assist the Italians as soon as the French replaced them at the Dardanelles (a sign of the difficult relations between Italy and France), while the French were also to provide the Italians with a dozen destroyers and other craft. The Italians took responsibility for patrolling the Otranto Straits and the Adriatic, while the French forces were to act independently and be on standby to support the Dardanelles forces in case the Austrians broke out into the Aegean. On 23 May, Italy formally declared war on Austria, but not on Germany[1] or Turkey. Austria reacted relatively quickly: on 24 May, Austrian cruisers and destroyers ventured out and bombarded the Italian coastal ports of Corsini, Ancona and Barletta, causing minimal damage and sinking one old Italian destroyer, the *Turbine*.

Even zigzagging at 18 knots was not necessarily a guarantee against submarine attack, as *Dublin* found out on 8 June, when patrolling off the Albanian coast opposite Brindisi. At 9.32 a.m., one of two torpedoes from *UIV*, under the command of Linienschiffsleutnant Rudolf Singule, hit her port side causing considerable damage. *Dublin* was able to effect repairs and managed to return to base. On the following day, *UB15* (which was to become *UXI*), on its maiden voyage under the command of von Heimburg, was off Venice when she sighted the Italian submarine *Medusa*, which she promptly sank, rescuing six survivors. After sinking a torpedo boat on 26 June, von Heimburg was once again successful near Venice, when on 17 July he sank the Italian armoured cruiser *Amalfi* (9,956 tons). German submarine officers had scant regard for the fact that Germany was not at war with Italy, and there were numerous occasions when Austrian flags were flown as a cover.

Naval activity evolved into one of containment, with occasional sorties against the enemy rather than a major engagement that might risk Allied battleships. So on 18 July Italian cruisers and destroyers led by the armoured cruiser *Giuseppe Garibaldi* (7,294 tons) headed out to destroy a railway bridge, some barracks and a suspected radio station. After bombing the railway bridge for an hour, they headed seaward. At this point, Singule in *UIV*, who had been on patrol looking for a downed aircraft, intercepted the naval force. After passing the cruiser and destroyer screens, his periscope having been fired upon, he finally managed to fire two torpedoes, one of which hit and sank the armoured cruiser.

Meanwhile, the Senussi living in the Italian North African colonies of Tripolitania and Cyrenaica were under pressure from the Turks to rebel. *B6* under the command of Lieutenant Macarthur and *B11* under the command of Lieutenant Holbrook, in company with the armed steamer *Heroic*, were sent to patrol the coast, and on 16 August the two submarines anchored 700 yards off-shore from Cape Lukka. A party was seen on shore and Holbrook rowed towards them until he became suspicious and started to return to his submarine. As he approached *B11* the shore party fired at him, sinking his boat and forcing him to swim to his submarine. While Holbrook was boarding *B11*, he was hit in the face by a ricochet and one sailor was killed aboard *B6*. Subsequent negotiations resulted in an apology from the Senussi, but U-boats were to continue to supply them with arms until they were defeated in a decisive battle on 26 February 1916.

Almost halfway up the Adriatic and near its centre lies the island of Pelagosa, and closer to the Austrian shore is the island of Lagosta. The Italians decided that these islands should be taken, given their strategic position for providing information on enemy movements; so for the next month these became the focal point of naval activity. On 11 July a small force was landed on Pelagosa without opposition (Austrian signalmen were found hiding in a cave). The next day the Austrians countered by attacking with a few torpedo boats supported by a plane. The garrison was reinforced and the idea of landing on Lagosta was abandoned.

The Austrians therefore arrived in greater force on 28 July, with one cruiser and four destroyers. While the cruiser remained off-shore, on the look-out for any intervening Italian force, the destroyers went in to bombard the garrison and sent a party ashore, which was driven off. The Italians were slow to respond and a naval force did not arrive till late that evening, when it was too late. Again the Italians did nothing when daily aircraft reconnaissance indicated that a strong Austrian force of four battleships, three cruisers and sixteen destroyers was heading south from Pola on 31 July. A submarine was sent to defend the island, although the Austrians never went as far as Pelagosa and returned to port forty-eight hours later. Logistical support of the island would prove to be costly when, on 5 August, one of the newer Italian submarines, *Nereide*, was torpedoed by *UV* while she stopped in the water unloading supplies.

The laying of mines became increasingly important, both as a defensive measure to protect ports and offensively, by laying traps at the entrance of enemy harbours. On 8 August, *UXII* ventured too close to Venice and struck a mine with all hands lost.[2] A few days later, on 12 August and under the command of Linienschiffsleutnant Karl Strand, *UIII* was patrolling the Otranto Straits when she sited the Italian auxiliary cruiser *Città di Catania* and fired several torpedoes at her without success; at this point the Italian rammed her, damaging her to the point where she could no longer submerge. The next morning, having been told of the submarine's presence, a patrol of destroyers sighted her and the *Bisson* opened fire, with the third round hitting the submarine and sinking her. Although twelve of her crew managed to survive, her captain was not among them.

On 17 August the Austrians finally made a major assault on Pelagosa. Two light cruisers, *Helgoland* and *Saida*, and twenty destroyers arrived in the early morning and over a two-hour period fired 7,000 rounds at the garrison, but, as in the lessons learnt at Gallipoli, the impact was negligible: one water-tank split, one anti-aircraft gun damaged, one officer and two men killed and about fourteen wounded.[3] Although the garrison had successfully defended the island against the Austrians without the support of the navy, which once again failed to go out and meet the enemy, the Italians lost confidence in holding the island and shortly afterwards withdrew their forces.

With the Otranto Straits still virtually open to submarine movements, and following *U21*'s successful voyage, a further five ocean-going submarines made the journey from Germany to Cattaro via the Mediterranean between

August and November. *U34* and *U35* left Heligoland on 4 August. *U34* was under the command of the very successful Kapitänleutnant Claus Rücher while *U35* was under the command of Kapitänleutnant Waldemar Kophamel. Both arrived at Cattaro on 23 August. Four days later *U39* under the command of Kapitänleutnant Walter Forstmann departed on her journey and, southwest of Fastnet, damaged the British barque *William T. Lewis*. When she reached the North African coast on 9 September, she sank three cargo vessels: the French *L'Aude*, the British *Cornubia* and the French *Ville de Mostaganem*. *U33* under the command of Kapitänleutnant Gansser left Borkum on 28 August; but, unlike Forstmann, Gansser did most of his damage while in the Atlantic, sinking six cargo vessels on the way.

U35 was the first to go on patrol on 31 August in the southern Aegean, and during a three-week period Kophamel was to sink three ships of 10,600 tons, including the *Ramazan* carrying Indian troops to Mudros, the French *Ravitailleur* and ex-Austrian *Gradac*.[4] On 1 September *U34* also departed on patrol, but only succeeded in sinking *Natal Transport* and the merchant cruiser *Indien*. In September *U39* departed for her first patrol, and by the time she returned to port on 12 October she had sunk a total of eight ships. During the first week of October, *U33* also headed through the Otranto Straits sinking two ships. Then she unsuccessfully chased the 46,359-ton liner *Olympic* with 5,500 troops on board, which had stopped to rescue survivors from a French collier previously sunk by Gansser. Over the next week she sank another eight ships. With this level of losses, more French destroyers were sent to the Adriatic, plus the submarine *H2* and the *Clacton*, designed to act as a Q ship (see Appendix II).

On 20 October *U38* left Germany under the command of Kapitänleutnant Max Valentiner and, when off the North African coast, she started her Mediterranean score by sinking two British cargo steamers, *Buresk* and *Glenmoor*, the French troopship *Calvados*, with the loss of 700 lives, and a French transport. On 7 November Valentiner caught the Italian liner *Ancona*, en route to New York. While passengers and crew were abandoning ship, he fired a torpedo, which produced the loss of 203 lives, including twenty Americans. This caused a serious diplomatic incident, as Valentiner was flying the Austrian flag.[5]

Attempts were made to close off the Otranto Straits not only to enemy surface ships but also to what were becoming more important: enemy submarines. The approach taken was to enlist steam-powered drifters,[6] which normally hung out large drifting nets. Steel nets were to be employed in the hope of 'catching' an enemy submarine by fouling its propellers, rudder or hydroplanes, or at least in the hope of showing the presence of a submarine and thus acting as a deterrent to those travelling through the straits.

Initially, thirty-one drifters set off from England in May, arriving in Lemnos on 23 June, and soon afterwards went on to lay their nets off Helles and Gaba Tepe and, later, off Suvla for the landings. It was not long before it became apparent that it was better to lay out nets supported by buoys, thus allowing the drifters the freedom to patrol up and down their nets. Ultimately the nets proved to have little success in catching enemy submarines. The Admiralty also expected too much of them, but over time, as the depth of the nets increased in some cases to 250 feet, their effectiveness, at least as a deterrent, improved.

In August, the first of sixty drifters set off for the Adriatic, arriving on 22 September at Taranto. By 1 October it became imperative to send some of the drifters to Mudros, to support the Allied landings at Salonika and so to improve the operations at Otranto; the drifters and their support vessel, the transport *Gallipoli*, were moved to Brindisi. With increasing reliance on the limited number of drifters, it was decided to arm them gradually with 5-pound guns. Shortly after the arrival of the drifters and until 9 October, the U-boats had been busy with the sinking of ten merchantmen. Having become aware of the drifters' presence on 12 October, while returning to base, *U39* surfaced and sank the unarmed *Restore* before she could be chased away by two other nearby drifters. The battle would intensify over time, as the straits became more and more difficult for the U-boats to navigate.

At this juncture the land battles between Italy and Austria became more fierce and there was concern that the Austrian naval forces might venture out of Pola to attack the Italian army's right flank from the sea. The Italian submarines were not up to the task of engaging the enemy due to their light construction; two of them returned to Venice on 1 November with sea damage. By the end of October, five out of a flotilla of six British B class submarines (*B6, 7, 8, 9, 10* and *11*) had arrived in Venice for support.[7] The first operational patrol, undertaken by *B9*, occurred on 18 October and until the end of 1915 a total of thirteen patrols was carried out. Little success was achieved until *B11* attempted to destroy a downed Austrian seaplane by ramming, on 11 November. Ironically, on 17 January she sighted an Austrian naval force looking for another downed seaplane, but she was unable to attack because of a faulty periscope. However, that afternoon she sighted the downed seaplane; before being rescued by *B11* the crew sank their plane.

Drifters went in support of the landing of Allied troops in Salonika on 5 October, after Bulgaria had declared war on 21 September. With little assistance from Greece, it became increasingly important for the Allies to support Serbia with military supplies by rail from the Greek sea port of Salonika at the northern end of the Aegean. By 10 October the Austrian–German forces had taken Belgrade, while Bulgarian forces had advanced from the east. The Serbian units were forced to move across to the Aegean coast. On

15 and 16 October Britain and France declared war on Bulgaria and instituted a blockade. On 21 October a force consisting of the *Doris*, cruiser *Theseus*, the seaplane carrier *Ben-My-Chree*, four destroyers and drifters bombarded Dedeagach, where the Salonika–Adrianople railway came to the sea, with modest results. With an increasing naval presence at Salonika, the railway was an obvious target for German U-boats. On 23 October, some 36 miles south of Salonika, *U35* attacked and sunk the British transport *Marquette*, with the loss of 167 lives.

The situation continued to deteriorate when on 14 November the Bulgarian forces from the east met up with the Austrian–German forces from the north. Ultimately the evacuation of the Serbian forces became more pressing as the supply line from Salonika had been cut at a time when plans were underway for the evacuation of Gallipoli. On 22 November the Italians occupied the Albanian town of Valona, on the other side of the Otranto Straits from Brindisi. To the north of Albania lay Montenegro, whose partially blocked port of Antivari was unsuitable, given its location close to Cattaro. Sixty miles to the south of Cattaro in Albania was the port of San Giovanni di Medua, 30 miles north of Durazzo, which was a further 30 miles north of Valona. Supplies were now to be transported across the straits primarily to San Giovanni di Medua, in support of the hard-pressed Serbians, as they made their retreat.

An Austrian naval force attempted to disrupt operations and attacked and sank a number of schooners on 23 November. On 1 December, the first of a planned force of 30,000 troops left Brindisi, arriving safely at Valona. Fortunately, at that time enemy submarines were busy in other parts of the Mediterranean, although a number of mines had been laid in the approaches to the harbour. Their presence was discovered on 4 December when the transport *Re Umberto* hit a mine and sank; fortunately some 500 troops were saved. The Italian destroyer *Intrepido* also struck a mine, but luckily the drifter *Manzanita* was nearby, to help rescue the crew and to push the stricken destroyer onto a nearby shore.

At this time there was also some concern over the neutrality of Greece and the potential threat to the Allied troops at Salonika. So on 20 November a special squadron was constituted in Malta, under Admiral Le Bris, comprising three French battleships, three British battleships and an Italian and Russian cruiser. The squadron then headed for the island of Milos, some 90 miles away from Athens, arriving there on 25 November, in a show of force to the Greeks. This proved to be effective, so that by 11 December the Greeks agreed to remove all but one of their divisions from Salonika.

On 5 December, the Austrians once again made a sortie, with the light cruiser *Helgoland* and the armoured cruiser *Sankt Georg* escorted by destroyers. Although they failed to intercept any of the transports crossing the straits, they entered the harbour of San Giovanni di Medua, sinking several transports. The French submarine *Fresnel* had been sent to protect the harbour from just such an attack, but had become caught on a shallow sandbank and was destroyed by the Austrian squadron which also captured her crew. By 11 December, the last of the troop reinforcements had reached Valona, and the supply of food and materials to the Serbian army, of some 130,000 plus 25,000 Austrian prisoners and 12,000 refugees, was now conducted through the port of Durazzo, as the small port of San Giovanni di Medua had become blocked from the ships sunk on 5 December.

By 14 December the evacuation of the Austrian prisoners had begun, and lasted until the first week of January. Italian troops that had landed at Valona marched north to Durazzo, and refugees began to be transported across the straits. The Austrians once again undertook a sortie, this time against Durazzo, on the evening of 28 December. After leaving Cattaro, the *Helgoland* and five destroyers intercepted the first of two French submarines, namely the steam-powered *Archimede*: this one, after having successfully torpedoed an Austrian steamer, was chased by the destroyers and damaged, but she managed to get home safely. Next to be sighted on the surface was the submarine *Monge*, under the command of Lieutenant de Vaisseau Roland Morillot, which was fired at by the destroyer *Balaton* and then finally rammed. With the conning tower leaking badly from the ramming, the submarine sank to 200 feet before the drop keel was released. When the submarine reached the surface, the crew abandoned ship while Morillot remained below as she sank, to ensure that the submarine wasn't captured. Arriving at daylight on the 29th, the Austrians found no shipping in the harbour and, after the destroyers had shelled the port, on the way out they ran into an Allied minefield. The destroyer *Lika* hit a mine which disabled her steering; when next she hit a second mine, she caught fire and eventually sank. Ahead of her was the destroyer *Triglav*, which also hit a mine but didn't sink, and was taken in tow by *Czepel* until this latter fouled one of her own propellers and *Tatra* had to take up towing duties.

When news of the events reached Italy, the British light cruiser *Dartmouth* and the Italian light cruiser *Quarto* headed to sea at 7.45 a.m. to intercept the Austrians, with French destroyers to follow later. *Dartmouth* headed north-north-east to head off the Austrians, when at 12.30 p.m. it sighted the Austrian heavy cruiser *Kaiser Karl VI*, which, with *Novara*, had headed out of Cattaro to lend assistance. Some seven minutes later the French destroyers joined the *Dartmouth*, while the British light cruiser *Weymouth* and the Italian light cruiser *Nino Bixio*, with Rear Admiral Bellini, had also departed from Brindisi in the company of four Italian destroyers shortly before, at 9.30 a.m.

The scene was now set for a major naval engagement. By 1 p.m. the *Dartmouth* and the *Weymouth* were in sight of each other and made towards the enemy. At 1.40 p.m. Captain Seitz, on the *Helgoland*, ordered the abandoning of the *Triglav*, while the partially disabled *Czepel* headed directly for home. Seitz had the advantage of speed and needed to stay out of range of the more powerful Allied ships until nightfall at around 5.30 p.m. At 2 p.m. *Weymouth* was given permission by Admiral Bellini to close on the enemy. This was the only signal that the admiral gave; he also failed to inform superiors of the enemy's course and speed, which resulted in other available naval units not joining in the chase.

At 1.43 p.m. the destroyer *Tatra* was falling behind, so *Helgoland* turned back to protect her. At this point *Dartmouth*, at a range of 14,000 yards, opened fire and hit her twice. Although *Helgoland* replied, her shells fell short and over the next hour the ships fired at one another sporadically. Attempts were made by the Allied destroyer to get close enough to engage *Tatra*, but without success. Seitz continually altered direction and used smoke to confuse his enemy. At 4.30, as *Tatra* finally caught up, *Weymouth* opened fire at extreme range, but with darkness setting in the engagement finally finished at 5.50 p.m. and the Austrians returned to port. By the first week of February Admiral Bellini was relieved of his command.

Valona became increasingly important for the removal of people and personnel back to Italy. When possible, San Giovanni was still being used to a limited extent. On 6 January the steamer *Brindisi* arrived off San Giovanni, carrying supplies and 425 Montenegrin reservists from Canada; but she ran into an Italian minefield and hit a mine, suffering the loss of 266 lives. Two days later the Italian merchant cruiser *Città de Palermo* left Brindisi, bound for Durazzo and carrying troops, when she ran into a minefield set by *UC14* and suffered the loss of some 100 lives. Drifters nearby came to their rescue, but both the *Freuchny* and the *Morning Star* hit mines and sank.

The final contingent to leave San Giovanni departed on 21 January 1916; the Austrians occupied the town a week later. By the evening of 26 February, the last of the Italian forces were removed from Durazzo. In the meantime the small force of steamers had succeeded in evacuating the Serbian army, the last of them through Valona on 11 April. Austrian and German submarine activity, particularly through mining, had caused a number of casualties, but the Austrians had failed to inflict a significant blow against the Allies. With the French at Corfu, the Italians at Valona and Allied forces at Brindisi, there was now little reason for the Austrian surface forces to venture out from the safety of their ports.

11

Final Submarine Phase

With the failure of the Suvla landings, the continued containment of the Allies both at Helles and at Anzac, and the impotency of the fleet (due to fear of possible U-boat activity), pressure intensified on the submariners to achieve even greater success in their campaign. But, although the number of submarines operating in the Sea of Marmara increased and aggressive commanders such as Nasmith continued to sink enemy transports, the last five months of operation in the area were to result in the loss of three Allied submarines.

The submarine force in the Sea of Marmara was never going to be a deciding factor in halting enemy supplies. The alternative land route provided, albeit under difficult conditions, a nearly uninterrupted flow of men and materials to the Turkish front. The narrowing of the isthmus at Bulair did provide a location from which naval forces in the Gulf of Saros could have significantly impaired the flow of supplies. However, once again, concerns over possible U-boat activity, combined with the difficulty of effectively interceding during the hours of darkness, meant that little was done. The submarine forces attempted, in their own limited way, to attack the supply route, but this was always going to be a dangerous and unrewarding course of action.

E11's second war patrol – 5 August to 3 September

On 5 August, *E11*, still under the command of Lieutenant Commander Nasmith, commenced its second cruise, departing from Kephalos at 1.30 a.m., escorted by *Basilisk*. Shortly after diving, at 4.07 a.m., while she was abreast of Suan Dere and proceeding at periscope depth, she fouled a wire stretched between two buoys. On surfacing for an inspection, fortunately no damage was found. Submerging again to a depth of 70 feet, *E11* continued through the Kephez minefield, until a heavy bump was heard along the starboard side at 4.45 a.m. Nasmith pressed on without stopping, and at 6.30 a.m. was taken to

Figure 11.1: Location of Allied and Turkish ships sunk

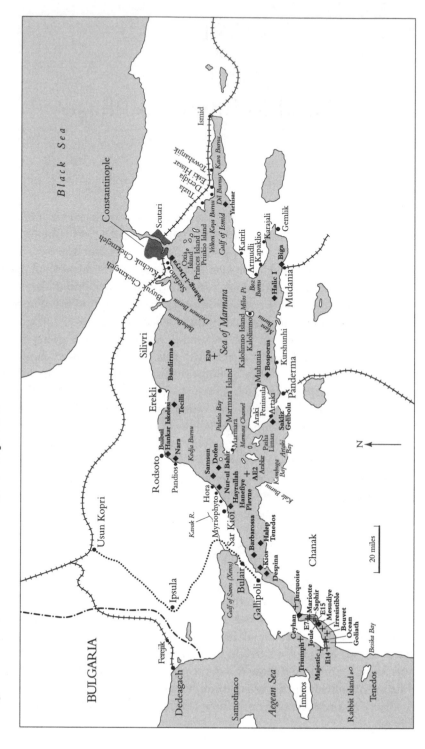

110 feet, as she rounded Nagara Point. Twenty minutes later her bow hit the net and was lifted to 90 feet, at which time a crack was heard. It was thought that this might have been the 5-inch thick footrope at the bottom of the net parting, but, as it turned out, this rope had slid over the boat, clearing her bow. A later inspection found that the submarine had been polished from her top down to a depth of 7 feet.

Passing Ak Bashi Liman, Nasmith sighted several targets and a number of sailing ships.[1] The starboard torpedo was fired at a transport, hitting her on the forward port side. She sank in shallow water and settled on the sea-bed with her superstructure still showing.[2] After passing the town of Gallipoli at 11.20 a.m., Nasmith headed north-east and, at 12.30 p.m., attempted to communicate with the contact ship *Aster* without success. *E11* was then forced to submerge by a gunboat, in the early afternoon.[3] When she surfaced again, the gunboat reappeared and immediately came in to attack, but the range was too great and *E11* too fast, so the gunboat's shots fell short. By 6.30 p.m. the gunboat gave up the chase, so, after recharging her batteries and allowing the crew to bathe, *E11* returned to the south-west. At dawn on the following day, she tried again unsuccessfully to communicate with *Aster*.

At 6.30 a.m. on 6 August, while still on the wireless billet, *E11* was forced to submerge: she was surprised by an enemy plane,[4] which dropped two bombs within 100 yards of her position.[5] The plane had not been heard, as it descended from a great height, with its engine probably throttled back. Fortunately, Chief Petty Officer William Dowell sighted it in time for evasive action to be taken. At 3 p.m. *E11* met with *E14*, to plan for a coordinated attack on Turkish shipping. Smoke was observed on the horizon and both submarines went in to attack. *E11* submerged and at 4.30 p.m. fired its port bow torpedo, which hit the cruiser *Peyk-i Sevket* on her starboard side amid-ships, sinking the ship in shallow water and killing four crew members.[6] Seeing that the ship had not sunk, Nasmith fired the starboard bow torpedo at 5.30 p.m., but this one missed, passing close to her stern.

E11 had been fitted with a larger 12-pound gun and, having noticed the movement of troops along the coastal roads at Dohan Aslan, at the northern entrance to the Narrows, Nasmith opened fire on a passing troop column at 11.30 a.m. on 7 August, scattering the troops. The captains of both *E11* and *E14* had been advised of the planned landings at Suvla, and had been ordered to attack any Turkish reinforcements marching along the Marmara shore near the Bulair Isthmus. Any movements from the seaward side were to be the responsibility of the armoured cruiser *Cornwall* and her accompanying destroyers. After submerging and observing the coastal road, *E11* surfaced again at 12.30 p.m. and, supported by *E14*, fired several rounds at the troops. The bombardment recommenced later, when a large column was observed marching along the road near the town of Gallipoli. After half an hour of firing, *E11* was forced to withdraw after coming within range of a field gun, but not before leaving a large number of dead and wounded alongside the road. Later that afternoon, Turkish troops were spotted resting, upon which *E11* surfaced, firing on and dispersing the troops, until a field gun once again forced her to withdraw. Although the extent of casualties caused by the two submarines may have been modest, they did disrupt the movement of troops and forced the Turkish army to station valuable field artillery near the shore, to protect the road.

At 4.40 a.m. on the following day, a battleship and destroyer in escort were sighted 5 miles to the north-east of the town of Gallipoli. By 5 a.m., near Bulair, Nasmith succeeded in torpedoing the battleship *Barbaros Hayreddin* using the port bow torpedo, which hit amidships. *Barbaros* immediately began to list to starboard; then shortly afterwards, at 5.20 a.m., a large flash was observed and the ship capsized and sank.[7] Minutes later, a second destroyer was observed approaching from Gallipoli. Nasmith attacked it, firing the starboard beam torpedo, but this passed harmlessly beneath the target.[8]

Later that morning, Nasmith established wireless communications with *Jed* to report his success, and then headed off once again to shell enemy troops on shore; but he was repulsed by shore guns. By 12.45 p.m. *E11* was in another engagement, firing on a ship which had been forced ashore by *E14*, then torpedoed.[9] At the last round fired by *E11*, the upper half of the gun-mounting fractured because of a flaw in the metal, throwing overboard the gun layer, Petty Officer John Kirkcaldy, with the gun almost going over with him. Nasmith was therefore forced to find a quiet spot, where his chief engine room artificer, Leonard. C. Allen, managed to remount the gun on a lower pedestal, although initially the task had appeared hopeless.[10]

Between 8 and 10 August, Nasmith was only able to find two small sailing vessels to sink. On the 9th they did benefit from the success of *E14*, when she transferred a case of tobacco to *E11* from a previous sinking. That night Nasmith once again used the fresh water/salt-water layer to rest the crew, with the submarine altering its depth by less than a foot. On 10 August at 1.21 a.m. *E11* received the following signal from the flagship:

> Large merchant ships reported off Ak Bashi Liman evening of 9th. Enquire in the morning if still there. *E2* will bring as much ammunition as possible. Excellent news from Home. Ends.[11]

At 9 a.m., in the company of *E14*, the hospital ship *Zia* was intercepted. The ship was directed to send a boat, and Lieutenant D'Oyly-Hughes was sent on board with a party of three hands to examine her. Before boarding, the entire crew of the hospital ship was ordered to one end of the vessel, while the submarine's guns were trained on them. One of the crew members of *E11* was Leading Seaman Axworthy, who stood guard over the hospital ship's crew. In his pocket he carried a small hand flag, which he was to use in directing fire from *E11*'s deck gun, in case of trouble, by pointing at the part of the ship *E11* was to fire at; fortunately this was not required, no contraband was found and she was allowed to proceed. *E14* then transferred two torpedoes to *E11*, as she herself intended to return to base the next day.

At 9 a.m. on the following day, 11 August, while *E11* was on the surface, a small destroyer[12] was encountered close to Stefano Point. Nasmith closed on her until he was seen, at which point he turned away from shore and increased speed to 14 knots, drawing the destroyer away from the protection of the shore-based guns. At a range of 7,000 yards Nasmith opened fire, and immediately came under return fire from the destroyer. Neither vessel made any hits as the range closed; eventually it became necessary for *E11* to submerge. At 10.30 a.m., after the destroyer had gone, she resurfaced, and then overtook and burnt six small sailing vessels.[13] The next day Nasmith continued his surface bombardment, this time with Mudania railway station as the target, but at 4 a.m., after making three hits, shore guns drove him off. Later that morning, another sailing vessel, laden with timber, was taken and burnt. At 7.30 p.m., off Stefano Point, *E11* was forced to dive after sighting an enemy aeroplane. It dropped two bombs, but these exploded harmlessly after the submarine had reached a depth of 40 feet.

The following morning, 13 August, having communicated with *Aster* and received news that *E2* was coming to join her, a hospital ship was stopped. She was inspected by D'Oyly and a boarding party, and proved to be the old Great Eastern steamer *Cambridge*. Nasmith then proceeded to the harbour at Artaki, which he found empty, except for a small steamer alongside the slipway. Surfacing, *E11* opened fire on the ship, but was again driven away by shore fire. Not to be dissuaded, she submerged, surfaced at longer range, fired three rounds at the shore gun, putting it out of action, and then proceeded to fire only a few rounds at the steamer; this was due to a shortage of ammunition before departure. The shortage was remedied the next day, when *E11* had a rendezvous with *E2* and received several hundred rounds of additional ammunition.

Nasmith then headed to the entrance of the harbour at Constantinople, where he observed a steamer alongside the Haidar Pasha Pier at 9 a.m. on 15 August. *E11* proceeded slowly towards her, and at 10.20 a.m. fired the starboard bow torpedo, hitting the target on the port side abreast the main mast. The steamer was observed to settle immediately by the stern.[14] Later that day, prior to the rendezvous with *E2*, two empty sailing vessels were burnt. At that time a rifle was lashed to *E11*'s 12-pound gun, and rifle-aiming practice was carried out, with spotting done by wireless from *E2*. Shortly after the practice, at 7 p.m., smoke was observed; it proved to come from a small steamer sailing from Constantinople towards Panderma. *E2* was the first to attack, using its deck gun, until the steamer altered course towards the shore guns at Stefano Point. Unfortunately *E2* only got off a few rounds before its gun-mounting gave way. *E11* continued the attack on the steamer, which had turned back to her original course once *E2*'s bombardment ceased. *E11* opened fire at a range of 6,000 yards, and the steamer again turned towards the shore. However, after she had been hit twice, she turned once more towards *E11* and, surprisingly, started an accurate return fire, forcing the submarine to submerge.

In the early hours of the next day, *E11* surfaced opposite a viaduct on the Baghdad railway and managed to fire fifteen shots, several of which hit the bridge supports, before fire from shore guns again forced her to submerge.[15] At 6.30 a.m. *E11* surfaced off the entrance to Ismid, to destroy a sailing vessel filled with hay, but, again, shore fire forced her to travel under water. At 9.30 a.m., in one of those classic First World War scenes, Nasmith sighted an enemy aircraft and submerged until only the conning tower was above surface, perhaps in the hope that his submarine would remain unobserved. However, when the aircraft got quite close, Nasmith waved to the pilot and submerged to 40 feet, with no follow-up attack from the aircraft.

Over the next few days, *E11* continued to try and disrupt troop movements, but with little success. On 20 August she headed eastward, in the hope of finding more worthwhile targets. That afternoon, at 3.30 p.m., *E11* stopped off Kalolimno Island, and a raft was constructed for a new and daring attempt to disrupt the flow of troops and materials on the railways. The raft was made from materials such as wood and kegs, which had been salvaged from the sailing ship burnt in Artaki Bay. That afternoon *E11* proceeded to the Gulf of Ismid, arriving as the moon was setting.

E11 approached the shore, about half a mile to the east of the Eski Hissar village, near a railway viaduct. Trimmed down so that only the conning tower was showing, she entered a small cove, surrounded by cliffs high enough to hide her. *E11*'s bow grounded just three yards from the rocks on the shore. In calm seas, the already constructed raft was lowered into the water, and loaded with 16 pounds of gun-cotton explosive. At 2.10 a.m. D'Oyly went over the side abreast the conning tower, armed with a revolver, a bayonet, an electric torch and a whistle, and swam ashore, pushing the raft with all the equipment in front of him. He landed 60 yards off the port bow of the submarine. His first point of contact with the shore proved too steep to climb, so he swam further along till he found a suitable landing spot. Once ashore, D'Oyly climbed the cliffs to the top and then continued for half an hour, until he reached the railway line. He kept going for another five or six hundred yards to reach the viaduct, staying a little above the line on the northern side, only to find that it was blocked by a three-man patrol. After watching them for some time, he left and made a detour inland, to inspect the viaduct.

After falling into a hen house and causing considerable noise (yet fortunately without waking up the nearby households), he came eventually within 300 yards of the viaduct and sighted a stationary engine. This engine was apparently under repair, so that he was again unable to set his charge. He finally chose a small culvert, 150 yards from the Turkish patrol, and placed the gun-cotton under the track. Muffling the fuse-pistol with a piece of rag, he set off the fuse, but the noise was still loud enough to give him away, and the patrol gave chase. After running a short distance he fired two shots at the pursuing guards, in an attempt to slow them down, but without any apparent effect; they in return fired several shots at him. With the enemy in close pursuit, he decided that to try and clamber down the cliff face would be suicidal, so he ran eastward for about a mile along the railway line, until it got close to the shore. Here, about three quarters of a mile to the east of the small bay in which *E11* was lying, he plunged into the water just as his charge exploded.

D'Oyly swam straight out for about 500 yards and desperately blew his whistle, but this was not heard by the submarine look-outs. With daylight approaching, he swam back to shore. After resting for a short while, he discarded all his equipment, re-entered the water and swam along the coast towards the bay. Once he turned into the bay his whistle was heard, but at the same time he heard shouts from the cliff tops and rifle fire which, unknown to him, was directed at *E11*. At this point, as *E11* reversed out of the bay, shrouded in the morning mist, he mistook her conning tower, bow and gun for small Turkish rowing boats. He swam ashore, but while he was trying to hide under a cliff face he realized his mistake, shouted, and re-entered the water. Rescued in the nick of time, around 5 a.m., 40 yards from the rocks, he was suffering from extreme exhaustion, having swum for a mile in his clothes. For this action D'Oyly was awarded the Distinguished Service Order, although it is a moot point whether what he did was worth the risk of exposing *E11*.[16]

Later that morning, 21 August, three sailing vessels loaded with fruit and vegetables were burnt, and at 6 p.m. *E11* met up with *E2*, after which *E11* headed again towards Constantinople. At 9 p.m., a convoy was sighted, consisting of a destroyer and three steam tugs towing eight small sailing vessels.[17] With the recent paucity of targets, this convoy offered a tremendous opportunity. Nasmith reconnoitred on the surface, using low buoyancy to remain unobserved. He came to the conclusion that the moonlight was in the enemy's favour, which greatly reduced the chances of a successful night attack. He therefore decided to station himself ahead of the convoy, as it headed on a straight course from Constantinople to the channel between Marmara Island and the northern shore.

By 4.30 a.m. on the following morning, having calculated that the convoy's speed would not enable them to reach shore by daybreak, Nasmith decided to attack. His target was the lead destroyer which had now started to zigzag. The first attack failed due to a poor approach, so Nasmith turned to attack again, but, as he came into firing position, the periscope dipped below the water briefly and, when depth was restored, the destroyer had once again changed course. *E11* increased speed and turned for another attack, when Nasmith observed that the reason for the change of course was to give assistance to one of the dhows and to the third tug, which apparently had broken down. Nasmith kept within range of the rest of the convoy, while at the same time increasing his distance from the destroyer.

He finally surfaced between Hora and Marmara Island, opened fire on one of the two remaining tugs, hitting her twelve times, and then damaged several dhows. The destroyer returned and *E11* was forced to dive, by which time the remaining two tugs were already heading for the shore. The destroyer then apparently directed one of the undamaged tugs to go to the assistance of the broken-down tug and dhow. Nasmith followed this tug and surfaced at close range, to find her towing the other two vessels. However, before he was able to use his deck gun, the towed tug opened fire, again forcing *E11* to submerge. As she did so, the leading tug slipped her tow lines and headed off to the safety of the destroyer. Nasmith then surfaced and, at a range of 6,000 yards, fired a few rounds at the two stranded vessels, until the dhow got under sail and also headed towards the shore. When the dhow was outside of the tug's gun range, Nasmith closed to within 50 yards and sunk her with the deck gun. The crew of twenty jumped overboard as the first shot was fired, and were picked up by Nasmith.[18]

Nasmith stowed the new passengers below, dived, and once again moved towards the broken-down tug. Through the periscope, he observed that it had been deserted, except for one man who was hiding under the gunwale. *E11* surfaced and, despite coming under fire from the undamaged tug, which was returning in an attempt to make a rescue, he quickly sank the abandoned tug *Dofen*. *E11* left the scene, and during the afternoon intercepted a sailing vessel carrying a cargo of water melons. The prisoners were placed on board the sailing vessel; they were made to throw the cargo over the side and then, to their surprise, allowed to go.

During the next two days there was little activity. On communicating with *Aster* (at the considerable distance of 90 miles, given the quality of the radio sets), Nasmith was advised that there were transports presently in the Dardanelles. Having failed to rendezvous with *E2*, Nasmith turned westward, and topped up the batteries in preparation for an attack in the Dardanelles. At 3.45 a.m. on 25 August, with low buoyancy, he proceeded to an area within 8 miles of Ak Bashi Liman, making one short dive in the vicinity of the town of Gallipoli in order to avoid being detected by a destroyer. At 7 a.m. he fired a starboard torpedo at a gunship, but the torpedo ran under the ship and exploded amongst other shipping, though Nasmith was unable to observe what damage had been done.[19] The gunboat and a destroyer gave chase, charging overhead several times, while *E11* proceeded first to the north and then returned to the attack, close to shore. At 10.15 a.m., Nasmith fired both bow tubes and hit two large transports, both of which were seen to settle and then capsize.[20]

Nasmith's run of success then faltered slightly as he moved *E11* back to Gallipoli, where at 12 p.m. he fired the starboard beam torpedo at a large transport but missed. However, thirty minutes later, after *E11* had turned, he fired the port beam torpedo, which hit the ship by the foremast. The transport settled by the bows and was last seen with her propellers revolving out of the water.[21] Later on that same day, at 3 p.m., Nasmith fired his last remaining torpedo, from the stern tube, at a large transport, which was hit under the forecastle and seen to settle by the bows.[22] At 6.20 p.m., *E11* met with *E2* again and it was arranged that *E2* should proceed to Ak Bashi Liman the following day.

For the next week *E11* patrolled near Dohan Aslan but encountered few targets, and so she continued to shell coastal railway installations, particularly around Mudania. On the 27th she found nothing in Mudania Bay,[23] and on the following day she fired on the Mudania railway station until the shore batteries forced her to submerge. Later in the day *E11* again met up with *E2*. The two submarines positioned themselves 6,000 yards from the railway station and, together, carried out a bombardment from outside the range of the shore guns.

The next day *E11* made her way to the Gulf of Ismid, where on that very morning she burnt a sailing ship laden with fruit, before unsuccessfully investigating the Zeppelin shed near Constantinople. Returning to the Mudania Bay on 30 August, she stopped and set four small sailing ships on fire. Nasmith realized from his previous observations that shipping traffic from Constantinople followed the shore closely until it reached the Gulf of Ismid, and so he decided that this was the place to patrol after nightfall. By 9 p.m. that evening he encountered three sailing vessels, one of which escaped in the dark. The two captured vessels carried valuable cargoes of coke and coal. The bigger of these was sunk, but due to the large number of prisoners taken,

Nasmith was forced to use the remaining vessel, but not until the prisoners had jettisoned a large part of the cargo.

On the following day, Nasmith headed to Prinkipo Island and, rising to the surface at 7.20 a.m., intercepted four sailing vessels. Nasmith fired only one round at the captured vessels before he was forced to submerge, again by fire from the shore. He was lucky, as the shore battery lobbed a shell within 10 yards of the aft hydroplanes which, if damaged, would have put the boat at great risk. Later that afternoon, *E11* opened fire on a three-masted sailing ship off Katirli village, hitting her a large number of times before she took refuge in the Gulf of Ismid. The following day, 1 September, *E11* rose to the surface at 5 a.m., and commenced the bombardment of the Ismid railway viaduct. At a distance of 6,000 yards, she was just outside the range of the shore guns. This continued for one hour but, although a number of hits were observed, the level of damage was not apparent. *E11* was finally made to withdraw when a larger field gun was brought into action. Finally, later that day two more sailing vessels were burnt, their crews being transferred to a sailing vessel found in the lee of Arablar Island. The next day the batteries were charged, the gun dismantled, extra jumping wired fitted, and preparations made to return to base at Mudros.

On 3 September, at 2 a.m., *E11* headed out of the Sea of Marmara. Once again, Nasmith employed the tactic of charging his batteries as he passed through the Narrows, trimmed down with the decks awash, and then pressed on to within 8 miles of Nagara, before having to submerge. *E11* initially approached the Nagara net at half speed and at a depth of 80 feet, when at 6.25 a.m. she hit an obstruction and increased speed to 8 knots. The boat was taken up to 60 feet before it broke free, but was only deflected a few degrees off course. While action to free the submarine was being taken, D'Oyly studied the net through the conning tower glass-scuttles. He found that a number of 2.5-inch wires had been crossed and securely joined together, forming a mesh about 10 feet square. On the port side, a dark object was observed, which was probably a sinker.[24] *E11* came to the surface off Helles at 9.15 a.m. and, escorted by *Bulldog*, returned to base at Mudros by 8 p.m., to a rousing reception from a number of nearby ships.

Nasmith included a number of observations in his patrol report, one of which concerned the ability of the submarine to 'float' below the surface, at the boundary layer between the different densities, throughout the Sea of Marmara. He listed the locations of enemy guns, the presence of aircraft and dirigibles, and the nightly routine of enemy transports. He also suggested that propaganda leaflets be dropped in small villages, as he had observed from the prisoners on board the submarine that the feelings of the locals towards Germans were very bitter. Perhaps more importantly, he noted that only one of his torpedoes had effectively sunk a major ship and he submitted that all torpedoes should be fitted with dynamite (trinitrotoluene/TNT) warheads rather than gun-cotton.

E2's first war patrol – 13 August to 14 September

Under the command of Lieutenant Commander David de Beauvior Stocks, *E2* arrived at Mudros on 4 August and, after loading provisions and exchanging her 6-pound gun for a more effective 12-pound gun, set off for Kephalos on 11 August, arriving there at 6.30 p.m. Leaving the next day for Suvla Bay, she tied up alongside *Euryalus*, took on additional ammunition, and left Sulva for her first patrol of the Sea of Marmara at 1.15 a.m. on 13 August. With a destroyer escort to Sedd el Bahr, she submerged at 3.55 a.m. for the remainder of the trip to Nagara.

At 6.25 a.m., during her passage through the Narrows, *E2* was caught on a 3.5-inch wire, which was observed through the conning tower scuttles to have wound itself around the submarine's gun in a half turn. A smaller wire had also wound itself around the forward part of the conning tower, holding her fast at 80 feet. Later observations were to show that another wire had wound itself around the wireless standard. Stocks ordered the boat to back up, and then went at full speed and simultaneously turned hard to starboard, which resulted in clearing the half turn on the gun. All wires then gave way and trim on the submarine was lost instantly, which caused her to dive to 140 feet before control could be regained. This was the first occasion on which detection of movement at the nets resulted in Turkish patrol boats dropping bombs which exploded on contact. Fortunately, although the crew heard small explosions while *E2* was still entangled, none came close enough to cause any damage. However, damage had been done to the gun mounting, which, even after much effort, was never again fully serviceable, each firing having caused further loosening of the rivets at the base of the gun.[25]

An hour later, when *E2* submerged off Ak Bashi Liman, a destroyer was encountered which fired a number of shells, falling harmlessly into the water. After losing the destroyer, *E2* dived to the bottom half an hour later to allow the crew to have dinner and a rest. The submarine again came to the surface at 2.20 p.m., and started charging her greatly depleted batteries. Later that afternoon she successfully made contact with *Aster* by radio, while she was off Dohan Aslan. The enemy destroyer once again forced *E2* to submerge, at 6.30 p.m., and she remained on the bottom for the rest of the night. At 5 a.m. on the following day, 14 August, she intercepted the minelayer *Samsun* (a converted tug), which was returning to Constantinople, but on sighting the submarine's periscope the minelayer fled. Stocks, however, still pressed on with his attack, and by 5.30 a.m. he had come into a firing position and fired his starboard beam torpedo, which hit *Samsun* on the starboard side-engine room, sinking her within five minutes and killing two officers and eight crew members.[26]

Later that morning, at 9.40 a.m., *E2* was forced to submerge, as a German seaplane similar in appearance to a Farman type approached from Gallipoli. Although the appearance of aircraft in the Marmara was increasing, it still remained infrequent, and then it occurred only when the weather was fine. Had the Turkish Air Force been better equipped and more aggressive, the Allied submarine offensive could have been greatly restricted. At noon, *E2* sank a dhow carrying provisions and telegraph wire and, around 2 p.m., she met with *E11* off Kalolimno Island, the sort of event that was becoming more frequent as the number of available submarines increased. Before continuing her patrol, *E2* transferred an extra 300 rounds of ammunition to *E11*, and in return received a bag of apples.

Early in the morning of the next day, off Kalolimno, *E2* was once again forced to submerge on sighting a seaplane which dropped some bombs but caused no damage. Only ten minutes later, Stocks attempted to attack a destroyer which was zigzagging, but, as the weather started to deteriorate, the destroyer moved away. It is possible that the aircraft and destroyer were working together in a search for the submarine. Shortly before noon a dhow was intercepted and chased into Kalolimno, where she opened fire on *E2* with her 3-pounders. The submarine returned fire, silencing the guns and ultimately sinking the dhow. She then used a small boat to send off the dhow's crew and six other prisoners, captured from the previous sinking. That evening, *E2* became engaged in a gunfight with the *Iskenderun*,[27] but, after firing six rounds, her deck gun pivot broke, and she was forced to submerge to safety.

The next morning, *E2* proceeded to the Gulf of Ismid, and on the way sank two dhows loaded with wooden spars and barbed wire (important war materials for the Turks), then put the captured crews on board a third dhow. On the way up the gulf, *E2* was forced by shore gunfire to submerge off Deridja, and again, later in the early afternoon, by artillery fire from the railway line near the town of Towshanjik. With the gulf empty, *E2* was able to make further repairs to her gun,[28] and on the following day she continued her patrol. While she was near Kalolimno Island, a steamer was sighted and *E2* dived to attack. However, the steamer had sighted the submarine, so she surfaced and gave chase. *E2*'s gun was still not adequately repaired and, when the steamer returned fire, Stocks had little choice but to disengage and dive, as he watched the steamer make for the Marmara Channel. The next day only a hospital ship was sighted off Buyuk Chekmejeh and, given the scarcity of suitable targets, Stocks was able to continue repairs on his deck gun.

On 20 August, at 3.56 a.m., Stocks fired a torpedo at a vessel[29] as she lay moored alongside the pier at Artaki. (He believed that this was the steamer which had fired at him on the 17th.) The beam torpedo hit amidships, immediately sinking the ship, with no apparent loss of life. Stocks believed her to be of 1,500 tons and armed with three or four guns, but in reality she had a displacement of only 142 tons, although she was 115 feet in length and may have given the impression of a greater displacement.

Given Stock's continuing difficulties with his deck gun, the requirement to keep the bilge pumps running all the time on account of leaks and a paucity of suitable targets for his valuable torpedoes, the remainder of *E2*'s patrol proved to be uneventful, difficult and disappointing. To make matters worse, fuel was leaking from the No. 1 fuel tank into the A main ballast and then on into each tank up to the bow, including the fresh-water tanks. This resulted in the loss of half the fresh-water supply, which forced the men into severe rationing over the last two weeks of the patrol, with the last pint being consumed as they passed Chanak on the way home.

On 21 August, a planned torpedo attack against the small target *Gelibolu* could not be carried out due to the position of an existing wreck in Rodosto Bay. Later that evening, *E2* again met up with *E11*. The following morning, a steamer discovered in the Mudania Bay proved to be high and dry on the shore. However, that afternoon at Mudania Pier a vessel was sighted and the starboard beam torpedo fired at 3.09 p.m., sinking the target.[30] This was followed shortly afterwards by a torpedo attack on the *Edremit*, which proved unsuccessful because she, too, was sheltered by another wreck. To add to Stock's frustration even further, he was fired on by shore guns while chasing a dhow near the town of Armudli. These guns were silenced by return fire, and an extra round, fired close to the village, had the desired effect of halting any further interference on the next few occasions when the submarine passed within firing range of the town. The next morning a periscope was sighted at a distance of 3,000 feet, but no attack was made, given the uncertainty over its origin. An hour later another unsuccessful attack was made, on a steamer near Panderma.

The next major opportunity occurred on 26 August when, near the town of Gallipoli, Stocks observed the wrecks of several steamers in Ak Bashi and a nearby patrolling gunboat. At 11.45 a.m. he fired a bow torpedo at the gunboat; the torpedo missed and exploded amongst the wrecks.[31] Desperate to achieve some success, Stocks continued to manoeuvre for the next two and a half hours, trying to get into a new firing position, but he had to give up as his batteries began to weaken. At 1.54 p.m. he sighted a transport on the Asiatic shore near Bergaz Iskalessi and fired his starboard beam torpedo, apparently hitting the transport abreast the ship's funnel. However, Stocks got the impression that the torpedo may have hit a smaller vessel alongside, as the ship didn't appear to sink before *E2* was forced to depart due to the activities of a nearby torpedo boat. By the end of the day, when *E2* surfaced at 8.15 p.m., she had covered an impressive 59.5 miles submerged.[32]

On 27 August, with a decrease in seaborne targets, Stocks began shelling artillery batteries near the town of Sar Kioi, firing twenty rounds. His use of shrapnel rounds on the target to the east of the town proved effective; later he saw stretcher parties removing bodies. He therefore proceeded towards the town's pier and scored several hits on a few small steamers nearby. Early next day a dhow was sunk and three prisoners taken on board, which was followed by the bombardment of the railway station at Mudania, undertaken in company with *E11*. *E2* fired thirty-five rounds, in the hope of doing some damage to the railway lines. After the short engagement, Stocks submerged to test the pressure hull, which proved still to be leaking badly, so he decided that something more radical had to be done with the deck gun.

A cutter was stopped that evening and the prisoners were transferred to make way for the major repairs that were to be undertaken the next day, Sunday 29 August. The gun was moved aft and the gun support ring was placed on top of Number 3 firing tank (a compressed air tank), as there were no longer any torpedoes to be fired from this tube. Holes were drilled into the tank and the gun attached, but the lower position of the gun resulted in very little freeboard (the height above the waterline). The next day work continued on the gun, so only one dhow was stopped and burnt, the prisoners being once again transferred to a passing cutter. Work on the gun continued during the day, and it was not until that night, at 10 p.m., that an attempt was made to attack a large sailing ship at Kalolimno. However, she proved to be too vigilant and the attack had to be aborted. Finally, at 8.50 a.m. on 31 August, the gun was satisfactorily tested by firing twenty-three rounds at a steamer at Kalolimno. After checking that there was no shipping at Gemlik, six rounds were fired that afternoon at the facilities at Boz Burnu, until a patrolling seaplane forced the submarine to submerge at 6.45 p.m.

The next two days resulted in little activity other than jettisoning some bran from a dhow, which was then allowed to proceed as it carried Greek refugees and a priest who had fled from Constantinople. On 3 September at 6 a.m., after *E2* reached Constantinople, four dhows were destroyed, three by fire and a fourth one by ramming,[33] and all the crews were placed on a fifth dhow, whose cargo of provisions had been removed. Next morning a dhow carrying melons was sunk and four prisoners were taken. While they were near Sar Kioi, two further dhows, crowded with female refugees, were stopped, the four prisoners put on board, and the dhows allowed to proceed. The occupants were so grateful that they insisted on giving the crew of *E2* live fowls and other gifts. *E2* then investigated the nearby pier in the hope of destroying it, but discovered that a house at the end of the pier had ostensibly been made into a hospital, so the bombardment was aborted.

On 4 September at 7 p.m. a dhow was sunk off Rodosto, with a nearby torpedo boat chiming in and firing on *E2*. The torpedo boat, however, kept its distance, remaining outside the range of *E2*'s gun. The same thing happened next morning near the town of Marmara, where a torpedo boat fired at long range, but *E2* submerged and made her way to Panderma. A steamer was sighted, but a closer investigation showed her to be stranded on the shore. On *E2*'s surfacing in Pergamo Bay, a cutter was stopped and the prisoners transferred from the previously sunk dhow. *E2* then went on to the arranged rendezvous with *E7*, which she thought should have reached the Sea of Marmara by this time; then she tried unsuccessfully to communicate with her by wireless.

The following day, 6 September, proved to be both fruitful and very active. Although small in tonnage, the number of dhows sunk by gunfire and ramming was a record eleven. In achieving this, *E2* fired a total of 192 rounds. These activities are described by Stocks in his patrol report thus:

7 a.m.	Sank 2 large dhows under Boz Burnu.
9 a.m.	Sank dhow on way to South Coast Mudania.
10 a.m.	Sank one dhow and one Brigantine.
Noon	Sank one dhow off Kapaklio.
2 p.m.	Sank dhow off N. Coast.
2.45 p.m.	Sank 5 dhows off Kapaklio.
6.20 p.m.	Attacked dhows off Karajali. Driven off by rifle fire.

On 7 September, *E2* dived into Armudli and moved in as close as possible to the shore, within 50 feet, to allow Lieutenant Harold V. Lyon to swim in and destroy two dhows. *E2* then proceeded into Kuchuk Chekmejeh Bay after sinking a dhow off Oxia Island, and rested on the bottom that evening, with conning tower and gun just out of the water.

Following the example set by *E11*, and perhaps due to the paucity of good targets and Lyon's previous good showing in the water, Stocks decided to attempt similar tactics on 8 September, at the nearby viaduct for the railway line from Constantinople. At 2.15 a.m., Lyon swam ashore with explosives, planning to blow up the railway line. Lyon was watched until he was 70 yards away and could no longer be seen. No sounds of any kind were heard, and the early morning was so absolutely still that noises on shore were distinctly audible. It had been agreed that, if he were to run into any trouble, Lyon would fire his Webley pistol and *E2* would show a red light from her station 300 yards away. *E2* remained on station until 7.15 a.m., when, in broad daylight, she was driven off by shore fire. She returned an hour later, in the hope of finding Lyon swimming off-shore or in a boat or dhow, several of which were at the nearby village, but without success. No onshore explosion had been observed or heard, and that evening *E2* returned again to look for Lyon, but he was never seen or heard from again.[34]

On the next day *E2* returned at dawn, with the aim of bombarding the railway station, but, as day began to break, Stocks suddenly sighted a torpedo boat only 800 yards away, heading directly towards him. The boat crash-dived and, though in shallow water, was able to reach a depth of 40 feet in time to avoid being rammed. Surfacing again at 8 a.m., he found nothing in sight and, particularly, no sign of Lyon. Later that morning four dhows were sunk. Their cargoes included a variety of goods such as soap, grapes, eggs, silks and manufactured goods; but most, importantly, the fresh food they carried gave *E2* the opportunity to restock her own dwindling supplies. The weather conditions were now starting to deteriorate and the seas increased to such an extent that, during the afternoon, when a tug towing two dhows opened fire at 3,500 yards straddling the submarine, she could not respond due to her much lower remounted gun.

The next day the seas became so much rougher that waves were breaking over the conning tower. Heavy seas and wind continued on the 11th and 12th, with no shipping observed. *E2* was unable to communicate with *E7* at the rendezvous; on 12 September she did manage to make contact with *Aster*, and was finally informed that there was to be no meeting with *E7*. By 13 September, with the bad weather abating, preparations were made to return to base. That afternoon, towing wires were fitted as jumping wires and all other large wires available were fitted round the submarine, to help avoid fouling the anti-submarine nets on the return journey. The deck gun, which had given them so much trouble, was finally secured.

The next morning, while on the way down the Dardanelles, Stocks sighted the *Aydin Reis* near the town of Gallipoli, and at 9.57 a.m. he fired the port torpedo, but was unable to observe the results on account of the activity of nearby torpedo boats.[35] Stocks then tried to get into position to attack a gunboat, but, mindful of the need to conserve his battery, decided to break off the engagement. After finding that Ak Bashi Bay near Nagara was devoid of targets, he set a course of 242 degrees at a depth of 80 feet with plenty of negative buoyancy, and headed for Maidos Hill. At 11.48 a.m. an obstruction was encountered, which subsequently proved to be a wire. It ran along the port side and overhead of the submarine, but did little to check her way, although it did tear away the forward hydroplane guard. This caused further leaks, which had to be managed by hand pumps. Ten minutes later, while still at 80 feet, she turned, passed close to Kilid Bahr at 12.30 p.m., and then surfaced off Sedd el Bahr at 2.40 p.m. The guns at Kum Kale on the Asiatic side opened fire, and *E2* was again forced to submerge, fouling the British anti-submarine nets as she did so. This forced her to surface once more and, again, brought her under fire from the shore batteries, which continued until the obstruction was cleared. She passed Cape Helles at 3 p.m., but ten minutes later the steering gear failed and she had to be taken in tow by *Scourge*. At 5.30 p.m. the towing wire broke, but by then makeshift repairs had been made to the steering, so *E2* was able to avoid any further embarrassment and make her own way into the harbour at Kephalos, returning to Mudros the next day.[36]

E7's second war patrol – 4 September

At 2 a.m. on the morning of 4 September, under the command of Lieutenant Commander Cochrane, *E7* departed from Kephalos and headed for the Dardanelles. Diving at 5 a.m. abreast of Achi Baba, in very calm seas and in bright moonlight, *E7* was seen by the coastal batteries,[37] but proceeded without difficulty until, as she passed Kilid Bahr at a distance of 200 yards, the nearby forts finally fired on her periscope, although without effect. At 7.30 a.m., Cochrane sighted the buoys of the recently strengthened submarine nets off Nagara Point and altered course, so that the path of the submarine was at right angles to the net. He then dived to 100 feet and increased speed to 7.5 knots, in an attempt to crash through.

As *E7* moved forward and the bows started cutting through the net, the starboard propeller fouled, forcing the starboard motor to stop. Cochrane increased the port motor to full speed to maintain the forward momentum, but this resulted in the submarine's bow swinging to starboard. To compensate, the rudder was put hard over to port, but the boat continued turning to starboard as before. After ten minutes the starboard propeller was finally free, but by this time *E7* was lying parallel to the net, on its northern side, and, most alarmingly, had become completely entangled at a depth of 100 feet, between buoys No. 13 and 14.

The motor gunboats *Nos 18* and *20*, and the patrol boat *No 32*, stationed on guard duty at the mine barrage between Nagara and Bigalli, noticed at 7 a.m. that two buoys were being dragged under the water and reported it to the naval base at Chanak. Meantime, Cochrane had decided to turn the boat's bow to the south, in an attempt to keep the propellers free, and continued to push her through the net. At 8.30 a.m., a mine exploded a few hundred feet away, but the boat was not damaged. However, by this time the starboard motor was badly strained, and occasionally molten copper would spray out.

This in itself was not dangerous, but on one occasion it landed on a bale of cotton waste and, were it not for the prompt action of some of the crew in putting out the fire, the submarine might have been lost at that moment. Attempts to get free continued for the next six hours, during which time the detonation of another mine occurred at 10.30 a.m., and battery reserves were almost exhausted, as is described by Cochrane in his report to the Admiralty, after the war:

> After about two hours manoeuvring, the boat was turned to the Southward, and repeated attempts to get clear of the net were made at depth from 60 to 130 feet by going alternately full speed ahead and astern. Although several messes of net were carried away it was impossible to gather sufficient weight to clear completely the main parts which were holding the boat fore and aft.
>
> 10.30 a.m. A mine was exploded close to the boat, the explosion was violent but no damage was done to the hull. After this explosion the boat was considerably freer than before, and in the hopes that further attempts to blow up the boat might result in completely freeing her, I decided to remain submerged at a good depth until after dark, when it might be possible to come to the surface and clear the obstruction. Burned all confidential papers.
>
> By 2 p.m. battery power was much reduced and further attempts to clear were given up for a time.[38]

As previously mentioned, *UB14* also arrived in the Dardanelles on the same day as *E7*. An unverified story relates how Oberleutnant Hugo von Heimburg, the commander of submarine *UB14*, then stationed at Chanak, slowly rowed out that afternoon, with his boat's cook, Herzig, along the line of the net-marker buoys.[39] While von Heimburg rowed, Herzig, who was 'a very capable fellow and a natural born fisherman to boot', sat in the stern with a plumb line, searching for the trapped submarine. When he believed that he had found it, he lowered a charge, which exploded and nearly capsized the dinghy. The embellished story goes on, reporting that this explosion was the one that forced *E7* to the surface.[40] However, later at 7.30 p.m. (Cochrane states 6.40 p.m.) further explosives were dropped by patrol boat *No 32*, detonating at 100 feet,[41] and exploding only a few feet from the hull, breaking electric lights and other small fittings. At this point Cochrane hoped that the nets had been damaged and he made one last effort to escape, but to no avail. The presence of enemy craft meant that coming to the surface at night to remove the obstructions was no longer practical, so Cochrane decided to surface, with the aim of removing the crew and blowing up *E7*. In Cochrane's words:

The boat was brought to the surface without difficulty and when the conning tower was above water Lieut. John Scaife RN went on deck to surrender the crew; fire was immediately opened on him from light guns on shore and 3 motor boats which were lying around *E7*. As soon as the excitement had died down and the officers had regained control of their men, 2 motor boats came alongside, and the officers and men were taken off without difficulty. This operation being carried out under the orders of German Submarine Officers.

The boat was sunk immediately she was clear of the men, and a time-fuse having been fired subsequently blew up.

The boat contained a large amount of explosives and it was hoped that the explosion would be sufficiently heavy to wreck the net; this however was not the case and was probably due to the rush of water down the conning tower having washed the fitted charge away from the other explosives.[42]

The explosive device consisted of thirty tins, each holding 6 pounds of gun-cotton. A fifteen-minute fuse was prepared by Petty Officer Bob Sims, running from the explosives to the base of the periscope, to which was attached a firing pistol and a detonator.[43] All that Cochrane needed to do to fire the pistol was to pull on a string. Cochrane was the last to leave and, after opening the external vents and firing the pistol, he clambered onto the deck, where he was nearly washed overboard and had to jump for gunboat *No 18*, which picked up both him and his crew.[44] They were all sent initially to Constantinople (where, coincidentally, Lieutenant Scaife had been born), and later interned at various prison camps for the remainder of the war.

E12's second war patrol – 16 September to 25 October

Not long after the loss of *E7*, and following an overhaul in Malta, *E12* proceeded to the Dardanelles on Thursday 16 September, under the command of Lieutenant Commander K. M. Bruce. Diving off Suan Dere at 5 a.m., *E12* rounded Kilid Bahr at 6 p.m. and passed through the nets at 7 p.m., at a depth of 80 feet. Bruce was to report later that it appeared that the net had parted on the knife-edge of the foremost periscope standard. After passing through the nets, *E12* proceeded to patrol along the Asiatic coast. She was carrying a 4-inch gun, the largest mounted on a submarine operating in the Sea of Marmara to date. At 9 a.m., Bruce rose to periscope depth and successfully torpedoed and sank a large steamer. The ship, which was at anchor in Bergaz Bay, sank quickly by the bows and took with her two sailing ships which had been tied alongside to act as an anti-submarine defence.[45] Bruce was unable to observe the results of his attack due to the presence of small patrol craft in the area, but he was able to confirm the sinking on his return journey down the straits. After the successful attack, *E12* surfaced at 2 p.m. near the town of Gallipoli, to recharge her batteries and to transmit back her report.

On 18 September, *E12* continued her patrol along the European shore, past the harbour of Rodosto (which proved to be empty), and then on to Kalolimno Island, where she intercepted the *Sivrihisar*. At a range of 8,000 metres, the two boats opened fire. On firing the fourth round, Bruce observed what he believed to be a hit on the stern of the torpedo boat, which then turned and proceeded at high speed to Constantinople.[46] On 19 September, *E12* shelled the railway station and the tug *Eftimos* at Mundania,[47] firing eight rounds and silencing the shore batteries before she moved on and sank two sailing craft.

In increasingly bad weather, Bruce proceeded to Marmara Island, where the next day he intercepted a steamer[48] carrying cattle and sheep and other provisions such as flour and candles. The steamer initially refused to stop, until she was fired at and hit by the submarine's 4-inch gun. After allowing the crew time to abandon ship, she was sunk by further gunfire. Later that day six small dhows were sunk off Panderma. Over the next six days, bad weather and heavy seas made conditions difficult for the crew of *E12*, but also forced enemy shipping to remain in port – except for those which had little choice, such as hospital ships. Two were sighted on 23 September, and another four steamers were chased the following day, but they also proved to be hospital ships. On 26 September two destroyers were sighted patrolling from the Zeitun powder factory to the Princes Islands.

The next day, just before daylight, *E12* was preparing to bombard the factory at Stefano when she was forced to submerge by a destroyer. A further three sailing vessels, carrying fruit and wood, were sunk in the Gulf of Ismid on 28 September, but the arrival of two destroyers, combined with a thick fog which engulfed the area, prompted Bruce to decide not to proceed further up the gulf. The fog was at least a precursor to improving weather conditions, and the following day a dhow was sunk off Rodosto. Proceeding to the west in order to undertake radio communication, *E12* was fired upon near Sar Kioi but returned fire until the shore guns were silenced. Continuing westward, a further four dhows were intercepted and sunk, at which point *E12* was finally free to send her radio report. About half an hour before sunset, *E12* luckily avoided a near fatal encounter with a spotter plane, possibly a German Taube, which dropped two bombs, one of them exploding only 10 metres astern. The aeroplane came very close before it was observed, and Bruce reported that it appeared to have a silencer on the engine, as it was not audible when climbing. It seems more likely that, as mentioned earlier, the plane descended with its engine throttled right back. The incident was particularly lucky for the crew, as all but six were on deck at the time, though they managed to get below without incident before the submarine submerged.[49]

Two days later, on 1 October, after the fog had lifted, another aeroplane attack was made on *E12*, although no bombs were dropped this time. On Monday 4 October, Bruce attempted to attack another destroyer, but the torpedo was not fired as the safety gear on the torpedo tube failed. Just before dark, *E12* met with *H1*, the first submarine of this type to enter the Sea of Marmara, and Bruce, as the senior officer, ordered her to patrol the eastern area and to rendezvous on 7 October.[50]

The next day a small steamer was sunk, followed by the sinking of seventeen small sailboats in Rodosto Bay. Again, half an hour before sunset, *E12* was attacked by an aeroplane which dropped a bomb, though this time she had already reached a safe depth of 40 feet. The following day *E12* was once again attacked by an aeroplane, late in the afternoon. The rendezvous with *H1* was made on 7 October, and was used to undertake running repairs and to allow the seamen to take baths and wash their clothes. Over the next four days, although a few steamers were sighted, Bruce could not get close enough to carry out any effective attacks. Then on 12 October a determined attack was made on a small gunboat near Gallipoli, but the boat changed course and the torpedo missed. A little later, perhaps revealing his increasing frustration at the lack of reasonably sized targets, Bruce fired two torpedoes at a steamer in Lampsaki Bay, and the second one fortunately hit the target. The ship was seen to list to port, but Bruce was unable to confirm the hit as *E12* was forced to dive by small enemy craft. For the next three days no significant contacts were made, due to bad weather, and on 16 October *E12* had a rendezvous with *H1* and proceeded to the Gulf of Ismid.

On the following day, shortly after daylight, the gunboat *Tasköprü* was sighted coming from Constantinople, and both submarines approached in the hope of launching a torpedo attack. When it became apparent that they would not be able to get close enough, *E12* rose to the surface and commenced firing, trying to drive the torpedo boat towards *H1*. With the larger 4-inch gun, it was not difficult for *E12* to outrange her, and she appeared to be hit several times, a fact confirmed by *H1*'s observations. For the next two hours, the fire fight between *E12* and the gunboat continued, with over 200 rounds fired. *E12* achieved one direct hit, which killed one crew member and injured others.[51] The gunboat seemed to lose control at one point, running aground at Kalolimno. The pursuit continued, however, with *E12* trying to drive the torpedo boat round the island down the eastern side, until finally *H1* was able to fire a torpedo, which missed, as a heavy rain squall arrived, allowing *Tasköprü* to get away. But the chase was still not over; it continued when the quarry was sighted an hour later on the way towards Panderma, which she finally reached safely by 2.30 p.m. Heavy fog made it impossible for the submarines to pursue her any further that day.

While the submarines were patrolling off Panderma the following day, a large explosion was heard just after daylight, and then the shore batteries fired into the bay, although *E12* and *H1* were 8 miles away. A little later two destroyers, the *Yarhisar* and *Basra*, came out, and the two submarines were forced to dive as they watched the destroyers head for Constantinople. On 19 October, *E12*, in an aggressive move, also headed for Constantinople, and surfacing at 5.20 a.m. opened fire on the Zeitun powder factory, at a range of 8,000 yards. After the third shot found the range, three more rounds were fired, apparently hitting the target. However, immediately after the first shot, the shore batteries had returned fire and straddled the submarine with their second salvo, forcing her to submerge, as shells, apparently from 6-inch guns, fell dangerously all around her.

The next day, with the continued lack of suitable targets, Bruce attempted to torpedo a berthed steamer surrounded by several sailing vessels, on the northern side of Mudania, but the torpedo missed and appeared to hit one of the sailing vessels or, more likely, the pier. At this time Petty Officer Samuel Bazill caught his arm in the hydroplane gear, which resulted in a serious injury, so *E12* withdrew to render first aid to the injured man.

E12 met with *H1* and the French submarine *Turquoise* on 22 October and on the following day with *E20*. The sinking of a steamer by *E12* on its way up the straits was then confirmed by *E20*. After assigning the other submarines to their respective patrolling areas, *E12* reported by wireless that she was preparing to return to base. By 24 October *E12* had made her final preparations, while off Gallipoli, where she was surprised by the *Akusar* and forced to dive.

The return journey commenced at daylight on 25 October, and was to prove one of the most eventful of the campaign, with *E12* immediately forced to submerge by an armed tug. Passing Gallipoli at 7.30 a.m. in very calm seas, *E12* came to periscope depth near Karakova Burnu to get a bearing, and discovered a destroyer 200 yards off her beam. Twenty minutes later, the destroyer was still nearby and opened fire. The next time Bruce put up the periscope, he discovered that the destroyer had now been joined by two tugs. He decided that he had to lose the pursuers, and so lay on the bottom off Moussa Bank for an hour.

Bruce then set course for the net, but he was observed, while still about a mile away, by a small guard boat which fired on his periscope, forcing him to proceed towards the net without having got a good fix on the best course to take. However, the submarine successfully passed the first net barrage at 80 feet, although Bruce did observe subsequently that they were towing part of the net. Quite suddenly, about two minutes later, trim was lost, and the boat became heavy in the bow and stated to descend rapidly. Bruce ordered full speed, hoping to force the bow up, as the foremost hydroplanes were jammed at about 10 degrees. At the same time he blew the main ballast. The boat's bow was brought to a 7 degrees up angle, with a positive buoyancy of 40 tons at a depth of 160 feet, but she continued to descend, and she reached 245 feet before the descent was arrested.

During the uncontrolled descent the external tanks were once again blown individually, to make sure that they were both empty. As the pressure increased, the conning tower glass-scuttles burst and water began to enter the submarine through other weakened seals, particularly in the forward compartments. The increasing level of water in the boat and her up bow angle caused the water to rush to the after compartments, threatening to cascade over the coaming of the door to the battery area; this could have resulted in the production of chlorine gases. The forward compartment, which was leaking badly, was closed off to stem the flow, but to make matters worse one of the watertight hatches to the battery compartment itself had previously been removed, to test the density of the batteries. Fortunately, the quick-thinking of Lieutenant Reginald Brooke-Booth saved the day by diverting the approaching water until the hatch could be replaced. To add to Bruce's difficulties, both diving gauges had been broken by the pressure, although they had been shut off at 100 feet. The steering gyrocompass had failed, and the magnetic compass on the bridge was flooded and useless. The only serviceable gauge was the one by the periscope, and the boat had to be conned by using the main gyrocompass.

Three men were now placed on the forward hydroplane hand gear, and using brute force were able to move the planes through 10 degrees each way, to allow for some level of control. After ten minutes at 245 feet, the submarine began to rise and was finally brought under control at 18 feet. Six enemy patrol boats were in the area and started firing at *E12* when she reached a depth of 50 feet. This suggested to Bruce that she must have been towing something that gave away her position. Very little progress had been made beyond Nagara Point when he set course for Kilid Bahr. The submarine remained unmanageable, frequently taking up big inclinations, and on two occasions sinking to 120 feet before she could be brought under control. However, when just south of Kilid Bahr, *E12* ran into a mine-mooring chain at 80 feet. At this point Bruce put the rudder hard over, went to full speed, and after about four minutes heard the chain rattle its way aft along the submarine, and she was free. However, more than just the mooring had parted. The obstruction *E12* had been towing down the Dardanelles also let go, the boat suddenly took a steep inclination by the bow and rapidly rose through the water.

The bow was now exposed on the surface for about two minutes and the conning tower for about one minute, until the flooding of the tanks took effect and the submarine submerged again, but not before she had come under fire from the nearby forts and patrol vessels. Submarines under intense fire at short range (the fort at Kilid Bahr was only about 150 yards away) have little chance of survival once the pressure hull is penetrated. The conning tower was hit, and the casting cracked by a small shell, while the bridge was hit several times by shells and fragments, but no serious damage resulted so the submarine was able to submerge to relative safety. Not long after, a torpedo fired from Kilid Bahr was observed, and then heard, passing over the submarine 10 yards aft of the conning tower, followed by a second torpedo, which passed 50 yards astern. *E12* submerged to 80 feet, regaining her trim, which no longer presented any difficulty. At about 5 p.m., *E12* finally rose to the surface off Cape Helles and proceeded to Imbros under escort. As Admiral de Robeck wrote later in his report:

> The passage down the Straits, when the control of the boat is entirely vested in the Commanding Officer, was an experience the like of which few officers have had to undergo, and the successful accomplishment of the journey speaks volumes for Lieutenant Commander Bruce's determination.[52]

H1's first war patrol – 2 October to 31 October

Under the command of Lieutenant W. B. Pirie, *H1*[53] departed from Kephalos at 2.45 a.m. on 2 October, under the escort of *Pincher*, and arrived abeam of Helles at 4.35 a.m. Three quarters of an hour later, 2 miles west of Suan Dere, she submerged to a depth of 80 feet and got under way at a speed of 6 knots. At 6.10 a.m., *H1* rose to periscope depth, and Pirie was able to fix her position and set course for Kilid Bahr, which was reached at 7.25 a.m. When only 150 yards away, the boat began to swing to starboard, most likely because of a local eddy, and Pirie was forced to use full rudder for one minute and a half, until her direction could be stabilized. *H1* continued on her course, and at 8.05 Pirie made one last observation and set a new course to pass through the net. He descended to 80 feet and increased speed to 8 knots to crash through. However, six minutes later the submarine hit the bottom and was immediately thrown up to 28 feet, at which point Pirie stopped the port engine, turned hard to port so that the bow turned 120 degrees to the west, and she gradually slid off into deeper water. Pirie was again faced with some difficulty in fixing his position before he headed once more for the net. At 8.44 a.m. the tightening of net wires was heard, but after a slight pause they parted. A wire (observed through the conning tower scuttles to be 2.5 inches in diameter) was also heard to foul one of the propellers, but luck was with her, and the wire cleared the propeller.[54]

Having passed the net and also the newly laid 47-mine minefield off White Cliffs, Pirie rose to periscope depth at 9 a.m., but was immediately fired on. A while later, while he was submerged at 80 feet and with the submarine momentarily stopped, the hydroplanes, which had been turned in prior to the passage up the Dardanelles to reduce the risk of catching any unwanted wires, were now turned out. The boat then became much easier to control. After coming to periscope depth, *H1* was again fired on and, as she went to a safer depth, propellers were heard overhead. The town of Gallipoli was reached at 1.25 p.m., but, not surprisingly, no targets were observed. By 4.20 p.m., *H1* was on the surface in the Sea of Marmara charging her depleted batteries when she was forced to submerge by the arrival of a torpedo boat.[55] After the torpedo boat had departed, *H1* returned to the surface, spent four hours recharging her batteries, sent a signal that was never received, and then retired below the surface for the remainder of the night.[56]

On Sunday 3 October, *H1* attempted to rendezvous with *E12* without success, and remounted her gun. On the following day, after failing to get within firing range of a small steamer in Panderma Bay, *H1* headed again for the rendezvous point. Seeing exhaust smoke from *E12* at 4.30 p.m., they met and planned for joint activities in the Sea of Marmara. Some success was achieved on 5 October, with the sinking of three small sailing vessels, by gunfire, between Mara Burnu and Sazkaveh Burnu. However, more meaning-ful results were achieved on the next day, with the torpedoing of the *Edremit* along the western side of the Mudania pier. She exploded when hit, damaging the *Rehber* on the eastern side of the pier, and then sank, leaving her super-structure still exposed.[57] Soon after the initial hit, shore batteries opened fire on *H1*, which was forced to abandon her attack and then had to depart, as the gunboat *Yarhisar* arrived upon the scene.

On 7 October *H1* and *E12* met again for a rest day, during which time repairs were made, and then *H1* headed for Kuchuk Chekmejeh. On the following day a shore-based factory was placed under scrutiny, and later, after sunset, *H1* came to the surface but, due to poor light, failed in its attack on a tug pulling two lighters. Over the next two days, in worsening weather conditions, *H1* jettisoned the cargo of one dhow, and on 10 October she intercepted a two-masted sailing vessel. After the crew was forced into two small boats, *H1* rammed the ship on both sides, as the weather was so bad that she could not risk boarding by coming alongside. With the vessel almost cut into two, four rounds from the 6-pounder finished her off.

During this period of her patrol, *H1* had continuing problems with a number of defects; these culminated on 11 October in the discovery of a leak in the forward battery tank. It therefore became necessary to proceed to the centre of the Sea of Marmara, where work on the Number 2 main ballast tank, the source of the leak, could be undertaken without interruption. The tank was opened, and Engine Room Artificer Arthur Harvey, under difficult conditions, entered the tank and searched for the leak, but without success. Fortunately for *H1*, when an enemy destroyer did approach, the cover had just been replaced and *H1* was able to submerge to safety. A temporary section was then rigged to the battery tank to help contain the leak, but the spare freshwater tank had already been contaminated.

Over the next four days, in difficult weather conditions, only one steamer and a dhow were sighted and no successful attacks were launched. The heavy seas, however, did result in a steering failure (which was repaired) and, when *H1* met again with *E12* on 16 October, half a ton of fresh water was transferred to *H1*, the boat was dried and the men bathed and rested for the day.

As previously described, the next day proved eventful in a joint patrol of the Gulf of Ismid with *E12*. Around daybreak they intercepted the gunboat *Tasköprü* near Kalolimno Island, and at 7.15 a.m. *H1* fired a torpedo at a range of 900 yards, missing the gunboat as she altered course. *E12* surfaced and pursued the enemy vessel as she tried to make for Panderma; she opened fire on her at 9.50 a.m., causing the gunboat to turn toward *H1* just as there appeared to be two successful hits by *E12*. A few minutes later *H1* submerged and steered a course to prevent the gunboat from doubling back, but she was sighted passing down the western side of Kalolimno Island, so *H1* rose to the surface again and steamed down the eastern side, to cut her off from the Mudania Bay. An hour and a half later, *H1* was fired upon by two guns from Kalolimno and was forced to move further away to get out of range. By 11.40 a.m., it became apparent that *H1* had cut her off, and the gunboat altered course. Having seen that *E12* had dived to the west of Kalolimno, Pirie tried to drive the gunboat in that direction, but under the cover of a rain squall she returned to the protection of the shore batteries off Panderma at 2.30 p.m.

On seeing the enemy's retreat, *H1* sent a signal to *E12* by way of her Fessenden underwater sound signalling gear, perhaps the very first such submarine signal during enemy action, and, on receipt, *E12* surfaced. When the weather cleared an hour later, an attempt was made to attack the *Tasköprü* and a nearby steamer, *Hüdavandigar*, but heavy rain and poor visibility prevented success.[58] That evening *H1* submerged for the night and informed *E12* of her movements, again using the Fessenden equipment. For the next few days, the submarines continued to hunt as a pair around the Marmara islands and near Constantinople, but with limited success.

On 18 October a small sailing craft was destroyed by fire and, after examining what looked like a pile driver in Panderma, the submarines tried and failed to get within range of two fast-moving torpedo boats heading for Constantinople. The next day they sighted smoke off Khairsis Ada, and fired a torpedo at a gunboat at a range of 750 yards. Although the torpedo broke surface at 150 yards, the gunboat remained on course, but the torpedo either ran just in front of the target or beneath it. *H1* then headed off to Sar Kioi, and at 9 a.m. on 20 October discovered the steamers *Plevne*, *Gelibolu* and *Hanefiye*, all at anchor, unloading provisions into barges for the 5th Army. Moored nearby was the minelayer *Intibah*. At 11.40 a.m., *H1* fired her first torpedo and sank the *Plevne*, the resultant explosion suggesting that she was carrying explosives. An hour later, after reloading a torpedo, *H1* returned for what proved to be a more difficult shot due to gunfire received from the shore each time the periscope was raised. However, at 1.30 p.m., the next torpedo was fired, hitting and sinking the *Hanefiye*. A third torpedo was fired at a range of 600 yards but failed to hit the *Gelibolu*, probably going under her.[59] The *Intibah*, with boilers unlit, made no effort to intervene.[60]

Little was sighted the next day, and on Friday 22 October *H1* met with the French submarine *Turquoise* and, later, with *E12*. The following day, while still in company with *E12*, they met up again with *Turquoise* and also with *E20*, creating the unprecedented event of four Allied submarines coming together in the Sea of Marmara. *E12* communicated to base by wireless, while *H1* passed on mail to *E20*. The group was finally interrupted by the appearance of a torpedo boat, and later that day *H1* sent a signal to *E12* using her Fessenden equipment. The signal was intercepted by *E20* from 45 miles away, which not only testified to the capabilities of the equipment, but also perhaps indicated the effect of different density layers in the Sea of Marmara. The next day, with weather conditions improving, *H1* proceeded into Artaki Bay, where the boat was ventilated in quiet water to rid herself of the build-up of damp. Over the next two days an attempted attack on a steamer had to be aborted when she was found to be a hospital ship, and an intercepted sailing ship was released after she proved to be carrying female refugees.

Things improved on 27 October, with *H1* sighting smoke coming through the Marmara Channel at 6.15 a.m. By 7.10 a.m., Pirie had made out the torpedo boat *Berkefsan* and the steamer *Hüdavandigar*, close in shore.[61] He altered course to pass between Muhunia on the eastern tip of Kapu Dagh and the nearby island to the east (the likely route to Panderma), increased speed to 10.5 knots, and dived to 40 feet to get into a firing position. After twenty minutes he rose to periscope depth and discovered that the torpedo boat was only 300 yards astern, so was forced to dive back to 40 feet to avoid her. By 8.15 a.m., *H1* was in an attacking position and Pirie fired a torpedo at the patrol boat but missed, as she altered course. Pirie still persisted, trying to get a shot at the more valuable steamer, but the defensive activities of the torpedo boat prevented him, until the steamer reached the safety of a mole. Pirie therefore directed his attack back to the torpedo boat, and for over an hour tried in vain to get into position, before retiring to the east, to rendezvous later that afternoon with *E20*.

Early the next day Pirie went on board *E20*, to plan activities for the few remaining days that *H1* had left in the Sea of Marmara. By 11.10 a.m., *H1* had returned to Panderma to attack *Hüdavandigar* once again, but a hospital ship had in the meantime moored in a position which prevented a torpedo attack. Not to be thwarted, Pirie waited, observed the hospital ship leaving the next day, and, at noon, dived into Panderma Harbour. By hugging the western shore and turning at the last moment, he was able to fire off a torpedo at the bow of the steamer, causing only minor damage.[62] A torpedo boat then suddenly appeared from behind the steamer and pursued overhead for the next hour, as *H1* made her escape. That evening, *H1* informed *E20* of the day's activities, using Fessenden at a distance of 30 miles without any difficulties. On the following day, 30 October, *H1* sunk a small sailing vessel and then met with *E20* for the last time. As she headed for the Dardanelles, her deck gun was removed and two extra jumping wires and guards were set, to help penetrate the increasingly difficult net defences.

The return journey commenced on the next day when, at 2.15 a.m., a steamer was heard to pass overhead. Surfacing in calm conditions at 3.30 a.m., *H1* proceeded towards the town of Gallipoli, submerging 3 miles off the town at 5.30 a.m. By 7 a.m. she was passing the town in a rainstorm when the gunboat *Aydin Reis* sighted her and alerted the enemy defences. Over the next two hours a number of steamers and small brigantines were sighted, but no attacks were made. At 8.50 a.m., the port main motor was observed to be sparking badly, and it was decided that it was unfit for any further use; fortunately this did not impede the submarine's progress. In mid-morning, while coming to periscope depth to fix his position, Pirie discovered a torpedo boat very close astern, heading straight for him. Luckily he was able to dive the extra 10 feet in time, so that the boat passed harmlessly overhead.

Pirie took the submarine to 80 feet for the passage through the net and increased speed to 7.5 knots, the safest maximum speed on one motor. At 10.06 a.m. the submarine passed through the net, not fouling any of the 1.5-inch diameter wires, which were observed through the conning tower scuttles. Pirie used dead reckoning for the next 30 minutes, then fixed his position by sighting Kilid Bahr and Chanak and went to 60 feet, to round an obstruction at Kilid Bahr which he had been informed about while on patrol. At 11 a.m. he once again fixed his position by observation (which coincided with his dead reckoning), as the submarine rounded Kilid Bahr at a distance of 300 yards, having missed any obstructions. He then dived to 80 feet to avoid the minefield. *H1* surfaced off Sedd el Bahr at 1 p.m., where she was fired at by shore batteries on the Asiatic side, before being met by her escort *Pincher* for her return to base.

Turquoise[63]

After mooring off the Dardanelles on 19 October, the French submarine *Turquoise*, under the command of Lieutenant de Vaisseau Ravenel, left for the Narrows at 3 a.m. on 20 October, submerging to a depth of 85 feet to run the gauntlet of nets and mines. At 7 a.m., off Chanak, the submarine grounded in shallow water and was forced to surface, coming under fire from motorboats *No 19* and *No 20*. Fortunately the gunboats scored no hits, and *Turquoise* was able to submerge and make the rest of the passage without difficulty, to be the first French submarine to navigate the straits successfully. Near the town of Gallipoli two steamers were spotted and an attack was immediately attempted, but difficulties with the day periscope caused her captain to abort the attempt.

At this time, problems (which had occurred previously) with the electric motors forced *Turquoise* to travel on the surface across the Sea of Marmara, to meet up with *E12* and *E20* on 20 October. The electrical motor problem continued for the remainder of the patrol, and resulted in short circuits and associated fires onboard. Other problems included a leaking periscope, an out-of-action gyrocompass and almost unusable forward hydroplanes. The poor performance of the submarine during the patrol was highlighted by her failure to achieve any significant success; several sailing boats escaped thanks to the submarine's poor gunfire. On 25 October *Turquoise* met up with *E20* and, after separating, intercepted the patrol boat *Bahr-i Sefid* at 4 p.m., but after an initial exchange of fire she broke off the attack and moved away. Fortunately *Turquoise*'s inability to press her attacks to a successful conclusion held her in good stead when, on 26 October, a torpedo attack on a small sailing vessel near Rodosto failed. It was later discovered to be filled with Greek refugees.

On 30 October, *Turquoise* began its journey back down the Narrows,[64] passing the town of Gallipoli at 9 a.m. before submerging. When she approached the nets at Ak Bashi Liman, she raised her periscope for a sighting and gave away her position; in consequence, the shore batteries fired at her. Although initially these caused no damage, control was lost and the submarine hit the bottom, then overcompensated and broke the surface. The shore batteries of 3-inch guns fired at the conning tower and, after hoisting a white flag, the crew abandoned ship and were rescued. Not only was the submarine captured intact, but a German officer who boarded the boat found that no attempt had been made by either the submarine's officers or her crew to destroy any of the boat's logs or code-books![65]

Turquoise was salvaged by the tug *Sana* and by the pumping tug *Kurt* on 2 November. On the following day she was towed to Constantinople by *Nusret* and *Samsun*. The convoy was blacked out to avoid any possible contact with other Allied submarines. During the night, while zigzagging, the two escorting ships collided, with the *Samsun* having to be rescued herself. The tow line also broke, which necessitated starting the submarine's engine, after which she and the other boats finally reached Palatia. The *Gayret-i-Vataniye* took *Turquoise* in tow on 4 November and delivered the submarine to the docks at Constantinople the following day. On 11 November, the *Turquoise* was transferred to the Ottoman navy and renamed the *Mustadieh Ombashi* (*Mustecip Onbast*), after the artillery commander who was responsible for her quick capture.[66]

E20's first war patrol – 21 October to 5 November

The submarine *E20* left for her first and last patrol on 21 October, under the command of Lieutenant Commander C. H. Warren, and reached the Sea of Marmara without difficulty. The submarine had been fitted with a 6-inch howitzer. As discussed, during the following ten days *E20* met with a number of other submarines, including *E12* on 23 October, *Turquoise* on 25 October and *H1* on 31 October. *Tasoz* reported sighting torpedo tracks near Marmara Island on 27 October, and *Durak Reis* made a similar report on the same day. These tracks were probably from torpedoes fired by *E20*.[67]

It is known that the logs and code-books recovered from the captured *Turquoise* provided the German and Ottoman navies with details of the rendezvous locations and of the times of meeting with the other British submarines. On 5 November, Oberleutnant zur See Hugo von Heimburg, commanding *UB14*, set out from Constantinople to one of the rendezvous positions and at 4 p.m. sighted a conning tower, 5 miles to the north. At 5.10 p.m., and at a distance of 550 yards, he fired one torpedo which hit and sank *E20*. (For more details see the section on *UB14*.) At 5.20, *UB14* surfaced and rescued two officers, including Warren, and six sailors from *E20*'s crew.

E11's third war patrol – 6 November to 23 December

At 3 a.m. on the morning of 6 November, still under the command of Lieutenant Commander Nasmith, *E11*, in the company of *Savage*, headed off for the third time to pass through the defences of the Narrows. Submerging at 5.35 a.m. off Suan Dere, *E11* passed Chanak at 6.30 a.m. and at 7.15 a.m. at a depth of 80 feet, broke through the net without difficulty and surfaced off the town of Gallipoli at noon.

After reporting her position by wireless, *E11* was fired on by a tug, but the shots fell short and she continued on to recharge her batteries and rest for the night. Nasmith's previous good fortune had not deserted him and, on the following day near Kara Burnu, he overhauled the sailing vessel *Exliyadifis*,[68] which carried wine in large vats. The crew and three women were put into lifeboats and she was set on fire. After failing to make contact with *E20*, unaware that she had already been sunk, Nasmith headed towards Panderma, where, in a departure from previous operations, he was to put an agent ashore. However, when the submarine came to the surface, the Berthon boat,[69] which was carried on the upper deck, was blown away by the violent wind, a mishap which delayed the clandestine operation.

The next day, 8 November, Nasmith attempted to complete the transfer of the agent by taking the boat from a small sailing vessel which he had captured; but in rough seas the boat was lost when it was swamped before it could be secured. (The captain of the confiscated vessel swore in perfect English at his loss – a legacy from his seven years in the British Merchant Navy.) That afternoon Nasmith approached another small sailing vessel and attempted once again to take her boat, but was forced to give up and dive when the shore guns on Kale Burnu opened fire.

On 9 November, two Bosphorus ferries were sighted heading from Artaki towards the Rhoda Channel. At 7.35 p.m., Nasmith fired the port bow torpedo at the leading steamer but missed. Four hours later, the sailing vessel *Hildon*,[70] carrying oil, was stopped and sunk by explosives. The crew were taken on board, and her boat fastened to the submarine's deck. At 1.30 a.m. on the following day, the agent was finally put ashore in Artaki Bay.[71] In the early hours of the same morning, prisoners from the *Hildon* were allowed to leave in their small boat, near Pasha Liman Island. Half an hour later, at 5.35 a.m., a tug was observed towing a large three-masted barque. Nasmith fired one round at each ship, but the flash from the deck gun was so bright that the gun crew lost their night vision, and also the location of the tug. Nasmith therefore gave the order for *E11* to submerge for a short dive. On returning to the surface, the tug had already made off while the crew of the barque were taking to their lifeboats. The barque was found to be loaded with hay and was quickly destroyed by gunfire.

The next afternoon, while *E11* was heading towards Rodosto, a small tug was observed towing a steamer towards Gallipoli, and then a schooner was found anchored at Panidos. *E11* surfaced to sink her by gunfire, but, to Nasmith's surprise, the schooner was well armed with four guns, which returned heavy and accurate fire. Nasmith was forced to retreat to a distance of 8,000 yards, and after half an hour abandoned the gun action, assuming that some damage had been done.

On 12 November Nasmith patrolled the entrance to Constantinople and observed that a destroyer and torpedo boat were lying inside the pier in Haidar Pasha Harbour. He considered an attack on the boats at their berths, but found it was not possible to get into a position to fire his torpedoes effectively. After observing the movements of ferry traffic in the area, *E11* moved on to Oxia Island, where on the following morning six small sailing boats were sunk which carried an assortment of supplies, including stakes to be used for barbed-wire entanglements. The next day was Sunday 14 November and, as on all Sundays, religious services were held, including prayers and hymns which were played on a gramophone.

On 15 November, after proceeding past the town of Gallipoli and finding that the harbour at Ak Bashi Liman was void of shipping, *E11* headed back to the Sea of Marmara and, on the way, found two steamers lying in Bergaz Bay. Nasmith manoeuvred *E11* into position, and at 11.35 a.m. fired his port bow torpedo at the innermost of the two ships. The torpedo struck her on the starboard bow, creating a large hole in her side and demolishing a small sailing vessel nearby. The ship sank in shallow water, but several weeks later was raised and repaired.[72] Nasmith then turned his attention to the nearby *Lilly Rickmers*, firing his starboard beam torpedo at 11.38 a.m., but it exploded prematurely, destroying two schooners. The torpedo attack had failed because of protective torpedo netting; it caused only minor damage to a steamer, which was subsequently repaired in Constantinople. By 3.35 p.m. Nasmith had added to his run of successes by entering Chardak Liman and firing his port beam torpedo, which sank a steamer.[73]

However, even Nasmith was unable to overcome the bad weather between 16 and 22 November, which restricted his sinkings. On 17 November, a small empty sailing vessel was captured and burnt; this was followed on 22 November by the capture and destruction through gunfire of a small sailing vessel. Earlier that morning, while in the Mudania Bay, Nasmith observed perhaps one of the most extreme examples of the different water densities in the Sea of Marmara. With the engines stopped and the hydroplanes set in a horizontal position, the submarine remained at a depth of 23 feet, with the top of the periscope just showing above the surface and the depth not varying by more than 6 inches. These pronounced conditions were only found in the bay, and were accentuated by the influence of a strong north-easterly wind. The next day, a small sailing vessel was set on fire and two more were sunk by ramming, which happened less frequently than might have been expected, given the frailty of the targets.

On 24 November, Nasmith missed a major opportunity when at 10.30 a.m., after leaving Artaki and heading for Gallipoli, he found a convoy of tugs and lighters proceeding towards Sar Kioi. When he was sighted, the convoy immediately broke up and scattered. He chose to follow the ships heading for Rodosto but was unable to attack as the enemy vessels moved into shallow water close inshore. The next afternoon a small sailing vessel was captured and sunk by gunfire; but it was on the following morning, 26 November, that Nasmith's next major encounter occurred.

On that morning, *E11* dived and moved into the anchorage at Artaki; there she discovered two steamers, the *Gelibolu* and the *Edremit*,[74] close to shore and protected from torpedo attack by a ring of dhows. At 11.45 a.m., *E11* rose to the surface and opened fire at a range of 8,000 yards, achieving several hits on the two ships, although, unintentionally, some of the rounds went over the targets and hit the nearby town. The shore guns and a gun on one of the steamers returned fire, but all their rounds fell short. *E11* dived and headed further into the anchorage, where Nasmith saw that little damage had been inflicted by his gunfire. At that time the naval tug *Sana* arrived on the scene, patrolled for about an hour and then, surprisingly, left. This gave Nasmith the opportunity to recommence his surface bombardment from a range of 6,000 yards. Again, several hits were observed, one of the steamers being set on fire. The resultant smoke and flame masked the location of the other steamer, so *E11* dived again and made her way into the harbour to examine the damage. There Nasmith discovered that the ship which was on fire (the *Gelibolu*) had sunk. Leaving the harbour, *E11* rose to the surface and, at a range of 4,000 yards, recommenced the bombardment of the remaining ship. With the approach of darkness the engagement was broken off, but by then the *Edremit* had been damaged.

Again bad weather, including gales and snow, interfered with operations for the remainder of the month; *E11* had to take shelter wherever she could, while still trying to check various locations for enemy shipping. In the early afternoon of 1 December, three small sailing vessels were captured and destroyed south of the Princes Islands. Then a small motorboat was captured, whose supply of potatoes, eggs and butter was happily confiscated by *E11*. Also on board was an English-speaking Greek captain captured for the second time; the first time had been on 8 November, when his lifeboat was confiscated and then lost. Another sailing vessel was sighted and destroyed, and all the crews were then loaded onto the small motorboat and allowed to go. The next day in the Gulf of Ismid the railway line was placed under scrutiny and a night-sight was later rigged on the deck gun. *E11* waited till midnight at a distance of 400 yards off-shore, when a goods train was spotted on its way from Constantinople. Only two rounds were fired, although one round did manage to set one wagon ablaze.

On 3 December, at 1 p.m., after moving out of the Gulf of Ismid, *E11* spotted the destroyer *Yarhisar* heading from the west towards the gulf. Nasmith quickly manoeuvred into position, fired the starboard beam torpedo and made a perfect hit, blowing the ship in two, with both halves sinking in less than a minute. *E11* then surfaced to pick up the survivors, two officers and forty men including the ship's captain, from a total complement of eighty, of which fifteen were Germans,[75] all of whom were later transferred to a captured sailing ship. By 6.10 p.m., *E11* was involved in another engagement, this time with an armed tug which in all likelihood had set out from Mudania to find out what had happened. After firing a few rounds at long range, Nasmith broke off the engagement and withdrew in failing light.

The following morning, a two-masted steamer was sighted trying to get to Panderma before daybreak. At 8.10 a.m. and a from distance of 2,000 yards, *E11* opened fire with its deck gun and hit the steamer with her third round, upon which the ship's crew took to the lifeboats and abandoned ship. Immediately a fast-moving torpedo boat approached from the north, firing rapidly at *E11* and forcing her to dive, but not before it was clear that the steamer was burning fiercely.[76] The torpedo boat then circled the steamer at a distance of 3,000 yards. When the torpedo boat was on the other side of the steamer, *E11* surfaced on her port side, within 20 yards, and fired one round under the water-line, to make sure that the steamer would sink. On realizing what was happening, the torpedo boat immediately opened fire and hit the steamer on its other side, while *E11* submerged. After half an hour, the torpedo boat departed and *E11* surfaced at 10.30 a.m., to watch the steamer sink by the bow. Nasmith's run of luck still continued next day, when at 2.20 p.m., in a sea of diminishing targets, he rose to the surface near Kamir Liman and bombarded the bark *Elenora*[77] until she was ultimately gutted by fire.

At 7.15 p.m., a small steamer was observed near the town of Gallipoli, so Nasmith trimmed *E11* down, hoping to remain unnoticed while he inspected the steamer as she continued on her course. She carried no lights and it was obvious that she was not a hospital ship, so Nasmith moved at full speed to get ahead, and at 8.45 p.m. opened fire at a range of 500 yards. After firing three rounds, the first of which destroyed her lifeboats and the second of which hit her boiler, Nasmith brought *E11* alongside the burning steamer (Number 40)[78] and rescued six members of the crew (one of whom died of burns shortly after boarding the submarine and was subsequently buried at sea). Among the survivors was the ship's French-speaking captain, who informed Nasmith that another ferry was due the next day. He also provided Nasmith with a good deal of interesting and somewhat embellished information, which gave some insight into the situation from the Turkish viewpoint at that time:

- All munitions of war and troops moved by land: food and less costly munitions were sent by sea.
- *Turquoise* was in Constantinople having been caught in the Nagara net.
- Ten submarines were based in Constantinople, including three large ones.

- Only three large merchant ships remained, two in Constantinople and one in Khelia Liman, and eight Shirket steamers of 200 tons displacement, all of which travel at night.
- *E20* had been torpedoed by a German submarine, with three officers and thirteen men saved.
- Aeroplanes worked daily from Rodosto, Gallipoli and Constantinople (weather permitting).

On 6 December Nasmith proceeded to Artaki Harbour, where he found the other steamer, mentioned by the previously captured captain. *E11* opened fire at a range of 5,000 yards, hitting her several times before reducing the range to 4,000 yards; then the steamer caught fire.[79] Shore batteries then opened fire, and forced *E11* to submerge and move away.

The following day, still near Artaki, *E11* rammed and sank a small empty sailing vessel before proceeding to Sar Kioi. There she trimmed down to remain unseen while observing a dispatch vessel, then took station behind her stern. Cruising within 500 yards at a speed of 12 knots, at 8 p.m. *E11* opened fire with three rounds; the first hit his target,[80] but the latter returned fire and *E11* was forced to submerge. Nasmith continued to follow the vessel and at 1 a.m. the next morning he saw it moving along the northern shore of Marmara Island. Increasing speed, and keeping in the shadow of the island, Nasmith was able to bring *E11* within 300 yards of the minelayer on her starboard quarter. Three rounds were fired hitting her twice, but she returned the fire and turned hard to starboard in an apparent attempt to ram the submarine. Nasmith turned his submarine slightly and crash-dived, with the minelayer passing harmlessly overhead. Nasmith was not willing to give up at this time and surfaced ten minutes later, only to see that the ship had taken shelter close to shore.

At sunrise it became apparent that the minelayer had taken refuge in Palatia Bay. At a range of 4,000 yards. *E11* once again opened fire, but was quickly forced to retreat to a range of 6,000 and then 7,000 yards, due to the accurate fire from the shore guns. The third round fired by *E11* at this greater range was seen to hit the minelayer's forecastle, putting her gun out of action and setting her on fire. With enemy shells falling all around, Nasmith finally had to withdraw, although the minelayer had not been put out of action.

Later that afternoon, while patrolling towards Panderma, *E11* was attacked by an aeroplane which approached by a silent volplane out of the sun and was not observed until it was right overhead; then it dropped two bombs, which exploded about 100 yards off the port bow. In Nasmith's typical fashion, he submerged until only the upper section of the conning tower was above water, grabbed a rifle, fired at the circling aeroplane, and then submerged at the last minute, as the aircraft came in for her second attack. *E11* dived safely while the bombs dropped in her wake.

The next day, 9 December, around 8 a.m., the risk of an attack came from below the sea. Leaving Panderma on the way out, luckily still submerged, Nasmith saw another periscope pass slowly by at a distance of 200 yards, on its way in. The top of the periscope was of a design similar to those fitted on earlier E boats, and he assumed that it was most likely *E2*, herself checking out of the port, prior to their rendezvous later that day. However, at that time *E2* was still passing through the Dardanelles, and certainly could not have been the submarine that Nasmith observed; while *E20* had already been sunk by then. The submarine that Nasmith saw was *UB14*, under the temporary command of von Dewitz. *E11* was not seen by von Dewitz, but later that day, around 1.30 p.m., he sighted her on the surface and attempted, over the next three hours, to get into an attacking position – without success.[81]

On 10 December, after searching for shipping in Palatia Bay, *E11* had a rendezvous with *E2* at 4.15 p.m. and collected some equipment and also ammunition. The next day no enemy activity was observed, and the moon proved too bright to allow an attack on the railway on the shore of the Gulf of Ismid. However, at 1 a.m. on the following morning, the bright moon enabled Nasmith to observe a tug towing a large heavily laden bark and a dhow. Taking station on the starboard quarter, *E11* opened fire at 4.20 a.m., at a range of 300 yards, firstly on the tug and then on the bark, whose crew quickly abandoned ship.[82] The shore batteries then opened fire with their first round hitting the bark, so after firing a few more rounds *E11* submerged. Coming back to the surface ten minutes later, Nasmith saw no trace of the bark, which had sunk, while the tug was ablaze and later sank.

The next day Nasmith took *E11* into the entrance to Constantinople, and observed nothing all day except hospital ships. Later that evening, when stationed 6,000 yards from the gun factory,[83] *E11* fired one round to test the Turkish response, but little occurred apart from a light being turned on at Stefano Point. At 8 a.m. on 14 December, *E11* once again dived into the entrance to Constantinople, where Nasmith discovered a steamer docking at Haidar Pasha Pier behind the breakwater. Never one to miss an opportunity, Nasmith manoeuvred *E11* into a firing position, getting ever closer to the breakwater as he waited for a small tug towing a string of dhows to pass by. Finally he got a clear shot and fired the port bow torpedo, which hit the steamer in the bow, so that she immediately began to sink. Nearby vessels quickly came to her aid and managed to prevent her from sinking.[84] It was now important to get out of the harbour, when *E11* hit the base of a breakwater at a depth of 19 feet. Fortunately this caused no major damage, although the periscope was showing 'above water' for several minutes. Nasmith manoeuvred *E11* to safety and then headed back to the Gulf of Ismid.

South of Tuzla, at 4.25 a.m. on the morning of 16 December, after a fruitless search of the Gulf of Ismid on the previous day, *E11* fired three rounds at a passing train on the Constantinople–Ismid railway,[85] at a range of 500 yards, but owing to poor light Nasmith was doubtful whether any rounds had hit. The next day he again took *E11* to Constantinople but, because no observation could be made in the mist, he came to the surface and captured a small sailing vessel. Once again Nasmith lashed the craft to the side of the submarine nearest to Constantinople, and travelling on the surface, captured another vessel. Then he departed, burning one of the captured vessels and knocking holes in the other to sink her.

E11 proceeded to Mudania and on the next day found nothing, so Nasmith decided to have a rendezvous with *E2*, but on the way he became wary when he saw a torpedo track passing well ahead of his submarine.[86] That afternoon, *E11* and *E2* parted company, with *E2* taking the eastern half of the Sea of Marmara. On 20 December at 10 a.m. off Erekli, *E11* sank one sailing vessel by ramming. She spent the following day searching for *E2* around Mudania, without success.

At 11.30 a.m. on 22 December near Mudania, *E11* rammed and destroyed another sailing vessel, and during the afternoon she rigged net-cutting gear on the upper deck for the return journey.[87] In the early hours of the next morning, *E11* dived off Dohan Aslan and rested on the bottom in 15 fathoms of water before surfacing at 5 a.m., passing the town of Gallipoli at 6 a.m., and then diving once again at 7 a.m. off Bergaz Bay. At 10.17 a.m., *E11* burst through the chain net, having avoided the older wire net, which appeared to have been extended only halfway across the Narrows, with the half nearest to Nagara either removed or swept away. At 10.50 a.m., *E11* rounded Kilid Bahr and at 1 p.m. she rose to the surface off Cape Helles for the last time, to be escorted to Mudros by *Comet*. On this mission, by Nasmith's reckoning, *E11* had sunk eleven steamers, five large sailing vessels and thirty small sailing vessels. Over the three missions, which lasted ninety-six days, *E11* had, by their reckoning, accounted for a total of 122 vessels sunk. Nasmith survived the war and eventually attained the rank of admiral during the Second World War, during which he was commander-in-chief of Western Approaches and was responsible for the fight against the U-boats in the Atlantic.

E2's second patrol – 9 December to 3 January

After a five-week refit at Malta, *E2* arrived at Mudros on 30 November, and moored alongside *Adamant*. On Wednesday 8 December the boat was ready for another mission, and Admiral Wemyss came aboard to wish the crew luck. *E2* proceeded to Rabbit Island under escort by *Racoon*, and secured alongside the monitor *Roberts* till the following morning. At 4 a.m. *E2* left Rabbit Island under the command of Lieutenant Commander D. de B. Stocks and proceeded up the Narrows, diving at 5.50 a.m. after being forced down by a French searchlight on the peninsula. By 7.47 a.m., *E2* was passing Kilid Bahr in very foggy conditions, which made it more difficult for Stocks to locate his position. Having negotiated the minefields without difficulty, at 8.45 a.m. *E2* struck the chain net at an initial depth of 80 feet, but after getting caught momentarily, was forced to go up, rising to 60 feet before control was established. At that point the chain snapped and passed overhead on the starboard side of the submarine, with 'much jarring and scraping'. The nets, which *E2* had broken through, were new ones, laid after *E11* had passed through. *E2* missed the second net and proceeded up the straits by dead reckoning, due to the thick fog. Unknown to Stocks, the submarine was spotted by the coast guard in the early hours of the morning, the anti-submarine force was alerted, and a Gotha spotter plane was dispatched. The plane sighted *E2* off Gallipoli at 1.45 p.m., and patrol boats were directed to her reported position, but without success.[88]

Meanwhile *E2* passed the town of Gallipoli, sighted the aircraft at 3.30 p.m., and at 4.05 p.m. surfaced and proceeded into the Sea of Marmara. After ventilating the boat, charging batteries and sending a wireless signal, *E2* submerged for the night. On the morning of the following day, off Sar Kioi, *E2* sank a large dhow carrying a cargo of salt and olive oil, and took four prisoners on board. In the early afternoon, *E2* was harassed again by a Turkish plane off Rodosto before meeting up with *E11* (as has been mentioned) to transfer stores and ammunition. Stocks then took *E2* to the harbour at Artaki on 11 December, where the prisoners were transferred to a small empty caique. On the following day, *E2* was once again forced by an aeroplane to submerge and that evening she continued through the Marmara Channel, resting on the deeper salt-water layer for the night.

Stocks then went on to Panderma on 13 December, where a search revealed no enemy shipping. The next day an unsuccessful attempt was made to destroy the submerged military telegraph-cable, which ran from Constantinople through the Sea of Marmara, then down the Dardanelles, passing near Marmara Island. An obstruction was encountered and destroyed by using a grappling hook to which an explosive charge was attached, but it proved not to be the cable. Back in Artaki Bay on 16 December, a small steamer, armed with a 3-pounder gun, came out from behind Point Papu on Pasha Liman and bravely opened fire at a range of 8,000 yards, but the range was too long and her shot fell short. *E2* replied with her 4-inch gun, and after fourteen rounds the steamer was ablaze and sank in shallow water at 5 p.m.[89] The nearby watch posts, on seeing the action, lit their smoke beacons and signal rockets, and shortly afterwards a torpedo boat arrived, chasing *E2* on the surface. When the range reduced to 10,000 yards, *E2* dived and, as was often the case, the torpedo boat made no attempt to continue the attack. At midnight that evening *E2* surfaced at her radio billet and made contact to check whether the evacuation of Gallipoli was still to proceed. A Turkish hospital ship was sighted, so *E2* submerged to avoid detection.

On the morning of 17 December, *E2* sank two dhows off Hora Burnu and by 2 p.m. was engaged in sinking the schooner *Emanetullah*.[90] After transferring the crew and prisoners to a small boat, she sank the schooner by charges and set her alight, until the arrival of the torpedo boat *Akhisar* forced *E2* to leave. On the following day, at midday, *E2* sank another dhow and later that afternoon met again with *E11*. The pair proceeded together on the surface for about one hour before they approached each other to compare notes and discuss new areas of activity; then they agreed to meet again on Christmas Day.

At 6 a.m. on 19 December, *E2* intercepted the tug *Tarik* with barges in tow, proceeding into Constantinople. She opened fire with her deck gun, noting two hits before the tug's 2-inch gun proved too effective and *E2* was forced to break off the engagement.[91] That afternoon, while she was submerged, the sounds of what were believed to be the propellers of an enemy submarine were heard close alongside.

On the next day *E2* entered Mudania Bay only to find it deserted; so in the afternoon Stocks decided to enter Mudania Harbour. He grounded his submarine in misty conditions but fortunately was able to get off and move away safely. A few hours later a large dhow was caught and burnt, followed by another dhow, which was carrying a cargo of figs; these were jettisoned but the dhow was allowed to proceed, as she also carried several women. Given the spirit of chivalry of the time and the inconvenience of taking women on board a submarine, the presence of women was perhaps intentional: with them on board, captains would only lose their cargoes but not their boats. That night, when *E2* was proceeding up the Gulf of Ismid, a German submarine was sighted off Boz Burnu, but she dived when she saw *E2* preparing to attack.

December 21 proved a relatively fruitful day. At 8 a.m., a large dhow was caught carrying Greek and Armenian women and children passengers, so that only the cargo of figs was jettisoned. Shortly afterwards, two dhows were destroyed, and later that evening the cargo of another dhow comprising 160 large tins of petrol (a valuable commodity at the time) was destroyed, while the prisoners taken earlier were transferred to the dhow and released. On the following day another dhow was sunk, and another one carrying women and priests was allowed to proceed, after the cargo was jettisoned. At 1.25 p.m. on 23 December the regular ferry service between Constantinople and Mudania was stopped and, after a search which revealed that the steamer was only carrying passengers, was allowed to continue. That night, in heavy seas, E2 once again searched for the enemy submarine off Boz Burnu, but without success.

The next day the heavy seas persisted, and E2 headed for her rendezvous with E11, but by this time E11 had left the Sea of Marmara, after having unsuccessfully tried to communicate with E2 by wireless. On the following day, which was Christmas Day, Stocks tried again, without success, to find the German submarine and to rendezvous with E11. In the evening the crew had a Christmas dinner of tinned turkey and plum pudding. The next day, encountering no enemy shipping, E2 proceeded down to the town of Gallipoli and finally managed to communicate with Aster, which clarified the situation of E11. On 27 December she ventured into Artaki Bay and, although she searched all the bays and even the harbour itself, she sighted no enemy shipping. This was, to some extent, testimony to the effectiveness of the Allied submarine offensive.

Early next morning, after she moved up Rhoda Channel, she sunk a dhow off Rhoda Harbour. This was followed next day (29 December) by the destruction of three dhows in the Gulf of Ismid. The last had refused to stop, so she was chased down and rammed; this resulted in the death of one of her crew, who became entangled in her main sail. The constant threat of an enemy submarine dwelled on Stocks' mind, so once again, in the early hours of 30 December, E2 returned to Boz Burnu searching for the elusive submarine. Although she was, once more, unsuccessful in locating the submarine, E2 was able to intercept a small dhow carrying charcoal, which was jettisoned, and in return E2 was able to jettison her cargo of prisoners. E2 then attempted an attack on a steamer near Mudania, but this proved to be a hospital ship.

On 31 December, E2 fired sixteen rounds at the Mudania railway station; Stocks noticed that it caught fire in eight separate places, although little damage was caused. The shore guns didn't return fire on account of their own low supplies of ammunition.[92] At 11 a.m., while near Makri Kioi, E2 was able to sink one dhow, capture a cargo of fresh fish from a second one and then sink a third. All of these dhows were carrying food cargoes bound for Constantinople – an effect of the increasing food shortages at the capital. E2 then made for Constantinople, arriving on 1 January, but this was too late to see the last transport convoy leaving for the front. E2 then remained off

Kuchuk Chekmejeh for the night and, on 2 January, as the weather deteriorated considerably, Stocks elected to pursue a westward course along the north coast of the Sea of Marmara.

That afternoon, after communicating with *Aster*, he received orders to return, and set about fixing *E2*'s jumping wires and knife cutter for the return journey. At 6 a.m. the next morning she set course for the Dardanelles, charging her batteries as she went. She dived at 8.45 a.m., and by 10 a.m. was passing the town of Gallipoli. At 1.30 p.m., when off Ak Bashi Liman, *E2* dived to 80 feet and found that the nets had apparently been removed; then she hit bottom at 70 feet off Maidos. Stocks turned *E2* to a heading of 165 degrees and went ahead but hit bottom again, running up to a dangerous depth of 20 feet, fortunately without being sighted. Taking bearings, Stocks fixed his position, turned *E2* to a heading of 125 degrees, and moved out of the straits, passing Chanak at 3.25 p.m. and surfacing off Cape Helles at 6.05 p.m. *E2* had travelled a distance of 1,480 miles, sunk nineteen dhows and one steamer, and caused damage to another steamer and a railway station; but, perhaps even more importantly, there were now no Allied submarines in the Sea of Marmara for the first time in ten months.

12

The Last Act

In August, Hamilton admitted to Kitchener that his offensive had failed and that he needed another 95,000 men to win. In reply, Kitchener informed him that Gallipoli had been given its chance and had lost, and that attention was now turning back towards France. The aim was to place more pressure on Germany's western front and thus to take pressure off the Russian front, where Warsaw had recently been captured by the Germans. However, had Turkey fallen, badly needed supplies could have been provided to Russia, which may have had a greater and more immediate impact than increasing pressure on Germany from the west. Of mounting concern was the possibility of Bulgaria siding with the Central Powers and the prospect of Germany being able to supply significant quantities of guns and ammunition to Turkey.

Hamilton's prospects improved briefly when, on 2 September, the French announced that four new divisions would be sent to the Dardanelles to attack the Asiatic side in conjunction with their existing forces at the Dardanelles. The British government then announced that two new divisions would be sent to replace the French divisions moving to the Asiatic front. But, by the end of September, all these additional troops were either promised or diverted to other theatres of war. In the meantime, the month of September had been cold, and a gale blew up on 8 October, warning the Allies of impending difficulties in keeping the troops supplied. Then, to make matters worse, on 25 September Kitchener informed Hamilton that two English and probably one French division would be taken from Gallipoli to reinforce Salonika, as Bulgaria had mobilized.

Hamilton's reputation was also starting to diminish, not only from the lack of success, but also through Stopford's criticism after his return to London. Further criticism by the war correspondent Ashmead-Bartlett, in a reported interview in the *Sunday Times* on 17 October, correctly foresaw the potential problems which would arise from a winter campaign on the peninsula. Keith Murdoch, the Australian reporter, wrote a scathing letter to the Australian

Prime Minister after visiting the Australians at Anzac, which further exacerbated the situation. This letter was seen by Lloyd George and sent to the Dardanelles Committee. On 11 October, Hamilton was asked to give his estimate of losses from an evacuation, and he replied on 12 October that the step was unthinkable to him. At this time Lieutenant General Robertson, the chief of the Imperial General Staff, was recalled from France to give his opinion. He advised that the Allies should cut their losses and evacuate and that 'it ought nevertheless to be a feasible operation provided that careful arrangements were made, especially with respect to secrecy'.[1] As there was no prospect of withdrawal from Gallipoli while Hamilton remained in command, on 16 October he received a cable recalling him to London; he left Imbros with good grace and was replaced by General Sir Charles Monro, former commander of the Third Army in France.

Monro took his time to study filed reports in London before he headed for Gallipoli. At the same time Commodore Keyes arrived in London, once again advocating an attack by the navy in case the army failed, although de Robeck was still against such a move. Monro was instructed to evaluate the Gallipoli situation and to decide on military grounds whether to attack or withdraw; this included saying how many men were needed to win and how many men would be lost if he withdrew. At the time there were 114,000 soldiers at, or around, the Dardanelles; when at full strength, this force should have numbered 200,000. When Monro arrived at Imbros on 28 October, the General Staff provided him with a plan of attack which would require 400,000 troops, and could not commence till the spring of 1916. If evacuation was decided upon, losses of up to 50 per cent of men and 66 per cent of equipment could be expected.[2] Monro visited all three combat sites in one day on 30 October, having received a telegram from Kitchener the day before asking for his decision. The short one-day inspection of Helles, Anzac and Suvla convinced him of the Allied army's precarious position and, perhaps more importantly, he believed in the strategy of 'killing Germans' to win the war; so on the next day he sent a telegram to Kitchener recommending an evacuation.

With the exception of the Australian and New Zealand Army Corps the troops on the Peninsula are not equal to a sustained effort, owing to inexperienced officers, the want of training of the men, and the depleted condition of many of the units.

We merely hold the fringe of the shore, and are confronted by the Turks in very formidable entrenchments, with all advantages of position and power of observation of our movements. The beaches are exposed to observed artillery fire, and in the restricted areas all stores are equally exposed. We can no longer count upon any action by surprise as the Turks are in considerably stronger force than they were, and have had ample time to provide against surprise landings.

Since the flanks of the Turks cannot be attacked, only a frontal attack is possible and no room is afforded on any of the beaches for the distribution of additional divisions should they be sent, nor is there sufficient space for the deployment of an adequate force of artillery, the action of which would be impaired by poverty of observation and good positions for searching or counter battery effects. Naval guns could only assist to a partial degree.

In fact, an attack could only be prosecuted under the disadvantages of serious lack of depth, and of absence of power of surprise, seeing that our line is throughout dominated by the Turks' position. The uncertainty of weather might also seriously hinder the landing of reinforcements and regularity in providing the artillery ammunition to the amount which would be required.

It is, therefore, my opinion that another attempt to carry the Turkish lines would not offer any hope of success; the Turkish positions are being actively strengthened daily. Our information leads to the belief that heavy guns and ammunition are being sent to the Peninsula from Constantinople. Consequently by the time fresh divisions, if available, could arrive, the task of breaking the Turkish line would be considerably more formidable than it is at present.

On purely military grounds, therefore, in consequence of the grave daily wastage of officers and men which occurs, and owing to the lack of prospect of being able to draw the Turks from their entrenched positions, I recommend the evacuation of the Peninsula.[3]

Kitchener's response was to ask for the views of the three corps commanders. Only Birdwood recommended against a withdrawal, particularly given the unreliable weather, where on the previous evening the destroyer *Louis* had been blown ashore at Suvla, and broken up in a storm. The corps commanders' views were forwarded to Kitchener on 2 November.

In the meantime in London, Keyes met Admiral Oliver, the chief of the Naval War Staff on 29 October, with his new plan of attack. This was followed by a meeting with Sir Henry Jackson, the First Sea Lord. At 5 p.m., he met Arthur Balfour, the First Lord. He was proposing a two-pronged attack at the Dardanelles. The first part consisted in using destroyers and mine-sweepers under the cover of a smokescreen at dawn, to press on through the minefields no matter what, while the monitors and new battleships pounded the Turkish guns from the mouth of the Dardanelles. Once the straits were swept, the ships would enter the Sea of Marmara, set a course for the Bulair Isthmus, and cut off the single road, which was heavily used by military traffic heading for Gallipoli.

This was the location where a number of submarines had previously attempted to make a small impression with their deck guns. The position of Turkish minefields was now believed to be better known thanks to aerial reconnaissance (although this was not reliable), and many of the shore guns had been removed because the Turks felt that another attack through the Dardanelles was unlikely. Finally, losing several battleships but possibly winning the war was better than losing lives through an unsuccessful evacuation.

On Saturday 30 October Keyes met Balfour again at 3 p.m.; two and half hours later, Balfour rose from his chair and said: 'It is not often that when one examines a hazardous enterprise – and you will admit it has its hazards – the more one considers it the better one likes it.'[4] After continued discussions with the admirals, he finally met Churchill on 2 November and in the afternoon Kitchener. With Monro's report on possible evacuation losses in mind, Kitchener agreed to support Keyes's proposal, as long as it had Admiralty support. By the next day Keyes was able to report that the Admiralty had given partial support as long as the army would attack, and that Kitchener was determined not to evacuate the troops from the Dardanelles, due to the high losses expected. At this stage Kitchener decided to visit Gallipoli, and at a farewell meeting with Cabinet on 4 November he discovered a high level of disagreement within Cabinet over Gallipoli, while Balfour made it quite clear that the navy would do nothing unless the army attacked.

Kitchener had previously informed Birdwood – who had been left in command while Monro met Maxwell in Egypt – that he, Kitchener, would come to Gallipoli; that Birdwood would take command of the Allied forces in Gallipoli; and that Maxwell would be sent to Salonika. Further, the forces at Helles, Anzac and Suvla would remain at the lowest manning levels possible and a new force would be formed, to land north at Bulair and thus encourage the navy to attempt another forcing of the Dardanelles. As Kitchener was now no longer sure if the army could attack, he sent another message to Birdwood, telling him to make secret preparations for an evacuation. While on his way to the Dardanelles Kitchener stopped off in Paris, to learn that the French were against an evacuation; he cabled Keyes to meet him, so that they could discuss plans for a combined attack. Due to an administrative error, Keyes never received the message. When Keyes failed to arrive to join him, Kitchener assumed that this was a sign that the navy no longer supported the idea. Meanwhile Keyes, who thought the plan would proceed, had arranged for additional warships both from England and France.

Birdwood was not in favour of the proposal that he should replace Monro, and gradually accepted the idea that evacuation was the only alternative. A landing at Ayas Bay, 800 miles from the peninsula, was suggested as a ruse to help to limit casualties, but it was used rather to convince Kitchener of the futility of any further landings on the peninsula. By this stage, the ructions within the British government had also become severe, with those supporting the evacuation gaining the upper hand when it became apparent that the navy was unlikely to act. After having visited each of the three landing sites, Kitchener sent a telegram to the Cabinet on 15 November, outlining the poor strategic position of the Allied troops and the strong defensive positions of the Turkish forces. Cabinet replied on 19 November that the Ayas Bay landing would not proceed; two more divisions were to be sent to Salonika; and Kitchener was to give his considered opinion on the evacuation. On 22 November he replied that Suvla and Anzac should be evacuated and Helles retained 'for the present'. On leaving, Kitchener was to comment that he felt the evacuation would be pulled off without losing a man. Monro was put in charge of the eastern Mediterranean, except for Gallipoli, where Birdwood was in command and carrying responsibility for the evacuation – which now also included the possibility of evacuating Helles. Wemyss also replaced de Robeck. As Keyes was to state later:

> Thus the Admiral and the General who were really entirely responsible for the lamentable policy of evacuation left the execution of this unpleasant task to an Admiral and a General who were strongly opposed to it.[5]

The month of November was very quiet on all three fronts and, although the weather was generally fine, there was the occasional short but violent storm, such as the one on 17 November, which destroyed the main piers at Anzac and W Beach. At the port of Kephalos, the piers and jetties were wrecked and small craft driven ashore, as the storm smashed through the breakwater from the north. The submarine *H3* was seriously damaged and, to avoid further mishap, she submerged to the bottom of the harbour to ride out the storm.

Again, on 27 November a violent storm resulted in so much flooding that both British and Turkish troops jumped on to their parapets opposite each other, without firing a shot, to avoid drowning. Two days later a blizzard struck, freezing to death 200 soldiers who were not equipped to deal with the sudden cold and causing 16,000 cases of frostbite. Conditions were so bad that there was some equivocation regarding the withdrawal. Monro telegraphed London on 1 December that the evacuation had to be immediate, while Keyes and Wemyss opted for another combined strike, by both army and navy, which strained relations further. On 28 November, Wemyss telegraphed the Admiralty with his proposal for an attack on the Dardanelles. His subsequent account of the somewhat optimistic plan recounted that

In it I explained that the operation in view would be undertaken for the purpose of opening the Straits and *keeping them open*. To effect this, a squadron of eight battleships, four light cruisers and ten destroyers, with four more older battleships, to act as supply vessels, and merchantmen carrying coal and ammunition – all fitted with mine bumpers – would enter the Straits at dark, at such a time as to arrive above the Narrows at earliest dawn. Under cover of darkness and veiled from the searchlights on Kephaz Point by a smoke screen, they would rush through the minefields, past the Forts, and the first act of the survivors would be the destruction of all depots on the beach and of the small craft capable of laying mines, after which they would attack the forts, taking them in reverse. A second squadron of six more modern battleships, the *Lord Nelson*, the *Agamemnon*, two King Edwards, the *Glory* and *Canopus* with destroyers sweeping ahead of them, would attack the Forts from below the minefields as soon as it was sufficiently light; whilst a third squadron, consisting of the *Swiftsure*, two monitors and five cruisers would cover the Army and join in the attack on the Forts from across the Peninsula. The co-operation of the Army was required to contain the Turkish forces and prevent them from turning their mobile artillery on to the ships and mine-sweepers; and herein lay the advantage we had gained from the occupation of our present positions. I believe, I added, that such a sudden attack, especially if, as hoped, the enemy were taken by surprise, must have a demoralizing effect on the Turkish Army and on the population of Constantinople.[6]

Munro was not convinced by Wemyss' proposal, as he felt that the action would only be of use if he could put direct pressure on the Turkish positions, and he believed that a squadron above the Narrows would have little effect on the Turkish army and could not stop supplies at night. By 2 December, Kitchener was again having second thoughts and telegraphed General Monro:

The Cabinet has been considering the Gallipoli situation all day. Owing to the political consequences, there is a strong feeling against evacuation, even of a partial character. It is the general opinion we should retain Cape Helles.

If the Salonika troops are placed at your disposal up to four divisions for an offensive operation to improve the position at Suvla, could such operations be carried out in time with a view to making Suvla retainable, by obtaining higher position and greater depth. The Navy will also take the offensive in co-operation.[7]

In the meantime, the impact of the submarine campaign had resulted in the construction by the Turks of an improved road system to Kavak at the head of the Gulf of Saros, where bullock wagons or camels transported all supplies by road across the Bulair Isthmus. On 2 December the *Agamemnon, Endymion* and a monitor succeeded in destroying a number of spans of the Kavak Bridge as well as the road, greatly interrupting the flow of supplies to the Turkish forces.

On 8 December, the Joint Staff Conference sitting at the French General Headquarters decided unanimously to defend Salonika and withdraw from Gallipoli immediately. Monro was therefore finally ordered to evacuate Suvla and Anzac. The following day Wemyss was again fighting a rear-guard action in order to proceed with his plan to force the straits. However, it was too late, as the decision to evacuate was now one of political rather than of strictly military considerations.

Fortunately Monro had had the foresight to start preparations for evacuation six weeks earlier, and managed to get his general and administrative staff together, to work on plans to remove 80,000 men, 5,000 animals, 2,000 vehicles and 200 guns from Sulva and Anzac. In Egypt, 12,000 hospital beds were made ready and 56 ships were turned into hospital ships to collect the wounded. The plan called for the steady departure of troops by night, while at the same time making every effort to convince the Turks that there was no change. The Turkish defenders did see troop movements, but were unsure whether they were coming or going. The Allies changed their routine so as to include two days of quiet, with activity on every third day. Although suspicious at first, the Turkish defenders discovered, after probing the lines, that the Allied troops were still there, and believed that this pattern of quiet time followed by activity was a possible prelude to further attacks. Back in England, Lord Milner asked a number of questions in Parliament on how well the plans for evacuation were progressing, but not even this alerted the Turks or the Germans, who probably thought this question was meant to mislead them, believing that no one could possibly be so stupid as to put the Allied troops at such great risk.

By 18 December, only 40,000 troops remained at Anzac and Suvla, after excellent weather had allowed the evacuation of troops and materials without the enemy becoming suspicious. On the night of 18 December a further 20,000 troops were withdrawn, the remainder being due to leave the following night. The tension was palpable on the last night as the troops left their posts closing barbed wire behind them and followed flour and salt trails which indicated the quickest way to the shore through the maze of trenches. Rifles were rigged to fire at intervals without human intervention, to give the impression that troops were still there. The trenches and paths to the beach were muffled with blankets and trench coats to limit the noise, and the two nights of little activity aroused no suspicion amongst the Turks. At each of the beaches, a small flotilla of 100 vessels, made up of trawlers, motor-lighters, small naval steamboats and pulling boats ferried the men to fourteen troop carriers, each capable of holding on average 1,200 men, two old battleships, *Mars* and *Magnificent*, and two cruisers. By 4.10 a.m., the evacuation of Anzac had been successfully completed, and at Suvla, around 5.15 a.m., the rear party, with Major General Fanshawe, was the last to leave the beaches. The final act was the firing of the supply depot and, perhaps unnecessarily, of a mine at Chunuk Bair which killed seventy Turkish soldiers. The last picket boat to leave the bay in the glow of the fire carried Captain Unwin, VC and Colonel Beyon, the principal embarkation officer. On the day after the evacuation a storm completely destroyed the piers at Anzac.

Although von Sanders now had a much larger force at his disposal, the Turkish troops were understandably reluctant to attack the remaining forces at Helles, when it seemed likely that they would also eventually withdraw. The French insisted on their forces withdrawing immediately, and so 29 Division was sent to Helles to replace them. Cabinet finally agreed on 27 December that Helles should be evacuated. Birdwood decided that the garrison should be reduced to 22,000 and that the remaining force should be withdrawn in two stages – 7,000 on the night of 7 January and the final 15,000 on 8 January, the minimum thought necessary to hold the line and, coincidentally, the maximum the navy could embark in one night.

On 7 January, von Sanders delivered the first attack of his campaign to drive the British forces from Helles. At midday a massive bombardment fell on 13 Division at Gully Spur, which was countered by the few guns remaining on shore and by the navy off-shore. At 4 p.m., two enormous onshore Turkish mines were exploded on Gully Spur, and the bombardment increased in intensity. Shortly afterwards the Turks charged, but the British machine-guns were still intact and the navy, unhampered by concerns over ammunition usage, cut down the Turkish troops before they made any progress. By 6 p.m. the fighting was over.

On the night of 8 January, the seas rose as the weather deteriorated, but by 4 a.m. on 9 January the last 35,268 officers and men, 3,689 horses and mules, 127 guns and 1,600 tons of stores were successfully evacuated, again without the Turkish forces becoming aware of what was happening.[8] A great feat had been accomplished through the successful evacuation of so many men with so few losses. But this suggests, or perhaps imposes, the obvious remark: if the same level of competence and preparation had been applied from the beginning of the campaign, how different the outcome might have been!

13

Conclusions

For all its faults, the Gallipoli campaign was perhaps one of the few strategic ideas of the First World War which, if successful, could have led to a shortening of the conflict. Perhaps its potential to deliver so much, followed by its eventual failure, is the reason why the campaign continues to be of such interest. It was also the first major modern seaborne landing of troops on hostile territory and offered many valuable lessons for military strategists as well as providing experienced personnel for the D-Day landings during the Second World War; for these reasons it is still studied by military planners today.

The relative importance of the Dardanelles, and Churchill's role in the campaign, continue to be debated. But, as Admiral Tirpitz wrote after the landings at Suvla: 'The situation is obviously critical. Should the Dardanelles fall, the World War has been decided against us.' The chief of the German general staff, Falkenhayn, writing to the Austrian General Headquarters, stated: 'It is incomparably more important that the Dardanelles should be secured and, in addition, the iron in Bulgaria struck while it is hot.'[1] Had it been successful, the importance of the Dardanelles campaign may have become more obvious to the Allies; but during the entire operation, at all levels of command, there was never the sense of an absolute determination to succeed. The western front was always dominant in allied strategic planning.

Once the element of surprise was lost, the Allies were left with a tactical advantage but no longer a strategic one. If the strategic advantage had been preserved, then a naval enterprise might have had a better chance. In 1917 de Robeck received a report from Naval Intelligence which suggested that the Turks felt that Gallipoli could have been taken if the element of surprise had been maintained – but given the logistics involved, was that ever likely?

If the Allied fleet, or, more importantly, its commander, had had the fortitude to press home the attack more vigorously on 18 March, accepting the losses from mines, this more determined action might have resulted in the enemy running out of larger calibre ammunition (although this is still debated), and in the fleet then reaching Constantinople without the support of ground troops. Even so, could victory have been won? From the comments of Morgenthau, the US ambassador of the time, this may have been possible:

> A political committee, not exceeding forty members, headed by Talaat, Enver, and Djemal, controlled the Central Government, but their authority throughout the empire was exceedingly tenuous. As a matter of fact, the whole Ottoman state, on that eighteenth day of March, 1915, when the Allied fleet abandoned the attack, was on the brink of dissolution. All over Turkey ambitious chieftains had arisen, who were momentarily expecting its fall, and who were looking for the opportunity to seize their parts of the inheritance.[2]

Morgenthau also related discussions he had with Enver, who had asked for President Wilson to intercede and end the war, as 'Turkey was war-weary and its salvation depended on getting an early peace'.

On the other hand, revolutions on a national scale are not easy, as Ellison noted:

> In these circumstances a revolution depended on the Turkish Army mutinying and refusing to obey orders. But a mutiny in the presence of an enemy is an unlikely event, especially when a nation, as was the case with the Turks in 1915, knows it is fighting for its national existence.[3]

Moreover, even if the navy had been successful in reaching the Sea of Marmara, it is difficult to see what it could have achieved in the longer term, unless the government was overthrown. It was against international law to bombard an undefended city, and even the destruction of a number of selected targets, such as the ammunition factories or the Turkish War Office, would probably have had little effect. Such an immediate threat to Turkey also assumes that Germany would have stood idly by and not brought in her own troops, first attacking Serbia and then advancing into Turkey.[4] From a political viewpoint, if the Allies had managed to persuade Turkey to become neutral, this would have deprived them of the chance to make any future territorial claims.

Without surrender by the Turkish government, the navy would have been forced to withdraw, and again run the gauntlet of the Narrows where further losses could have been expected. Even if the loss of ships was acceptable, the loss of their crews, who represented a significant pool of experienced men for the home fleet, was probably something which could never be countenanced.

In the end it had to come down to a combined army and naval attack on the peninsula, supported by submarines in the Sea of Marmara.

Once a decision was made to land troops, the navy took on a supporting role and later demonstrated, on two occasions, its ability to land a large force on hostile shores. Importantly, it was to prove its ability, initially with some difficulty, to remove the wounded (31,100 in a two-week period during August alone). It then transported them directly to facilities in Malta and Alexandria, and in some cases to England. The navy supplied the landing force with all of their food and ammunition, and also with fire support, perhaps not as effectively as it was hoped, but still critically. Gradually, over time, the navy became more efficient in incorporating the use of aircraft and balloons to direct fire at the enemy, and better coordinated in its fire support for the troops, which was to be the forerunner of amphibious landings in the Second World War. Under the threat of submarine attacks, it was also able to change its mode of operation so as to maintain support for the landed troops.

For the Gallipoli land campaign to have succeeded, there were a number of crucial elements in addition to naval support which should have been resolved right at the beginning. The overall objective was to take and hold Constantinople and, to do this, control of the straits had to be gained by capturing the forts. It is always important to have a good plan of attack; when working in combination with forces from other countries, this required cooperation and a unified command. Hamilton considered it better to land his army intact (with minimum casualties), in a worse position, rather than suffer crippling losses gaining a better position. Therefore there was no true tactics other than to gain ground with minimum possible loss and to be prepared to seize the advantage if the opportunity arose. Although opportunities did arise, they were rarely seized.

Hamilton was concerned over possibly being pushed back into the sea,[5] and he planned his landings with a number of feints, to keep von Sanders guessing as to where the weight of his attack was going to be. He knew that he would have supporting naval fire from three sides at Helles, while at Anzac or Bulair, or even later at Suvla, fire support could come only from the west. Had the Anzacs been in a position to cut across from the north of Gaba Tepe, following a successful landing, the Turks would have been forced into fighting on two fronts. The Turks to the south might have been cut off and made dependent on being supplied from the Asiatic shore. This appeared to offer a better chance of success than landing at Bulair, where the Turks could have been more easily resupplied and the landing force was under attack from two sides.

A landing on the Asiatic side (which, as von Sanders suggested later, was a better alternative) would have been opposed by two divisions, but an advance probably could have been made, moving parallel to the coast, with the fleet supporting off-shore to the west. However, over time, the Turks would have brought in more troops in defence and would have attacked the eastern flank of the advancing army, while the Turkish guns on the Gallipoli side would have continually harassed the Allied troops (as the Asiatic guns later did the troops at Helles). The Anzac landing, however, was too far north and became entangled in difficult terrain with too small a force. When the men became bogged down, they should have been brought out and sent to Helles. Although they tied down Turkish troops, logistically it was always easier for the Turks to redeploy their forces where and when they were needed.

By placing the weight of the attack on Helles, Hamilton assumed that taking Achi Baba would afford a direct observation point overlooking the straits. It was not realized until later that Achi Baba would only have been helpful for observing the intermediate forts. In addition, the ridges ran north–south, parallel to the shore, preventing the flat trajectory of naval fire from being truly effective, while the earlier landings on 25 February had given the Turks ample warning and time to prepare their defences.

To the north of Anzac and around Suvla, there was little defence, ample ground to assemble, and protection for ships in rough weather. If Sari Bair could have been quickly taken and held, the attacking troops would have been in an excellent position to cut off the defenders in the south, near Kilid Bahr. They would still have to cover a distance of 15 miles to get there, which would have proved a formidable task. There was limited information on shoaling or the terrain, so this proposal was not included in the initial landings at Gallipoli. When it was decided in August that a landing at Suvla should proceed, secrecy was too high, troops were inexperienced and untrained and Stopford proved to be unequal to the task. Perhaps even more disappointing was the fact that Hamilton's failure to learn from his experiences of the previous three months meant that he did not take an active part in the operation right from the beginning.

Once the decision on where to land had been made (and it would seem that Hamilton chose the best available option), it was critical that a sufficient concentration of firepower be assembled to ensure a successful landing, using superior forces with clear and determined objectives. To this must be added the unquestioned continuing support from senior command, which in this case was ultimately represented by Kitchener, either to get the job done or to withdraw as soon as the objectives were no longer obtainable. Unfortunately, an intrepid spirit and a single-minded intention to win were lacking in both Hamilton and de Robeck, while by comparison von Sanders and Kemal were both determined to win, no matter what the cost.

The hurried nature of preparation for the land battle has already been noted. The failure to possess adequate knowledge of the ground and of the forces to be met is perhaps best summarized by Ashmead-Bartlett:

> It is no use evading the facts. We landed on the Gallipoli Peninsula in entire ignorance of every essential factor on which success or failure depended. We had no certain knowledge of the enemy's true strength, we knew little about his defence works immediately protecting the selected landing points, and still less of the lines he had constructed inland, and we were ignorant of the topography of the country, of the broken nature of the ground, the nullahs, river-beds, woods, and dense scrub, all of which lent their aid to the Turks.[6]

But there was more information available when the landings were undertaken than Ashmead-Bartlett and others would suggest, and, while the initial maps were not as accurate as perhaps desired, these were greatly improved upon especially with the capture of enemy maps. The level of intelligence gathering at Gallipoli did improve and at times was impressive, with a large part of that information coming from Turkish prisoners.

The other recurring theme is that Hamilton always lacked adequate artillery (initially, only one third of the usual number of guns), but he did have significant, although constrained, naval firepower. He had almost no howitzers, few trench mortars and insufficient hand grenades and high explosive ammunition. The lack of effective and on-demand artillery was no doubt a limiting factor on the Allies' ability to advance, although on the western front massive artillery support initially didn't prove to be the answer. Such lack of artillery support was not always the case in Gallipoli either, as shown in the attack on 4 June, when over 12,000 shells were fired over a 5,000-yard front. For the size of the advance, this situation was favourable when compared to the western front.[7]

The terrain which Hamilton's forces had to overcome was difficult, with ravines and ridges covered in dense scrub, many of which were impassable. There was always the problem of locating the enemy, directing the naval or shore fire, while ensuring that Hamilton's own troops were not hit in the process. Communications were a problem, and attacking uphill, with the enemy located on the reverse slope, limited the effectiveness of naval fire. Best results were achieved when spotting could be done at right angles. This was possible at Helles but not at Anzac. Where observation was good, naval bombardment could have a devastating effect.

It was important also for objectives to be kept simple as well as clearly communicated. In this respect, the Suvla and Anzac operations were perhaps too ambitious and complex. The Allies were also, at critical times, having problems with an inadequate water supply, and in addition they were unable to rest their troops properly. Overall, it could be said that Turkish troops were better led, more disciplined than expected, and motivated to defend their country. They held the high ground, had plenty of water and room to rest their troops. The terrain favoured them and made it difficult to detect their movements, particularly at night. The Turkish artillery was also more effective, due to their spotting from higher ground, although many of their shells failed to explode. Four years after the landing, a Turkish staff officer was to comment on the Allied objectives at Anzac that '[i]t would have been almost impossible to reach those objectives even in an operation of peace time'.[8] However, the feint on Gaba Tepe initially proved to be more successful than Hamilton had hoped, in that it drew all the local reserves as it represented such an immediate threat. The Anzac position, given its hilly terrain and small beaches, never offered the logistical benefits of those at Helles.

The real problem was that, once the trench warfare started, the troops would become holed up. Whatever the situation, action had to be quick to gain objectives without delay. This concept did not enter into the thinking of commanders of the time. The old military philosophy still survived at the beginning of the war that an aggressive attitude and the belief in human courage could surmount all else, including the machine-gun. The need for new weapons such as mortars and grenades, to overcome the enemy's machine-guns when suppressive artillery fire was not available or effective, was not as yet part of the military doctrine, as it lessened the importance of rifle and bayonet. Technology was favouring the defensive capabilities of trench and machine-gun, but these, together with artillery, were seen as secondary support weapons. It was not till much later in the war that tanks and aircraft, in conjunction with machine-guns and artillery, became the primary weapons, with infantry in support. Those in charge of the Gallipoli campaign had not had the time or, in some cases, the ability to appreciate and accommodate the changing momentum of war. Under the given circumstances, structural rigidity of the existing chain of command limited the flexibility that was required. As Head was to comment:

> Unforeseen contingencies of every variety were bound to arise in the strange and novel conditions of the circumstances, and it was essential that leaders of commanding authority be right on the spot to deal with them. If our leaders were determined to sit under cover far behind their troops, no scheme of operations was likely to get us to the Straits.[9]

Commanders concentrated on sending reinforcements in support of troops who were not progressing well, rather than to the weakest point of enemy resistance, where there might be a chance of success. There was also a preference, particularly with Hunter-Weston, because of his lack of battlefield skills, to attack simultaneously along the whole front, a tactic which resulted in heavy losses. Infantry had not learnt to follow behind a moving barrage, and artillery had not learnt to fire on enemy trenches up until the last moment before an attack.

It has been suggested that, although the Dardanelles campaign was not a victory for the Allies, it did tie up nearly 300,000 Turkish troops, who would otherwise have been engaged elsewhere. Offsetting this was the fact that up to 500,000 Allied troops were used to contain the Turkish forces, requiring the expenditure of huge amounts of money, munitions and materials. There was likewise a huge deployment of naval and maritime forces. As the Dardanelles Commission pointed out, 'we do not think that from a military standpoint our gain in one direction compensated for our losses in the other direction'. The commission went on to say:

> We think that the difficulties of the operations were much underestimated. At the outset all decisions were taken and all provisions based on the assumption that, if a landing were effected, the resistance would be slight and the advance rapid. We can see no sufficient ground for this assumption. The short naval bombardment in November, 1914, had given the Turks warning of a possible attack, and the naval operations in February and March of 1915 led naturally to a great strengthening of the Turkish defences. The Turks were known to be led by German officers, and there was no reason to think that they would not fight well, especially in defensive positions. These facts had been reported by Admiral de Robeck and Sir Ian Hamilton.

Further it was to say:

> We are of the opinion that, with the resources then available, success in the Dardanelles, if possible, was only possible upon condition that the Government concentrated their efforts upon the enterprise and limited their expenditure of men and material in the Western theatre of war. This condition was never fulfilled.[10]

After Gallipoli, only the Anzac troops headed for Europe, while all the others remained in the east. By 1918, a total of three quarters of a million Allied soldiers had been sent to Salonika and another 280,000 fought from Egypt to Jerusalem and Damascus. If only a portion of these resources had been deployed originally at Gallipoli, it is possible that the war could have been shortened and perhaps many lives saved.

But was a land-based victory ever plausible? The combination of a lack of space, a lack of men and materials, weakened navy support, difficult terrain and a determined enemy meant that, with the loss of surprise after the first naval bombardment, no victory was possible unless an overwhelming force was sent to the peninsula, and that was never going to happen.

Hamilton was overly optimistic in his reports to London, submissive to Kitchener, whom he didn't want to offend. Kitchener was too secretive, underestimated the enemy, relied too much on the navy and thought Gallipoli was a subsidiary campaign, so he failed to quickly supply sufficient adequately trained and equipped troops. Although troops were available by June, there was limited room to accommodate them on the peninsula and they couldn't be brought in by sea fast enough when required. The transports which were required to remove the large number of casualties at the same time created a bottleneck at the beaches, which was always an issue given the relatively small area occupied by the Allies.

The price of failure was high for the 500,000 Allied soldiers landed at Gallipoli during the nine-month campaign. Casualties for the Australians numbered 26,094 (7,594 killed), for New Zealand 7,571 (2,341 killed), for the British 205,000 (43,000 killed or dead from their injuries), and for the French 47,000 (about 5,000 killed). On the Turkish side, estimates of casualties are 216,000 (66,000 killed).

Perhaps Wemyss best summed up the critical issues of the overall campaign:

Politically and strategically the conception of the campaign was correct, and had it been properly planned and methodically carried out there is no reason why it should not have been crowned with success; but, rushed into as it was, without forethought or preparation, devoid of plan, treated as a side-issue, with improvisation as the only means whereby daily requirements could be met, it was little less than a crime, which could hardly have been committed had the body of men who sanctioned its inauguration been properly organized with a view to carrying out the work committed to their charge.

The blame for this tragedy cannot be laid at the door of any one individual, but must be attributed to system, the system that places the direction of naval and military operations solely in the hands of men devoid of the knowledge and experience necessary for the task, and immune, moreover, from the consequences of their actions; for the exercise of authority with the assurance of never being brought to account must ever be fraught with fatal results; and it is a noteworthy fact that not one of the members of the War

Council responsible for the campaign but has held high office since its disastrous termination.[11]

Meanwhile, thirteen Allied submarines had managed to complete twenty-seven successful passages through the Dardanelles (with the loss of eight submarines), and had succeeded in sinking two Turkish battleships, five gunboats, one destroyer, nine transports, thirty steamers, seven ammunition and stores ships, and numerous sailing vessels. Turkish sources claim that, in addition to the naval forces sunk, only twenty-five steamers were sunk, ten damaged and 3,000 tons of smaller vessels sunk. The discrepancies are primarily accounted for by the beaching, repairing and refloating of vessels, some of which were then sunk or damaged again.

Importantly, the Turks were forced to use a large number of small boats, which moved along the coast at night and sheltered in the bays and harbours during the day. Overland transport from the nearest railhead at Usun Kopri via the Bulair Road was confined to camel trains and army wagons, as there were no motor vehicles available, but overall, when combined with water transport and materials from the Asiatic side, sufficient supplies were conveyed to the Turkish Fifth Army. All heavy equipment had to be carried by sea, while two months of food-stocks were maintained, in case the Sea of Marmara was ever closed. Near the front lines, sixteen days supply of food, fifty-three days of baking supplies and eight days of animal fodder were maintained, so Turkish units generally endured no major food shortages. But the production of cloth materials was a continuing problem which meant that no winter clothing could be provided, nor was there a sufficient supply of sandbags.

Did the Allied submarines make a material difference to Turkey's ability to fight the war at Gallipoli? The answer in its strictest terms has to be that they did not. There is no question that the submariners displayed great courage and tenacity in getting into the Sea of Marmara, and caused considerable difficulty for the enemy. Ian Hamilton mentions that the submarines accounted for losses of 25 per cent of the enemy's supplies by sea.[12] But 25 per cent is nowhere near enough to bring an army to its knees, particularly when alternate land routes via the Asiatic side and Thrace were available. However, the difficulties of supplying and reinforcing the Turkish forces were greatly increased. As Liman von Sanders commented:

The bringing of food to the Fifth Army was especially difficult. The railway station in Usunköpri [Uzun Kupru] in Thrance was seven marches distant and the means of transport were very limited. In those days the armies in Turkey had no auto trucks and it was with much difficulty that the columns of camels, pack animals and Turkish ox wagons managed to get a few tons to the front. Hence the Fifth Army had to depend for its supplies almost completely on water transport through the Sea of Marmara where British and French submarines tried to close this line. It was fortunate that the submarines could not do it, otherwise the Fifth Army would have died of hunger.

In judging the action of the submarines it should be noted that in the narrow and open Sea of Marmara four or five submarines operating at the same time were unable to stop transportation by boat. Several Turkish ships were torpedoed, but the majority came through and reached their destination by steaming at night from etape to etape. Various things came to the debarking stations by sailboat and towed mahones.[13]

The relatively small operating zone of the Sea of Marmara meant that one submarine could travel from one end to the other in a day. This no doubt gave the impression of a number of submarines operating at any one time, but the reality was that for most of the time there was no more than one submarine. Even so, by June, Turkish troops were down to 160 rounds each and the German official history, *Der Krieg zur See*, stated that by late August

The British submarines succeeded for the first time in raising the losses (among supply ships; all troops were at that time sent by road) to a point that caused anxiety. If this destruction of tonnage had been maintained at anything like the same level during the next few months the resistance of the Fifth Army would have come to an end.[14]

The greatest danger for the Turks was the loss of ships rather than of the supplies they carried, as their official history stated:

The chief harm done by submarines was to the naval transport which was considerably interfered with. The number of ships in Turkey was limited, and it was absolutely impossible to provide new ones when they were sunk. Furthermore, ships seriously damaged could not be repaired.[15]

As has been previously stated, many of the ships the submariners thought they had sunk were subsequently brought back into operation. Increasing use was made of small shipping inshore at night where most of the submarines often did not operate. And, although the number of submarines in the Sea of Marmara did increase by late August, there were never enough of them to ensure that several were in continuous operation, given the need to service them and rest the crews. With the opening of the Bulgarian land route,

supplies from Germany increased (see Appendix III). A report by German
General Pieper also indicated that tremendous efforts were being made in
Turkey to increase production of munitions from existing and converted
factories; the manufacture of flame throwers and gas shells occurred too late
for the campaign.[16] Had the Dardanelles campaign continued through 1916,
the increases in war materials would have created an even greater reliance on
submarines, but the lack of a sufficient number of them and an alternative
land route that was being increasingly used to avoid the Sea of Marmara meant
that adequate supplies were always likely to reach the Fifth Army.

Although success was never within their grasp, Winston Churchill perhaps
best summed up the efforts of the submarines when he commented:

> The Naval History of Britain contains no page more wonderful than that
> which records the prowess of her submarines at the Dardanelles. Their
> exploits constitute in daring, in skill, in endurance, in risk, the finest
> examples of submarine action in the whole of the Great War, and were,
> moreover, marked by a strict observance of the recognized rules of
> warfare.[17]

Epilogue

Following the high drama of the battles of 1915, it might have been expected that, after the departure of the Allies, the backwaters of Gallipoli would remain uneventful for the remainder of the war. For much of the time this was the case, but in early 1918 there was one further small flurry. By that time, the naval force left on station was a destroyer patrol of four to six ships and two pre-Dreadnoughts, *Lord Nelson* and *Agamemnon*, all based at Mudros, under the command of Hayes-Sadler, now rear admiral. These were supported by a naval airbase at Imbros which was flying daily reconnaissance missions and by extensive mining designed to keep the *Goeben* and *Breslau* from moving out of the Dardanelles.

However, on the evening of 20 January 1918, under the new German commander, Vice Admiral Hubert von Rebeur-Paschwitz, *Goeben* and *Breslau* moved quietly down the Dardanelles, unobserved and unimpeded, reaching Cape Helles at 5.40 a.m.[1] The plan called for *Goeben* to bombard Mudros, while *Breslau* kept watch. It also included the use of a U-boat to lay mines in that area. After destroying the radio station at Kephalos Point, *Goeben* hit a mine at 6.10 a.m., having just cleared the straits. She suffered only minor damage (compartments X and XI), and both ships continued towards Kusu Bay at the north-eastern corner of Imbros Island. At 7.20 a.m., the British destroyer *Lizard* challenged *Breslau*, which had taken station ahead of *Goeben*. With the British ships unable to send any warning, *Goeben* opened fire and sank two monitors in Kusu Bay, *Lord Raglan* and *M28*, before they could return effective fire. *Lizard* and another destroyer, *Tigress*, did attempt to put up a smoke screen to help protect the monitors, but to no avail.

The two ships then proceeded to their primary objective, attacking the large collection of shipping at Mudros. Prior to all of this, Hayes-Sadler, rather than using a destroyer or waiting until his yacht *Triad* returned from repairs, had taken *Lord Nelson* to Salonika on business. He was now too far away to intercept the German ships, while *Agamemnon* was ineffectual, due to her slow speed and particularly to lack of support from *Lord Nelson*. Shortly after leaving Kusu, heading south on a reciprocal course to the outward run, *Breslau* was harassed by recently arrived British planes. At 8.31 a.m., as she moved unnecessarily past *Goeben* to clear the way for her anti-aircraft fire, she hit a mine on her starboard side. Her steering and starboard low-pressure turbine were put out of action and she was brought to a standstill. As *Goeben* went to her assistance, and while she was still under attack from the air, she hit a second mine at 8.55 a.m. *Breslau* now attempted to manoeuvre out of the minefield, but in doing so hit three more mines, then another one at 9.05 a.m., and finally, began to sink, thus ending a four-year partnership.

Admiral Rebeur-Paschwitz now chose to return to the safety of the Dardanelles and asked the Turkish destroyers *Basra*, *Muavent-i Milliye*, *Numune-i Hamiyet* and *Samsun* to come to assist him. As they did so, at 9.20 a.m. *Lizard* and *Tigress* attacked, inflicting considerable damage on the lead destroyer *Basra* and forcing them to return to the Dardanelles. *Lizard* then stopped, to pick up survivors from the *Breslau*, until a reported periscope sighting ended the rescue.[2] As the *Goeben* finally turned to make her way back up the straits, she hit a mine at 9.48 a.m. which flooded compartments III and IV and, although she was not seriously damaged, she did take a 15 degrees list and appeared to settle at the stern. Heading up the straits and fending off continued air attacks, *Goeben* finally rounded a buoy just off Nagara, mistakenly thinking it was the end of the net barrage, and at 11.30 p.m. ran aground on a sandbank at 15 knots, and held fast.

Over the next five days, Allied aircraft repeatedly attacked the stranded *Goeben*, dropping over 15 tons of bombs, although only 16 direct hits were claimed. Given the relatively small size of the bombs, which were little more than 100 pounds each at best, the ship suffered no significant damage.[3] No effort was made to use *Lord Nelson* or *Agamemnon* to shell her, and an attempt to use the monitor *M17* failed. On the early morning of 28 January, a flight of three seaplanes from *Ark Royal* and one from *Express* took off with 18-inch torpedoes. Only one succeeded in getting to the target and, although not able to see *Goeben*, the pilot dropped his torpedo and heard a major explosion. Despite this *Goeben* was still intact, and an alternative approach was needed in order to ensure that she was put permanently out of action.

The submarine *E12* was stationed at Mudros, and her captain, Lieutenant F. Williams-Freeman, had been flown over the *Goeben* on 22 January, to reconnoitre the situation. Unfortunately, while on exercises the previous month at Lemnos, the submarine had fractured its main port shaft, which reduced her surface speed. A new shaft had been shipped from Malta on board the *Louvain*,[4] but she had been torpedoed by *UC22* on 20 January, in the Aegean Sea. Given the importance of the mission, *E12* had been given permission by the Admiralty to undertake the operation. However, Admiral Hayes-Sadler at this critical moment decided not to allow *E12* to go ahead, because of the risks of the strong currents and its own mechanical problems.

Of the other submarines available, *E2* was at Malta completing a dockyard refit, while *E14* was stationed at Corfu, to patrol in the Straits of Otranto. So, by 22 January, *E14*, now under the command of Lieutenant Commander Geoffrey Saxon White (the senior captain of the three submarines), was on its way, as Admiral Gough-Calthorpe, the commander-in-chief of the Mediterranean, had accepted responsibility for the mission. With *E14*'s arrival, preparations were made for the attempt to run the Narrows (including fitting jumper wires and knives to cut the nets). It was planned that the aerial attacks would be continued, in the hope that they would draw the enemy's attention away from the submarine's presence. If *E14* could get past the strengthened minefields, the nets, and the increased number of surface patrols, she would attempt to torpedo the *Goeben* with a beam shot from the European side. White had flown over the area and observed the *Goeben* before setting out, and felt confident that success could be achieved.[5]

On Friday 25 January, prior to entering the Dardanelles that night, *E14* was ordered to go alongside the aircraft carrier *Ark Royal*, due to a strong gale. While doing so *E14* ran aground, and it was not until Sunday 27 January, at 6.30 p.m., that *E14* left Imbros. She submerged at 11.45 p.m., entering the straits near Rabbit Island in total darkness, and dived to 100 feet to go under the minefields at Kephez. On entering, she was sighted by British look-outs on Mavro Island who, mistaking her for a U-boat, raised the alarm. Although this was immediately cancelled, the message had gone on air and possibly alerted the enemy to the submarine's presence. Occasionally going to periscope depth to locate his position, White found it too dark to discern any meaningful landmarks, and was forced to use dead reckoning. A number of times he heard scraping on the hull, which indicated that *E14* was in the minefield; this was confirmed by the absence of surface traffic in the area. White then decided to go to 150 feet, to try to ensure that he got below the mines, and when this was done the scraping stopped. By 5.30 a.m. he estimated he was clear of the minefield and went to periscope depth. Though still in darkness, he was able to make out cliffs on his port side and low-lying land to starboard, so he concluded that he was in the Narrows. Once again *E14* went to 150 feet and increased speed to get through the nets.

At 3 a.m. *E14* passed the first of the nets, which only momentarily retarded her progress, though at one stage it was necessary to go full astern and dive to a depth of 160 feet to get clear. At 6 a.m., another net was encountered, but this time *E14* could not get clear and was deflected into a strong current, which pushed her onto a sand bank. With daylight fast approaching, White decided to surface, to investigate the situation. *E14* could go astern but could not go forward, so White gave orders to First Lieutenant Jack Blissett to dive while White was on deck if any problems were encountered, in order to ensure the safety of the crew and submarine. Once there, White removed the obstruction from the bow of the submarine, ordered full astern with both motors, and *E14* slid off the bank.

While on deck, White saw that they were opposite Chanak, but fortunately the searchlights were busy looking for aircraft so *E14* remained undetected. White was also able to observe 'the gate' which consisted of two buoys marking the passage through the nets. This enabled him to set what looked like a safe course through the minefield, and he decided to travel at a depth of 170 to 190 feet, as added insurance. At 7.30 a.m., after having been submerged for about an hour, White rose to periscope depth as the day broke, to find that he had cleared the Narrows and was just below Nagara Point. To his great surprise, *Goeben* was no longer to be seen. Until that moment, he had been completely unaware that she had recently been re-floated. He considered proceeding further up the straits, in the vain hope of finding the *Goeben*; but, with a weakening battery, he decided that he would have to make his way back down the Narrows in daylight. However, White was determined to make his presence felt, stating: 'I am not going back without firing a fish after coming all this way. I'll have a look at Nagara.'[6]

The starboard bow torpedo was made ready, and by 8.45 a.m., with the aid of the fast-moving current, *E14* had passed back through the Narrows and was nearing Chanak. While checking his position, White sighted a Turkish ship, the *Intibah*, which had been used to offload *Goeben*'s munitions in order to lighten her for re-floating. White fired the torpedo and eleven seconds later an immense explosion[7] was heard, so close that gauges and light bulbs exploded and the fittings on the fore hatch were sprung, leaking badly until the clips could again be screwed tight. With the explosion so close, *E14* was lifted to a depth of 15 feet and had her conning tower exposed. The Turkish forts immediately opened fire and believed that they had succeeded in hitting the submarine. Nearby, *Husret*, *Intibah* and the gunboat *Kemal Reis* rushed to the spot where she was last seen.

White immediately ordered *E14* to dive and descended to 150 feet, although depth keeping had become more difficult with the boat wanting to go deeper. White took *E14* to periscope depth on several occasions, to check her progress down the straits. It was soon apparent that she had suffered further damage, as it became increasingly difficult to maintain trim and direction. At 1.13 p.m., after finishing a game of cards, White ordered periscope depth for another sighting and, while blowing the ballast, *E14* heaved to starboard, almost capsizing. White immediately re-flooded external tanks 3 and 4, so that the boat could be righted. The downward dip of the bow now increased until she could no longer be held, and she plunged to 165 feet before being brought under control by partially blowing the main ballast, using more of the dwindling supply of precious high-pressure air (only three bottles remained).

The situation was now critical, and White decided that his only course of action was to bring the submarine to the surface and make a dash for it, using her diesel engines. The last of the remaining air was used, and after being submerged for nearly eighteen hours, *E14* surfaced between Cape Helles and Kum Kale with open sea ahead. As soon as the conning tower was above the surface, he ordered the hatches opened to allow air to enter the submarine, so the diesels could be started. However, the conning tower was full of water, due to previous enemy fire puncturing its sides (this was probably responsible for the poor depth keeping). An enemy round hit the submarine over the ward room, making it now impossible to submerge, as the pressure hull had been breached. The explosion also created difficulties and delays in opening the fore hatch, which would have been necessary in order to allow air in so that the engines could be started, and the boat could get underway.

Meanwhile, the Turkish gunners at the nearby forts had plenty of time to find the range on the still slowly moving target. (Turkish estimates were that 250 rounds per minute were fired at the submarine.) White, his navigating officer, Lieutenant Drew, and a few crew members went on deck and took some cover on the port saddle tank, as most of the fire was coming from Sedd el Bahr on the starboard side. Able Seaman Mitchell (the only Australian on board) went up onto the conning tower, where White and the other officers where now stationed, to report that the steering wheel was not connected.[8] This prevented them from manoeuvring the submarine more rapidly away from the shell fire which exploded around them as she picked up speed. The first direct hit on the bow had caused only modest damage, so White ordered *E14* to turn to starboard and head for shore, to give his crew some chance of escape. A shell then hit the muffler box, releasing steam into the engine room and badly injuring Ordinary Telegraphist Pritchard, who fell unconscious on deck. After giving the order to steer amidships, White and Drew[9] were killed by the next enemy round, while further hits penetrated the pressure hull, causing the submarine to slowly sink.

The order was then given on deck (probably by Petty Officer Perkins) to turn 25 degrees to port, with the final shell hitting the starboard saddle tank as *E14* started to sink into deep water. Able Seaman Mitchell, who by this time was in the water, saw *E14* go down bow first, with her propellers thrashing on the surface. He found Pritchard, and later, helped by Seaman Trimball, kept him afloat. Several other sailors, including the coxswain, Petty Officer Robert

Perkins, got into the water before *E14* sank. Lieutenant Jack Blissett was last seen in the engine room, still directing the men at their posts, as the submarine sank with him and twenty other members of the crew. A Turkish tug later picked up nine survivors, three of whom, Pritchard, Mitchell and Trimball, were injured.

On the same day at 11 a.m., an Allied aircraft had reported seeing what looked like a submarine under fire from the shore batteries, surrounded by white splashes of water and smoke. An explosion was then observed, followed by increasing water disturbance, until finally nothing remained on the surface.[10] It was not until the next day, 29 January, that a Turkish communiqué announced the sinking of the submarine. At the same time, Flight Lieutenant Harvey in a long-range DH4 aircraft reported that *Goeben* was in a dockyard at Constantinople.[11]

In May, a letter written by Petty Officer Perkins finally arrived from a prison camp in Asia Minor, detailing the events of 28 January. On 24 May 1919, after the prisoners had been repatriated and the Admiralty had recovered the full story of White's actions, he was posthumously awarded the Victoria Cross. This created history, as *E14* is the only vessel in the Royal Navy for which two different commanders have, at different times, both been awarded the medal. Meanwhile an ill Hayes-Sadler had been relieved of his command due to his indecisive action.

On 15 September 1918, the Bulgarian front collapsed after the opening of the Allied offensive a few days earlier at Salonika, and on 30 September the Bulgarians asked for an armistice. With the British victorious in Palestine, Turkey was forced to seek an armistice on 20 October, and by 30 October agreement was reached. The armistice was signed on board *Agamemnon* at Mudros. Clearing of minefields commenced immediately, and on 12 October the combined Allied fleet sailed up the straits, finally to anchor off Constantinople the following day.

After the war, *Goeben* was formally handed over to Turkey and was anchored in shallow waters in the Gulf of Izmid, in case her bulkheads failed. By 1930 she had been fully repaired and modernized, and was renamed the *Yavuz Sultan Selim* in 1936. She was decommissioned in 1950, and in 1966 was offered for sale at US $2.8 million (much to the protestations of many who felt she should become a museum piece, as the last remaining major warship of the First World War). However, she failed to sell and was left to decay at the naval base at Golcuk, 40 miles from Istanbul. She was finally broken up in 1976, sixty-five years after her launching. The butterfly had finally come to rest.

Appendix I: Submarine Fact File

Submarine Design

The general design and operating principles of the submarine (called a boat rather than a ship) have changed little since the First World War, although the technology has evolved in dramatic ways. The submarine should be viewed as a long watertight cylinder, designed to withstand the pressure below surface, which increases by one atmosphere (15 pounds per square inch) every 33 feet of depth. The cylinder or pressure-hull crush-depth is the depth where the outside pressure is greater than the strength of the pressure hull, as the resisting pressure inside is only one normal atmosphere.

Surrounding the pressure hull is a superstructure which allows for a flat deck for the crew to walk on, a conning tower for observation and navigation, and, mostly but not always, saddle or ballast tanks attached to the sides of the pressure hull, which can be flooded with water and emptied by compressed air. The watertight cylinder houses the crew, the propulsion systems and the armament, primarily torpedoes. Because the inside of the cylinder is at atmospheric pressure, there is no need for decompression of the crew if the submarine surfaces rapidly. Some pressure build-up does occur due to the leaking of compressed air tanks, but this is only minimal.

There are three basic designs with respect to the pressure hull and the ballast tanks, which are filled with water to submerge. In the single-hull type, all the tanks are arranged in the pressure hull, which gives optimum submerging time and higher underwater speeds, but makes crew conditions cramped and has a low reserve buoyancy (that is, difference in displacement between being on surface and being submerged). It is also less seaworthy and hence more difficult to control in rough sea conditions. In the saddle-tank configuration, the ballast tanks (and possibly the fuel tanks) are outside the pressure hull, which provides more internal room, greater reserve buoyancy, and hence better sea-keeping.[1] However, diving time is increased and underwater speeds are lower. The third type is similar to the saddle-tank arrangement in that the ballast tanks are outside the pressure hull, but, rather than having the tanks placed like saddles on the side of the hull, an outer, more streamlined, hull surrounds the pressure hull and holds the water ballast between the outer hull and the pressure hull.

There are numerous penetrations through the cylinder's pressure hull, such as hatches for men and materials, piping, periscopes, torpedo tubes and drive shafts for the propellers. Each has to be designed so as to prevent unwanted sea-water from entering the cylinder. To ensure the integrity and safety of the boat, watertight transverse bulkheads separate the submarine into a number of compartments, so that, if one is flooded, the others remain dry, to allow for escape for the crew. During the First World War, the first of the British submarines to be provided with transverse bulkheads was the E class, which had two bulkheads, while its German counterparts had up to eight bulkheads. The central compartment located under the bridge is usually the control room, which houses all the means for controlling the submarine's operations, such as steering, operation of hydroplanes, all of the valves and vents which control the boat's buoyancy, and, most importantly, the periscope.

Wireless communications for British submarines during the First World War consisted of a 1 kilowatt Morse code transmitter, which later in the war was increased to 3 kilowatts. Due to the low-power rating, it was necessary to have a mast near each end of the boat, with an aerial suspended between them. Each mast was a three-piece telescopic pole, the first section of which was wound up into a vertical position from within the boat; then, using pulleys and wire, the second and third pieces were extended upwards. In the case of an emergency dive, the masts could be left up and lowered while the vessel was submerged.

Propulsion and Endurance

At the beginning of the First World War, the main form of propulsion for submarines was either petrol or a diesel engine for travel on the surface, and a battery-powered electric motor(s) for travel underwater. Due to the inherent dangers of petrol engines, these were eventually superseded by the diesel, which was safer and far more efficient and reliable. It should be remembered that most surface ships at the time used coal-fired steam engines. The German submarines during the First World War had more efficient diesel engines, producing 200 to 300 horsepower per cylinder thanks to their blast-injection systems, while the British submarine diesels only produced 100 horsepower per cylinder, due to solid injection. All diesels were four-stroke, as lighter two-stroke engines could not be built at the time because of lack of materials able to withstand the extra stress.

The only supply of air, when submerged, was contained within the cylinder, therefore electric motors were the only form of propulsion available (combustion engines require 200 cubic feet of air for every pound of fuel burnt). Underwater endurance for the crew was therefore limited to the available oxygen in the air, which was sufficient for about 24 hours, after which asphyxiation would occur. The boat therefore had to surface regularly and ventilate, to refresh the air in the submarine.

The other endurance factor was that of the batteries. As mentioned below, forward motion of the submarine is important in maintaining depth, unless the submarine finds a major change in water density or rests on the ocean floor, depth permitting. The batteries were, and still are today, lead acid batteries, not too dissimilar to car batteries. The endurance of the batteries is a function of the power drawn by electrical items in the submarine, such as lights, but, most importantly, the power drawn by the electric motors. The faster the submarine travels, the greater the power consumed. For submarines of the First World War travelling at a speed of 1 knot, the endurance could be up to 50 hours, although a submarine would have to surface before that, in order for the crew to get fresh air. If the boat travelled at maximum speed of about 8 knots, then the battery would last only 5 hours. It should be noted that early submarines were less efficient when travelling underwater. This was due to their design, which concentrated on their less efficient surface-going capabilities. In simple terms, the submarines of the First World War (and the same is true for all but one German design of the Second World War) were surface-going boats which had the capability to submerge for a limited time.

The batteries were recharged by a generator(s), which was driven by the diesel engine(s). It was therefore possible, out of two diesel engines, to use one for recharging while on the surface, and the other to propel the boat through the water. Both diesel engines could be used to minimize the recharge period, if the submarine remained stationary. At best, the charge necessary to replace the preceding discharge was 110 per cent, and therefore batteries had a limited life, which was a function of the number of recharges.

Due to their weight, batteries were carried low in the boats, which often meant that they were difficult to service and were in poor environments, where moisture accumulates, causing further deterioration to the already troublesome batteries. They had to be properly ventilated, particularly during recharging, as explosive hydrogen gas could be produced. Any contact with sea-water also had to be avoided, as it could result in the creation of poisonous chlorine gas.

Submerging and Maintaining Depth

Submerging and maintaining a constant depth, particularly when using the periscope, is crucial for a submarine, and no different today from what it was in the First World War. The filling of the ballast tanks with sea water does not result in the submarine becoming heavier than the water it displaces, and thus in her sinking to the bottom (although in time of war a submarine could have a slight negative buoyancy to aid in a more rapid dive). Rather, the flooding of the ballast tanks and the partial flooding of the auxiliary tanks result in the boat having small positive buoyancy (reserve buoyancy); which means that it just floats on the surface. The boat can then be trimmed by pumping water between the bow and stern trim tanks, so that she remains on an even keel. The submarine is then literally driven below the surface by its forward momentum and the diving planes. The diving planes act like horizontal rudders, which, when pushed into the forward position, cause the bow to descend and the stern to lift, forcing the submarine down. Trim tanks are also regularly adjusted to compensate for the consumption of items such as diesel, fresh water and torpedoes, which over time would otherwise alter the trim. Once the boat has been trimmed for the day, the ballast tanks are blown (water removed by compressed air), and the boat rides high in the water, affording the look-outs the best view of the horizon.

If an enemy is sighted, the ballast tanks are opened to let the air out and sea-water in. The diesel motors are shut down and the electric motors started, and the hydroplanes put into the full forward position to get the submarine underwater as quickly as possible, usually within a few minutes. The ballast tanks are usually compartmentalized, to maintain an orderly rush of sea-water into the tanks. Vent valves are fitted along the top of the ballast tanks and are opened, to allow the sea-water to come in through the bottom of the tanks, which are open to the sea. One or two of the ballast tank compartments may have a Kingston valve on the bottom. This can be shut when in port, to ensure that no accidental submerging of the submarine should take place. (In an emergency, if the tank is flooded and there is no compressed air to empty the ballast tank, the Kingston valve could be closed and electric pumps used, to pump the water out.) 'Q' tanks for quick diving are flooded only in an emergency, to get the submarine submerged by effectively producing a negative buoyancy, but they are then emptied once submerged. (During the First World War only the H class of British submarines incorporated Q tanks, which reduced diving time from 93 seconds to 82 seconds.)

Once the boat is submerged, its depth is maintained by achieving a balance between forward speed and the hydroplanes, counteracting the boat's slight positive buoyancy. If the submarine stopped its forward motion, she would either float to the surface or, if she were trimmed with negative buoyancy, sink to the bottom. Water density can vary with depth, and therefore the auxiliary and trim tanks may have to be adjusted to maintain depth. At all times, records are kept of all the materials consumed, so that the compensating tanks can be adjusted to maintain trim. To surface, sea-water is forced out of the tanks by air from compressed air bottles (at pressures of 3,000 to 4,000 pounds per square inch), which are recharged when on the surface. To save as much pressurized air as possible, once the conning tower hatch is above water, it is usually opened and a low pressure (LP) blower used, to pump surface air into the ballast tanks and to finish expelling the remaining sea-water. This facility was first installed in submarine *E7*, and thereafter in all the submarines of this class.

Torpedoes

The submarine's main offensive weapon is the torpedo. This is a long narrow cylinder (for the First World War, the Mark VI was 18 inches in diameter and 17 feet long), with a rounded front and a propeller at the back. The motive power was provided by compressed air, which turned the propellers but also left a telltale track of bubbles as it escaped from its tanks, while keeping the propeller turning. The speed of the Mk VI was about 35 knots, with a range of 6,000 yards, or 45 knots with a range of 3,500 yards, and a total weight of 1,490 pounds, including a 200 pound warhead.

On the front of the torpedo was a small set of propellers or 'whiskers', which were turned by the flow of water passing over them as the torpedo progressed through water. The whiskers were a safety device to ensure that the explosive charge would not be primed to go off prematurely, but would be primed once the torpedo had travelled a safe distance from the submarine. As the whiskers turned, a threaded shaft moved a firing pin closer to the detonator. The torpedo exploded on impact with the target, as the pistol or firing pin was driven back into the primer or detonator with considerable force, thus activating the explosive.

To maintain the correct depth, so that the torpedo would not pass under the target, yet still remain deep enough to ensure that damage was caused below the water-line, the first torpedoes used a simple bellows to measure the hydrostatic pressure; the operating depth of the torpedo was inferred from it. This depth information controlled the horizontal rudders, to correct any depth error which occurred. Unfortunately, this arrangement was unstable. The next innovation was to add a pendulum so as to sense the pitch angle and to combine the pitch and depth information so as to control the horizontal rudder. The result was a stable, but not an optimized, system, which was usually referred to as 'pendulum and hydrostat' control. The depth setting was initiated before the torpedo was loaded into the tube. Correct direction was maintained by an internal gyrocompass.

The torpedo was expelled or fired from the submarine via a torpedo tube. The torpedo was loaded into the torpedo tube through an inner door, which was connected by an interlocking gear to the outer door. This prevented the inside and outside doors of the torpedo tube from opening at the same time. The inner door was closed, and the torpedo tube was flooded from water carried in the WRT (water round torpedo) tanks, so as not to upset the boat's trim and to equalize the pressure; then the outer door or bow cap (stern cap) to the tube was opened. During the First World War the torpedo was fired by compressed air, which was not vented back into the submarine (thus giving away a boat's position, due to the large bubble of air observed on the surface). Between the wars, technology was developed which allowed for the venting of the air back into the boat. Additionally, as the torpedo was fired, the submarine became lighter and hence the boat's trim needed to be compensated, to ensure the submarine didn't broach the surface. If the torpedo was not fired, then the outer doors would be closed, the water pumped out of the tube into the holding tank and the torpedo removed from the tube back into the boat, so that it could be dried of any sea water. The torpedo and the torpedo tube would then be re-greased before the next firing.

Some First World War submarines, especially German U-boats, were fitted with mines as an offensive weapon. German coastal U-boats carried twelve mines in six open, free-floating, nearly vertical tubes in the submarine's centre line, and eventually some U-boats carried up to forty-two mines in dry storage, at the stern of the submarine. Following the success of the minelaying U-boats, the British converted some of their E class boats to carry twenty mines in open vertical tubes, arranged in their saddle tanks.

The British E Class Submarine

One of the most successful and reliable submarines during the First World War, and the one utilized most frequently during the Gallipoli campaign, was the E class boat. A total of fifty-six boats were active during the war, of which twenty-three were lost (excluding three, which were scuttled). The submarines can be divided into two groups, with salient features summarized in Table A1.1 below.

Table A1.1   *E class submarines: common and specific features*

	Group I	Group II
Number	E1 to E8 including AE1 & AE2	E9 to E56
Displacement	625/796 tons	662/807 tons
Dimensions	176×22.5×12 feet	180×22.5×12.5 feet
Armament	4×18-inch torpedo tubes	5×18-inch torpedo tubes
	1 bow, 2 beam, 1 stern	2 bow, 2 beam, 1 stern
	8 torpedoes carried	10 torpedoes carried
Engine	Vickers diesel/electric; 2 screws; 1,600/840 hp = 15.25/9.75 knots	
Fuel	diesel oil, 45 tons with max of 50 tons	
Battery	224 cells, each cell weighing half a ton	
Range (surface/underwater)	3,225 nautical miles at 10 knots, 85 nautical miles at 5 knots	
Complement	31 (including three officers)	

Comparisons with the German counterparts are difficult, but the Group I E class and U23 class were both intended for action in the North Sea, and are compared in Table A1.2. Generally, the German construction was considered superior to the British, but, as Table A1.2 below shows, there were many similarities; there were also some major differences which gave the U-boat an advantage, primarily in endurance, speed, diving depth and safety.

Table A1.2   *Comparison between English and German submarines*

	E Class Group I	U23 Class
Constructed	1910–11	1910–11
Displacement (ton)	625/795	669/864
Design	saddle tank	double hull
Diving depth (feet)	100	165
Safety factor	2.0	2.5
Length (feet)	180	212
Beam (feet)	22.5	20.75
Armament – torpedoes/tubes	4×18 inch, 8 carried	4×19.7 inch, 6 carried
Propulsion (hp)[a]	1,600/840	1,800/1,200
Speed (kt)[b]	15.25/9.75	16.7/10.3
Fuel (ton)	50	98
Battery (no. of cells)	224	220
Range on surface (nm[c]/kt)	3,225/10	7,620/8
Range submerged (nm/kt)	85/5	85/5
Complement	31	35

[a]hp = horsepower   [b]kt = knot   [c]nm = nautical mile

A further advantage enjoyed by the U-boats was their far more reliable type G torpedo, which carried a warhead of 440 pounds, compared to the unreliable Mark VI, which had a warhead of 200 pounds. The type G also had a longer range of 6,560 feet at 36 knots, compared with the Mark VI's range of 6,000 feet at 35 knots. Although the U23 class originally carried fewer torpedoes, this capacity was increased to ten later in the war. The U-boat construction was stronger, had better sea-keeping capabilities, better periscope optics, better ventilation, including air purifiers, and the bridge afforded better look-out positions, particularly in bad weather.

Table A1.3   *Characteristics of Dardanelles submarines*

	ENGLISH *B11*	ENGLISH *E7*	FRENCH *Saphir/ Turquoise*	FRENCH *Joule/Bernoulli*	GERMAN *U21*	GERMAN *UB8*	GERMAN *UC1*
Completed	1906	1914	1908	1902	1913	1915	1915
Length	142 ft 2½ inch	178 ft 1 inch	147 ft 4 inch	170 ft 11 inch	211 ft 10¼ inch	92 ft 9 inch	112 ft
Beam	13 ft 7 inch	22 ft 8½ inch	12 ft 10 inch	17 ft 9 inch	20ft 1½ inch	10 ft 7 inch	10 ft 6 ins
Surface displacement	287 tons	655 tons	392 tons	397 tons	650 tons	127 tons	168 tons
Dived displacement	316 tons	796 tons	425 tons	551 tons	837 tons	142 tons	183 tons
Torpedo tubes	2×18 inch	4×8 inch	6×45 cm	1×45 cm plus 6 torpedoes external	4×50 cm	2×45 cm	12×mines
Surface speed	12 knots	15.25 knots	11.5 knots	13 knots	15.4 knots	6.5 knots	6.2 knots
Dived speed	6.5 knots	9.0 knots	9. 2 knots	8.8 knots	9.5 knots	5.5 knots	5.2 knots
Surface endurance	1,300 miles at 9.0 knots	3,000 miles at 10 knots	2,000 miles at 7.3 knots	1,700 miles at 10 knots	7,600 miles at 8 knots	1,650 miles at 5.0 knots	750 miles at 5.0 knots
Dived endurance	50 miles at at 4.5 knots	99 miles at 3 knots	100 miles at 5 knots	84 miles at 5 knots	80 miles at 5 knots	45 miles at 4 knots	50 miles at 4 knots
Crew	15	30	21	29	35	14	14

Appendix II: Anti-Submarine Warfare

Ramming, Firing and Sub-diffusion

At the beginning of the war all sides were ill prepared, and the technology for anti-submarine warfare was basic, to say the least. The first step was to issue orders to ships to ram, or fire on, any enemy submarine sighted. An illustration of the type of order issued, and to some extent of its hopelessness and naivety, is shown in the following Turkish example:

> *Opening Fire on Submarines* – If a submarine is on the surface she will be put under by ordinary gunfire. If she is submerged, after carefully ranging on her periscope, fire will be opened. If the submarine fires a torpedo in the direction of the ship (when the torpedo is in motion it leaves a trace which shows its direction) the ship will at once go with full speed towards the submarine and cast anchor. In this way the chain will catch in the propeller and render the submarine helpless.[1]

To improve their chances of success against the U-boats, the British enlisted the services of trawlers and drifters (by war's end, the total number of vessels grew to 3,174), as part of their defensive network of surface ships – although these were only slowly painted in navy colours and armed. The aim was for the surface vessels ultimately to force the U-boats to run out of electrical power or air and so to need to come to surface, where they could be engaged. This seldom occurred, but it did make navigation more difficult for U-boats, which resulted in a number of strandings in shallow waters. A further variation by the British was to arm heavily a disguised merchant ship, in the hope that a submarine would surface to sink the helpless merchantman by gunfire, and so fall into a deadly trap. These decoys or 'Q' ships, as they were known, on some occasions towed a submerged submarine, which would be cast off when a U-boat approached, and would then attack the unsuspecting U-boat.

Nets

Another approach to the containment and possible destruction of submarines was through the deployment of heavy steel nets, such as those used across the Narrows in the Dardanelles. The tops of the panels of steel mesh were held in place by large floats on the surface, between buoys, which were moored to the bottom by cables and anchors. The sides of the mesh panels were then fixed to the buoy cables. Lighter, and thus weaker, nets were often employed as indicator nets, which were designed to provide a signal when broken through by a submarine. They were not intended to stop or foul a submarine's progress, although a navy patrol had to be at hand to pursue the submarine. Indicator nets were also often towed behind trawlers, in the hope of snaring a submarine.

Nets were also used to protect capital ships; they came into general use around the 1880s. These nets were deployed along each side of the ship and were suspended 30 feet out by booms, with the aim of causing torpedoes to explode harmlessly before striking the ship. The nets themselves weighed about 50 pounds per square yard. They were supported by booms made of mild steel tubing about 30 feet long and over 6 inches in diameter, with a spacing of 30 feet between each. When not in use, the nets were rolled up and stored on the main deck, while the booms were swivelled to the side of the ship.

The Explosive Sweep and Lance Bomb

Since 1910, the British had been experimenting with explosive sweeps and lance bombs to attack submerged U-boats. The sweep consisted of a hydroplane (or kite), towed behind a surface ship at a depth of about 40 feet. On the hydroplane was an 80 pound gun-cotton charge which could be detonated electrically, once the cable fouled some part of a submerged submarine. No successful sinkings were recorded.[2] The less effective lance bomb consisted of a 7-pound amatol charge attached to a 4-foot wooden handle. The bomb would be thrown down into the water and explode on contact with a hard surface such as a U-boat's hull.

The Germans developed an explosive anchor, which consisted of a grappling hook attached to a hydroplane strung between two boats 50 feet apart, and travelled at a depth of 30 feet. If the grappling hook snagged a submarine, an explosive charge from one of the boats would be guided to the submarine. An explosive sweep (UD15) was also developed. This was attached to a hydroplane and towed on a 300-foot cable, at a depth of 8 feet, carrying a 200 pound charge. The device was fired electrically on contact with the submarine, but was very unreliable.

The Paravane

A more advanced version of the explosive sweep, the paravane, came into service in 1916. Like the sweep, the paravane was pulled behind a ship, but it would remain at a pre-selected depth regardless of the ship's speed or direction, and it would maintain at a fixed distance from the side of the ship. Paravanes were towed in pairs, one on each side of the ship, and each one carrying a 400-pound charge of dynamite (TNT), which would detonate on contact or could be fired electrically by the operator. The paravane could be towed at greater speeds than a sweep and to a greater depth (up to 200 feet). Although the device was employed on a number of occasions, no confirmed sinking of a U-boat was achieved. The mass introduction of depth charges later in the war limited the paravane's use, but it was the precursor to the 'Otter', used by mine-sweepers, which was a paravane without explosives but with the ability to cut a mine's anchor cable.

Depth Charges

Developed by the British in 1914 and in use by early 1915, the first design consisted of a float and a line that unravelled as the mine sank below water. Once the line was fully extended, the buoyancy of the float would pull the trigger of a pistol within the mine firing it and setting off the explosive charge, of between 35 to 100 pounds of gun-cotton. The size of the explosive charge was not large enough to be effective, and the availability of mines was restricted. The Germans also had a float and line depth charge, C15, which carried a 200-pound charge and a timer which fired the charge if the float and line failed. For all that, the depth charges failed 50 per cent of the time after their general introduction in early 1916.

By early 1916, the type D of depth charge became available in two sizes: 120 pounds for slow-moving vessels and 300 pounds for faster-moving vessels, which could get far enough away to avoid damage when the depth charge exploded. A hydrostatic fuse was attached to the type D, which allowed for detonation at a preset depth of 40 or 80 feet. However, supply was still limited, and by the end of 1916 only four depth charges per vessel were available.[3] The French also developed several designs which were unreliable, while the United States copied and improved on type D. In 1918, the US also introduced the depth-charge rack, which allowed for the timed dropping of depth charges. A total of twenty-nine U-boats were sunk by depth charges during the war.

To increase the killing zone, depth-charge throwers were developed, which enabled a destroyer to fire a pattern of depth charges to either side, as well as rolling them off the stern of the ship. By mid-1917, the Thornycroft thrower could launch a type D depth charge as far as 40 yards; it was later improved by the Americans with the Y-Gun, which was simpler to construct and use. For smaller and slower ships, the British developed howitzers, which fired artillery rounds either exploding on contact, or at a depth of 20 feet. The 7.5-inch howitzer fired a 100-pound shell. Bomb-throwers were also developed which fired a bomb attached to a stick. These were placed into the smooth bored barrel of a cannon (not too dissimilar to the hedgehog throwers of the Second World War). A 3.5-inch stick thrower had a range of 1,200 yards, firing a 200-pound bomb.

Mines

The most effective anti-submarine warfare device was the mine. Minefields, or barrages, were placed in strategic positions, to intercept patrolling submarines and U-boats. The mine consisted of a cased explosive device that was attached to an anchor on the sea floor by a length of anchor cable, so that the mine floated at a predetermined level below the surface. The early British mines suffered both from defective firing mechanisms and from weak anchor cables. These were easily parted by a submerged submarine before the mine could be drawn down to the submarine's hull, to explode on contact. It was not until November 1917 that the British introduced the H2 mine (a 300-pound charge), and the H4 (a 150-pound charge), which were copies of a German design. Floating mines could also be deployed in areas which had the appropriate currents. The mines floated at, or just below, the surface.

The German anti-submarine mine was based on the standard E mine for surface ships, but carried a smaller charge of 44 pounds and featured the effective Hertz horn, which was ultimately copied by the British. Major production of mines didn't occur until 1916. The Hertz horn consisted of a glass tube filled with an electrolyte, which was located within the lead horn protruding from the mine. If a horn was bent on contact with a ship or submarine, the glass vial inside broke and the electrolyte flowed to the bottom of the horn and completed an electrical connection between two wires, setting off the explosive.

Estimates of the number of mines laid during the First World War vary, but the British, American and Germans are estimated to have released 116,000, 56,000 and 44,000 mines respectively. In the North Sea and English Channel, Germany lost 150 naval vessels and auxiliaries, including 35 U-boats, while worldwide a total of 1,047 vessels were sunk and a further 541 were damaged. British losses to German mines were 46 major warships, 259 merchant ships and 63 fishing vessels, with a further 84 merchant vessels being damaged. A total of 586 Allied merchant ships are estimated to have been lost to German mines, to a total of 1 million tons.[4]

Hydrophones

First introduced by the British by late 1915, these listening devices were non-directional, and hence were not very accurate in determining the direction or distance of other vessels. The operator could turn the listening device and hear the sound in one ear, then turn it 180 degrees and hear it in the other ear, and know it came from one of two reciprocal directions, but not which one. The device had to be lowered from the side of the vessel and noise minimized, so the searching vessel needed to remain stationary. By 1917, directional hydrophones became available and could be used by vessels travelling at low speed. To reduce noise, several variants were designed, to be towed behind the vessel. The Germans developed two hydrophones, one directional and one not, but these were not as advanced as their British equivalents.

Appendix III: Supplies Received by Turkey from Germany and Austria

	Supplies	Pre-Bulgarian entry (Nov. 1915)	Post-Bulgarian entry	Sent to Gallipoli
Guns	Austrian mortar, -24cm/10 cal.		4	4
	Austrian howitzer, QF.,* 15 cm		20	2
	Austrian heavy field gun, 10.4 cm		2	—
	Coast gun, Krupp QF., 21 cm/40 cal.		—	1
	Coast gun, Russian QF., 10.2 cm/45 cal.		4	2
	Coast gun, Russian QF., 15 cm/40 cal.		8	6
	16 type field gun, 15 cm/43 cal.		2	—
	Heavy field howitzer, 15 cm		76	—
	'Vawuz', 15 cm/45 cal.		2	2
	Coast gun, QF., 10 cm/53 cal.		2	2
	Heavy coast gun, 10.5 cm/35 cal.		12	—
	Circuit testers	5	—	—
	Case of explosive	5	—	—
	'Gehenhem' exploder	5	—	—
	Machine-guns	87	732	530
Ammunition	Coast, QF., 23 cm/35 cal.		4,944	3,274
	Coast, QF., 24 cm/22 cal.		500	202
	Austrian mortar, QF., 24 cm/10 cal.		1,500	725
	Coast gun, QF., 21 cm/40 cal.		500	500
	Coast, not QF., 21 cm/22 cal.		700	526
	Russian coast gun, QF., 15.2 cm/45 cal.		2,000	2,000
	'Messoudie' gun, QF., 15.2 cm/45 cal.		2,000	2,000
	'Yawuz' QF., 15 cm/45 cal.		371	371
	Coast gun, QF., 15 cm/40 cal.		11,732	10,232
	Mortars, not QF., 21 cm/6–4 cal.		7,934	7,394

*QF. = quick firing

Supplies	Pre-Bulgarian entry (Nov. 1915)	Post-Bulgarian entry	Sent to Gallipoli
16 type heavy field gun, 15 cm/43 cal.		470	—
Inclined recoil, not QF., 15 cm/43 cal.		24,843	13,700
Old Krupp, QF., 15 cm/14 cal.		1,300	—
Heavy field gun, QF., 15 cm		140,268	—
Austrian howitzer, 15 cm		6,800	1,880
Bulgarian, not QF., 12 cm/30 cal.		14,438	4,000
Pedestal mounted, not QF., 12 cm/24 cal.		20,260	3,870
Light Russian howitzer, 12 cm		2,983	—
Krupp howitzer, not QF., 13 cm/1.6 cal.		40,540	12,800
'Breslau's', QF. Gun, 15.5 cm/45 cal.		3,209	3,209
'Peyk-i Shevket', QF., 10.5 cm/40 cal.		3,800	2,000
'Barbaros', Q.F., 10.5 cm/30 cal.		7,200	5,110
14 type heavy field gun, 10 cm/30 cal.		15,734	—
Coast gun, QF., 10 cm/23 cal.		1,888	1,888
Naval QF., 8.8 cm/45 cal.		3,000	3,000
Naval QF. gun, 8.8 cm/30 cal.		4,860	4,860
Mantilli gun, 8.8 cm/24 cal.		111,108	41,000
Naval QF., 7.5 cm/40 cal.		3,300	3,300
Naval QF., 5.7 cm/40 cal.		2,000	2,000
Field, mountain, gun and howitzer, and bomb throwers		350,332	117,034
New pattern mountain howitzers, 7.25 cm mountain, not QF.		388,310	—
Bulgarian hand grenades		227,950	227,950
Explosive detonators	4,000	—	—
Illuminating rockets	161,990	—	—
Very light pistols	1,000	—	—
Percussion primer	2,000	—	—
Electric primer	1,150	—	—
Gutta percha insulator	2,000	—	—
Elastic insulator	1,114	—	—
Engineer's pliers, covered	1,527 and 25,450	—	—
Searchlight carbides, 1.5 metre	806	—	—
Covered engineer's hand-bag	346	—	—

Appendix IV: Turkish List of Vessels Sunk by Submarines

Date	Place of sinking	Tonnage (tons)	Type and Name
13.12.1914	Dardanelles	9,200	battleship – *Mesudiye*
1.5.1915	Near Myriophysto	198	gunboat – *Nur-ul Bahir*
23.5.1915	Near Makri Kioi	585	gunboat – *Peleng-i Derya*
24.5.1915	Near Rodosto	474	steamer – *Naga*
24.5.1915	Near Rodosto	n.a.	ferry – *Hünkar İskelesi*
28.5.1915	Silivri	474	steamer – *Bandirma*
2.6.1915	Venedek Rocks	390	steamer – *Tecilli*
7.6.1915	Near Chanak	3,510	steamer – *Ceyhan*
25.6.1915	Near Mundania	144	Golden Horn ferry – *Halic I*
2.7.1915	Rodosto	93	tug – *Bulbul*
10.7.1915	Mundania	469	steamer – *Biga*
27.7.1915	Sar Kioi	139	steamer – *Hayrullah*
8.8.1915	Near Gallipoli	10,060	battleship – *Barbaros*
22.8.1915	Near Hora	124	tug – *Dofen*
25.8.1915	Near Gallipoli	3,304	steamer – *Kios*
25.8.1915	Near Gallipoli	3,648	steamer – *Halep*
25.8.1915	Near Gallipoli	3,564	steamer – *Tenedos*
14.8.1915	Near Hora	275	minelayer – *Samsun*
19.8.1915	Araki	142	guard vessel – *Sakiz*
20.9.1915	n.a.	438	steamer – *Kesendire*
20.10.1915	Sar Kioi	506	steamer – *Hanefiye*
20.10.1915	Sar Kioi	1,154	steamer – *Plevne*
15.11.1915	Chardak Liman	774	steamer – *Despina*
26.11.1915	Artaki	284	steamer – *Gelibolu*
3.12.1915	Near Dil Burnu	300	destroyer – *Yarhisar*
4.12.1915	Near Panderma	2,995	steamer – *Bosporus*
Total		43,244	

Appendix V: Glossary

Ada = island
Bahr = Sea
Bair = slope or spur
Boghaz = channel
Burnu = cape or point
Chai = river
Dere = valley, stream
Dil = point
Kale = fortress
Kapu = gate
Kuyu = well
Liman = harbour
Nullah = gully
Sirt = slope
Tepe = hill

Notes

Chapter 1: The Beginnings

1 Taylor 1966, p. 16.
2 Fewster 1983, p. 36.
3 Langensiepen 1995, p. 14.
4 Ibid., p. 17: the total cost for the destroyers and battleships was 25 million marks, a sum which was raised from public subscriptions and credits of 13 million marks held by Deutsche Bank.
5 A 23,000-ton 14×12-inch-gunned battleship, with the second ship, of a 27,500-ton displacement, to be armed with ten of the latest 13.5-inch guns.
6 *Goeben* was a Molke class battlecruiser with a displacement of 22,640 tons; it was launched in March 1911 (22,640 gt, 1911: this is to be the short hand notation for gross tonnage and year launched in future references). A top speed of 28 knots, an 11-inch armour belt amidships, 10 inches of armour on her five-gun turrets and a skirt of armour plate below the water-line made her superior to all the British battlecruisers. She had ten 11-inch guns which, due to a higher muzzle velocity, where not noticeably inferior to the British 12-inch guns. The *Breslau* was a lightly armoured cruiser of 4,550 tons launched in May 1911. She carried ten 4.1-inch guns, well below the standard 6-inch guns of the British navy, but with a top speed of 28 knots she could outrun them.
7 Halpern 1987, p. 9.
8 Ibid., p. 13.
9 Lumly 1970, p. 369.
10 Namely *Indomitable* and *Indefatigable*; in the meantime he remained with his flagship *Inflexible* in Malta.
11 Van der Vat 1985, p. 102.
12 Milne did not make upmost speed, apparently because he felt that *Goeben* was too quick.
13 Lumly 1970, p. 143.
14 For a dramatic account of the actions involving *Goeben*, see Dan van der Vat 1985.
15 Miller 1997, p. 246.
16 On board a passing Italian steamer, *Sicilia*, was the daughter of the US ambassador to Turkey, who was quizzed by the German and Austrian ambassadors on her arrival in Constantinople; there she described her first-hand observations of this engagement.
17 Djemal Pasha 1922, p. 110. It is probable that this ship was sent from Constantinople after Captain Hamann, naval attaché to the German embassy, received permission from Djemal Pasha to borrow five or six thousand tons of coal on 8 August.

18 Kannengiessr 1926, p. 25, reports that he was present when the German military attaché, Lt Colonel von Kress, put pressure on Enver Pasha to give permission to allow the German ships to enter the Dardanelles. Enver hesitantly made the decision to allow the ships to enter without consultation with the grand vizier. Von Kress then asked if the English ships should be fired upon in case they followed. Enver initially felt that the decision was one for the council of ministers, but, under further pressure, he made the fateful decision that the forts could fire at the British. It was not until later that evening that he reported his decision to Grand Vizier Talaat and to Djemal. During their discussions on how to allay the Allies' fears, someone came up with the idea that the ships had been previously bought from the Germans.

19 Chatterton 1936, p. 19: 2,264 tons, 1899.

20 Wilson and Kemp 1997, p. 29.

21 Morgenthau 1918, p. 78.

22 Hoyt 1976, p. 25.

23 Marder 1952, p. 292. Admiral Carden had been the superintendent of the Malta Dockyard. Admiral Limpus, the former head of the British Naval Mission in Turkey, would have been the better appointment, because he had greater understanding and knowledge of the Dardanelles defences – he had advised the Turks on their minefields. But the British, in particular Ambassador Mallet, didn't want to offend Turkey; as Limpus had left while it was still neutral, although he had been prolific in providing reports on the defences while he was in Turkey. Admiral Carden was generally considered to be poorly qualified to command in combat, hence his previous posting at Malta.

24 Cassar 1971, p. 42. On 1 September, Churchill had called for a report on the viability of a landing by the Greek army supported by the British navy. It was believed that Turkish strength had declined since the general staff survey of 1906 and that possibly 60,000 troops might accomplish the task, although with great difficulty.

25 Hankey 1961, p. 223.

26 The Dardanelles Commission 1917, Part I, p. 54.

27 In September 1914 consideration had been given to the use of Greek soldiers in capturing the Gallipoli Peninsula by landing men to the south of Gaba Tepe and then striking eastwards, to capture the Kilid Bahr batteries from the rear. However, this plan failed when the Greeks made it clear that Turkey would have to be simultaneously attacked by Bulgaria.

28 Churchill 1923, p. 116.

29 Hankey 1961, Vol. 1, p. 265: 'The idea caught on at once. The whole atmosphere changed. Fatigue was forgotten. The war council turned eagerly from the dreary vista of a slogging match on the western front to brighter prospects, as they seemed, in the Mediterranean.'

30 James 1984, p.40: 'Two Australian sergeants, Little and Millington, had cut a rubber stamp with the initials "A. & N.Z.A.C." for the purpose of registering papers at the Corps headquarters, situated in Shepherd's Hotel, Cairo. When a code name was required for the Corps, a British officer, a Lt White, suggested "Anzac". Little later claimed that he made the original suggestion. It was in general use by January, 1915.'

31 Churchill 1923, p. 184.

32 Hankey 1961, p. 283.

33 James 1984, p. 44.

34 Dittmar and Colledge 1972, p. 82. 280/310 tons submerged, 135×13.5×10 ft, 600/190 hp (horse power) petrol/electric, 2×18-inch torpedo tubes. *B6, 7, 8, 9* and *11* were converted into surface patrol boats in the Mediterranean in 1917, after having the motors removed, the hull raised and the conning tower replaced by a wheelhouse. The class was renamed S6 to S11 respectively.

35 The main surface current from the Sea of Marmara into the straits at the northern end near Gallipoli enters at 1 or 2 knots in a southerly direction and then varies depending on the width of the straits, increasing up to 2 or 4 knots between Kilid Bahr and Chanak, which is the narrowest point. Strong winds can have a marked affect on the surface currents: they can increase the maximum speed at Chanak to 5 knots and, if they are sufficiently strong from the south, they can reverse the current back up the straits. Approximately 66 feet below the surface is a submerged current of denser salt-water, which runs in the opposite direction up the straits. Eddies and submerged currents are also apparent in many of the bays.

36 Guttman 1995, p. 91.

37 This was the *Mesudiye* ('Happiness'), built in 1873 in London and then refitted in 1903; she had a displacement of 9,190 tons, a length of 102.4 metres and a top speed of 17 knots. Armament consisted of two 9-inch, twelve 6-inch and fourteen 3-inch guns. She was anchored off Nara near the Hauslar estuary, as a floating battery, to cover the minefields from attack by British destroyers or mine-sweepers, with the *Intibah* and *Nusret* assigned to provide her with protection.

38 Liddle 1976, p. 30.

39 Usborne 1933, p. 14.

40 James 1965, p. 12.

41 Gray 1988. According to rank, the officers and crew of *B11* shared a bounty of £3,500 for sinking the *Mesudiye*: Holbrook as Captain received the greatest share, which was £601 10s. 6d, while the lowest rating received £120 6s. 1d (the equivalent of a full year's wages for an average factory worker). By statute, the bounty dated back to Henry VIII in 1649 and was mentioned in the Prize Act of 1708: 'If in any action any ship of war or privateer shall be taken from the enemy, five pounds shall be granted to the captors for every man which was living on board such ship…'. In 1805, the word 'taken' was amended to 'taking, sinking, burning or otherwise destroying' of an enemy man-of-war.

42 Jameson 1962, p. 28.

43 Langensiepen 1995, p. 34.

Chapter 2: Naval Attack on the Dardanelles

1 Chatterton 1935, p. 54.

2 Turkish General Staff 2004, p. 275. Flight Officer Fazil was the first Turkish pilot to undertake aerial reconnaissance of the Allied naval build-up in Lemnos as early as 5 October 1914.

3 James 1984, p. 16.

4 *Report of the Committee Appointed to Investigate the Attacks Delivered on the Enemy Defences of the Dardanelles Straits, 1919* (Admiralty Naval Staff… 1921), p. 484.

5 Chatterton 1935, p. 68.

6 Von Sanders 1928, p. 48.

7 Morgenthau 1918 , p. 195.

8 Corbett 1929, Vol. II, p. 148.

9 Layman 1996, p. 142.

10 On 9 April *Monica* arrived at Mudros, the first kite-balloon ship successfully to provide gunnery observation at a maximum altitude of 1,500 feet. It was not until the arrival, in April, of No. 3 Squadron of the Royal Naval Air Service (RNAS), under the command of Air Commodore C. R. Samson, that a more meaningful aircraft presence was established (a French squadron, L'Escadrille 98T, arrived on 1 May).

A new airstrip was built on the island of Tenedos and, for the rest of the campaign, the squadron was able to provide aerial reconnaissance, naval artillery spotting and aerial bombing of enemy positions. At the start Samson had twenty-two aircraft at his disposal, but only five were of any practical use. Samson was to tell General Hamilton that the minimum requirement was thirty good two-seater machines; twenty-four fighters; forty pilots; and 400 men.

The initial difficulty encountered was the bad maps, and it was only towards the end of the fighting that an excellent map was produced, from the photographs taken by the squadron itself. By the time of the landings, a total of forty-two reconnaissance flights and eighteen photographic flights had been made in preparation; had there been more aircraft available and additional cameras, considerably more could have been accomplished. Hamilton and Hunter-Weston visited the squadron to assess the information gained from the limited number of aerial photos.

Difficulties were also encountered in fitting reliable wirelesses in the aircraft and in establishing procedures for naval fire control, but these were to improve over time. Unhappily, some naval units tended to ignore the information supplied; but ships such as *Prince George* and *Agamemnon* were regarded as getting the best results from aircraft spotting. Spotting to pinpoint shore artillery also proved accurate, but was often not effective because of ammunition shortages. The result was that the guns were ceasing fire once the daily allowance of shells was expended. Turkish battery commanders, over time, also learnt to cease fire when aircraft were overhead, so as not to give away their positions.

The perspective afforded by flying over the peninsula and by seeing at first hand the terrain and the difficulties likely to be faced was not utilized by any senior officer apart from Birdwood, who flew over Anzac Cove with Samson on 18 September: too little and too late. Indeed, prior to the landings, Samson recalled how impressed he was with Hamilton's suggestion that army casualties of up to 50 per cent could be expected upon landing on the Gallipoli Peninsula and upon gaining a foothold – when, as a result of his constant flying over the peninsula, Samson thought that the landing would be impossible.

In July, No 3 Squadron moved to Kephalo Point on Imbros, and by late August another squadron arrived, under the command of Wing Commander Gerrard; but this new wing came under the command of Colonel Fredrick Sykes, RNAS. Little has been written on the support provided by the aircraft during the battle for Gallipoli and, in retrospect, perhaps not enough use was made of it. However, support of this kind was evolving into a new type of war; the plane's role and its development were still in their infancy. The RNAS was at that time a poor cousin to the navy, and many exploits went unrewarded. However, one VC was won by Lieutenant R. B. Davies, who, while on a bombing raid on 19 November of Ferejik Station in what was then Bulgaria, landed his aircraft behind enemy lines, to rescue another downed pilot.

11   This was a family of propellants made by combining two high explosives, nitro-cellulose and nitroglycerin. The primary shell explosive was lyddite, which was based on picric acid, with 10 per cent nitrobenzene and 3 per cent vaseline.

12   Puleston 1927, p. 32.

13   Naval guns were never designed to fire up and over a target but directly at it, and thus at a range of 15,000 yards from Gaba Tepe, the angle of descent for *Queen Elizabeth* was 17° 18', while against Chanak it was still a modest 20° 20'. The naval guns also had the advantage of a greater striking force. When a 12-inch Mark X shell from *Lord Nelson* or *Agamemnon* was used, it had a range of 16,000 yards and a velocity of 1,369 feet per second, compared with a range of only 11,000 yards and a velocity of 970 feet per second for a 12-inch howitzer. The higher velocity of these naval guns allowed for greater accuracy, and at 12,000 yards the 15-inch shells of the *Queen Elizabeth* would have had three and a half times greater probability of hitting a target than the 15-inch howitzer had at 11,000 yards. Ironically, the high penetration of the projectiles worked against the naval bombardment, as most of the defences were made of earth. Hence the shells buried themselves before exploding (or, sometimes, before not exploding) and the energy was dissipated, which resulted in little damage.

Additionally, at that time the 15-inch shells did not carry a high-power charge such as lyddite but only powder, and therefore had only one third of the explosive effect of a howitzer. To knock out a gun, a near direct hit was required and this was very difficult to achieve, given the angle of trajectory. At closer range, the odds were greatly improved, with the fleet's 6-inch guns being capable of hitting their targets once for every two shots fired. At 1,000 yards, if the ship was anchored and the gun was new, accuracy increased to 97 out of 100 times. The difficulty was to get close enough, or within range, so as to able to spot the enemy's guns accurately and, most importantly, to hit them directly.

14   Chatterton 1935, p. 85.
15   Taffrail 1935, p. 32.
16   Bush 1975, p. 45.
17   Chatterton 1935, p. 92.   Some 4,000 shells were fired at the battery between 26 February and 16 March without destroying any of the five 6-inch guns encased in steel turrets.
18   Moorehead 1997, p. 48.
19   Marder 1965, p. 240.
20   Launched in Germany in 1911, she joined the Turkish navy in 1913 and was commanded by Lieutenant Hakki.
21   Keyes 1934, p. 209.
22   Bean 1921, p. 191.
23   Hankey 1961, p. 304. At this time the army on the western front counted 546,000 men and was making no progress.
24   Stewart and Peshall 1918, p. 38. The picket boats used a 'sweep' which consisted of a grappling hook or grappling iron fitted with a small gun-cotton charge fired by a battery in the boat when the sweep held fast to an object such as a mine.
25   Not long after that, Venizelos was forced to resign by King Constantine of Greece, who was determined to remain neutral as he was married to Kaiser Wilhelm's sister and was therefore considered to be pro-German.
26   Beesly 1982, p. 81. At this time the head of Room 40, Captain Hall, was also negotiating with the Turkish government at the Thracian port of Dedeagatch in neutral Bulgaria – negotiations carried through with the help of George Eady, a civil engineer, and Edwin Whittall – to break with Germany and allow the Royal Navy a free passage through of the Dardanelles. Eady was authorized to offer £3 million and had discretion to go as high as £4 million if the Turks would agree. The negotiators were not authorized to guarantee that Constantinople would remain in the hands of the Turkish government. This was a major obstacle to the negotiations, since, unbeknownst to the Turks or to the negotiators, the capital had been promised to the Russians. By 16 March negotiations had come to an end and the agents departed for Salonica.
27   Marder 1974, p. 17.
28   Chatterton 1935, p. 132.
29   Swing 1964, p. 71.
30   Aspinall-Oglander 1929, p. 97.
31   Chatterton 1935, p. 140.
32   Corbett 1929, Vol. 2, p. 222.
33   On 18 May, special ceremonies are now held in Turkey to commemorate the Battle of Chanakkale. On the British side, supposedly, one unnamed officer and several other sailors were court-martialled. They were found guilty of failure to do their duty in clearing the mines prior to 19 May and were executed. The truth of the matter was only discovered later.
34   Travers 2004, p. 29. It had been suggested earlier that destroyers should be fitted with sweeps rather than trawlers to remove the mines; however, the commanders of both the British and French destroyer flotillas rejected the suggestion.

35   Keyes 1934, p. 264.
36   Ibid., p. 266.
37   Aspinall-Oglander 1929, Vol I, p. 105.
38   It was not until Bulgaria entered the war against Britain, on 18 October, that the level of munitions greatly increased; see Appendix II for details.
39   *AE2* was one of two E class boats, designated *AE1* and *AE2*, purchased by the Australian government in December 1910. The boats were commissioned into the Royal Australian Navy on 28 February 1914. On 2 March the two submarines were convoyed to Colombo by *Eclipse* and were crewed by Royal Navy officers and a mixture of Royal Navy and Royal Australian Navy sailors. Some technical difficulties were experienced en route, particularly with propellers, but, overall, the submarines performed very well. A collision nearly occurred between the two submarines while they were on the way from Malta to Port Said, during heavy weather. Difficulties continued with the propellers particularly on *AE2*, with a spare propeller having to be shipped from England to Aden. At Colombo, the escort *Yarmouth* replaced the *Eclipse*, and on 14 April they headed east for Singapore. From Singapore the *Sydney* escorted the submarines, and, while in the Lombok Straight, the two submarines and the *Sydney* nearly collided again. The submarines reached Darwin on 5 May, and after a few days of rest proceeded to Cairns and then to Sydney, arriving on 24 May. Each of the submarines had travelled about two thirds of the 12,000-mile journey under their own power. At the outbreak of war, an Australian naval task force which included *AE1* and *AE2* was sent to Rabaul in New Guinea. While there, *AE1* was lost, most likely through collision with a submerged reef; her possible resting place was discovered by the Australian Royal Navy in early 2007. *AE2*, having been offered to the Admiralty, returned to Port Said escorting the second contingent of the First Australian Imperial Force and arrived on 28 January 1915. The submarine was then ordered to Tenedos, arriving on 5 February. She had travelled over 30,000 miles in just twelve months!
40   *E1–E6* and *AE1–AE2*: 660/810 tons, 176×22.5×12 ft, 4×18-inch torpedoes and, later, one 12-pound gun. *E7–E56*: 662/835 tons, 181×22.5×12.5 ft, 5×18-inch torpedoes and one 12-pound gun. All submarines were powered by diesel/electric 1,600/840 hp = 15/10 knots with two screws. Theoretical submerged endurance was 50 miles at 2.5 knots.
41   Brodie 1956, p. 13.
42   White 1992, p. 46. *AE2* ran aground, entering the Port of Mudros at 9.45 p.m. on 10 March, after returning from patrolling the Dardanelles. The light at the entrance to the harbour had been extinguished and Stoker had not been informed. Stoker made the turn on the basis of a spurious light and struck Sagandra Point, where *AE2* was stuck fast for three hours; during this time it was feared that the boat would be lost. *Chelmer* got a wire across and succeeded in towing *AE2* off at 2 a.m. on 11 March. In dry dock at Malta, the boat's tanks were found to be severely damaged and took a month to repair. Stoker was exonerated of any fault in the accident.
43   C. G. Brodie, the twin brother of T. S. Brodie, was on Commodore Keyes' staff, as his assistant; since he had submarine command experience he became Keyes' liaison for the submarine force at Mudros.
44   Brodie 1956, p. 24.
45   Ibid., p. 32.
46   The first pilot ever to take off from a moving ship.
47   The order read: 'Two picket boats from *Triumph* and *Majestic* are to attack *E15* tonight with torpedoes fitted to dropping gear. Lieutenant Commander E. G. Robinson of *Vengeance* will be in charge of operations. Only volunteer crews to be sent.'
48   Gray 1971 suggests that, instead of the submarine being lightened, her tanks were flooded, so that she may not be too readily affected by the quick-flowing current and hence easily dislodged; but this would seem inconsistent with other reports.

49 *E15* was stripped and lay on the beach until she was recovered for scrap in 1920.
50 There is some inconsistency over the casualties suffered in the loss of *E15*. Chatterton, Edwards, Keyes and Usborne mention the asphyxiation of six people. Langensiepen reports that a second shell hit the submarine, killing three crew members. Keyes reports that the Turks buried Brodie and two others of *E15* in a Greek ceremony at Chanak and provided coffins and a Greek priest to read a sermon. Einstein (1917) mentions that the English dead were buried on the beach but when Djevad Pasha heard of this he had them re-interred in the British cemetery.
51 Morgenthau 1918, p. 258. In early January 1916, Fitzgerald was held in the basement of the War Office in Constantinople. The American ambassador, hearing of his plight, had him released on his own recognizance, for eight days, before Fitzgerald had to return to a prisoner of war camp. As it happened, he was also engaged to the daughter of the British minister to the Vatican, and Enver agreed to free him after he gave his word not to fight against Turkey.
52 Avci 2003, p. 65, states that, when Palmer was recognized by his captors, he was threatened with death as a spy, unless he told them where the Allies were going to land at Gallipoli. Palmer reportedly misinformed them that the landing would be at Bulair, which was in line with von Sanders' view of the most likely landing place. Einstein 1917 also mentions the threat to Palmer and writes that, when Brodie was hit by the shell, he was cut into half, with the lower part of his body falling at Palmer's feet. Travers 2004 mentions a message sent by the commander of the strait's forts, which confirmed that Palmer, in order to mislead the Turks, told them that the Allies had originally planned to land at Gaba Tepe and Sedd-el-Bahr, but when they learnt that the Turks had discovered their intentions the landing had been delayed and moved to Bulair.
53 Stoker 1925, p. 100.
54 Ibid., p. 105.
55 Brodie 1956. p. 54.

Chapter 3: The Gallipoli Landings

1 Liddle 1976, p. 91.
2 Hamilton 1920, Vol. I, p. 80.
3 The Turks had attacked the Suez Canal at the end of January 1915, and after a few days of fighting in February were repulsed mainly by Indian troops. By 11 February the canal was reopened for night traffic.
4 Davies 1992, p. 37.
5 Chasseaud 2005, p. 100.
6 Carlyon 2001, p. 91. Hamilton received information from the War Office to the effect that the office knew that the water supply on shore was poor: this was based on an official document from 1905 and a report from an admiral that water was scarce in the villages. Kannengiesser 1926 mentions that ample clean fresh water was always available to the Turkish defenders from springs in the hills.
7 Chasseaud 2005, p. 67.
8 Hamilton 1917, p. 74.
9 James 1984, p. 88.
10 Ibid., p. 91.
11 The ships providing covering fire were given only general instructions to support the landings. It was therefore up to the individual captains how they would interpret their orders. Some captains, were very aggressive – for instance those of *Triumph* and *Bacchante*, which came right up against Gaba Tepe and stayed there all day, firing on selected targets and giving excellent support to the troops. Other ships were less supportive.

12 Frame 2000, p. 185, also suggests that the maps of the time were inaccurate by some 500 yards to the north.
13 Bush 1975, p. 112.
14 Ibid., p. 114. Lieutenant Tom Phillips had suggested putting a submarine off Gaba Tepe and showing a light to direct the boats. This was rejected at the time, but implemented for D Day during the Second World War.
15 Travers 2004, p. 95.
16 Ashmead-Bartlett 1928, p. 81.
17 Hamilton 1917, p. 42.
18 Bean 1921, p. 229.
19 A total of 6 Victoria Crosses were awarded to the Lancashire Fusiliers.
20 Unwin, who had come up with the idea of using a collier to land the troops, and five others were awarded the Victoria Cross on that day for helping to land soldiers or to retrieve the wounded.
21 Stewart 1918, p. 89.
22 Samson 1930, p. 235.
23 Unfortunately, for some unknown reason, destroyers had been ordered not to fire in support, even though ships such as the *Scorpion* were only 500 yards from Turkish trenches at Sedd el Bahr.
24 Hunter-Weston had located his command on the *Euryalus* and failed to move around to find out the true situation at all the landing places.
25 Bean 1921 p. 458.
26 Ibid., p. 460.

Chapter 4: Breaking into the Sea of Marmara

1 Report written by Stoker to the Admiralty, after the war.
2 Brodie 1956, p. 55.
3 White 1992, p. 52.
4 Stoker 1925, p. 56.
5 Langensiepen 1995 mentions that the attack may have been made against the battleship *Torgud Reis* at anchor off Kilya, which seems unlikely. White does refer to a battleship that was firing against the landing forces, although Chatterton states that the Turkish naval fire didn't commence till 27 April. White's correspondence describes a report by Turkish authorities at the time, which stated that the gunboat *Peyk-i Sevket* was torpedoed and this caused a jammed rudder. (Avci names *Aydin Reis* as the boat torpedoed, although she was only involved in the early part of the search and was withdrawn on account of her low speed.) Listing to port, the boat was beached. The *Peyk-i Sevket* was also referred to as a torpedo cruiser (hence Stoker's reference); it was built in Kiel and launched in 1906, with a displacement of 775 tons and 3×18-inch torpedo tubes.
6 Chatterton suggests that the cause of the grounding was a fault with the gyroscopic compass, although Stoker makes no mention of it. White points out that it has never been established whether the cause was the compass or just the result of strong currents in the area. However, a report to Vice-Admiral de Robeck in January 1919 from the former commanding officer of submarine tender *Adamant*, A. Sommerville, does mention that the Sperry gyrocompass ceased working after they passed the first minefield.
7 Fort 24 on the Asiatic side, above the Narrows.
8 No information is provided by Stoker as to the reason for the second grounding except the tongue-in-cheek '. . . I observed that *AE2*, with an apparent liking for forts, had chosen one on the western shore under which to run'. Stoker 1925, p. 113.

9   It should be remembered that depth charges were unknown at that time. See Appendix II for more information on anti-submarine warfare.

10   Stoker sighted the *Barbaros Hayreddin*, a battleship of the Torgud Reis class, with displacement of 10,670 tons and 6×280mm guns, launched in Wilhelmshaven in 1891. She was escorted by the Antalya class torpedo boat *Kutahya* (165 tons, launched 1904, 2×18-inch torpedo tubes). The sighting occurred near the Dohan Aslan Bank (Langensiepen 1995, p. 35).

11   Stoker 1919.

12   Ibid.

13   Langensiepen 1995, p. 35. It is likely that this was a Samsun class destroyer, namely the *Yarhisar* (284 tons, launched 1907).

14   Wheat's unpublished diary, written possibly in 1915, states (p. 12) that in the afternoon three lighters containing soldiers were sighted but with no deck gun nothing could be done.

15   Langensiepen 1995, p. 36. It is likely that this destroyer was the *Muavent-i Milliye* (765 tons, launched 1908).

16   Wheat, p. 13, states that an unknown ship signalled *AE2*'s call sign that night, but, without knowledge of any Allied ship in the Sea of Marmara, they refused to reply.

17   Ibid., p. 13. The diary of J. Wheat tells a slightly different story. He claims that an hour was spent in the attempt to get a clear shot at the gunboat, and just as *AE2* was leaving the harbour area a transport arrived, which Stoker unsuccessfully attacked with the starboard tube. He turned the submarine and fired from the stern tube, but was then forced to go deep, to avoid being rammed by a destroyer. Returning to periscope depth five minutes later, Stoker observed that destroyers were still pursuing him, so he ran deep to avoid them. On returning to the surface to recharge his batteries, he observed six destroyers, escorting two or three small transports, coming towards them from the direction of Constantinople. There was only one torpedo left, and Stoker decided to remain on the surface and to close in on the destroyer. When the range had closed to within 800 yards, the first shot was fired by a destroyer. This fell 100 yards off the starboard bow and was followed by another shot above their heads. *AE2* was then forced to dive to avoid ramming by the destroyer. They remained submerged for about twenty minutes, then surfaced and headed towards Marmara Island. About ten minutes later they sighted the *E14*, which had already surfaced.

18   Kannengiesser 1926, p. 123. One of the transports sighted was possibly the *Plevne*, which had on board German Colonel Kannengiesser, on his way to Gallipoli; there, at 2.30 p.m., he observed the track of a torpedo, 'a bubbling line in the water', crossing the bows of his transport.

19   Brenchley 2001, p. 91. The *Sultan Hissar* was used to transport Liman von Sanders from the town of Gallipoli to Maidos nearer the front line each day, but had been ordered back to Constantinople on that fateful day.

20   Bell 1918 mentions that at this point a hole was reported aft and a leading seaman put his hand over the hole, but another hole followed about 8 inches from it. These may have been small calibre holes, or rather he may have been confused by the sequence of events, given the more serious damaged suffered later.

21   Bell 1918 reports that Stoker told someone to get something white and that A. B. Cheater, the officer's servant, was the man who opened the conning tower. When the blow was stopped and the vents opened, those remaining on deck were three officers – two E RAs (Engine Room Artificers) and Stoker; the latter said: 'Come on then, it is no use stopping here', and they all proceeded to jump into the water.

22   Wheat, p. 15, notes in his diary that the Turkish torpedo boat fired two torpedos and the gunboat one, all of which missed the submarine. Able Seaman Albert Knaggs describes in his diary that, when the torpedo boat was boarding, both torpedo tubes were empty, and an English-speaking German sailor said that both torpedos had been

fired at *AE2* but missed, while a third one had been fired by one of the other gunboats.

23 Frame 1990, p. 87.

24 Stoker 1925, p. 139.

25 Langensiepen 1995, p. 36. The other torpedo boat was the *Zuhaf*, which reportedly was about to ram the submarine before the crew commenced to abandon ship. The location of the sinking is given at 27°25′ E, 40°35′ N (Avci quotes 27°25′ E, 40°31′30″ N). The submarine was discovered in 1998 in 72 metres of water.

26 The officers and crew were initially transported to Gallipoli and were prisoners for the remainder of the war. All but three of the crew survived their three years of imprisonment.

27 Jose 1943, p. 247.

28 Wheat's unpublished diary, p. 15.

29 Brodie 1956, p. 75.

30 Wilson 1988, p. 134.

31 Jameson 1962, p. 46. A torpedo may have been fired at a Turkish destroyer.

32 Stanley 1915. The remaining stanchion was not removed when the submarine submerged and was not discovered until in the Sea of Marmara. Without anyone's knowledge, this had increased the hazard of catching on any obstructions such as nets while travelling up the Dardanelles.

33 Langensiepen 1995, p. 36, suggests that the ship fired at and missed by *E14* at 6 a.m. near Maydos could have been the *Barbaros Hayreddin*. However, this was a battleship of 10,670 tons and would not have been confused with a 850-ton torpedo cruiser. It is possible that the *Barbaros Hayreddin* was in the area at the time and the Turkish authorities thought it was the target. Jameson 1962 suggests that the gunboat sunk was the *Berki-Satvet*, but this gunboat did survive the war.

34 This story of the attempted 'catching of the periscope' has been embellished over time. Kemp 1952, p. 67 tells a version according to which, shortly after firing the torpedo, Boyle was unable to see through his periscope, so he raised his second periscope and 'watched an elderly Turkish fisherman in a rowing boat trying to pull the first periscope out of the water. His hand was over the top glass, shutting out all light.' Edwards 1939, p. 128, relates the same story in the following form, vouching for its truth: 'the same cannot be said of the tale of a submarine which, finding herself blind, eventually surfaced to find out what was wrong with her periscope – only to discover that a Turkish fisherman had hung his fez on it.'

35 Haskins 1915 mentions that the first torpedo was fired accidentally, while the crew were waiting for the order to fire; the second torpedo was fired a minute or two later. *E14*'s log also notes that two torpedoes were fired.

36 Stanley 1915.

37 Kemp 1952, p. 66, Usborne 1933, p. 133 and Edwards 1939, p. 127.

38 Kipling 1916, p. 113.

39 Jameson 1962, p. 43.

40 Submarine Patrol Report.

41 Ibid., p. 45, suggests that a second torpedo was fired before going deep.

42 Langensiepen 1995, p. 36. Turkish records suggest that the attack on the steamer *Ittihat* (921 tons, 1883) failed. Haskins 1915 also states that the torpedo did not run straight and missed its target.

43 Submarine Patrol Report.

44 Submarine Patrol Report.

45 Langensiepen 1995, p. 36. Launched in 1898, with 450 tons displacement.

46 It is not clear from Boyle's report whether both torpedoes were fired or the second one ran erratically, but the ship's log does mention the firing of two Mark V torpedoes, both of which missed.

47 Langensiepen 1995, p. 36.

47 Chatterton 1935, p. 229. Referred to by the British as *Gul Djemal*, it was originally the British White Star liner *Germanic*, built in 1874, with a displacement of 5,017 tons.

49 Langensiepen 1995, p. 36.

50 Carr 1930, p. 29. By 1917, Boyle had learnt who the *Gulcemal* was and what she was carrying, and applied for 'blood money' for sinking it. The Admiralty paid 'blood money' to submarines for every member of the enemy they put out of action. For example, if a submarine sunk a battleship with a crew of 1,000, then the Admiralty would award £5,000. The £5,000 was to be divided among the crew according to rank. This money was only paid, however, if the vessel was offensively armed. Commander Boyle at the time argued that the transport was armed with 3-inch field guns and under the convoy of a destroyer, so he made a claim for £30,000 – £5 for each Turkish sailor and soldier aboard. With a submarine crew of 35 officers and men, the average amount expected to be received was about £1,000 each – a great deal of money at the time. Unfortunately, long before the Admiralty had approved the claim, most of the crew had already spent their share. The Admiralty Prize Court considered the claim and turned it down on the grounds that the transport was defensively, not offensively, armed. Some months after the war the Prize Court finally awarded a total of £31,000 (see Chatterton 1935, p. 229).

51 James 1984, p. 167.

52 Haskins 1915.

53 Formerly German ship *Weissenberg*, 9,000 tons and 6×11-inch guns, launched in 1893, purchased from Germany.

54 Halpern 1979, p. 139. The VC was awarded to him on 16 May, on the strength of a wire sent by Admiral de Robeck and by Keyes to the Admiralty on the night of the 14th. The wire said that he deserved the greatest credit for his persistence in remaining in the Sea of Marmara while he was hunted day and night, as well as for sinking the enemy's biggest transport, which probably had 2,000 men on board. Boyle dined with the admiral and the commodore on the evening of the day of his return, and he left the ship just before the admiral had official confirmation of Boyle's award. Keyes hoped that Boyle would get the VC but he rather doubted it. He was all the more pleased that it happened without an official recommendation, after his return.

55 Wilson 1988, p. 135. A new intermediate shaft had arrived from England on the *Reliance* and was machined to size, the submarine's pressure hull opened, the old shaft removed and the new one installed. The pressure hull was then closed and tested for watertightness.

56 Brodie 1956 , p. 84.

Chapter 5: Gallipoli Action

1   Fewster 1983, p. 70.

2   James 1984, p. 136.

3   Hall *c.*1915–16.

4   His being aboard a ship of this size meant that he was never able to get close to the action – a disadvantage which might have been overcome by moving to a destroyer or a light cruiser.

5   Davies 1967, p. 121.

6   Wester Wemyss 1924, p. 98.

7   James 1984, p. 152.

8   Ibid., p. 179.

9   Churchill 1923, p. 432.

10 Chatterton 1935, p. 222.

11 Langensiepen 1995, p. 159: destroyer class (765 tons, 1909).

12 Ibid., p. 31.

13 Goodchild 1917, p. 151.

Chapter 6: German Submarine Activity

1 Halpern 1987, p. 72.
2 Ibid., p. 75.
3 Rössler 1981, p. 40.
4 Sokol 1933, p. 173. The captain of the *Novara*, later Admiral Miklos Horthy, mentions in his memoirs a sailing date of 2 May, and wooden deckhouses as method of camouflage.
5 Submarine Patrol Report.
6 Halpern 1987, p. 116. Some authors, notably Chatterton, mistakenly attribute the loss of *Merion* to *U21*.
7 Samson 1930, p. 247, writes that, on the morning of 4 June, one of his pilots on returning to base reported sighting a submarine. Samson immediately took off and located the shallow submerged submarine in Morto Bay heading for the French battleship *Henri IV*. Samson descended and attacked the submarine by dropping a bomb, which exploded harmlessly on the surface. The submarine continued on its way, passing directly underneath the battleship and disappearing as it went deeper. Then she was not sighted again until later that afternoon, when Samson, once again on patrol, saw her this time on the surface off Ak Bashi Liman, under escort of a torpedo boat. Unfortunately this time Samson was not carrying a bomb and, having no time to go back to base to get one, he descended and, out of frustration, fired a few rounds from his rifle at the submarine before returning back to base. The date is consistent and, although no report of being attacked by a plane was made by von Voigt, it may have been his submarine that was sighted.
8 Submarine Patrol Report.
9 The misfires may have been caused by the strong sea-swell and the currents near the straits, while the first torpedo had previously displayed low boiler pressure (steam driven torpedo), which may have affected the depth-keeping chamber. The second torpedo was a bronze type that had shown even lower pressures and may also have gone deep.
10 Chatterton 1935, p. 246 suggests that *UB3* was almost certainly blown up by a Turkish mine on 9 April entering Smyrna, but this is not consistent with the date at which the submarine was lost.
11 Wilson 1988, p. 137. Immediately after this mission, the *Gazelle* underwent another conversion, to become a minelayer, and then laid the first British minefield off Smyrna, which may have been the cause of the loss of *UB3*.
12 The ship began to list immediately after being torpedoed and many of the men on deck raced down below to get their life vests, as they had not been required to wear them; this produced a log jam with those attempting to get out. The lifeboats could not be lowered because of the list, and many men who could not swim landed in the water without their vests and drowned. Official reports at that time stated that 132 men were lost, including her captain, Commander P. M. Watton, RNR. The loss of life was far greater. The *Dictionary of Disasters at Sea 1824-62* published by Lloyds Register of Shipping states that 'of the 1,586 on board less than 500 were rescued'.
13 Submarine Patrol Report.
14 Originally the *Vanderland* passenger ship (11,889 tons), she was requisitioned as a troop ship in 1915 and renamed the *Southland*. She returned to White Star – Dominion Liverpool – Quebec – Montreal service in August 1916, but on 4 June 1917 was torpedoed and sunk by the German submarine *U70* off the Irish coast, with the loss of four lives.
15 Grant 1964, p. 152.
16 Halpern 1987, p. 149.

17 Grant 1964, p 54. She was lost to mines while returning home to the Zeebrugge base in Belgium under the command of Feddersen on 3 October 1917.

18 Hoover 1976 suggests that Hersing was the main proponent of the mission; after having volunteered, through his persistence he convinced the admiral's staff of the mission's merits.

19 The *U21* was 210 feet long, with a draft of 12 feet displacing 840 tons when submerged and 650 tons when on surface. Surface speed was of 15 knots; submerged speed, 9 knots. She carried 8 torpedoes, several guns and was commissioned in 1913.

20 Thomas 1929, p. 52.

21 Hoover 1976, p. 36.

22 Ibid.

23 Thomas 1929, p. 58.

24 Chatterton 1935, p. 249.

25 Hoover 1976, p. 38.

26 Beesley 1982, p. 82.

27 Dittmar 1972, p. 31. Lord Nelson class, launched on 23 June 1906; 16,500 tons, 443.5×79.5×27 ft, 16,750 hp = 18.5 knots, 4×12-inch guns, 10×9.2-inch guns, 12×3-inch guns and 5×18-inch torpedo tubes, armour of 12-inch sides, 3-inch on decks and 12-inch on main guns.

28 Keyes 1934, p. 353.

29 Thomas 1929, p. 63.

30 Dittmar 1972, p. 31. Launched 15 January 1903; 11,985 tons, 479.5×71×24 ft, 14,000 hp, maximum speed 20 knots, 4×10-inch guns, 14×7.5-inch guns, 14×14-pounders, 2×18-inch torpedo tubes, armour 7 inches on sides, 3-inch armour on decks and 10-inch armour on main guns.

31 The destroyers were the *Chelmer* nearest; possibly the *Wolverine* under the command of Adrian Keyes, younger brother of Commodore Keyes, which also sighted the periscope; and *Grampus*, which had Commodore Keyes on board.

32 Chatterton 1935, p. 255.

33 Hickey 1995, p. 186.

34 Dittmar 1972, p. 29. Launched 31 January 1895; 14,900 tons, 421×75×27.5 ft, 12,000 hp = 17.5 kts, 4–12-inches, 12–6-inches, 18–12 pdr, 5–18-inches TT, 9 in sides, 4-inch deck and 14-inch gun armour.

35 Goodchild 1917, p. 169. Petty Officer Cowie reported seeing the periscope and part of the conning tower just astern of the minesweeper *Reindeer*.

36 Schreiner 1918, p. 262, in an interview with Hersing, stated that he was surprised to have got the *Majestic* so easily.

37 Goodchild 1917, p. 179.

38 Ashmead-Bartlett 1928, p. 113.

39 Macintyre 1965, p. 32. Hersing was to rise to the rank of vice-admiral on 1 April 1942 and though retired was kidnapped by the Russians at the end of the Second World War and died as a prisoner in 1945.

Chapter 7: The Next Land Phase

1 The monitors consisted of those with displacements of 1,260 tons with 6-inch guns and those of 6,150 tons with 14-inch guns.

2 Ashmead-Bartlett 1928, p. 130.

3 Travis 2004, p. 130.

4 It is interesting to speculate what impact these vehicles in large numbers would have had, had they been landed during the first few days after 25 April.

5 Daily support was to consist typically of a destroyer at each flank of a bay, supported

further out by a torpedo proof monitor or cruiser, with drifters and trawlers on patrol for enemy submarines.

6   Kannengiesser 1926, p. 178.

7   Churchill 1923, p. 413.

8   Von Sanders 1928, p. 79.

Chapter 8: Submarines Take Control of the Sea of Marmara

1   Compton-Hall 1991, p. 322. He added another family name, Dunbar, towards the end of his career, to become Admiral Sir Martin E. Dunbar-Nasmith, VC, KCB, Vice-Admiral of the United Kingdom and Lieutenant of the Admiralty.

2   Brown was a reservist from the merchant navy, and famous for having been born on a sailing ship, while she was rounding Cape Horn.

3   Lambert 2001, p. 302: at a depth of 84 feet in position Lat 40° 28' N, Long 26° 51' E.

4   Carr 1930, p. 32. A story goes that Nasmith reprimanded the individual crew member whose responsibility it was to have the radio working, and he did it in front of as many of the crew as could be fitted into the control room. Having admonished the crew member for dereliction of duty, he went on to confess to his own inefficiency for being unable to tell the crew man how to fix the problem.

5   Plowman 1915.

6   Langensiepen 1995, p. 158. The torpedo gunboat was the *Peleng-i Derya* (900 gt, 1890), which sank with the loss of two lives. Launched in Kiel, she sank in shallow water near Makri Kioi and was salvaged. She was towed to Constantinople in 1915 and broken up in 1920.

7   The periscope can be seen at the Nasmith exhibit at the Royal Navy Submarine Museum in Portsmouth.

8   Nasmith also hoped that, if a spare was available at Mudros, a seaplane might fly it out to *E11* while she was out on patrol. Although a spare was provided for, it had been sent to Port Said by mistake and was not available at the time.

9   Langensiepen 1995, p. 178: *Nara*, 450 tons transport, sunk at 40° 51' N, 25° E off Rodosto.

10   Raymond Swing became a well-known BBC broadcaster during the Second World War. The name 'Silas Q' was recorded in numerous newspaper articles, particularly after Rudyard Kipling wrote about it, and can be attributed to D'Oyly, who gave Swing this nickname. D'Oyly also found Swing's typewriter on board the steamer and kept it with him until it was lost in the sinking of his own ship during the Second World War.

11   Swing 1965, p. 92.

12   Submarine Patrol Report.

13   Schreiner 1918, p. 253.

14   Langensiepen 1995, p. 36.

15   Shankland 1964, p. 100. The ferry was re-floated on the next day and made to proceed to Rodosto (see also Langensiepen 1995, p. 36).

16   Jameson 1962, p. 63. Nasmith was to return to Constantinople properly some five years later, as captain of the battleship *Iron Duke*.

17   Lambert 2001, p. 307. The deck log of the USS *Scorpion* reports sighting a periscope at 12.40 p.m., at a distance of 330 yards, heading north for 1,800 yards before submerging and firing two torpedoes, one of which ran on the surface and another just below the surface; this one missed the *Scorpion* by some 30 yards.

18   Gray 1971, p. 128.

19   Langensiepen 1995, p. 37. One torpedo exploded on a pier, which caused some panic amongst the populace: they thought that the Allied fleet was attacking the city. The second torpedo wrecked a barge and ripped a 6-metre by 4-metre hole in the merchant ship *İstanbul* (3,559 gt, 1904), which was quickly repaired. More importantly, at the

time there were eight merchant ships tied up at Galata Pier, at which Nasmith fired, and a further six merchantmen at the nearby Sirkeci Pier. These were intended to be used to transport the Turkish 1st Division to the Dardanelles front. After the attack the troops were sent overland: the submarine threat was considered too great.

20 Carr 1930, p. 39. Carr suggests from his conversations with Nasmith that it was not so much in the direction the boat turned, but rather that it was able to turn rapidly at a depth of 30 feet, which suggested that they were resting on a shoal under Leander Tower. Either the submarine was being turned by the current or they had been hooked by something that was towing them; so Nasmith, out of concern, started the motors to descend to a greater depth.

21 Shankland 1964, p. 37.

22 Ibid., p. 37.

23 Langensiepen 1995, p. 37. The large steamer was the *Bandirma* (474 gt, 1879), ahead of a convoy of three Bosphorus ferries supported by the torpedo boat *Akhisar*. The steamer sank with the loss of 250 lives, the largest loss suffered by the army at sea.

24 Ibid. The steamer was the *Dogan* with 500 passengers aboard, travelling from Constantinople to Panderma.

25 Harris 1997, p. 194. This was a breach of international law.

26 The safety mechanism for the torpedo consisted of a small set of propeller-blades, or 'whiskers', on the nose of the torpedo; these would revolve as the torpedo moved through the water. The torpedo would be in a 'safe' state where it could not be detonated, as the firing pin was too far from the detonator. It would take some forty-five yards of travel through the water to reach the 'unsafe' position where the whiskers had revolved far enough, working down the thread of a fitted sleeve, to bring the firing pin down to a point about one sixteenth of an inch from the detonator (which contained fulminate of mercury). Once in this position, any contact with the hull of a ship would cause the firing pin to strike the detonator, which would then ignite some gun-cotton, and this in turn would detonate the primary explosive of Trotyl, a generic of TNT (= trinitrotoluene).

27 This was not the first time in Nasmith's career that a torpedo had failed to explode on hitting a target. Early in the war, Nasmith fired at what he believed to be a German U-boat, but fortunately the torpedo failed to explode on hitting what proved to be a neutral Danish submarine. Both he and the Admiralty always denied the submarine was ever fired upon.

28 Plowman 1915.

29 This was demonstrated in 1958, when the US submarine *Bergall* was handed over to the Turkish navy. During a torpedo practice run, the American commander asked his Turkish counterpart what he would have done if the peacetime target had inadvertently turned towards the submerged submarine. He replied that he would have surfaced and not attempted to go deeper, due to the difficulty in getting the submarine below 100 feet in time.

30 Langensiepen 1995, p. 37. The ship was the *Madeleine Rickmers* (3,431 gt, 1913), which had been tied up at the Panderma Pier. It was beached and later salvaged and taken to Constantinople for repairs.

31 Ibid. The ship was the *Tecilli* (390 gt); it was sunk with the loss of its entire crew of eighteen, which was escorted by the *Samsun*.

32 Ibid. The ship was the third ship of the convoy, *Baslangic* (381 gt, 1854).

33 Submarine Patrol Report.

34 Langensiepen 1995, p. 37. The ship was the *Ceyhan* (3,509 gt, 1890), acting as a guard ship to anchored battleships.

35 Plowman 1915. He suggests that Lieutenant D'Oyly went into the conning tower and was the first to spot the mine. He then called for the captain to have a look, though they kept it quiet from the crew. When *E11* was about to surface, Plowman was sent to

the conning tower, where he was to get some flags. On spotting the mine he informed Nasmith, who laughed and told him to get a hammer. When they surfaced, Nasmith and Plowman went on to the deck to release the mine, but it had detached of it own accord as the submarine reversed.

36 Langensiepen 1995, p. 38. The ship at the pier was the *Ittihat*, as was reported by *E11*, and not the *Madeleine Rickmers*, stranded by Nasmith on 1 June. Langensiepen reports that neither the ship nor any of the dhows were hit, but rather the torpedos hit the jetty.

37 Ibid. *Kutahya*, a torpedo boat of 165 tons.

38 Edwards 1939, p. 145. 22 June, 1 dhow; 23 June, two-masted sailing ship; 24 June, 2 dhows.

39 Langensiepen 1995, p. 38. *Kutahya.*

40 Ibid.

41 Named after the seventeenth-century physicist, this class of submarine carried a crew of twenty-nine and was launched in 1911 with 4×18-inch torpedo tubes and two external 18-inch torpedoes. The submarine weighed 530 tons on surface, 630 tons submerged, had a top speed of 14 knots on surface, and a record 11 knots submerged.

42 Avci 2002, p. 167.

43 The sections were attached to buoys with a buoyancy of 12 tons, and these, in turn, were moored to the bottom with two anchors and two chain cables. The nets were made of 3-inch wire, while the head, foot and side ropes were 5 inches in diameter. The mesh of the net was 4 square metres. To keep the foot of the net down in the high current, four sinkers per section were attached, each one weighing 100 pounds. The head of the net was 5 feet below the surface. Maintenance was a never-ending task, with 120 men ashore and 80 men afloat on two crane ships, one of 25-ton capacity and the other of 10-ton capacity. A passage was left, in the shallow waters, to a depth of 24 feet, which was closed by a torpedo net gate.

For the defence of the nets, and to attack any entangled submarine, five motor gunboats were stationed at the nets. Each of these mounted a 18-inch searchlight and a 1.5-inch automatic gun, and was capable of a top speed of 12 knots. One boat was always on duty, moored at the buoy closest to Nagara; a second one was moored near the centre. On shore were five 3-inch guns at Nagara, two 2.2-inch guns at Bokali Kalessi, a quick-firing 3-inch gun manned by Germans at Khelia Tepe and two 1.9-inch guns at Abydos Point. A 36-inch searchlight on rails at Nagara was kept turned on all night.

44 Kemp 1952, p. 77; this incident is not mentioned in Bruce's patrol report.

45 Langensiepen 1995, p. 38.

46 Ibid.; the *Halic 1* (144 gt, 1910) and the *Halic 3* (141 gt, 1910).

47 Stanley Wilson, gunlayer; John Williams, sightsetter; and Ernest Burton, loader.

48 Langensiepen 1995, p. 38.

49 Hallifax 1915.

50 Submarine Patrol Report.

51 Langensiepen 1995, p. 38: it was sighted by *Aydin Reis* and, after a short search of the area, the gunboat headed back to Constantinople.

52 Hallifax 1915.

53 Langensiepen 1995, p. 38; the tug *Bulbul* and the brigantine *Ceylanibahri*.

54 Ibid.; the ferry *Biga* (784 gt, 1894).

55 Ibid.; the ferry *Nusret* (230 gt, 1873).

56 The enemy practice of grounding targets allowed for the quick shelling of hulls that would normally be below the waterline, but many of the boats were quickly repaired and returned to service within a few days.

57 Hallifax states in his unpublished diary (of around 1915) that it was the poor control of the helmsman, H. Kielynack, that resulted in the failed attack.

58   Hallifax c.1915: on arriving back at base Cochrane was informed by the flagship that
      the torpedo had hit a gunboat. Cochrane was unable to identify the gunboat from his
      'Janes' book of vessels, but he suggested that it might have been the *Nuin-i-saffer* with
      two extra rigged masts, although it is unlikely that any ship was hit.
59   Located some 20 nautical miles to the south-west of Constantinople near the coast,
      Zeitun was one of several gunpowder and projectile factories (*baruthanes*). Storage
      facilities were also believed to be located some 5 nautical miles further to the west and
      at Stefano to the south-west, near the coast.
60   Wilson 1988, p. 62.
61   Hallifax 1915. A week earlier, all the base-fused shells had been used and it was now
      necessary to fit time and percussion fuses, which had been shipped from Harwick for use
      against zeppelins. Each case held 11 shells, and when these fuses were fitted in the front
      and the shells placed back in the box the lids could no longer be closed. After completing
      the bombardment, six fuses were fitted, but Hallifax, who had the job of fitting them (in
      view of his incapacity to carry out other duties, because of his burns), discovered that
      only percussion fuses were left. These were 1.5 inches too long and would not screw in
      properly. Thus, of the thirty-three rounds left, only six were now usable.
62   Langensiepen 1995, p. 39 *Gülnihal* and *Ziya*.
63   Ibid.: the transport *Hayrullah* (139 gt,1879).
64   It is interesting to note that little effort seemed to have been made by the British
      submarines to intercept enemy shipping at night. Following the captured captain's
      tale, *E14* spent that night safely submerged.
65   Langensiepen 1995, p. 39; *Tenedos* (3,564 gt, 1889), *Bandirma* (474 gt, 1879) and the
      destroyer *Samsun*.
66   Ibid.; *Aydin Reis* – but no engagement between the two is recorded.
67   Boyle was the senior commander and had assigned *E11* to the northern position.
68   Submarine Patrol Report.
69   Langensiepen 1995, p. 39. *Mahmut Sevket Pasa* (2,690 gt, 1886), a steamer on its way
      to act as a picket ship for the battleship *Barbaros Hayreddin*, was ultimately re-floated
      and returned to service in 1917.
70   On 12 August, Flight Commander Charles Edmonds, in a seaplane from *Ben My
      Chree*, made the world's first successful torpedo attack from an aeroplane. At a height
      of 15 feet and at a distance of 300 yards, he released his 14-inch torpedo, which hit the
      ship amidships not knowing that the ship was already aground. Several more
      successful attacks on other vessels were made over the next few days, including by
      Flight Lieutenant D'Acre, who had to land in False Bay due to engine trouble and there
      he proceeded to taxi on the water to his target and fire his torpedo; then, being lighter,
      he was able to take off and return safely.
71   Axworthy (unpublished private diary, probably 1915). The two torpedoes were
      expelled from *E14*'s tubes, collected and transferred into *E11* via her stern tube and
      carried through the boat forward to her bow tubes.
72   Submarine Patrol Report.

Chapter 9: The August Land Offensive

1   James 1984, p. 262.
2   Kannengiesser 1926, p. 207.
3   James 1984, p. 297.
4   The navy had offered to land men to the north of Suvla Point (the northern
     promontory of Suvla Bay), so that the troops were near the important northern
     objective of the Kiretch Tepe Heights. On the night of 20 June, a small party of New
     Zealanders had landed, unopposed, to reconnoitre the area and found sources of good
     water, but the army rejected this proposal.

5   Von Sanders 1928, p. 88.
6   Within a few days it was discovered that water could be found by digging wells some 4 to 15 feet deep.
7   Hamilton 1917, p. 220.
8   Hamilton 1920, p. 91.
9   Their bodies were found after the war, well beyond the Turkish lines.
10 Von Sanders 1928, p. 87.

Chapter 10: Containing the Austrians

1   It was not until 28 August 1916 that Italy finally declared war on Germany.
2   On 3 January 1917 the submarine was raised and taken to Venice, where it was subsequently broken up. Its captain, Lerch, and his crew of 12 were buried with full military honours on the island of San Michele.
3   Chatterton 1936, p. 43.
4   Wilson 1997, p. 64.
5   Halpern 1987, p. 194.
6   North Sea fishing vessels, usually some 88 feet long and 19 feet wide, with a displacement of 30 tons. Powered by a triple expansion steam engine of 34 horsepower, they were capable of doing 9 knots.
7   *B10* did not arrive until March 1916, due to dockyard repairs in Malta. She was to become the first submarine ever to be sunk from the air, which happened on the evening of 9 August 1916 while she was moored at dockside.

Chapter 11: Final Submarine Phase

1   Langensiepen 1995, p. 39; the hospital ship *Ziya*, transport *Halep* (3,648 gt, 1181).
2   Ibid.; *Halep* was raised on 8 August and towed to Constantinople for repairs.
3   Ibid.; *Aydin Reis*, which was carrying Admiral von Usedom's staff.
4   Avci 2003, p. 203, mentions that the aircraft was a Gotha biplane WD1, No 286. The pilot, Flight Officer Jansen, and his Observer Thiele, on return to base at Chanak, did report the location of the submarine and what they believed (on observing oil on the surface) to have been a successful attack, so no follow-up seems to have been undertaken.
5   Chandler (unpublished private diary, probably 1915) reports that one bomb exploded 100 feet ahead of the submarine and the other bomb failed to explode quite close on the starboard side.
6   Langensiepen 1995, p. 39: a torpedo cruiser of 775 tons. On the following day, 7 August, Turkish salvage parties removed radio equipment, ammunition and guns from the ship, whose superstructure was still above water. A number of ships arrived to help in the recovery, including the *Sultan Hissar*, which arrived at 6.30 p.m. towing a diving barge and a salvage crew from the *Midilli*. At 7.30 p.m. the pumping tug *Liverpool* also arrived, followed by the pumping tug *Kurt* next day. By 7 p.m. on 8 August, the *Peyk-i Sevket* was raised and arrived at the No 2 dockyard in Constantinople on 9 August. The German flotilla commander, who had been aboard the torpedoed ship, praised the Ottoman crew members.
7   Langensiepen 1995, p. 39. Due to acute shortages of ammunition, the battleship had been risked in taking supplies to the front.
8   Langensiepen 1995, p. 39 states that the destroyer which Nasmith attacked was the *Basra*, which was picking up survivors.
9   Ibid.; the guard ship *Mahmut Sevket Pasa* near Dohan Aslan. Although hit by gunfire from both submarines, the ship was salvaged several days later.

10   Jameson 1962, p. 68.
11   Lambert 2001, p. 317.
12   Langensiepen 1995, p. 39: *Sivrihisar*.
13   Chandler 1915 reported that a French newspaper was recovered from one of the boats that told them that the ship they had sunk was the *Barbaros*.
14   Langensiepen 1995, p. 39; the *Isfahan* (843 gt, 1886) was unloading coal for the Baghdad railway at the Haydarpasa pier before she was sunk but was subsequently raised (re-floated). See Kemp 1952, p. 85. The story goes that the ship was unloading 3,000 tons of coal and Turkish officials were standing next to the jetty discussing how the coal should be distributed, when the ship blew up before their eyes, eliminating the need for a decision.
15   Chandler *c.*1915 reports that the bridge was of a 'Trellis work girders', so that little damage was probably done.
16   Compton-Hall 1991, p. 323. D'Oyly was later to command the aircraft carrier *Glorious*, which was sunk in the Norwegian Sea on 8 June 1940 together with her two escort destroyers by the German battlecruisers *Gneisenau* and *Scharnhorst*. D'Oyly was returning to port, to court-martial two of his commanders under orders from the Commander-in-Chief Home Fleet, and was killed in the action together with 1,500 other men, of whom only 39 survived.
17   Langensiepen 1995, p. 39, *Yarisar*, escorting the tug *Dofen* (124 gt, 1895) and four sailing barges.
18   One of the survivors was a German bank manager who was taking some money to the Chanak Bank. Chandler mentions that a total of twenty-five were picked up, which included a Turkish army captain, some soldiers and aeroplane builders. However, Langensiepen disputes the likelihood of any German banker or other personnel being on board the tug.
19   Langensiepen 1995, p. 39; Nasmith fired a torpedo at *Durak Reis* but missed, hitting instead the steamer *Kios* (3,304 gt, 1893), which had been bombed by British aircraft on the 17 August. The ship had already been grounded due to the aircraft attack and salvaged, but the torpedo attack finally finished her off.
20   Ibid., p. 40. *Halep* (3,648 gt, 1884) hit amidships, which then capsized and sank. It was followed in sinking by the *Tenedos* (3,564 gt, 1889).
21   Ibid.: *Sam* (3,662 gt, 1884), causing only minor damage; the steamer was ultimately towed back to Constantinople.
22   Ibid.: *Lilly Rickmers* (4,081 gt, 1910), again, only causing minor damage; the steamer returned to port under its own power. *E2* later observed the ship on shore.
23   However, Chandler does mention that the high power periscope was used to spy on two girls sitting on a beach and wearing white blouses, pale blue skirts and straw hats trimmed with feathers.
24   At the start of his patrol a month earlier, *E11* had struck a heavy horizontal wire at a depth of 110 feet, which Nasmith now thought was probably the lower jackstay supporting the sinkers. After considering all the information gathered from his two excursions, he came to the conclusion that the net might be safely passed without encountering any obstruction, if passage was taken between two buoys at a depth of 130 feet or more.
25   The netting had likely sheared off the holding-down bolts and, perhaps more seriously, had flattened the pressure hull in two places as a result of this; the hull leaked badly for the remainder of the trip.
26   Langensiepen 1995, p. 40.
27   Ibid.
28   These repairs initially included lowering the gun 2 feet from its original height and then re-bolting it. A total of fifty-six rounds were fired from this makeshift position, but the hull continued to leak badly.

29　Langensiepen 1995, p. 40; the patrol vessel *Sakiz*.

30　Ibid.; the ship was *Armagan*, but was reported by Turkish authorities as not being sunk.

31　Stephens 1915 reports that the torpedo missed the patrol boat but hit the nearby destroyer *Yarhisar*. This, as they were to learn later, had been incorrectly reported by the Turkish authorities as being sunk on that date. This is another example of the confusion of information – much of which has been clarified by Langensiepen: this information was based on the guesswork of sailors, who were not in best position to observe from a submerged submarine.

32　Stephens 1915.

33　Ibid.

34　Carr 1930 reports that an explosion was heard at daybreak. It is interesting to note that Stocks said little in his patrol report about the loss of Lyon except in a special mention of crew members, which in the case of Lyon stated, strangely: '… for his continual keenness and good work, his complete knowledge of the boat was of the greatest assistance'.

35　Langensiepen 1995, p. 40, reports that the ship was not hit.

36　Jackson (unpublished private diary, probably of 1915).

37　Langensiepen 1995, p. 40.

38　This comes from a short unpublished report to the Admiralty, by Cochrane, after the war.

39　Gray 1972, p. 99.

40　There is some confusion and possible myths associated with the presence of the German submarine officer von Heimburg and his activities at the scene, as the only mention of any German officers was made in Cochrane's report to the Admiralty. A possible reason for Heimburg's appearance at that time is described by Gray 1972, whereby *UB14* had been caught in British nets which had been placed across the Narrows to prevent German submarines from entering the Sea of Marmara. After a massive struggle and depth-bombs from British surface ships which weakened the nets, *UB14* escaped but suffered some damage. The submarine was forced to enter the harbour of a small fishing village, which had been renamed Hersingstand by the villagers in honour of Hersing's success. It was while *UB14* was undertaking repairs that the *E7* incident occurred.

　　German records do mention that Leutnant Prinz Heinrich Reuss (who did come aboard *UB14* when she arrived at Chanak) reported that an English submarine had been caught in the nets since 6 a.m. that morning, and that demolition charges were made by *UB14*. After the first charge failed, a second one was prepared, but *E7* surfaced before it could be deployed.

　　In his submarine log, Heimburg mentions that he suggested to the commander at Chanak that seaman Herzig, who was schooled in the field of demolition and had the equipment handy, should be utilized. Prince Reuss later informed Heimburg that Herzig, through his expertise, was very much involved in the destruction of *E7*.

41　It is not known for certain how these charges were set off, but this is most likely to have been done through electronic detonation, as the charge could have been lowered down to the appropriate depth by the firing wires and then fired. It is unlikely that a hydrostatic switch was incorporated, although, if it had, it would have been the first successful attack by the equivalent of a modern day depth charge.

42　Cochrane's unpublished report to the Admiralty.

43　Sims 1938.

44　Cochrane (a descendant of Admiral Lord Cochrane, the source of inspiration for Forester's Hornblower novels), and Stoker from *AE2* met up in a Turkish prison camp 300 miles inland in Asia Minor. They joined together in an attempt to escape, but were recaptured 10 miles from the coast and sentenced to a year's close imprisonment. On the day of their escape, the coxswain of *E7*, who was imprisoned 60 miles away from the coast, escaped from his prison and made his way to the sea, where he launched a small canvas boat. Unfortunately, he was blown back by a gale and was recaptured too. On 18 August 1918, Cochrane once again escaped and returned safely to England, where he became Unionist MP for East Fife in 1924, and Governor of Burma from 1936 until 1941. He had received the DSO for *E7*'s first patrol of Marmara, and a Bar (that is, a second DSO) following his successful escape from Turkey.

45   Langensiepen 1995, p. 40; the Austrian steamer *Bitinia* (3,125 gt, 1900), which remained half submerged for several weeks before it was salvaged and towed to Constantinople.

46   Ibid.; no hits were recorded. One possible explanation is that Bruce sighted exhaust gases resulting from the torpedo boat's increase in speed.

47   Langensiepen 1995, p. 40, claims that the shore batteries forced *E12* to leave after achieving little success.

48   Ibid.; *Kesendire* (438 gt, 1902).

49   Davies (unpublished private diary, probably of 1915).

50   Over the next few weeks, *E12* and *H1* met up on a number of occasions, sometimes remaining together for a full day at a time. These submarines are credited with performing one of the first wartime underwater experiments which tested the Fessenden sound signalling equipment. The equipment sent out underwater sonic transmissions, so that submarines could communicate over several miles.

51   Langensiepen 1995, p. 41.

52   Edwards 1936, p. 177.

53   The H class submarine was a coastal submarine (423 tons/510 tons, 11.5 knots/9 knots, 4×18-inch torpedo tubes) with the initial batch of ten, built in Canada, suffering from a low reserve of buoyancy. *H1* crossed the Atlantic in 1915, a record journey in its day.

54   It was discovered later, on coming to the surface, that the jumping wires were intact but the net wires had forced them down and then had cut themselves on the periscope standard, which had been grooved in the process. The magnetic compass, which was housed on the bridge and reflected onto screen in the control room, was also affected, and condensation made it difficult to read it when the boat was submerged. Midshipman Bethell, as boarding officer, was later to remove a compass from a dhow in order to provide some small additional assistance on the direction in which the submarine travelled. Unlike the E class submarines, *H1* had no gyrocompass fitted.

55   Langensiepen 1995, p. 41; possibly two boats, *Aydin Reis* and *Nusret*.

56   Moth 1987. It was not till a week later that *E12* sent a signal in a new code, given to her by *H1*, to the effect that it was known that she had made it into the Sea of Marmara. A signal was placed on the noticeboard of her parent ship, which stated: 'As a signal has been received from *E12* in a code taken to the Sea of Marmara by *H1*, it is presumed that the latter boat is safe.'

57   Langensiepen 1995, p. 41; both vessels were repaired and returned to service by the end of the month. Pirie made a claim for an award of Prize Bounty for the sinking of the ship on the western side of the pier, which he estimated at 1,000 tons; he estimated that she had a crew of not less than forty – the number affecting the amount of prize money to be awarded.

58   Langensiepen 1995, p. 41.

59   Pirie made a claim for an award of Prize Bounty for the sinking of the two ships. The larger one he estimated at 5,000 tons and, due to the sea conditions at the time, he felt it was unlikely that any troops, which he estimated at not less than 2,000, could have disembarked. He estimated the smaller vessel at 1,000 tons and her crew as having not less than forty members.

60   Langensiepen 1995, p. 42; *Plevne* (1,154 gt, 1892), *Hanefiye* (506 gt, 1879).
61   Ibid.
62   Pirie again made a claim for an award of Prize Bounty for sinking the ship; he estimated that it was 7,000 tons and a crew of not less than fifty, and that she was armed.
63   Built in Toulon, France, and commissioned in 1908, the 50-metre long submarine had a displacement of 390 tons when on surface and 447 tons when submerged, a surface speed of 11 knots and a range of 1,500 miles, and, when submerged, a maximum speed of 8 knots with a range of 12 miles. Powered by a 600 horsepower engine, it carried four 18-inch torpedo tubes, a 9-pound deck gun and a crew of twenty-five.
64   Bush 1975, p. 221. Ravenel had failed to inform anyone of his return journey and revealed his lack of determination when he wrote previously in his log: 'Good God what an atrocious prospect! We must remain here for 18 days. How are we to survive? It is terrible.'
65   A court marshal of Ravenel was conducted in 1919, but a panel of judges consisting solely of submariners acquitted him. Thomazi's 1927 *La Guerre Navale aux Dardanelles* makes no mention of the destruction of the documents or its consequences, but mentions instead the destruction of secret documents on board *Saphir* and *Mariotte*.
66   Langensiepen 1995, p. 42; after a number of short cruises on the Bosphorus for propaganda purposes, the newly acquired submarine saw no action, as her outdated equipment made it impossible to get spares and she spent the remainder of the war as a charging station for German submarines.
67   Ibid., p. 43.
68   Ibid.
69   A 14-foot collapsible wood and canvas lifeboat, invented by the Rev. Edward Lyon Berthon in the late nineteenth century.
70   Langensiepen 1995, p. 43.
71   Plowman 1915. Plowman and another crewman, Spiers, rowed the boat that landed the agent on shore. Plowman writes that the agent arrived on board dressed as a Greek, carrying a sack over his shoulder, but that on departure the Armenian was dressed as a Turkish soldier. He told Plowman that all his family had been massacred by the Turks and that he had agreed to spy for the English to get his revenge. Although Plowman claims that the agent had informed him of his orders, unfortunately no information was provided. The agent was to be dropped near a Turkish army base and, on his approaching the shore, several lights were observed. But, although the grounding of the boat made a considerable racket, which was then followed by the agent's pistol falling out of his overcoat into the boat and causing further noise, Plowman, Spiers and the spy were not detected.
72   Langensiepen 1995, p. 43; the Austrian steamer *Arimatea* (3,891 gt, 1912).
73   Langensiepen 1995, p. 43; *Despina* (774 gt, 1866). Struck on the starboard side, the ship broke into half and sank with her load of wheat, with the loss of three lives.
74   Ibid.; *Gelibolu* (284 gt,1867) was sunk and *Edremit* (414 gt, 1887) was damaged.
75   The numbers vary in different accounts; some give 42 or 43 survivors out of a total complement or total crew of 85. According to Plowman's recollections, each one of the rescued Germans was wearing the Iron Cross and had been aboard *Goeben*.
76   Langensiepen 1995, p. 43. She was the *Bosporus* (2,995 gt, 1911) and the torpedo boat was the *Berkefsan*.
77   Ibid.
78   Langensiepen 1995, p. 43, states that it was the ferry *Rehber* (287 gt, 1890).
79   Ibid.; the ferry *Eser-i Merhamet* (230 gt, 1982), which was ultimately recovered in 1916 and returned to service.
80   Ibid.; the minelayer *Intibah* reported only slight damage in the first engagement.

81 *UB14* Patrol Report.
82 Langensiepen 1995, p. 43; *Meno* and the *Cezlani Bahri.*
83 The gun factory was shown on the charts, but what the symbol referred to was unknown to the submarine captains.
84 Langensiepen 1995, p. 43; the steamer *Leros* (247 gt, 1915).
85 Ibid. The train was not a troop train, as British Intelligence thought, but a regular express service No 1678, although Nasmith reported it as a goods train.
86 Wilson 1997, p. 93, suggests that the torpedo could have been fired by *UB8*, under the command of von Voigt, although von Voigt did not fire a torpedo due to fading light.
87 As well as the jumping wire, it is also likely that a 'knife' was placed over the 4-inch gun, which consisted of a sharpened steel blade extending from the conning tower down and over the gun, and then to the upper deck, so that, if the jumping wire broke, the blade would cut through the net and prevent entanglement.
88 Langensiepen 1995, p. 44.
89 Bennet (unpublished private diary, probably of 1915).
90 Langensiepen 1995, p. 44.
91 Ibid.
92 Ibid.

Chapter 12: The Last Act

1 Robertson 1921, p. 269.
2 James 1984, p. 322; however, Nevison 1919, p. 387, states that he heard staff officers commonly estimating losses at 15 per cent.
3 Ashmead-Bartlett 1928, p. 219.
4 Keyes 1934, p. 448.
5 Ibid., p. 470.
6 Wester Wemyss 1924, p. 218.
7 Churchill 1923, p. 530.
8 James 1984, p. 347.

Chapter 13: Conclusions

1 Keyes 1934, p. 436.
2 Morgenthau 1918, p. 227.
3 Ellison 1926, p. 66.
4 Indeed by 1915 it became apparent to the Germans that, to keep Turkey in the war, Serbia would have to be defeated and, to do so, Bulgaria would have to be convinced to join Germany. While the Allies could not promise Bulgaria any new territory, Germany and Austria, on 6 September 1915, offered her a loan of 200 million francs, the return of lands lost during the 1913 war with Greece and Romania, and the annexation of Serbia–Macedonia. On 14 October Bulgaria declared war on Serbia; this was followed on the 16th by France and Britain declaring war on Bulgaria.
5 Fewster 1983, p. 169: Hamilton became increasingly fearful '… if the Germans bring down their heavy artillery. If they had enough big guns and ammunition they might blow us off the beaches.'
6 Ashmead-Bartlett 1928, p. 96.
7 Travis 2004, p. 227.
8 Bean 1921, p. 602.
9 Head 1931, p. 160.
10 Dardanelles Commission 1917, Part II, p. 292.
11 Wester Wemyss 1924, pp. 282 and 283.
12 Hamilton 1920, p. 342.

13 Von Sanders 1928, p. 73.
14 Keyes 1934, p. 416.
15 Mitchell 1921, p. 205.
16 Liddle 1976, p. 168.
17 Churchill 1923, p. 444.

Epilogue

1 Miller 1996, p. 310, comments that the British were aware, from intercepted messages and the re-coaling of the *Goeben*, that something might happen.
2 Ibid.: 14 officers and 150 men were rescued.
3 Langensiepen 1995, p. 32. On 22 January two bombs hit the *Goeben*: one hit the after funnel and the other hit the port net locker.
4 She started off as the *Dresden* (1,805 gt, 1897), and was taken over by the Admiralty as an armed boarding steamer and renamed *Louvain* in 1915.
5 Jameson 1962, p. 91.
6 Mitchell 1918.
7 Langensiepen 1995, p. 32, suggests that two torpedoes may have been fired, the last one at 9.13 a.m., and that the sound of the nearby explosion suggested that one of the torpedoes had hit a mine close by. If a second torpedo was fired, then it is likely that at least one torpedo hit the wreck of the *Grap*. The *Intibah* was not hit.
8 On the basis of the statement of senior survivors, Jameson 1962 suggests that the wheel had been severed by enemy fire; but Mitchell reports that it had been disconnected on the previous night, when they had dived, and that he had been the last one to use it. It is possible that Mitchell was a major contributor to the survivors' statements, which makes the situation even more confusing than one might expect it to be in the heat of battle.
9 A Turkish sailor informed Petty Officer Perkins later that Drew's body was found on a beach near Kum Kale. Perkins was with the two officers and saw White being almost blown to pieces.
10 Jameson 1962, p. 93.
11 She had been freed using the old Turkish battleship *Torgud Reis*, which had been made fast (that is, tied) alongside *Goeben*, and, by altering the direction of her screws, created sufficient disturbance on the sandbank to break the suction effect and to allow the *Goeben* to break loose.

Appendix I: Submarine Fact File

1 The performance of a vessel subjected to a sea state.

Appendix II: Anti-Submarine Warfare

1 Mitchell 1921.
2 Messimer 2001, p. 51.
3 Ibid.
4 See www.mcdoa.org.uk/DevelopmentofMinewarfare.htm (last accessed 2006).

Bibliography

Unpublished manuscripts

Axworthy, W. R., *c*.1915. 'H. M. Submarine E11 in the Sea of Marmara 1915: A Diary'

Bell, S.T., c.1918. 'Statement on Loss of HMA. Submarine AE2'

Bennet, A. C. M., *c*.1915. 'War Experiences in Submarines'

Chandler, S., *c*.1915. 'A Diary of Exploits with Submarine E1, in the Dardanelles'

Davies, T. G., *c*.1915. 'Diary of Stoker Petty Officer of E12'

Hall, P., *c*.1915–16. 'Letters'

Hallifax, O. E., *c*.1915. 'Diary, Vol. VII:: 28 May 1915–16 August 1915'

Haskins, J. T., *c*.1915. 'Aboard H.M. Submarine E14 – Dardanelles 26th March to 19th May 1915'

Holbrook, N. D., 1976. Audio tape

Jackson, T. W., *c*.1915. 'H.M. Submarine E.2: Diary of Able Seaman'

Knaggs, A.E., *c*.1915. Diary on the Voyages of AE2

Lohden E., *c*.1915. 'Diary of L/Tel Edgar Lohden HM S/M E11'

Loss of Submarine E14 at the Mouth of the Dardanelles, 28 January 1918: Statement by Senior Survivors', 1918

Nasmith, M. E., n.d. 'Some Recollections of Submarine Work in the Sea of Marmara in 1915'

Nasmith, M. E., 1963. Audio tape

Plowman, H., c.1915. Diary of HMS E11

Report of Proceedings – Commodore of Submarines for AE2, B6, B10, B11, E2, E7, E11, E12, E14 and H1, 1915 (Public Records Office)

Stanley, E. G., c.1915. 'Passage of the Dardanelles by "E.14", April 27th 1915.' First Lt.s Narrative

'Statement by A.C. Nichols on Loss of H.M.A. Submarine AE2', c.1918

Stephens, W. J., *c.*1915. 'Retrospective Diary 15/6/15 to 7/10/15' (Liddle Collection)

Stoker, H. G., *c.*1919. 'Report to the Commonwealth of Australia on the movements of H.M.A. Submarine "A.E.2", 9 January'

U-Boat Patrol Reports, 1915. US National Archives (Microfilm Series T1022)

Wheat , J. H., *c.*1915–19. 'Diary of Submarine AE2'

Printed works

Admiralty Naval Staff Gunnery Division, 1921. *Report of the Committee Appointed to Investigate the Attacks Delivered on the Enemy Defences of the Dardanelles Straits, 1919.* (= Mitchell Report), London: Government Printer (= secret government report)

Ashmead-Bartlett, E., 1928. *The Uncensored Dardanelles*, London: Hutchinson

Aspinall-Oglander, C. F., 1992. *Military Operations Gallipoli*, Vol. I, London: Imperial War Museum (original publication: 1929)

Avci, C., 2001. *The Epic Story of AE2*, Istanbul: Nart Yayincilik

Avci, C., 2002. *Thirteen Leagues under the Sea*, Istanbul: Nart Yayincilik

Avci, C., 2003. *The Skies of Gallipoli*, Istanbul: Nart Yayincilik

Bean, C. E. W., 1981. *The Story of Anzac*, Vol. 1, St Lucia: University of Queensland Press (original publication 1921)

Beesly, P., 1982. *ROOM 40: British Naval Intelligence 1914–18*, London: Hamish Hamilton

Brenchley, F. and E. Brenchley, 2001. *Stoker's Submarine*, Sydney: HarperCollins

Brodie, C. G., 1956. *Forlorn Hope 1915: The Submarine Passage of the Dardanelles*, London: Frederick Books

Bush, E., 1975. *Gallipoli*, New York: St. Martin's Press

Carlyon, L., 2001. *Gallipoli*, Sydney: Pan Macmillan Australia

Carr, W. G., 1930. *By Guess and by God: The Story of the British Submarines in the War*, London: Hutchinson

Cassar, G. H., 1971. *The French and the Dardanelles*, London: George Allen & Unwin

Chasseaud, P. and P. Doyle, 2005. *Grasping Gallipoli: Terrain, Maps and Failure at the Dardanelles, 1915*, Staplehurst: Spellmount

Chatterton, E. K., 1935. *Dardanelles Dilemma: The Story of the Naval Operations*, London: Rich & Cowan

Chatterton, E. K., 1936. *Seas of Adventure*, London: Hurst & Blackett

Churchill, W. S., 1923. *The World Crisis 1915*, New York: Charles Scribner's Sons

Compton-Hall, R., 1991. *Submarines and the War at Sea 1914–18*, London: Macmillan

Corbett, J. S., 1995. *Naval Operations*, Vols II–III, London: Imperial War Museum (2nd edn) (original publication 1929)

Dardanelles Commission, Parts 1 and 2, 1914–15, 2000. London: Stationary Office (abbr. edn; original publication 1917)

Davies, M. J., 1992. 'Military intelligence at Gallipoli', *Defence Force Journal*, 92, p. 37

Davies, R. B., 1967. *Sailor in the Air*, London : Peter Davies

Dittmar, F. J. and J. J. Colledge, 1972. *British Warships 1914–1919*, London : Ian Allan

Djemal Pasha, 1973. *Memories of a Turkish Statesman, 1913–1919*, New York : Arno Press (original publication 1921)

Edwards K., 1939. *We Dive at Dawn*, London: Rich & Cowan Ltd

Einstein, L., 1917. *Inside Constantinople*, London: John Murray

Ellison, G., 1926. *The Perils of Amateur Strategy*, London: Logmans, Green

Fewster, K., 1983. *Gallipoli Correspondent: The Frontline Diary of C. E. W. Bean*, Sydney : George Allen & Unwin

Fewster, K. et al., 1985. *A Turkish View of Gallipoli*, Richmond, Victoria: Hodja Educational Resources Cooperative

Frame, T. R., 2000. *The Shores of Gallipoli: Naval Aspects of the Anzac Campaign*, Sydney: Hale & Ironmonger

Frame, T. R. and G. J. Swinden, 1990. *First In, Last Out: The Navy at Gallipoli*, Kenthurst, New South Wales: Kangaroo Press

Goodchild G., 1917. *The Last Cruise of the 'Majestic'*, London: Simpkin, Marshall, Hamilton, Kent

Grant, R. M., 1964. *U-Boats Destroyed: The Effect of Anti-Submarine Warfare 1914–1918*, London: Putnam

Grant, R. M., 1969. *U-Boat Intelligence 1914–1918*, Hamden: Archon Books

Gray, E., 1988. *Captains of War: They Fought Beneath the Sea*, London: Leo Cooper

Gray, E., 2001. *British Submarines in the Great War*, Barnsley: Leo Cooper (original publication 1971)

Gray, E. A., 1972. *The Killing Time: The German U-Boats 1914–1918*, London: Pan Books

Guttman, J., 1998. *Defiance at Sea*, London: Cassell (original publication 1995)

Halpern, P. G., 1979. *The Keyes Papers. Volume 1: 1914–1918*, London: George Allen & Unwin

Halpern, P. G., 1987. *The Naval War in the Mediterranean 1914–1918*, London: Naval Institute Press

Hamilton, I., 1917. *Despatches from the Dardanelles*, London: George Newnes

Hamilton, I., 1920. *Gallipoli Diary*, Vols 1–2, New York: George H. Doran

Hankey, M., 1961. *The Supreme Command 1914–1918*, Vol. I, London: George Allen & Unwin

Harris, B., 1997. *The Navy Times Book of Submarines: A Political, Social and Military History*, London: Berkley Publishing Group

Head, C. O., 1931. *A Glance at Gallipoli*, London: Eyre and Spottiswoode

Hickey, M., 1995. *Gallipoli*, London: John Murray

Higgins, T., 1963. *Winston Churchill and the Dardanelles*, London: William Heinemann

Hoover, K. D., 1976. 'Commander Otto Hersing and the Dardanelles Cruise of S.M. U-21', *American Neptune*, 36.1, pp. 33–44

Hoyt, E. P., 1976. *Disaster at the Dardanelles, 1915*, London: Arthur Baker

James, R. R., 1984. *Gallipoli*, London: Pan Books (original publication 1965)

Jameson, W. S., 1962. *Submariners V.C.*, London: Peter Davies

Jameson, W. S., 1965. *The Most Formidable Thing*, London : Rupert Hart-Davis

Jose, A. W., 1987. *The Royal Australian Navy, 1914–1918*, St Lucia: Angus & Robertson (original publication 1928)

Kannengiesser, H., 1926. *The Campaign in Gallipoli*, London: Hutchinson

Kemp, P. K., 1952. *H.M. Submarines*, London: Herbert Jenkins

Keyes, R., 1934. *The Naval Memoirs of the Admiral of the Fleet, Sir Rodger Keyes*, New York: E. P. Dutton

Kipling, R., 1916. *Sea Warfare*, London: Macmillan

Lambert, M., 2001. *The Submarine Service 1900–1918*, Aldershot: Ashgate

Langensiepen, B., 1995. *Ottoman Steam Navy: 1828–1923*, London: Conway Maritime Press

Layman, R. D., 2002. *Naval Aviation in the First World War*, London: Caxton Editions (original publication 1996)

Liddle, P., 1976. *Men of Gallipoli*, London: Penguin Books

Liddle, P., 1985. *The Sailor's War 1914–18*, Dorset: Blandford Press

Lumly, E. W. R., 1970. *Policy and Operations in the Mediterranean 1912–14*, London: Navy Records Society

Macintyre, D., 1965. *Fighting under the Sea*, London: Evans Brothers

Marder, A. J., 1952. *Portrait of an Admiral*, Cambridge, MA: Harvard University Press

Marder, A. J., 1965. *From the Dreadnought to Scapa Flow*, Vol. II, London: Oxford University Press

Marder, A. J., 1974. *From the Dardanelles to Oran*, London: Oxford University Press

Messimer, D. R., 2001. *Find and Destroy: Antisubmarine Warfare in World War I*, Annapolis: Naval Institute Press

Miller, G., 1996. *Superior Force: The Conspiracy behind the Escape of Goeben and Breslau*, Hull: University of Hull Press

Miller, G., 1997. *Straits: British Policy towards the Ottoman Empire and the Origins of the Dardanelles Campaign*, Hull: University of Hull Press

Mitchell, R. J. E., 1918. Private letter to his parents, to be accessed at: www.cronab.demon.co.uk/reub.html (under title 'The loss of submarine E-14')

Moorehead, A., 1997. *Gallipoli*, Ware: Wordsworth Editions (original publication 1956)

Morgenthau, H., 1918. *Ambassador Morgenthau's Story*, New York: Doubleday

Moth, R. O., 1987. 'A month in the Sea of Marmara', *The Gallipolian*, 53 (Spring)

Mulligan, J., 2000–1. *Gallipoli*, National Defence University (Newsletter, Internet)

Nevison, H. W., 1919. *The Dardanelles Campaign*, New York: Henry Holt

Newbolt, H., 1918. *Submarine and Anti-Submarine*, London: Longmans

Poolman, K., 1981. *Periscope Depth: Submarines at War*, London: William Kimber

Puleston, W. D., 1927. *The Dardanelles Expedition: A Condensed Study*, Annapolis: United States Naval Institute

Robertson, W., 1021. *From Private to Field-Marshall*, London: Constable

Rössler, E., 1981. *The U-Boat: The Evolution and Technical History of German Submarines*, London: Arms & Armour Press

Samson, C. R., 1990. *Fights and Flights*, Nashville: Battery Press (original publication 1930)

Schreiner, G. A., 1918. *From Berlin to Baghdad*, New York: Harper

Shankland, P. and A. Hunter, 1964. *Dardanelles Patrol*, London: Collins

Sokol, H. H., 1933. *Osterreich–Ungarns Seekrieg 1914–18*, Vols I–II, Zurich: Amalthea

Spindler, A., 1932. *Der Krieg zur See 1914–1918, Der Handelskrieg mit U-Booten*, Vol. II, Berlin: F.G. Mittler

Stewart, A. T. and C. J. E. Pershall, 1918.*The Immortal Gamble*, London: A. & C. Black

Stoker, H. G., 1925. *Straws in the Wind*, London: Herbert Jenkins

Swing, R., 1965. *Good Evening! Raymond 'Gram' Swing*, London: The Bodley Head

Taffrail, T. D., 1935. *Swept Channels*, London: Hodder & Stoughton

Tarrant, V. E., 1989. *The U-Boat Offensive 1914–1945*, London: Arms & Armour Press

Taylor, A. J. P., 1966. *The First World War: An Illustrated History*, Harmondsworth: Penguin Books

Thomas L., 1929. *Raiders of the Deep*, London: William Heinemann

Thomazi, A., 1927. *La Guerre Navale aux Dardanelles*, Paris: Payot

Travers, T., 2004. *Gallipoli 1915*, Stroud: Tempus Publishing

Turkish General Staff, 2004. *A Brief History of the Canakkale Campaign in the First World War*, Ankara: Turkish General Staff Printing House

Usborne, C.V., 1933. *Smoke on the Horizon: Mediterranean Fighting 1914–1918*, London: Hodder & Stoughton

Van der Vat, Dan, 1985. *The Ship that Changed the World*, London: Hodder & Stoughton

Van der Vat, Dan, 1994. *Stealth at Sea: The History of the Submarine*, London: Orion Publishing Group

Von Sanders, L., 2000. *Five Years in Turkey*, Nashville: The Battery Press (original publication 1928)

Wester-Wemyss, R. E., 1924. *The Navy in the Dardanelles Campaign*, London: Hodder & Stoughton

White, M. W. D., 1992. *Australian Submarines: A History*, Canberra: Australian Government Publishing Service

Wilson, M., 1988. *Destination Dardanelles*, London: Leo Cooper

Wilson, M. and P. Kemp, 1997. *Mediterranean Submarines*, London: Crecy Publishing

Further reading

Akermann, P., 1989. *Encyclopaedia of British Submarines*, Liskeard: Maritime Press

Allen, G. R. G., 1963. 'A ghost from Gallipoli', *Journal of the Royal United Service Institution*, May, Vol. 108, No. 630, p. 138.

Bendert, H., *Die UB-Boote der Kaiserlichen Marine 1914–1918*, Hamburg: Mittler

Bennett, G., 1983. *Naval Battles of the First World War*, London: Pan Books

Blackburn, J. A. and K. Watkins, 1920. *The British Submarine in Being*, London: Grieves

Callwell, C. E., 1924. *The Dardanelles*, London: Constable

Culcu, M., 1997. *Gallipoli 1915: Bloody Ridge Diary of Lt. M Fasih*, Istanbul: Denizler Kitabevi

Denham, H. M., 1981. *Dardanelles: A Midshipman's Diary*, London: John Murray

Evans, M., 2000. *From Legend to Learning: Gallipoli and the Military Revolution of WW1*, Working Paper 110, April, Duntroon: Land Warfare Studies Centre

Fortescue, G., 1915. *What of the Dardanelles*, London: Hodder & Stoughton

Frothingham, T. G., 1971. *The Naval History of the World War. Vol II: The Stress of Sea Power 1915–16*, New York: Books for Libraries Press (original publication 1924–6)

Gibson, R. H. and M. Prendergast, 1931. *The German Submarine War 1914–18*, London: Constable

Halpern, P. G., 1994. *A Naval History of World War 1*, London: UCL Press

Hezlet, A., 1967. *The Submarine and Sea Power*, London: Peter Davies

Hurd, A. and H. H. Bashford, 1919. *Sons of Admiralty*, London: Constable

Jameson, W., 1965. *The Most Formidable Thing: The Story of the Submarine from its Earliest Days to the End of World War I*, London: Rupert Hart-Davis

Kemp, P., 1997. *U-Boats Destroyed: German Submarine Losses in the World Wars*, London: Arms & Armour Press

Kemp, P., 1999. *Submarine Action*, Stroud: Sutton Publishing

Kemp, P. and P. Jung, 1989. 'Five broken down B boats', *Warship International*, pp. 11–27

'Klaxton', 1933. *Dead Reckoning: A Story of our Submarines*, London: Rich & Cowan

Longstaff, R., 1984. *Submarine Command: A Pictorial History*, London: Book Club Associates

Mackenzie, C., 1930. *Gallipoli Memories*, New York: Doubleday

McLaughlin, R., 1974. *The Escape of the Goeben*, London: Seeley Service

1879–80 Map Mediterranean Sea of Marmara. Surveyed by Commander W. J. L. Wharton and the officers of HM Ships, Shearwater (1872) and Fawn, 1920 London: Ordinance Survey

Mascfield, J., 1916. *Gallipoli*, London: William Heinemann

Military Operations Gallipoli, 1992. Vols I and II, London: Imperial War Museum (original publication 1929)

Oliff, R., *Fastest to Canada: The Royal Edward*, Kettering: Silver Link

Pelvin, R., 1999. *First through: The Epic Voyage of AE2*, Canberra: Media Marketing Group (= Wartime Magazine, Australian War Memorial, Vol. 6)

Pelvin, R., 2000. *Suvla: Sea Power at Suvla, August 1915*, to be accessed at: www.iwm.org.uk/upload/package/2/gallipoli/pdf_files/Suvlanaval.pdf (= Joint Imperial War Museum / Australian War Memorial Battlefield Study)

Preston, A., 1982. *Submarines*, Greenwich: Bison Books

Smyth, D., 1974. 'The submarine *AE2* in World War I', Naval Historical Society of Australia, 30 April Lecture

Snelling, S., 1995. *VCs of The First World War Gallipoli*, Stroud: Sutton Publishing

Steel, N., 1999. *Gallipoli*, Barnsley: Leo Cooper

Stuermer, H., 1917. *Two War Years in Constantinople*, New York: George H. Doran

Taffrail, D., 1931. *Endless Story – Being an Account of the Work of the Destroyers, Flotilla-Leaders, Torpedo-Boats and Patrol Boats in the Great War*, London: Hodder & Stoughton

Talbot, F. A, 1915. *Submarines: Their Mechanism and Operation*, London: William Heinemann

Tarrant, V. E., 1989. *The U-Boat Offensive 1914–1945*, London: Arms & Armour Press

Index